RADICALIZATION IN BELGIUM AND THE NETHERLANDS

RADICALIZATION IN BELGIUM AND THE NETHERLANDS

Critical Perspectives on Violence and Security

Edited by
Nadia Fadil
Martijn de Koning
Francesco Ragazzi

I.B.TAURIS
LONDON • NEW YORK • OXFORD • NEW DELHI • SYDNEY

I.B. TAURIS
Bloomsbury Publishing Plc
50 Bedford Square, London, WC1B 3DP, UK
1385 Broadway, New York, NY 10018, USA
29 Earlsfort Terrace, Dublin 2, Ireland

BLOOMSBURY, I.B. TAURIS and the I.B. Tauris logo
are trademarks of Bloomsbury Publishing Plc

First published in Great Britain 2019
Paperback edition first published 2021

Cover design by Sara S'Jegers | sarasjegers@yahoo.com
Cover image: vecteezy.com

A catalogue record for this book is available from the British Library.

A catalog record for this book is available from the Library of Congress.

ISBN: HB: 978-1-7845-3889-7
PB: 978-0-7556-4123-9
ePDF: 978-1-7883-1619-4
eBook: 978-1-7883-1620-0

Series: Library of European Studies

Typeset by RefineCatch Limited, Bungay, Suffolk

To find out more about our authors and books visit
www.bloomsbury.com and sign up for our newsletters.

CONTENTS

LIST OF FIGURES

ACKNOWLEDGEMENTS

This edited volume is the outcome of two conferences that were held in Amsterdam and Leuven in January and September 2016. We would like to thank the invited keynote speakers, Arun Kundnani and Martha Crenshaw, and the conference participants for their contributions and stimulating comments which have made the realization of this volume possible. We would also like to thank the anonymous peer reviewer, as well as Tahni Candelaria for the copy-editing of the manuscript and Sophie Rudland from I.B. Tauris for her professional guidance and support throughout the process. The realization of the volume was made possible with the financial support of the University of Amsterdam and the Catholic University of Leuven.

LIST OF CONTRIBUTORS

Jaafar Alloul holds an MA in Middle East studies from the Belgian University of Ghent, along with a European MA of Excellence (Erasmus Mundus Joint Master Degree/EMJMD) in social science with a focus on migration studies (EMMIR), coordinated by the German University of Oldenburg. He is currently finalizing in a joint PhD program in social anthropology at the KU Leuven and the University of Amsterdam, working on migration, minorities and the inclusion-exclusion nexus across the EU and the Arab Gulf/Dubai. His broader research interests include political Islam, the globalization of culture(s), and the social hierarchies of the political economy of race in Europe and the greater Middle East.

Didier Bigo is Professor at King's College London Department of War Studies and research professor of International Relations at Sciences-Po Paris/CERI. He is also director of the Centre for Study of Conflicts, Liberty and Security (CCLS) and editor of the quarterly journal *Cultures et Conflits*, published by L'Harmattan, as well as founder and previous co-editor, with Rob Walker, of the ISA journal *International Political Sociology*. His work focuses on critical approaches to security in Europe and the relation between internal and external security, as well as the sociology of terrorism, antiterrorism and practices of surveillance. Some of his recent publications are *Extraordinary Rendition: Addressing the Challenges of Accountability* (with Elspeth Guild and Mark Gibney, 2018) and *Foucault and the Modern International: Silences and Legacies for the Study of World Politics* (with Philippe Bonditi and Frederic Gros, 2017).

Rik Coolsaet is Professor Emeritus of International Relations at Ghent University (Belgium) and Senior Associate Fellow at Egmont–Royal Institute for International Relations (Brussels). He was appointed a member of the original European Commission Expert Group on Violent Radicalization (established 2006) and the subsequent European Network of Experts on Radicalization (ENER). He was chair of the Department of Political Science at Ghent University from 2006 to 2014. He served as director of the Security & Global Governance programme at Egmont–Royal Institute for International Relations (Brussels). His most recent studies on radicalization and terrorism have all been released by the Egmont Institute: 'Returnees – Who Are They, Why Are They (Not) Coming Back and How Should We Deal with Them? Assessing Policies on Returning Foreign Terrorist Fighters in Belgium, Germany and the Netherlands' (with Thomas Renard, February 2018); 'Anticipating the Post-Daesh Landscape' (October 2017); '"All Radicalisation is Local": The Genesis and Drawbacks of an Elusive Concept' (June

2016); 'Assessing the Fourth Foreign Fighters Wave: What Drives Europeans to Syria, and to Islamic State? Insights from the Belgian Case' (March 2016).

Beatrice de Graaf is Professor of History of International Relations & Global Governance at the University of Utrecht. She is a leading expert in the field of terrorism, conflict and security and is a well-known researcher and discussion partner for governmental and societal institutions and the media. In 2007, she co-founded the Centre for Terrorism and Counterterrorism at Leiden University (Faculty Campus – The Hague). She was appointed professor for Conflict and Security History at Leiden University (2011), and received numerous grants, including an EU Consolidator Grant (SECURE) and the Stevin Prize (2.5 million euros). She has two research tracks: (1) the investigation into the origins and makings of a European Security Culture in the nineteenth century and (2) terrorism/counterterrorism from a historical perspective. She is a council member of the European Council of Foreign Relations, member of the Royal Netherlands Academy of Arts and Sciences, and sits on the editorial boards of *Studies in Conflict & Terrorism* and *Terrorism and Political Violence*.

Lili-Anne de Jongh studied communication studies and political science at Leiden University, American University in Washington, DC and Vrije Universiteit Amsterdam. She currently works as a policy advisor on security (radicalization and polarization in particular) for the City Council of Delft, the Netherlands, and as a part-time scientific researcher on the effects of security and counterterrorism measures on individuals, communities and human rights in general. Prior to that, she worked as the coordinator for the Institute of Security and Global Affairs (ISGA) Opening Conference of Leiden University and as a freelance researcher on counterterrorism measures at the Department of Human Rights Policy of Amnesty International, the Netherlands.

Martijn de Koning is an anthropologist. He teaches at the Department of Islamic Studies at Radboud University, Nijmegen, in the Netherlands and conducts research on lifestyles, identities and memories of Dutch Muslims in the UK. He is a post-doc researcher at the Department of Anthropology at the University of Amsterdam, where he is currently involved in the Netherlands Organization for Scientific Research (NWO) funded project 'Forces That Bind and/or Divide' (on how Muslims can claim a voice in the public debates on Islam), and in the European Research Council (ERC) funded programme 'Problematizing "Muslim Marriages": Ambiguities and Contestations'. Martijn de Koning has published on Moroccan-Dutch youth and identity formation, radicalization, Salafism, Islamophobia, racialization and activism among Muslims in the Netherlands, Germany and Belgium. He maintains his own weblog CLOSER: http://religionresearch.org/closer.

Nadia Fadil is Associate Professor of Anthropology at the IMMRC (Interculturalism, Migration and Minorities Research Centre) at the Catholic University of Leuven (KU Leuven) in Belgium. Her ethnographic focus is on the presence of Islam in Europe, both as a living tradition and as an object of governmental regulation and societal debate, on which she has published extensively in academic journals (such as *HAU, Ethnicities, Identities, Social Anthropology, Ethnic and Racial Studies* and *Feminist Review*) and edited volumes. More broadly, her theoretical interests pertain to questions of subjectivity and power, ethical selfhood, embodiment and affect, postcolonialism, race and secularism.

Mieke Groeninck holds a PhD in social and cultural anthropology from the Catholic University of Leuven, Belgium. Her doctoral research focused on Islamic religious knowledge transmission for adults in Brussels' mosques and Islamic institutes. She has published articles on the art of Quranic recitation, the history of the institutionalization of Islam in Belgium, and pious epistemology and subjectivization. Currently, she works as a full-time researcher at the Knowledge Centre Higher Institute for Family Studies, conducting a research project on resilience among Afghan, Iraqi and Syrian asylum seeking and refugee families in Belgium. Her next project starts in May 2019 as a Marie Sklodowska-Curie postdoctoral research fellow at the Leiden University, where she will work on informal imam education programmes in Belgium and the Netherlands.

Silke Jaminé is a PhD researcher in anthropology at KU Leuven and Université libre de Bruxelles (ULB). She studied social work (UCLL/Social School Heverlee) and social and cultural anthropology (KU Leuven). During her master thesis research, she conducted fieldwork among civil servants and youth workers who were developing a deradicalization project. After graduation, she worked as a social worker in Antwerp. Her current PhD research looks at the development of counter-radicalization policies among local municipalities and civil servants in Belgium.

Iman Lechkar is Fatima Mernissi Chairholder at the Vrije Universiteit Brussels and a postdoctoral research fellow at IMMRC (KU Leuven). She obtained a PhD in social and cultural anthropology on Neo-Sunnis and Neo-Shi'ites in Belgium, which looked into conversion and religious practices in a secular context. Her teaching and research engage with questions of Islam and gender, religion and secularism, conversion, religious practice, identities and authorities, ethnicity, citizenship, subjectivity, agency, affect and (visual) methodologies. Recent publications include 'Being a "True" Shi'ite: The Poetics of Emotions among Belgian-Moroccan Shiites', *Journal of Muslims in Europe* 6, no. 2 (2017): 241–59; and 'The Power of Affective Encounters and Events: Why Moroccan Belgian Sunni's become Shia', in *Moroccan Migration in Belgium: More than 50 Years Settlement*, eds. C. Timmerman et al., 367–80 (2017).

Annelies Moors studied Arabic at the University of Damascus and anthropology at the University of Amsterdam. She did fieldwork in Palestine, Yemen and the Netherlands, and holds the chair of contemporary Muslim societies at the Department of Anthropology at the University of Amsterdam. She is also the PI of the NWO programme 'Muslim Activism in the Netherlands after 1989' and of the ERC advanced grant 'Problematizing "Muslim Marriages": Contestations and Ambiguities'. She has published widely on gender, nation and religion, materiality, affect, and visuality of various aspects of the Muslim culture, including *Women, Property and Islam: Palestinian Experiences 1920-1990* (1995). She has edited special issues of journals such as *Islamic Law and Society* (2003), *Fashion Theory* (2008, with Emma Tarlo), *Social Anthropology* (2009, with Ruba Salih), *Material Religion* (2012) and *Anthropological Quarterly* (2014, with Jeanette Jouili); and edited volumes including *Religion, Media, and the Public Sphere* (2006, with Birgit Meyer), *Narratives of Truth in Islamic Law* (I.B. Tauris, 2008, with Baudouin Dupret and Barbara Drieskens), *The Colonial and Post-Colonial Governance of Islam* (2011, with Veit Bader and Marcel Maussen), and *Islamic Fashion and Anti-Fashion* (2013, with Emma Tarlo).

Francesco Ragazzi is Lecturer in International Relations at Leiden University and Associated Scholar at the *Centre D'Etude sur les Conflits, Liberté Security* (CCLS). He has published widely in peer-reviewed journals including International Political Sociology, Security Dialogue and Political Geography. He has been consulted as an expert on security by the European Parliament, the Council of Europe and the French Senate.

Ineke Roex studied anthropology at the Radboud University in Nijmegen. Her thesis was about the Arab European League (AEL) in Belgium. In 2007–9 she participated in a research programme about Salafism in the Netherlands at the University of Amsterdam. In 2009–11 she worked at FORUM, Institute for Multicultural Affairs, as a researcher in the context of the special FORUM Frank Buijs Chair on Radicalization Studies with professor Frank Bovenkerk. She has participated in a programme of education and research on the evaluation of the effectiveness of anti-radicalization policies. Her dissertation *Leven als de profeet in Nederland: Over de salafi-beweging en democratie* (2013) is based on her anthropological fieldwork in the Salafi movement in the Netherlands. She was involved in a research project focusing on Islamic activism in Western Europe, with a special focus on Sharia4Belgium. She is co-author of *'Als ik iemand beledigd heb, dan was dat mijn bedoeling': Sharia4Belgiums ideologie en humorgebruik* (2017). She is currently involved at NTA (*Nuance door Training en Advies*) as researcher and consultant, and she is guest researcher at the Department of Political Science at the University of Amsterdam.

Paul A. Silverstein is Professor of Anthropology at Reed College (Portland, USA). He is author of *Algeria in France: Transpolitics, Race, Nation* (2004) and *Postcolonial France: Race, Islam, and the Future of the Republic* (2018), among other publications. His ethnographic and archival work addresses issues of (im)migration, labour, popular culture, sport and identity movements in both Europe and North Africa, and he is completing an ethnohistorical monograph on Amazigh cultural politics in south-eastern Morocco. His new research investigates the history and politics of immigrant workers in the coal mines of northern Europe. In 2015–16 he was a Fulbright visiting professor in the Interculturalism, Migration and Minorities Research Centre at the University of Leuven. He chairs the board of directors of the Middle East Research and Information Project and is a co-editor of the Public Cultures in the Middle East and North Africa book series with Indiana University Press.

Floris Vermeulen is Associate Professor at the Department of Political Science at the University of Amsterdam. He has been chair of the department and co-director of the Institute for Migration and Ethnic Studies (IMES). His research focuses on the civic and political participation of immigrants and their descendants at the local level. He is also interested in local integration policies for immigrant communities and the manner in which these policies are often combined with preventive policy programmes to counter violent extremism. His work is published in different international volumes and journals such as *European Union Politics, Journal of Ethnic and Migration Studies, Terrorism and Political Violence, Nonprofit and Voluntary Sector Quarterly, Urban Studies, West European Politics, British Journal of Sociology,* and *Political Psychology.*

INTRODUCTION

RADICALIZATION: TRACING THE TRAJECTORY OF AN 'EMPTY SIGNIFIER' IN THE LOW LANDS

Nadia Fadil, Martijn de Koning and Francesco Ragazzi

In the spring of 2013, the mayors of the Flemish towns of Vilvoorde, Antwerp, Mechelen and Maaseik presented at a largely attended press conference the brochure *Beheersen van Moslimradicalisering: Handreiking voor Beleid en Praktijk* (*Controlling Muslim Radicalization: A Guide for Policy and Practice*). The brochure was a hasty publication that came out a few months after the news about a hundred Belgian Muslims, who had left the country in order to join the fighting forces in Syria against the regime of Bashar al-Assad, had started dominating the news coverage. While the initial reasons for this preoccupation were undetermined, many policymakers and commentators feared that some of these youths could return to take up arms against the local authorities – something that would be proven a few years later with the attacks in Paris in 2015 and Brussels in 2016. Yet what seemed to be of a bigger concern for the policymakers were the ideas that informed the youngsters' decision to leave, and which came to be captured by the concept of *radicalization*.

In the definition they offered of the term, the Belgian policymakers understood radicalization as the '*growing ability to strive towards and/or support deep-seated changes in a society that stand in contradiction with the democratic order and/or where undemocratic means are being used*' (p. 9).[1] The definition given by the Belgian policymakers was neither unique nor new, but directly borrowed from the Dutch coordinating agency of security and counterterrorism (NCTV – *Nationale Coordinator Terrorismebestrijding en Veiligheid*) which had employed the definition introduced by the Dutch security services (AIVD – *Algemene Inlichtingen en Veiligheidsdiensten*) in 2004. When coining the term in 2001, Dutch security officials had hoped to find a concept that would account for the possible relationship they saw between a failing integration of (especially Moroccan) migrants and what they categorized as growing security threats.

While this connection was highly hypothetical at the time of its introduction, the 9/11 attacks and especially the murder of Theo van Gogh in 2004 and the London bombings in 2005 were seen as evidence of this link, which spurred a further investment into this question. Radicalization thus became understood as a process that precedes the possible usage of violence, and fits within an ever more expanding reach into these preventive measures and policies by the security services. By the time the term, and its definition, had been used in the Belgian brochures mentioned above, it had become a well-established concept in several policymaking circles, the scientific literature and in the public debate throughout Europe.[2]

This book seeks to offer an account of how the discourse of radicalization has been introduced, adopted and disseminated and has reframed practices of power of authorities, scientists, social workers, Muslim preachers and civil actors since its introduction into the Dutch-speaking countries (Belgium and the Netherlands, also referred to as the Low Countries) at the turn of the twenty-first century. This critical take on radicalization, which is more attentive to interrogating the discourses, the policies and their effects rather than alleged forms of radicalization, has been at the heart of several recent scholarly contributions.[3] Over the years, several authors have indeed sought to account for the ways in which the 'war on terror' has come to produce its own discourses, vocabularies and policies which particularly target Muslim populations in the diaspora.[4] Recent scholarship has also addressed the increasing influence of the counterterrorism imperative in other professional fields, such as education,[5] healthcare,[6] social work[7] or prison and probation services.[8] Studies have indeed attended to the important paradigmatic shift that occurred in the discourse on security throughout the nineties, i.e. that the presence of political violence – especially that of opponents – becomes increasingly perceived and explained through the lens of belief systems and ideology, rather than political actions and causes.[9] The discourse of radicalization figures as the most recent articulation and materialization of this shift.

In what constitutes one the key genealogies of the discourse of radicalization, Arun Kundnani critically unpacks the circulation of this master signifier in the English-speaking countries to show how it generates analytical frameworks that fail to account for the political dimensions of the existing social and political tensions.[10] By subsuming these questions to a privileged focus on individual motivations, ideologies and religious views, radicalization becomes conceived of as a 'virus'[11] that can be reinforced by a mobilizing network of friends and theological beliefs and which can ultimately lead to the use of political violence. A similar critical take can also be found in the texts collected by Baker-Beall, Heath-Kelly and Jarvis,[12] who note that radicalization functions as an exonerating discourse that enables politicians to 'externalise responsibilities for, and the origins of, political discontent'.[13] The authors similarly highlight how the latter circulates through the construction of a religious, racialized Other. Building upon this critical turn, this edited volume seeks to expand the scope of these studies geographically and methodologically.

Geographically, first, this edited volume takes the Northern-European countries Belgium and the Netherlands, a linguistic ensemble often referred to as the 'Low Countries', as an empirical site to examine the discursive and material circulation of practices and policies around (de-)radicalization. Whereas the region of the

Low Countries carries a historical depth that continues to inform certain political and cultural imaginaries,[14] our interest in this region is more informed by the pioneering role of the Netherlands in the development of the discourses and policies of (de)radicalization worldwide. The influence of the Netherlands on Belgium is materialized in a shared political language that addresses the 'problems' of multiculturalism and integration, as well as a circulation of expertise between these two countries.[15] The bulk of existing studies on radicalization focuses on the UK and English-speaking countries such as Australia or the US. The geographical concentration of these studies, however, only partially reflects the dynamics of the policies' diffusion. The choice of these cases reflects more the domination of Anglo-American scholarship and the easy access to English-language sources rather than the prominence of these countries in the broader counter-radicalization international context. As this book will show, developments in several other European countries, such as France, Austria, Germany, Denmark – and of course Belgium and the Netherlands – have been important, if not more important, at least in the early years, than those in English-speaking countries. The aim of this book is thus not only to shift the analytical lens to understudied geographical regions relevant to the process, but mainly to contribute to de-centring current debates concerned with counter-radicalization policies and their impact, showing the importance of processes that have thus far remained out of sight for an English-speaking readership.

A second aim of this edited volume is of a theoretical and methodological nature, and is to reaffirm the importance of a critical, reflexive approach to counter-radicalization discourse and policies. This book intends to contribute to the often marginalized – yet ever more necessary in the current security context – approach that locates these policies within a broader reflection on the social construction of categories of knowledge and practice. Building on the traditions of critical security studies and critical studies on terrorism, the approach adopted in the current volume does not treat security as a given, but rather as a process.[16] Following the broadening and deepening debates from the 1980s,[17] it conceives of security as more than just the security of states, but as processes that affect individuals and ethnic groups. Building on the linguistic turn of the 1990s brought about by securitization theory, security is viewed as a signifier that is more often than not used to justify exceptionalist politics[18] which extends the notion of what security is,[19] and in some cases brings about new laws and suspends or transforms existing laws.[20] The current volume is however also attentive to the sociological dimension of security discourses and practices, and aware that 'radicalization discourse' does not occur in a vacuum: it is embedded in bureaucratic struggles and technological apparatuses and ultimately reflects the specific visions of social actors that have cards to play in the field of security.[21] As such, the perspective adopted in this book can therefore broadly be defined as 'social constructivist', in that it aims to examine the ways in which terms circulate and come to be used by social actors.

Lisa Stampnitzky explains that examining the social construction of key categories such as terrorism doesn't imply dismissing their empirical validity, but it rather concerns 'asking how problems, concepts and institutions came to be, and what makes them powerful'.[22] Inspired by this approach, and more broadly by the genetic structuralism of authors like Pierre Bourdieu and Michel Foucault,[23] this edited volume seeks similarly to denaturalize the usage and application of this term by unpacking its genealogical circulation among circles of expertise, and its diffusion at different levels of the state apparatus – not necessarily following a top-down trajectory but rather reinvesting the 'local' as a key site of political experimentation – and finally its translation in specific practices of power. Whereas the concept can be understood as a 'floating'[24] or an 'empty' signifier[25] – that is to say a word that might not necessarily refer to something existing in the real world[26] – in this book we propose to precisely analyse what the notion does, what it enables and how it (re)organizes and reframes the relation between political violence and the government of cultural diversity.

The focus on the Netherlands and Belgium

The Netherlands has played a pioneering role in the conceptualization of the term *radicalization.*[27] The introduction of this term in the 2001 BVD [*Binnenlandse Veiligheidsdienst*] (Internal Security Service) report was explicitly tied with the growing perception that the integration of postcolonial (especially Moroccan) migrants represented a particular challenge, and that the evolution towards a 'multi-ethnic society' could result in security hazards. An explicit reference to this question is made in the 1999 and 2000 BVD Reports, as the necessity to 'signal and (help) prevent threats linked with the integration process' was mentioned as a an important task of the BVD, which also fits in its desire to develop a more comprehensive approach in tackling security issues.[28] This view on multiculturalism, as a possible problem and threat, was not isolated but resonated with a broader change in the public rhetoric on cultural diversity that took place throughout the nineties and early noughties. Like several other Western European countries, the Netherlands attracted a significant number of migrants after the Second World War. Although the presence of migrants was initially tied to a shortage of labourers in the country, the worldwide recession from the seventies and the end of the Cold War produced an international climate wherein immigrants – especially from Muslim countries – were increasingly viewed as suspicious. In the context of the Netherlands, this was reflected in a growing questioning of the institutionalized presence of Islam. In line with the model of pillarization that prevailed in the country, Muslim minorities (often of Moroccan and Turkish background) had set up mosques, schools, civic organizations and media that explicitly aimed at catering to the needs of Dutch Muslims. The idea that migrants and their culture pose a danger was however asserted from the earliest days of the Dutch minority policies.

    The idea of danger initially pertained mainly to the idea that migrant cultures were a potential threat to the rule of law. For example, as Duyvendak and Scholten show, in the early eighties, members of the WRR [*Wetenschappelijke raad voor het Regeringsbeleid*] (The Scientific Council for Government Policy) had concerns about the relationship between 'cultural diversity' and the 'rule of law'.[29] According to them, the rule of law was the result of the codification of 'cultural achievements' – something that had to be protected. The 'compatibility of Islam and the rule of law' was challenged, and it was believed that a 'conflict of values and norms' could emerge. After internal deliberations, the threat presented by migrant cultures was acknowledged, but only conditionally. Rather than assuming such a threat was all pervasive, the WRR thus stated that the danger migrant cultures could present might occur when conflicts came about and, if this were to occur, 'cultural achievements' would have to be defended.[30] Later, during the nineties, political parties across a broad political spectrum questioned whether an increase in 'cultural diversity' would threaten social cohesion.[31] The involvement of the WRR in the early years and later on was also significant, as it helped politicians to treat the incorporation of migrants as a non-political issue that could be dealt with in a technocratic, problem-solving manner.[32] The idea that the culture and practices of migrants – and in particular Islam – posed a problem was also vehiculated by influential Dutch protagonists such as Frits Bolkestein (in the early nineties) and Pim Fortuyn (in the late nineties) who played a significant role in challenging what they considered as a period of 'laissez-faire' towards cultural diversity in general, and Islam in particular. This discursive shift towards a 'new realist discourse'[33] will state that a 'politically correct' attitude towards cultural diversity and Islam prevailed for too long, and that now the time for a more critical attitude had come. A strong attachment to liberal-secular values, combined with a growing hostility towards the presence of religious (and Islamic) norms within public life would characterize this new form of *parler-vrai* (frank discussion). Although this idea of the Netherlands as having been too accommodating and lenient towards any form of cultural diversity has been deconstructed and challenged by a number of analysts for being fraught,[34] this perspective would nevertheless continue to circulate and be adopted by politicians and analysts to discharge what they consider to be 'apologetic trends' within progressive milieus.

The southern neighbour of the Netherlands, Belgium, equally faced similar challenges related to the presence of cultural diversity at the turn of the twenty-first century. Like the Netherlands, Belgium also welcomed a significant number of migrants from North Africa (Morocco) and Turkey throughout the sixties and seventies. And although the country doesn't count as many Islamic schools as the Netherlands, the official recognition of Islam by the Belgian state in 1974 did result in the active inclusion of this religion in the Belgian institutional landscape.[35] From the eighties onwards, several tensions related to migration started capturing the public attention – especially through (and because of) the electoral successes of the right-wing party Vlaams Blok, an offshoot of the Flemish nationalist movement that would achieve important electoral successes from 1988 until 2004. Several analysts have described how the rise of this movement lay equally at the basis of a more generic semantic shift towards migration – which became increasingly viewed and framed as a problem.[36] In their important work *Debating Diversity*,[37] Jan Blommaert and Jef Verschueren describe how the dominant frame that prevailed in popular media and state politics throughout the late eighties/

early nineties drew on a similar set of presuppositions that considered 'migration towards Europe' as 'dramatic and exceptional'.[38] The dominant ideology that informed these policies – and that they describe as *homogeneism* – drew on a monocultural understanding of Belgian and Flemish society, which consistently marked 'others' as a possible threat or pollution to the social fabric that could only be overcome through integration. This was, in particular, the case for '*moslem cultures*' (i.e. Turkish and Moroccan migrants) whose values were consistently seen to conflict with those of the West. Their study furthermore shows how this ideology of *homogeneism* even extended to diversity-promoting institutions such as the Royal Commissariat for Migration policy, installed in 1988 right after the first electoral success of the Vlaams Blok. In the trainings offered by the institutions, migration is primarily approached and conceived as a problem and a general attitude was adopted that sought to curtail the cultural beliefs and practices of the minorities – especially when they were Muslim.[39]

The Flemish-Belgian and Dutch discussions on the multicultural model were, however, not entirely cut off from one another but were often deeply interlaced and interacting. A clear example can be found in Paul Scheffer's seminal essay 'Het Multiculturele Drama' published in 2000 in the Dutch daily *NRC Handelsblad* which provides a telling example of how critiques on multiculturalism circulated across the border to reinforce local dynamics. In this essay, Scheffer challenged what he viewed as a 'politically correct attitude' in the Netherlands. His critique not only gained resonance in the Dutch media but was also hailed by 'progressive' and 'left-wing' Flemish intellectuals who felt that a similar 'politically correct attitude' had been nurtured in Flanders in order to counter the electoral successes of the Vlaams Blok.[40] The 9/11 attacks, the escalation of the 'war on terror' and the murder of Theo van Gogh in 2004 would give further credence to the already circulating idea that the failure of integration not only poses a problem for social cohesion, but that it might occasionally also result in real security threats. Another example is the emergence of the Arab European League (1999–2005), a civil rights' movement created in the late nineties in Antwerp and which reverberated throughout the Low Countries and had chapters both in Belgium and the Netherlands.[41] A brief reference to this movement is noteworthy because of the importance this organization had in channelling some of the societal tensions on multiculturalism and security at the turn of the twenty-first century. The movement was an offshoot of the *Federatie Marokkaanse Verenigingen*, an established Belgian-Moroccan cultural organization in Antwerp, and gained national attention through its provocative stances – especially by its leader Dyab Abou Jahjah – on integration and racism. The organization also garnered quite a lot of media attention in the Netherlands and created its own local chapters there. Some of its actions consisted of the monitoring of police violence towards ethnic minorities and various anti-war and pro-Palestinian demonstrations. They also ran for the regional elections in 2003 on a joint ticket with the communist party (PVDA – Partij van de Arbeid). Its outspoken anti-racist and anti-Zionist positions were, however, considered controversial and Dyab Abou Jahjah was also briefly arrested on the accusation of having instigated riots in November 2002 (these claims were later proven unfounded). The climate of suspicion and criminalization that existed around the Arab European League lead to an active listing by both the Belgian and the Dutch security agencies.[42] The Dutch Christian-Democrats and the party of the late Pim Fortuyn (Lijst Pim Fortuyn) also called for banning the organization in the Netherlands in 2004.

The (inter)national trajectories of an 'empty signifier'

While the notion of 'radicalization' with its connotations of failed migrant integration, urban relegation and marginalization, religious fanaticism and ultimately political violence is not new, it has recently acquired an overwhelming pre-eminence in media and political discourse in Europe. As Baker-Beall, Heath-Kelly and Jarvis have suggested, we do, as we write this introduction, live in what could be defined as an 'age of radicalization'.[43] The omnipresence of the term however should not stop us from tracing its genealogy, and specifically how from its origins in the intelligence circles of the Netherlands, it gradually infiltrated the European policy arena in Brussels, ultimately finding its way into the everyday of ministries of interior and justice, prison and probation services, education boards and city councils across Europe and the world.

The Dutch counter-radicalization discourse and expertise, known as the 'comprehensive approach' (*brede benadering*) that had developed between the end of the 1990s and the beginning of the 2000s,[44] was promptly imported in the UK in the aftermath of the London bombings of July 2005. The Dutch influence is such that according to some, it served in large part as the basis for the British 'Prevent' section of the UK's comprehensive 'Contest' counterterrorism strategy devised under the leadership of Sir David Oman. It is only then, as Rik Coolsaet shows in more detail in Chapter 1 in this volume,[45] that counter-radicalization, as a particular structured project of broadening counterterrorism to societal actors beyond the law enforcement circles, broke onto the European scene with the British presidency of the Council of the European Union. In December 2005, the *European Union Strategy for Combating Terrorism* took up the British strategy virtually point by point, also defining four areas of action: Prevent, Pursue, Protect and Respond. Immediately afterwards, the Council of Europe adopted the *European Union Strategy for Combating Radicalization and Recruitment to Terrorism*.[46] While high policy was decided between ministers and heads of governments, counter-radicalization discourse spread through other, more horizontal networks.

Two networks are of particular relevance and both of them are tightly linked to the Netherlands. The first is the *Policy Planners Network on Countering Polarization and Radicalization* (PPN), a grouping of interior ministry mid-level officials from ten European countries (United Kingdom, France, Germany, the Netherlands, Denmark, Norway, Sweden, Belgium, Finland, Spain) and Canada, coordinated by the Institute for Strategic Dialogue, a think tank based in the United Kingdom. It was created in 2008 as a Dutch-British initiative to organize the sharing of information and 'best practices' among its members, to pool research and expert reports and ultimately to advise the Coordinator for Counterterrorism for the European Commission. The PPN still meets three times per year, and is a space for direct contact between actors that are directly linked to the day-to-day design and monitoring of counter-radicalization policies. The second is the better-known *Radicalization Awareness Network* (RAN), launched by the European Commission in September 2011 as an umbrella organization connecting several networks of actors involved in preventing radicalization and violent extremism (social workers, religious leaders, youth leaders, police officers, etc.). The aim of the RAN, discussed in more detail in the chapter by Rik Coolsaet (Chapter 1 in this volume), is again to exchange 'best practices' and share 'experience' among the different countries (European Union Member States plus Norway).[47] Since the early 2010s, the European Union has developed or participated in other smaller initiatives, such as the network 'Strong Cities'.[48]

While some countries in the EU resisted the notion that terrorism should be framed as a problem of radicalization – France, for example, until 2014 considered terrorism to be purely a law enforcement problem, before performing a 180-degree turn and adopting the Anglo-Dutch position. It has now become the dominant, single discourse through which terrorism and counterterrorism is conceptualized. In 2014, the United Nations (UN) adopted Security Council Resolution 2178, which gave the radicalization narrative a global resonance, and encouraged all UN Member States to adopt preventive policies.[49] The Global Counterterrorism Forum (GCTF), a counterterrorism organization launched in 2011 to shadow the UN's counterterrorism efforts, adopted a series of memoranda, listing 'best practices' in relation to radicalization. These memoranda were widely circulated within international organizations and around the mid-2010s, when several regional or international organizations felt they needed to engage in what was becoming a new policy paradigm, these texts served as a basis for many initiatives. The counter-radicalization discourse then started to proliferate: In 2015, the Council of Europe (the Strasbourg-based regional organization of the European Court of Human Rights, which counts forty-seven members, including Turkey and Russia) adopted an 'Action Plan on the fight against violent extremism and radicalization leading to terrorism' and issued in 2016 the *Guidelines for Prison and Probation Services Regarding Radicalization and Violent Extremism*. In 2016, the Organization for Security and Cooperation in Europe (OSCE) issued a 'guidebook' to community approaches to counter-radicalization,[50] and it is likely that the coming years will bring more handbooks, guidelines and best practices.

Radicalization and/as Islam

Despite its claims to the contrary, there exists a tacit – and at times explicit – link between the use of the term radicalization and the political militancy of Muslims in Europe. In its circulation in policy and scientific circles, and the further conceptualization as a process, the notion of radicalization has been largely developed in order to account for viewpoints and practices that might be considered as threatening within Islam, although connections have also occasionally been made with right-wing and other forms of militant actions.[51] Several scholars have noted how this focus on Islam and Muslims as threats to social cohesion has triggered a securitization of Islam and Muslims and an 'Islamization of security' – which means that any debate on Islam focuses on the threat it represents and that any debate about security is reduced to Islam. This makes Islam the centre stage in public debates and policies concerning national security.[52] This is certainly not an exclusively Dutch or Belgian development. Recently, several researchers throughout Europe have delved into the issue of the process of securitization of Islam[53] and how radicalization consists of an externalization of violence into racialized 'others'.[54] Transforming a particular social group from being treated as an ordinary political issue into a security matter legitimates the adoption of exceptional measures that may go beyond (or even undo) existing legal benchmarks and rights.[55] But, crucially, at the same time it also allows it to become part of the daily political, bureaucratic security logic.[56] In understanding how such current practices of surveillance seem to find a privileged entrance point towards Islam, it is important to not only situate them against shifting geopolitical conjunctures after the Cold War, which turned political Islam into a new global threat, but to also place them in an older (post)colonial framework, where Orientalist representations of Islam[57] have consistently informed the colonial administration in Muslim territories. Indeed, Hajjat and Mohammed[58] remind us that when French ethnologists, working for the colonial administrations in West Africa in the early twentieth century, coined the term Islamophobia, it was to describe a differential mode of treatment of Muslim subjects based on a view that Islam was fundamentally 'other'.[59] This view extended into several policies – of which the French Algerian civil code *Statut Juridique des indigènes en Algérie* (1865) remains the most telling example.[60] This decree administered the legal rights of the 'indigènes' whereby staunch distinctions were drawn on confessional grounds. Jews were naturalized after 1870, yet a similar naturalization for Muslims as a group remained inconceivable – even for Algerians who converted to Catholicism. One's identity as Muslim was indeed not viewed solely as a confession but something akin to what the French historian Patrick Weil describes as an 'ethnic-political' category,[61] and which strongly conditioned their access to French citizenship.[62] Orientalist representations of Islam as 'other' also fed into how violence was being framed and treated by the colonial administrations. Paul Silverstein describes how violent forms of resistance by Algerians were understood by the French colonials as a reflection of Islam's vindictive nature and the duty upon Muslims to be engaged in a perpetual 'holy war' against 'infidels'.[63]

Although in many cases we can find a problematization of Islam in its entirety, in many colonial policies a recurring distinction was made that boils down to a simple opposition between 'acceptable' and 'non-acceptable' Islam to a large extent determined by local and global interests of the ruling elites and their desire to maintain peace and order.[64] By the end of nineteenth century and beginning of the twentieth, the Dutch 'pillarized' society into socio-religious denominations, while in the colonies there was a strong preference for implementing secular rule (although the Dutch churches were by no means absent from the scene).[65] Albeit in different ways, Dutch administrators and missionaries made a distinction between an 'acceptable' and 'non-acceptable' Islam based upon ideas of what was compatible with Dutch colonial rule or Christianity.[66] Alexanderson's account of how the Dutch colonial authorities tried to regulate the hajj maritime networks between the East Indies and Jeddah shows how worried the Dutch authorities were about Hadrami Arabs and Meccan sheikhs who travelled within those networks on the same ships as the people from the East Indies.[67] In the words of the Dutch academic and alleged convert to Islam Snouck Hurgronje (who was particularly influential in shaping colonial policy and writing about the 'question of Islam' that emerged out of the necessity to prepare the indigenous population for modern culture and life), the distinction between 'acceptable' and 'non-acceptable' Islam was one between Islam as a religion and Islam as a political doctrine.[68] While the Islam of the local population was seen as apolitical and inferior to 'Europeanness', it was the Islam of the Hadrami Arabs and sheikhs that was seen as potentially disrupting the social order because of its pan-Islamic and anti-colonial ideas.

Such Orientalist representations, we want to argue, continue to resonate with contemporary surveillance practices. Indeed, (de)radicalization policies often draw on the presupposition that certain *belief systems*, which hold antagonistic views towards liberalism and secular modernity, can potentially stimulate forms of resentment that can translate into violence. And in this context, the focus on 'Salafism' emerges as one of the most telling examples of such continuities. While during the 1980s and 1990s Salafis shied away from any public visibility in the Netherlands, and certainly from participating in public debates, from 2002 onwards Salafi visibility increased in the public image of Islam and Muslims because of a number of incidents.[69] It wasn't until 2003, however, that the term 'Salafism' became apparent to a wider audience. That year, in the Netherlands, a trial took place that concerned twelve people accused of recruiting young men for military jihad, in particular for the violent struggles in Kashmir, after two young men from the city of Eindhoven were killed there in 2002. According to the newspapers, the public prosecutor stated that the twelve men belonged to 'Salafism', a 'radical Islamic branch with extreme ideas about Qur'an interpretation and Islamic law'. The question of how dangerous 'Salafism' is or 'Salafis' are has been in the background of much of the media coverage and policy attention. In the public debates, Salafism is often equated with radicalism and vice versa, so-called radical Muslims are often called Salafi or Salafists. In this way Dutch Salafi networks became *hyper-visible*,[70,] referring to processes which make racialized people intensely visible as objects of attention, fear and desire through the gazes of media and state. Hyper-visibilized subjects are invisible in their individuality but highly visible as repositories of fear and desire.[71] In this logic, gender and the body play an important role; Muslim men who refuse to shake hands are thought to be 'Salafi' and are often referred to as 'beards of hate' (*haatbaard*), and wearing the niqab is seen by the Dutch government as a symbol of a form of Islam that does not fit Dutch society.[72] These traits are often regarded as features of Salafism, and people who refuse to shake hands or wear the niqab are thought to be Salafi, albeit with a clear gendered difference.

Most of the policy reports about radicalization do not explicitly refer to gender, although some note that women may 'also' be open to radicalization and that some play an active role in, for example, translation work.[73] In the case of women however issues of radicalization are often raised in the context of other debates that are sometimes also exclusively linked to debates on Islam and/or Salafism such as forced marriage,[74] (the partial ban on) the face veil,[75] and 'Islamic marriages'.[76] These indirect links with radicalization and Islam/Salafism are important as they show how the debates on radicalization are often informed and shaped by broader concerns and fears about 'our way of life' being threatened: a phrase that is sometimes invoked after events of political violence and during integration debates. As Brown and Saeed note for the UK and USA, such fears and concerns are highly gendered and sexualized.[77] Not only does the stereotype of the oppressed Muslim woman prevail (but with the veiled Muslim woman as a threat at the same time), notions about freedom and 'our way of life' are also often raised in opposition to gender and gay rights in relation to Islam.[78]

Yet besides addressing how counter-radicalization projects selectively target and include Islam as one of the main centre points, this volume also seeks to show how such policies often draw on the active involvement of Muslim actors and organizations. Few studies have documented how Muslim networks as well as individuals have consistently cooperated with the state and local authorities to signal and prevent radicalization among 'vulnerable' youth.[79] Most have rather tended to place Muslim actors as the passive recipients of a repressive policy. Whereas such accounts are understandable in light of the hegemonic weight of discourses that primarily target Muslims as 'other', they do not offer a valid account of the complexity of these policies and how they are being implemented through the mobilization of a heterogeneous set of actors – Muslim and non-Muslim. With the instalment of a policy on radicalization in 2015, the Flemish government, for instance, also assigned a well-known and popular imam the task to coordinate a Flemish network of Islam experts to produce a counter-discourse on radicalization.[80] In the Netherlands, after the murder of Theo van Gogh in 2004, a large project was initiated by the government called 'Binding Society' (Maatschappelijke Binding), which required all the government departments to devise projects countering radicalization and furthering social cohesion. Mainstream Muslim organizations were partners in these endeavours, but all Salafi networks were excluded (although some local contact between the networks and local authorities remained, see Chapter 2 by Fadil and De Koning in this volume) as they were seen as the main agents responsible for radicalizing Muslim youth. Also, several prominent Muslims have been solicited by the Dutch authorities to take up individual cases to de-radicalize, and in 2016 the main umbrella organization of mosques was asked to organize meetings to create awareness among Muslims about 'radicalization and alienation'.

Such an active – and often prominent – inclusion of Muslim actors in public policies on de/radicalization is understandable in light of the pillarization model that prevails in the region and which understands religious movements as a vital component of civil society. But these examples also show how some Muslim actors often have a vested interest in producing counter-narratives and supporting state-sponsored initiatives on radicalization. The departure of youngsters from Belgium and the Netherlands to Syria from 2012 resulted, for instance, in an unprecedented series of Muslim-led initiatives on *jihadism* and radicalization in Belgium and the Netherlands.[81]

If we are to understand, following Foucault, radicalization as a *dispositif* or an apparatus, it is important to consider this critical alliance between these heterogeneous sets of actors, who seem to share a common agenda of creating distinctions between 'acceptable' and 'non-acceptable' forms of Islam, yet in many cases also often draw on distinct imaginaries and languages in doing so. What might appear at first glance as simply a co-optation of Muslims, who are consequently turned into governmental subjects or docile/good Muslims,[82] is equally mediated by intra-Muslim contestations.

Yet these are, we want to suggest, rarely taken into account in much of the literature. An example can be found in the current discussions about the Salafi *manhaj* or 'Salafism' as a clearly defined ideology. Salafi or Salafist as a label is highly contested among Muslims. Some refuse to use it, some use it to denounce other Muslims and some (even those who refuse to use the label in religious circles) use it in public debates to describe themselves. Furthermore, many groups of Muslims, other than the Salafis, regard the Prophet Muhammad and the first three generations of Muslims as exemplary Muslims and their teachings as an inspiration for current day reform. These range from other Islamic movements, to socialists and feminists in the Middle East. For many individual Muslims, whether affiliated with a particular branch or movement or not, the lives and teachings of the first generations and the Prophet Muhammad are attractive 'ideals'; there is no clear concept of what form they actually take. In recent years, the departure of youngsters to Syria from Belgium and the Netherlands has resulted in an exceptional series of discussions and 'internal debates' within the Muslim communities both in Belgium and the Netherlands on the circulating discourses and narratives concerning the obligation to perform the *hijra* or the *jihad* or the relationship to non-believers or what a Caliphate should be like.

These discussions often draw on older debates on the position of Muslim minorities in a non-Muslim majority context.[83] In some cases, they also explicitly target discourses produced by Salafi-jihadi groups by challenging their views on war, violence and non-believers through counter-examples from the Qur'an and the Sunna. These discussions have occasionally also resulted in calls for a 'reform' of the existing methodologies and ways of approaching religious texts.[84] One of the central aims of this volume is therefore to shed a complex light on the Muslim implication in the discourses and practices of (de)radicalization by documenting and demonstrating the public (and private) involvement of these actors in these policies. The perspective upon which we draw is one that understands Islam as a vibrant and complex discursive tradition,[85] where the question of how to behave properly as a Muslim has been a constant point of inquiry for lay Muslims and scholars. These discussions have often resulted in concepts and theological vocabularies that have sought to problematize modes of reasoning or practices that are seen to contradict the teachings of Islam and that occasionally seem to find new points of articulation in the current discussions on radicalization.[86] Our aim is to show how initiatives on radicalization provide a site of interaction (or even collusion) between state-led attempts at regulating (and securitizing) the Muslim field and intra-Muslim discussions and debates on 'acceptable' forms of Islam.

Outline of the chapters

This volume is organized in three sections, which all seek to address the history, practices and co-optation of these discourses and practices of radicalization. The first part of the volume offers a history of the term by showing both its starting point in the Netherlands and its expansion to other European countries. The contributions of Rik Coolsaet (Chapter 1) and that of Nadia Fadil and Martijn de Koning (Chapter 2) trace the evolution and dissemination of the concept in the European and Dutch context respectively. The contribution of Rik Coolsaet (Chapter 1) looks at the European trajectories of the term radicalization. It shows how the term was introduced shortly after the 9/11 attacks within European police and intelligence circles and found its way through the EU institutions, where it appeared for the first time in May 2004. The attacks in Madrid, two months before, and in London, in July 2005, pushed the concept to centre stage in EU counterterrorism thinking and policies. But Coolsaet equally contends that the concept – despite its spread and use – remains ill-defined, complex and controversial. This also applies to its American twin 'CVE', countering violent extremism. Both concepts are usually taken for granted and considered self-evident, but they are not. Because of its apparent simplicity, but also its ambiguity, it became entwined with the public disenchantment over immigration that had been developing since the 1980s, and with the unease over Islam and Muslims boosted by the 9/11 attacks. The concept was all the more tantalizing because of the pre-existent popular idiom: 'radical Islam' and the ubiquity since 9/11 of the 'clash of civilization' paradigm.

   In their contribution, Fadil and De Koning (Chapter 2) examine how the notion of radicalization was developed by Dutch intelligence in 2001 and how it came to gain scientific legitimacy in the Dutch scientific field from 2005 onwards. Their genealogical investigation shows that although the term radicalization was explicitly coined with reference to Islamic forms of militancy, a subsequent attempt at expanding it into other forms of activism will also consistently mark and characterize its trajectory. Yet despite these attempts at different articulations of the term, the dominant reference to Islam and Muslims continues to inform the primary usage of this term. They thereby conclude that the ambivalence of the term radicalization is similarly one of the persistent hallmarks of this floating signifier.

The concept of radicalization does not only circulate in and between policy and academic circles, translations also occur within mosques and other Islamic institutions as Mieke Groeninck (Chapter 3) shows. In her chapter, she describes the debates and discussions that followed the departure of youngsters to Syria and the Paris and Brussels attacks in Brussels-based Muslim circles between 2013 and 2015. Groeninck identifies two different discourses that dealt with the 'radicalist' and 'Salafist' sites of contestation, which were brought in direct relation to the resurgence of terrorism. A first position links radicalization (and terrorism) with a lack of knowledge of the *adab* (ethics) of divergence, which may lead to 'radicalism' understood as extremely exclusivist behaviour and dehumanization of non-Muslims and Muslims alike, possibly resulting in violence. Another position considers the main cause of radicalization to lie in the exclusivist behaviour promoted by a particular hermeneutical understanding of the Islamic sources, proclaimed by what they described as Salafism. Groeninck reflects in her chapter on both positions through ethnographic examples from teachers, fellow students and debates that clarify both lines of thinking.

The second part of the volume attends to the public policies and practices of deradicalization. As stated earlier: The perspective we adopt in this volume draws on a pragmatic theoretical and philosophical tradition, which seeks to understand how concepts and ideas reconfigure existing policies and material realities. In analysing how this notion of radicalization is introduced, recuperated and applied, our aim is two-fold. The first is to demonstrate how a securitization logic gradually becomes inserted as a fundamental prerogative of different kinds of professional activities – i.e. judges and lawyers, social workers, civil servants and local policies. Several authors have already pointed towards this development – and in re-posing this question in the Dutch and Belgian context, we seek to show how such dynamics take place in a particular setting. The contribution of Beatrice de Graaf (Chapter 4), who examines the juridical effects of the radicalization paradigm in the Netherlands, provides a case in point. Drawing on the preventive lens that figures as a starting point and core mission of the radicalization narrative in the notion of radicalization, this chapter seeks to show how an idea of 'preventive sanctioning' gradually seeps into the juridical domain transforming trials into ways of managing risk. De Graaf examines the terrorist trial as a performative space where potential future terror is imagined, invoked, contested and made real. By focusing on the cases against terrorism suspects involved in attempts to join or recruit for the Caliphate between 2013–16, she is able to show how present criminal offences involving terrorist aims and intent are constituted through the appeal to potential future violence, assemblages of evidence and linear projections of radicalization models. This chapter teases out how techniques of actuarial justice – including appropriating scholarly concepts and theories – are applied to transform these trials into instruments of managing the risk presented by the offender.

Equally, a second aim of this part is to demonstrate the active agency of local actors vis-à-vis these securitizing mechanisms. Indeed, the different chapters in Part II show that the adoption of the radicalization narrative is far from a straightforward process, but often entails an active negotiation – and contestation –

by the local actors. This is illustrated through the contribution by Ineke Roex and Floris Vermeulen (Chapter 5). Their chapter offers an account of how the implementation and instalment of public policies of deradicalization in Antwerp, Flanders, equally meant the rise and co-optation of new public actors that were otherwise deemed illegitimate. The growing anxiety around extremism and terrorist attacks as well as the Syria fighters provoked an unprecedented demand for pre-emptive measures that were considered as an adequate and indispensable anticipatory security practice to counter the threat. This also resulted in the need for new forms of partnership between local authorities and new organizations. Through the discussion of a few examples, the authors seek to understand to what extent these measures eventually result in certain 'democratic innovations' at the local level. In their chapter, Francesco Ragazzi and Lili-Ann de Jongh (Chapter 6) show how the demands made by radicalization policies place Dutch civil workers and front-line workers in a perpetual and unresolvable tension between their roles as 'confidants' and 'informants'. Their chapter, based upon empirical work, draws on the work of Simmel, Foucault and Bourdieu. Ragazzi and De Jongh argue that a project of bending, harnessing or hijacking existing or supposed relations of trust that form the basis of specific social settings is at the core of contemporary counter-radicalization rationality. This invites them to understand counter-radicalization as a form of 'government through trust' which opens up a new perspective wherein the management and instrumentalization of trust relations as a central anticipatory technology for both intelligence gathering and social control becomes a key site of investigation. The chapter by Silke Jaminé and Nadia Fadil (Chapter 7) examines, in turn, the practices of negotiation that lie at the core of the implementation of public policies of deradicalization. Set in a Flemish city among civil servants and a team of youth and family coaches in a youth care centre, it seeks to map the different ways in which radicalization becomes defined and apprehended in this particular context. Indeed, this work of constantly defining and determining 'whether someone is radicalized' was one of the main activities of the team. These negotiations also extended to the constant quest for a stable theoretical definition in the discussion with public servants, which was however rarely reached. The nature of deradicalization as negotiated practice can partly be explained by the fact that the field of deradicalization has emerged only recently and that public opinion is still divided. But the authors also locate these negotiations in a larger restructuring of the field of social work and youth work, where the question of expertise becomes an ever more important method of distinction.

The final part of this volume turns, at last, to the ways in which this *dispositif* of radicalization produces effects on Muslims – who often figure as the target of these policies. Whereas much has been written on the securitization effects of these measures, very few studies have explored the daily routines and practices which these forms of surveillance produce. Drawing on years of fieldwork with Dutch Muslim militant activists, the chapter by Martijn de Koning (Chapter 8) shows how these militant activists feel scrutinized not only by these state institutions, but also by the debates on Islam more generally. The chapter explores these two different modes of interpellation as forms of hard and soft surveillance (as they occur within the context of securitization of Islam). Based upon the question of how to live when defined as a 'security problem', De Koning's chapter shows how militant activists can have different types of responses: routinization and mobilization. Both routinization and mobilization are driven by a sense of injustice but pertain to different types of reactions. While the first response is invoked by the desire not to let surveillance affect daily life, the second one is conjured by the need to speak out. Muslims are not only the target of deradicalization strategies, but in many cases, they are also active actors in these policies. One of the main ways through which this idea of 'radicalization' resonates with Muslim practices is through a recurring concern about what counts as 'acceptable' forms of Islam.

The final two chapters, by Jaafar Alloul (Chapter 9) and Annelies Moors (Chapter 10), each try to disentangle the workings of the hegemonic de/radicalization discourse and explore the im/possibilities of letting the '*muhajir*' speak. Jaafar Alloul takes those who have been dubbed FTF ('foreign terrorist fighters') by the dominant political discourses and media as the starting point of a digital ethnography, and inquiries into some of their self-portrayals in new (online) media over the course of 2012–14. He observes how their digital portrayal remains fixated on Belgium and the Netherlands despite their relocation and the abundant public talk on their exogenous 'Islamist' nature. Rather than encountering substantiated ideas about Middle Eastern politics, one can trace an understudied social critique of the *home society* in Europe, not least the majority–minority relations and their treatment as an 'abjected' Muslim Other. In their online posts, a pertinent dialogical relationship can be identified in opposition to the political discourse of the far right in Europe. Syria, or '*sham*' as they romantically code their newly found 'home', facilitates a reconstitution of selfhood and community, of which the vernacular dispositions and ritual processions make *relational* testimony to, if not partly reproduce, a 'lived space' in Europe. As such, this contribution runs against the prevailing focus on the (ideological) 'pull factors' often found in security and terrorism studies by exploring how *hijra* to Syria constitutes a form of racial (emigration and) status exchange.

Whereas Alloul's contribution provocatively raises the Spivakian question about the possibility of letting the *muhajir* speak in the European public space, Annelies Moors' chapter reflects on this question through the spectrum of anthropological scholarship and the im/possibility of conducting fieldwork with subjects considered as abject, such as Islamic State (IS) fighters. Her auto-ethnographic account recounts her difficult journey through a public and political controversy, following the publication of an academic peer-reviewed paper in *Anthropology Today* on the marriage practices of the *muhajirat* under IS. The public controversy came about after a journalist accused one of the co-authors of Muslim background of having sympathies for Islamic State. According to the journalist this could have resulted in a bias, downplaying the danger of women who left for Syria. These accusations resulted in a public and political denunciation of the methodology and objectivity of the concerned researchers and led to a public and academic investigation. More than being simply incidental, Moors's account is telling of the risks scholars – and in particular anthropologists (and even more in particular, researchers with a Muslim background) – take in upholding a neutral and objective stand towards groups and individuals who have been called out as a public enemy. As she notes quite astutely in her auto-ethnographic entry, this raises important questions not only about scholarly deontology, but also about who is entitled to represent particular groups, and from which normative positions scholarship may or may not be conducted. She concludes with some reflections on the possibility of escaping this securitizing gaze, even within the most qualified academic scholarship.

Echoing Moors' contribution and reflection, one of the explicit hopes of this volume is that this geographically situated, historically informed and ethnographically grounded account of the deradicalization framework will enable a new, and critical, conversation about the operation of this discourse and its effects. We believe it to be our role, as scholars, to keep the possibility open for a complex understanding of the various predicaments of social life, also (and in particular) when these run against the dominant doxa. This volume is an experiment in this direction and, we hope, only the start of a new conversation.

Notes

1 Bart Somers, Bart De Wever, Hans Bonte and Jan Creemers, *Beheersen van Moslimradicalisering: Handreiking voor Beleid en Praktijk* (Antwerpen, Maasmechelen, Mechelen, Vilvoorde, 2013).

2 On the emergence of the 'radicalization' discourse, see Jonathan Githens-Mazer, 'The Rhetoric and Reality: Radicalization and Political Discourse', *International Political Science Review* 33, no. 5 (2012): 556–67; Charlotte Heath-Kelly, 'Counter-Terrorism and the Counterfactual: Producing the "Radicalisation" Discourse and the UK PREVENT Strategy', *The British Journal of Politics & International Relations* 15, no. 3 (2012b): 394–415; Arun Kundnani, 'Radicalisation: The Journey of a Concept', *Race & Class* 54, no. 2 (2012): 3–25; Peter R. Neumann, 'The Trouble with Radicalization', *International Affairs* 89, no. 4 (2013): 873–93; Alex P. Schmid, 'Radicalisation, De-Radicalisation, Counter-Radicalisation: A Conceptual Discussion and Literature Review', *International Centre for Counter-Terrorism* (The Hague: ICCT, 2013). For a nuanced take on the concept from a sociological perspective, see Eitan Y. Alimi, Lorenzo Bosi and Chares Demetriou, *The Dynamics of Radicalization* (Oxford and New York: Oxford University Press, 2015); Stephen W. Beach, 'Social Movement Radicalization: The Case of the People's Democracy in Northern Ireland', *The Sociological Quarterly* 18, no. 3 (1977): 305–18; Donatella Della Porta, *Clandestine Political Violence* (Cambridge: Cambridge University Press, 2013); Olivier Roy, *La sainte ignorance: Le temps de la religion sans culture* (Paris: Seuil, 2008).

3 See, in this context, Jonathan Githens-Mazer and Robert Lambert, 'Why Conventional Wisdom on Radicalization Fails: The Persistence of a Failed Discourse', *International Affairs* 86, no. 4 (2010): 889–901; Heath-Kelly, 'Counter-Terrorism and the Counterfactual'; and Arun Kundnani, *The Muslims Are Coming! Islamophobia, Extremism, and the Domestic War on Terror* (London and New York: Verso, 2014).

4 See, in this respect, Arun Kundnani and Ben Hayes, *The Globalisation of Countering Violent Extremism Policies: Undermining Human Rights, Instrumentalising Civil Society*

(Amsterdam: Societal Security Network, 2018). Most works have rather adopted a national focus. See, for instance, Nisha Kapoor, *Deport, Deprive and Extradite: 21st Century State Extremism* (London and New York: Verso, 2018); Yasser Morsi, *Radical Skin. Moderate Masks: De-Radicalising the Muslim and Racism in Post-Racial Societies* (London and New York: Rowman & Littlefield International, 2017); Jocelyne Cesari, *Muslims in the West after 9/11: Religion, Politics and Law* (Oxon and New York: Routledge, 2010); Tufyal Choudhury, *Impact of Counter-Terrorism on Communities: UK Background Report* (London: Institute for Strategic Dialogue, 2012); Ralph Grillo, 'Backlash against Diversity? Identity and Cultural Politics in European Cities', *COMPAS Working Papers* 14 (Oxford: Centre of Migration Policy and Society, 2005); Frank Peter, 'Political Rationalities, Counter-Terrorism and Policies on Islam in the United Kingdom and France', in *The Social Life of Anti-Terrorism Laws: The War on Terror and the Classifications of the 'Dangerous Other'*, ed. Julia M. Eckert (Bielefeld: transcript Verlag, 2008); Francesco Ragazzi, 'Suspect Community or Suspect Category? The Impact of Counter-Terrorism as "Policed Multiculturalism"', *Journal of Ethnic and Migration Studies* 42, no. 5 (2016): 724–41.

5   Vicki Coppock and Mark McGovern, '"Dangerous Minds"? Deconstructing Counter-Terrorism Discourse, Radicalisation and the "Psychological Vulnerability" of Muslim Children and Young People in Britain', *Children & Society* 28, no. 3 (2014): 242–56; Bill Durodie, 'Securitising Education to Prevent Terrorism or Losing Direction?', *British Journal of Educational Studies* 64, no. 1 (2015): 21–35; Shamim Miah, 'Preventing Education: Anti-Muslim Racism and the War on Terror in Schools', in *The State of Race*, eds. Nisha Kapoor, Virinder S. Kalra and James Rhodes (Basingstoke: Palgrave Macmillan, 2013); and Rights Watch UK, *Preventing Education? Human Rights and UK Counter-Terrorism Policy in Schools* (London: RWUK, 2016).

6   Neil Krishan Aggarwal, *Mental Health in the War on Terror: Culture, Science, and Statecraft* (New York: Columbia University Press, 2015); and Charlotte Heath-Kelly, 'Algorithmic Autoimmunity in the NHS: Radicalisation and the Clinic', *Security Dialogue* 48, no. 1 (2016): 29–45.

7   Basia Spalek and Robert Lambert, 'Muslim Communities, Counter-Terrorism and Counter-Radicalisation: A Critically Reflective Approach to Engagement', *International Journal of Law, Crime and Justice* 36, no. 4 (2008): 257–70; Charles Husband and Yunis Alam, *Social Cohesion and Counter-Terrorism* (Bristol: The Policy Press, 2011); and Francesco Ragazzi, 'Countering Terrorism and Radicalisation: Securitising Social Policy?' *Critical Social Policy* 37, no. 2 (2017): 163–79.

8   See Mark Hamm, *The Spectacular Few: Prisoner Radicalization and the Evolving Terrorist Threat* (New York: New University Press, 2013); and Tinka Veldhuis and Siegwart Lindenberg, 'Limits of Tolerance under Pressure: A Case Study of Dutch Terrorist Detention Policy', *Critical Studies on Terrorism* 5, no. 3 (2012): 425–43.

9   See Lisa Stampnitzky, *Disciplining Terror: How Experts Invented 'Terrorism'* (Cambridge: Cambridge University Press, 2013); and also Neumann, 'The Trouble with Radicalization'; Schmid, 'Radicalisation, De-Radicalisation'.

10 Kundnani, 'Radicalisation: The Journey of a Concept'.

11 Ibid., p. 21.

12 See also Charlotte Heath-Kelly, 'Can We Laugh Yet? Reading Post-9/11 Counterterrorism Policy as Magical Realism and Opening a Third-Space of Resistance', *European Journal on Criminal Policy and Research* 18, no. 4 (2012a): 343–60; Heath-Kelly, 'Counter-Terrorism and the Counterfactual'; and Heath-Kelly, 'Reinventing Prevention or Exposing the Gap? False Positives in UK Terrorism

Governance and the Quest for Pre-Emption', *Critical Studies on Terrorism* 5, no. 1 (2012c): 69–87.

13 Christopher Baker-Beall, Charlotte Heath-Kelly and Lee Jarvis, eds., *Counter-Radicalisation: Critical Perspectives* (Oxon and New York: Routledge, 2015), p. 7.

14 The concept of the 'Low Lands' continues to hold a symbolic reference for some political movements (especially conservative and nationalist movements) and in the literary field. For a further acccount of this concept, see Maarten Van Ginderachter, 'Trou de mémoire: De droom van Groot-Nederland', in *Het geheugen van de Lage Landen*, eds. Jo Tollebeek and Henk te Velde (Rekkem: Ons Erfdeel, 2009).

15 A concrete example of such cooperations in the domain of security are the so-called '*Burgemeesterconferentie over radicalisering en polarisatie*' (Mayors' conference on radicalization and polarization). Since 2014, Mayors from several Flemish and Dutch towns and diplomats gather on an annual basis to exchange expertise, policy tools and political strategies on this question.

16 Martha Crenshaw, 'The Causes of Terrorism', *Comparative Politics* 13, no. 4 (1981): 1–24; Richard Jackson, *Writing the War on Terrorism: Language, Politics and Counter-Terrorism* (Manchester: Manchester University Press, 2005); and Della Porta, *Clandestine Political Violence*.

17 Ken Booth, 'Security and Emancipation', *Review of International Studies* 17, no. 4 (1991): 313–26; and Keith Krause and Michael Williams, 'Broadening the Agenda of Security Studies: Politics and Methods', *Mershon International Studies Review* 40, no. 2 (1996): 229–54. For an anthropological take on this issue, see Hugh Gusterson and Catherine Besteman, *The Insecure American: How We Got Here and What We Should Do about It* (Berkeley, CA: University of California Press, 2010); and Zoltan Glück and Setha Low, 'A Sociospatial Framework for the Anthropology of Security', *Anthropological Theory* 17, no. 3 (2017): 281–96.

18 See c.a.s.e. collective, 'Critical Approaches to Security in Europe: A Networked Manifesto', *Security Dialogue* 37, no. 4 (2006): 443–87; and Ole Wæver, 'Securitization and Desecuritization', in *On Security*, ed. Ronnie D. Lipschutz (New York and Chichester: Columbia University Press, 1995).

19 Didier Bigo, 'Security and Immigration: Toward a Critique of the Governmentality of Unease', *Millennium* 27, no. 1 (2002): 63–92.

20 See De Graaf (Chapter 4 in this volume); and also Judith Butler, *Precarious Life: The Powers of Mourning and Violence* (London and New York: Verso, 2004); Marieke de Goede, 'The Politics of Preemption and the War on Terror in Europe', *European Journal of International Relations* 14, no. 1 (2008): 161–85.

21 Within the field of critical security studies, see Didier Bigo and Daniel Hermant, 'La relation terroriste', *Études Polémologiques* 47, no. 3 (1988); and Didier Bigo, Sergio Carrera, Elspeth Guild and R. B. J. Walker, *Europe's 21st Century Challenge: Delivering Liberty* (Farnham: Ashgate, 2013). For an anthropological perspective on the state as an assemblage between state and non-state actors, see Aradhana Sharma and Akhil Gupta, eds., *The Anthropology of the State: A Reader* (Malden, MA, and Oxford: Blackwell Publishing, 2006).

22 Stampnitzky, *Disciplining Terror*, p. 5.

23 Pierre Bourdieu, *Outline of a Theory of Practice*. Cambridge Studies in Social Anthropology 16 (Cambridge: Cambridge University Press, 1977); Michel Foucault, *Security, Territory, Population: Lectures at the Collège de France, 1977–78* (London: Palgrave Macmillan, 2007).

24 Claude Lévi-Strauss, *Introduction to the Work of Marcel Mauss* (London: Routledge & Kegan Paul, 1987); Jef Huysmans, 'Security! What Do You Mean? From Concept to Thick Signifier', *European Journal of International Relations* 4, no. 2 (1998): 226–55.

25 Ernesto Laclau and Chantal Mouffe, *Hegemony and Socialist Strategy: Towards a Radical Democratic Politics* (London: Verso, 1985).

26 Heath-Kelly, 'Counter-Terrorism and the Counterfactual'.

27 For a fuller account, see Fadil and De Koning (Chapter 2 in this volume).

28 BVD, *Jaarverslag 2001 [2001 Annual Report]* (The Hague: BVD, 2002), p. 15.

29 Peter Scholten, *Framing Immigrant Integration: Dutch Research-Policy Dialogues in Comparative Perspective* (Amsterdam: Amsterdam University Press, 2011). See also Jan Willem Duyvendak and Peter Scholten, 'Beyond the Dutch "Multicultural Model": The Coproduction of Integration Policy Frames in the Netherlands', *Journal of International Migration and Integration* 12, no. 3 (2011).

30 Scholten, *Framing Immigrant Integration*, pp. 143–4.

31 Alfons Fermin, *Nederlandse politieke partijen over minderhedenbeleid, 1977–1995* (Amsterdam: Thesis Publishers, 1997).

32 Fermin (1997) has shown how debates and deliberations about integration at the time were focused on (social) stability, inclusion and potential problems that could occur if integration failed, ranging from an increase in school drop-out rates to increased levels of crime and political violence.

33 Baukje Prins, *Voorbij de onschuld: Het debat over de multiculturele samenleving* (Amsterdam: Van Gennep, 2000).

34 See, in this respect, Duyvendak and Scholten, 'Beyond the Dutch "Multicultural Model"'; Sarah Bracke, 'Transformations of the Secular and the "Muslim Question": Revisiting the Historical Coincidence of Depillarization and the Institutionalization of Islam in the Netherlands', *Journal of Muslims in Europe* 2, no. 2 (2013): 208–26; Frank de Zwart and Caelesta Poppelaars, 'Redistribution and Ethnic Diversity in the Netherlands: Accommodation, Denial and Replacement', *Acta Sociologica* 50, no. 4 (2007): 387–99; and Frank de Zwart, 'Pitfalls of Top-Down Identity Designation: Ethno-Statistics in the Netherlands', *Comparative European Politics* 10, no. 3 (2012): 301–18.

35 For a further account of the institutionalization of Islam, see Nadia Fadil, Farid El Asri and Sarah Bracke, 'Islam in Belgium: Mapping an Emerging Interdisciplinary Field of Study', in *The Oxford Handbook of European Islam*, ed. Jocelyne Cesari (Oxford: Oxford University Press, 2015).

36 Mark Spruyt, *Wat het Vlaams Blok verzwijgt* (Leuven: Van Halewyck, 2000); Jan Blommaert and Albert Martens, *Van Blok tot Bouwsteen* (Berchem: EPO, 1999).

37 Jan Blommaert and Jef Verschueren, *Debating Diversity: Analysing the Discourse of Tolerance* (London: Routledge, 1998).

38 Ibid., p. 118.

39 Ibid., p. 156.

40 Nadia Fadil, 'Breaking the Taboo of Multiculturalism: The Belgian Left and Islam', in *Thinking through Islamophobia: Global Perspectives*, eds. Abdoolkarim Vakil and Salman Sayyid (New York: Columbia University Press, 2010).

41 Ludo De Witte, *Wie is er bang van Moslims? Aantekeningen over Abou Jahjah, etnocentrisme en islamofobie* (Leuven: Van Halewyck, 2004); Mohammed Benzakour, *Abou Jahjah, Nieuwlichter of Oplichter? De demonisering van een politieke rebel* (Amsterdam: L.J. Veen, 2004).

42 See, for instance, the 2004 AIVD '*Van da'wa tot jihad*', where the movement is described as a form of 'radical Islam', p. 40.

43 Baker-Beall, Heath-Kelly and Jarvis, eds., *Counter-Radicalisation*. See also Kundnani and Hayes, *The Globalisation of Countering Violent Extremism Policies*.

44 See also Fadil and De Koning (Chapter 2 in this volume).

45 See Coolsaet (Chapter 1 in this volume).

46 Raphael Bossong, 'The Action Plan on Combating Terrorism: A Flawed Instrument of EU Security Governance', *JCMS: Journal of Common Market Studies* 46, no. 1 (2008): 27–48.

47 See also Diana Davila Gordillo and Francesco Ragazzi, 'The Radicalisation Awareness Network: Producing the EU Counter-Radicalisation Discourse', in *Constitutionalising the Security Union: Effectiveness, Rule of Law and Rights in Countering Terrorism and Crime*, eds. Sergio Carrera and Valsamis Mitsilegas (Brussels: Centre for European Policy Studies, 2017).

48 'Strong Cities Network', http://strongcitiesnetwork.org/ (accessed 14 March 2017).

49 Kundnani and Hayes, *The Globalisation of Countering Violent Extremism Policies*.

50 Organization for Security and Co-operation in Europe, *Preventing Terrorism and Countering Violent Extremism and Radicalization that Lead to Terrorism: A Community-Policing Approach* (Warsaw, 2014).

51 See Fadil and De Koning (Chapter 2 in this volume) for a fuller account of these connections.

52 Beatrice de Graaf, 'Religion Bites: Religieuze orthodoxie op de nationale veiligheidsagenda', *Tijdschrift voor Religie, Recht en Beleid* 2, no. 2 (2011): 62–81; Sami Zemni, 'The Shaping of Islam and Islamophobia in Belgium', *Race & Class* 53, no. 1 (2011): 28–44.

53 Liz Fekete, 'Anti-Muslim Racism and the European Security State', *Race & Class* 46, no. 1 (2004): 3–29; Jocelyne Cesari, 'The Securitisation of Islam in Europe: The Changing Landscape of European Liberty and Security', *Research Paper no. 15* (2009), http://www.libertysecurity.org/IMG/pdf_The_Securitisation_of_Islam_in_Europe.pdf (accessed May 2018); De Graaf, 'Religion Bites'; June Edmunds, 'The "New" Barbarians: Governmentality, Securitization and Islam in Western Europe', *Contemporary Islam* 6, no. 1 (2012): 67–84; Stuart Croft, 'Constructing Ontological Insecurity: The Insecuritization of Britain's Muslims', *Contemporary Security Policy* 33, no. 2 (2012): 219–35.

54 Baker-Beall, Heath-Kelly and Jarvis, eds., *Counter-Radicalisation*, p. 7.

55 Edmunds, 'The "New" Barbarians'.

56 Mavelli, 'Between Normalisation and Exception: The Securitisation of Islam and the Construction of the Secular Subject', *Millennium* 41, no. 2 (2012): 159–81. See also the contribution of De Koning (Chapter 8 in this volume).

57 Edward W. Said, *Orientalism: Western Conceptions of the Orient* (London: Penguin, 1995 [1978]).

58 Abdellali Hajjat and Marwan Mohammed, *Islamophobie: Comment les élites françaises fabriquent le 'problème musulman'* (Paris: La Découverte, 2013).

59 Ibid., p. 74.

60 Todd Shepard, *The Invention of Decolonization: The Algerian War and the Remaking of France*, 2nd edn (Ithaca, NY, and London: Cornell University Press, 2008); Olivier Le Cour Grandmaison, *De l'indigénat* (Paris: La Découverte/Zones, 2010).

61 Patrick Weil, 'Le statut des musulmans en Algérie coloniale: Une nationalité française denature', *EUI Working Papers HEC* 3 (2003), p. 7.

62 For a fuller account of the 'politique musulmane' in the French colonies, see Naomi Davidson, *Only Muslim: Embodying Islam in Twentieth-Century France* (Ithaca, NY, and London: Cornell University Press, 2012), who describes how this collapsing of Muslims with their confessional practices produced a specific scholarship and policies under the colonies (especially chapter 1). Mayanthi Fernando in *The Republic Unsettled: Muslim French and the Contradictions of Secularism* (Durham, NC: Duke University Press, 2014) also traces how this convergence of 'race' and 'religion' in the case of Muslims continues to inform contemporary Republican practices towards this religious minority.

63 Servier and Anon, quoted in Silverstein, 'The New Barbarians: Piracy and Terrorism on the North African Frontier', *CR: The New Centennial Review* 5, no. 1 (2005): 50.

64 Marcel Maussen, Veit Bader and Annelies Moors, *Colonial and Post-Colonial Governance of Islam Continuities and Ruptures* (Amsterdam: Amsterdam University Press, 2011).

65 James Kennedy and Markha Valenta, 'Religious Pluralism and the Dutch State: Reflections on the Future of Article 23', in *Geloven in Het Publieke Domein: Verkenningen Van Een Dubbele Transformatie*, eds. W. B. H. J. van de Donk, A. P. Jonkers, G. J. Kronjee and R. J. J. M. Plum (Amsterdam: Amsterdam University Press, 2006).

66 Frans Wijsen, 'Indonesian Muslim or World Citizen? Religious Identity in the Dutch Integration Discourse', in *Making Religion: Theory and Practice in the Discursive Study of Religion*, eds. Frans Wijsen and Kocku von Stuckrad (Leiden and Boston: Brill, 2016).

67 Kris Alexanderson, '"A Dark State of Affairs": Hajj Networks, Pan-Islamism and Dutch Colonial Surveillance during the Interwar Period', *Journal of Social History* 47, no. 4 (2014): 1021–41.

68 Christiaan Snouck Hurgronje, *Nederland en de Islâm: vier voordrachten, gehouden in de Nederlandsch-Indische Bestuursacademie* (Leiden: E. J. Brill, 1911).

69 Martijn de Koning, 'The Other Political Islam: Understanding Salafi Politics', in *Whatever Happened to the Islamists: Salafis, Heavy Metal Muslims and the Lure of Consumerist Islam*, eds. Olivier Roy and Amel Boubekeur (London and New York: Hurst, 2012).

70 Maureen T. Reddy, 'Invisibility/Hypervisibility: The Paradox of Normative Whiteness', *Transformations: The Journal of Inclusive Scholarship and Pedagogy* 9, no. 2 (1998): 55–64; George Yancy, *Black Bodies, White Gazes: The Continuing Significance of Race* (Lanham, MD: Rowman & Littlefield, 2008).

71 Paul Amar, 'Turning the Gendered Politics of the Security State Inside Out?', *International Feminist Journal of Politics* 13, no. 3 (2011): 305.

72 Annelies Moors, 'The Dutch and the Face-Veil: The Politics of Discomfort', *Social Anthropology* 17, no. 4 (2009): 401.

73 AIVD, *Jaarverslag 2007 [2007 Annual Report]* (The Hague: AIVD, 2008).

74 Marguerite van den Berg and Willem Schinkel, '"Women from the Catacombs of the City": Gender Notions in Dutch Culturist Discourse', *Innovation: The European Journal of Social Science Research* 22, no. 4 (2009): 393–410.

75 Moors, 'The Dutch and the Face-Veil'.

76 Annelies Moors, 'Unregistered Islamic Marriages: Anxieties about Sexuality and Islam in the Netherlands', in *Applying Shari'a in the West: Facts, Fears and the Future of Islamic*

Rules on Family Relations in the West, ed. Maurits Berger (Leiden: Leiden University Press, 2013).

77 Katherine E. Brown and Tania Saeed, 'Radicalization and Counter-Radicalization at British Universities: Muslim Encounters and Alternatives', *Ethnic and Racial Studies* 38, no. 11 (2016): 1952–68.

78 Van den Berg and Schinkel, '"Women from the Catacombs of the City"'.

79 See, for instance, Francesco Ragazzi, 'Policed Multiculturalism in Europe? The Impact of Counter-Terrorism and Counter-Radicalization and the "End" of Multiculturalism', in *Counter-Radicalisation: Critical Perspectives*, eds. Christopher Baker-Beall, Charlotte Heath-Kelly and Lee Jarvis (Oxon and New York: Routledge, 2015).

80 http://onderwijs.vlaanderen.be/nl/deradicalisering and https://onderwijs.vlaanderen. be/nl/co%C3%B6rdinator-onderwijsnetwerk-islamexperten-tegendiscours.

81 In France: Dounia Bouzar (who is ambiguious about her Muslim identity), Sonia Imtoul, Rachid Benzine, Tariq Oubrou. In Belgium: Abou Youssouf, Michael Privot, Brahim Laytouss, Suleyman Van Ael, Khalid Benhaddou. In the Netherlands: Mohammed Cheppih and Yassin Elforkani, for instance.

82 Mahmood Mamdani, *Good Muslim, Bad Muslim: America, the Cold War, and the Roots of Terror* (New York: Pantheon Books, 2004).

83 Tariq Ramadan, *Être musulman européen: Études des sources islamiques à la lumière du contexte européen* (Lyon: Tawhid, 1999).

84 See contribution of Groeninck (Chapter 3 in this volume).

85 Talal Asad, *The Idea of an Anthropology of Islam*. Occasional Papers Series (Washington, DC: Georgetown University Center for Contemporary Arab Studies, 1986).

86 This occurs through the desire to develop an Islam of the 'middle-way' or by calling groups considered as extremist (such as ISIS) *khawarij*, a reference to seventh-century fighting groups that were excommunicated for their refusal to accept the proposed pacification by the Muslim leadership and who were accused of killing the fourth caliph, Ali. See, in this respect, Khaled Abou El Fadl, *The Great Theft: Wrestling Islam from the Extremists* (New York: Harper One, 2007).

Part I

THE CIRCULATION OF A CONTESTED CONCEPT

Chapter 1

RADICALIZATION: THE ORIGINS AND LIMITS OF A CONTESTED CONCEPT[1]

Rik Coolsaet

'Radicalization' has a twisted history. At every turn, it gained a new meaning without shedding the existing one. In the beginning, 'radicalization' meant Muslims espousing an anti-Western, fundamentalist stance, with Iran as the epicentre of a global Muslim insurgency. In the wake of the 9/11 attacks, it started to be loosely used as a synonym of 'anger'. A number of Muslims were said to become increasingly angry as a result of a wide variety of 'root causes'. But almost simultaneously, it became intertwined with 'recruitment' by foreign extremists, who tried to persuade these angry individuals to join foreign war zones. In 2004, another layer was added when 'self-radicalization' became the buzzword, since it appeared that one could also develop into a terrorist through kinship and friendship networks. That year, the EU officially embraced the concept. Myriad models and studies were financed to try to clarify the long, step-by-step process through which an individual radicalized into a terrorist. But, in a new twist, by 2015–2016 it became obvious that radicalization didn't require a long process after all. 'Flash' or 'instant radicalization' was introduced to elucidate how some literally in a moment jumped into jihadi terrorism without any previous phase of, well, radicalization. In the meantime, by 2018, the culprit behind the global Muslim insurgency had crossed the Gulf. Saudi Arabia was now seen as the villain that, through its multi-billion-dollar promotion of a newly coined 'Salafi-Wahhabism', has perverted the minds of millions of Muslims worldwide into a rejectionist, anti-Western stance.

As this chapter will illustrate, throughout the years 'radicalization' has gained even more layers than those succinctly exposed in the introductory paragraph. When the scale of Europeans travelling to Syria was publicly disclosed in early 2013, many were taken by surprise, even in countries like the Netherlands or the United Kingdom, which had taken a substantial lead in the field of radicalization studies. By mid-2014, the Dutch General Intelligence and Security Service (*Algemene Inlichtingen- en Veiligheidsdienst*, AIVD) consequently reported that the existing tools focusing upon profiles and indicators had proven to be of only limited use.[2] This observation should come as no surprise. The very notion of 'radicalization' has always been an oversimplification of an extremely complex phenomenon, and a source of ambiguity and confusion as a result of competing paradigms and multi-layered definitions.

The concept of radicalization in relation to terrorism has no long-standing scientific pedigree. It was born as a political construct, first raised within European police and intelligence circles, boosted by the 9/11 attacks and finally embraced in May 2004 in an internal EU counterterrorism document. The attacks in Madrid, two months before, and in London in July 2005, pushed the concept to centre stage in EU counterterrorism thinking and policies. Unlike the perpetrators of 9/11, these attackers did not come from abroad but were individuals who grew up in Europe and were often born there. How did they come to resort to terrorism and turn against their own countrymen? Why were they attracted by extremist ideologies? What made them vulnerable to recruiters? Something, it was argued, must turn a person from a 'normal' individual into a terrorist. Untangling this process became the essence of radicalization studies and the holy grail of European (and later worldwide) counterterrorism efforts. Fifteen years after its official adoption and notwithstanding its widespread usage, radicalization remains a sloppy notion, ill-defined, complex and controversial. The same questions are still being asked today: What exactly do we understand by radicalization? What are its drivers? How do we reverse or stop it? Are radical ideas a conveyor belt to radical action? How does religion relate to it exactly?

2001–4: The origins of a novel concept

The 9/11 attacks made terrorism once more a leading threat to the West. Initially, this was essentially considered an external threat. The West was a target for al-Qaeda and other jihadi groups, as well as a 'place for recruitment and logistical support for jihad in Afghanistan, Iraq and Chechnya', according to Europol, the Europe-wide police office.[3] Its international nature made it stand apart from the other forms of terrorism in the EU, dubbed 'domestic', such as separatist, extreme-left or eco-terrorism. The first official EU declaration on terrorism in the wake of the 9/11 attacks clearly testified to the external nature of the threat. Under the aegis of the United Nations, the EU affirmed that it would act in solidarity with the United States and that it would take and support

> actions ... targeted and ... directed against States abetting, supporting or harbouring terrorists. ... It is by developing the Common Foreign and Security Policy (CFSP) and by making the European Security and Defence Policy (ESDP) operational at the earliest opportunity that the Union will be most effective. The fight against the scourge of terrorism will be all the more effective if it is based on an in-depth political dialogue with those countries and regions of the world in which terrorism comes into being.[4]

But soon, counterterrorism experts in the Belgian police and in State Security (the civil intelligence service VSSE (*Veiligheid van de Staat-Sûreté de l'État*)) started noticing signs of 'radicalization' among youngsters in immigrant communities, particularly with Moroccan roots. 'Radical' was loosely used here. It covered the same observations described by Europol some time later as a 'toughening' (of Moroccan students in France).[5] The Belgian assessments were shared with the colleagues of the AIVD, who, in the months following the September 2001 attacks, had noticed a parallel trend of recruitment of young Dutchmen by foreign 'fundamental Muslims' who had fought in Afghanistan. In a public report released in December 2002, the AIVD attempted to draw a profile of these youngsters. Many of them were young men of Moroccan origin (aged eighteen to thirty-one), who were born in the Netherlands or grew up there from early childhood:

> These young people are often in search of their identity. They blame Dutch society for not having enough respect for their ethnic and religious community and not in the least for their parents and they themselves. Where other foreign youths opt for a more liberal confirmation of their Islamic belief and attach a lot of value to their social development in the Dutch society and others end up in a criminal environment, these youths find something to hold on to in very radical Islamic beliefs. Former Islamistic fighters who guide them in a recruitment process, give them a sense of self-respect, involvement, brotherhood and identity. They feel that they are involved in a fight between good and bad, which guides them into a certain direction and provides answers to existential questions they are dealing with. For some Muslim youths embracing a radical Islamic faith signifies a clear break with their former criminal existence, a way of life they want to leave behind for good.[6]

In this report 'radicalization processes' was incidentally mentioned. It was not altogether clear what exactly was meant, but from the earlier quote it can be assumed that it referred to Muslims 'embracing a radical Islamic faith'. In relation to Islam, 'radical' had indeed become a widespread term since the Iranian revolution of 1979. It was in this sense that the AIVD's precursor, the BVD, used it in the early 1990s when referring to the 'increasing radicalization or fundamentalization of Muslim communities'.[7] But here too, the concept was not further elaborated upon.[8]

In its *2001 Annual Report*, the Dutch service went one step further. It now explicitly linked extreme religious ideas to terrorism:

> Never before has it been so manifest that extreme religious convictions within part of the Muslim community also involve risks in the sphere of radicalization and terrorism, in addition to other security-related problems, such as a polarization between population groups or imported conflicts. ... The BVD's intensified attention for counterterrorism is partly focused on the identification of breeding grounds for radical ideas that might eventually lead to actual support to or participation in terrorist attacks by Dutch residents.[9]

The 'breeding grounds for radical ideas' seem to refer in the first place to the countries of origin of the immigrant communities in the Netherlands, in particular the Turkish, Kurdish and Afghan communities, but the 'phenomena that frustrate the integration of Muslims into the Dutch society' were also identified, albeit in lesser detail.

The Dutch intelligence service called for both dialogue and repression as measures to prevent radicalization processes from developing into terrorism. How exactly radical ideas transformed into violent acts was not spelled out, however. The previously mentioned December 2002 report was the first attempt to break down the process by which individuals decided 'to travel abroad to participate in or support the jihad'. Radicalization was described as part of a recruitment process led by foreigners and aimed at drawing individuals into participation in overseas terrorist campaigns. In other words, radical ideas possibly turned into terrorism through the patient endeavours of recruiters. This was considered a 'long process':

> A recruiter requires patience and social-psychological insight to gradually tighten his grip on the recruit and to be able to manipulate him towards a willingness to devote himself to the jihad. The recruitment process is a long process, that starts with making and intensifying the contact, in which the relation starts to look more and more like a recruiter–recruit relationship. Because recruiters have more impact on recruits than the other way around, it seems probable that the initiative for recruitment originates with a recruiter. . . . People recruited in the Netherlands who then travel abroad to participate in an ideological and military training elsewhere or in the Islamistic war, are also a huge threat for the international legal order.[10]

In the run-up to the 2003 Iraq War, some European intelligence agencies warned of potential consequences for Europe, contradicting the official American rationale for the war, summarized by George W. Bush as follows: 'We will strike the terrorists abroad so we do not have to face them here at home.'[11] Belgium's VSSE was apprehensive that the Iraq War would, on the contrary, boost resentment and unrest among youngsters on the streets of Europe, as indeed police officers in the field soon reported.

As it turned out, the American invasion of Iraq breathed new life into the waning jihadi scene. A new wave of radicals emerged, angered by the invasion. This wave was labelled 'home-grown'. By adding a layer of frustration that existed within Muslim communities worldwide, it also pushed jihadi terrorism into a new dimension that plugged into the ongoing fragmentation of the al-Qaeda network: a bottom-up dynamic of small self-radicalizing groups and individuals no longer directed by al-Qaeda but subscribing to its ideology. Foreign recruiters were no longer needed (even if this still happened), and recruitment became a more spontaneous local process, evolving through kinship and friendship bonds. The jihadi threat was becoming a decentralized, home-grown patchwork of scattered groups linked by a common world view and opportunistic connections. It thus represented an essentially bottom-up dynamic, increasingly replacing the earlier top-down strategy conducted via foreign recruiters.

Competing paradigms on the origins of terrorism were by now cohabitating within EU counterterrorism thinking. The original view of terrorism as an external security challenge was highlighted in the EU's first European Security Strategy (ESS), presented by Javier Solana in December 2003. A second view co-existed alongside the first, but initially only as a side issue, involving exploitation of domestic grievances by foreign extremists. The ESS also mentioned 'alienation of young people living in foreign societies'. That sentence was somewhat puzzling, since the precise meaning of 'foreign societies' was not explicit. Did it concern youngsters living in dire situations outside Europe or did it refer to European youngsters with migrant roots? Probably both. The ESS addressed the realm of external relations, but surprisingly, in a subsequent sentence it also mentioned that 'This phenomenon is also a part of our own society.'[12] That last view was soon to gain the upper hand.

The Madrid train bombings of March 2004 subsequently confirmed these early indications of a home-grown threat, even if the ensuing 'Declaration on Combating Terrorism' still largely described the threat of terrorism in terms of external threat. The perpetrators did not conform to the (implicit) standard terrorist profile of a fundamentalist Muslim coming from abroad, but originated from the important Spanish-Moroccan diaspora, without any proven link to al-Qaeda. With hindsight, this was nevertheless a major boost for what was to become a brand-new dimension in European counterterrorism: the identification of 'root causes'.

The Madrid attacks prompted the EU and its Member States to break new ground in their counterterrorism approach by delving into the mechanisms underpinning the recruitment of individuals into terrorism. The Council meeting of March 2004 called for a thorough assessment of 'the factors which contribute to support for, and recruitment into, terrorism'. The groundwork had been laid by the earlier intelligence and police assessments and the discussions within the EU counterterrorism working groups, but now the EU seriously embarked on the 'root causes' approach to terrorism.

By taking this route, the EU entered uncharted territory. Historically, Member States had always considered terrorism to be a crime that should be tackled through criminal law. 'Root causes', however, not only brought the EU into the realm of prevention, a policy domain that lay by and large within Member States' competence, but also, more importantly, pushed counterterrorism far beyond its traditional security-centred tools of policing, intelligence and law enforcement by linking prevention and security with the ultimate ambition of draining the breeding ground for terrorism. Counterterrorism now became a whole-of-government effort, encompassing complex societal issues such as integration, multiculturalism and social cohesion, and stitching it all together in a broadened security agenda.

Only with the passing of time would the implications of blurring the once-obvious dividing line between prevention and security, and their respective constituencies, become clear. It led to ambiguities and unintended consequences that still bedevil counterterrorism, prevention and community relations alike.

With the EU embarking upon a root cause trajectory, the United States instead privileged a global manhunt as its main strategy for combating international terrorism. The EU's burgeoning focus on upstream prevention through the identification of the underlying factors that could lead to (recruitment to) terrorism was generally rejected by the United States, since it considered that speaking of 'root causes' implied condoning certain terrorist acts. The idea of 'roots' was 'a taboo in the Bush administration, with "evil" the only acceptable explanation for the attacks of September 11'.[13]

Immediately after the Madrid bombings, a closed meeting organized in Brussels by the Belgian Egmont Institute – The Royal Institute for International Relations – at the request of the (rotating) Irish EU presidency brought together for the first time the two relevant EU working groups on terrorism (Council Working Group on Terrorism – International Aspects or COTER and the Terrorism Working Group or TWG) with the police and intelligence services of the Member States to discuss terrorist recruitment. Participants tried to determine whether top-down recruitment by international networks such as al-Qaeda or instead bottom-up self-recruitment were the main avenue by which individuals were drawn into terrorism.

The Irish EU presidency acted upon the discussions at this conference. In May 2004, a common (confidential) assessment of the 'Underlying factors in the recruitment to terrorism' by the two EU working groups (COTER and TWG) attempted to identify the root causes of radicalization. It was the very first time an official (albeit confidential) EU document mentioned 'radicalization' in relation to terrorism. In the assessment radicalization was essentially understood as 'anger among Muslims or Islamists'.

The potential causes of this anger were considered wide-ranging (but not put in any specific order of priority, nor really operationalized): regional conflicts and failed or failing states (and the perception of Western double standards), globalization and socio-economic factors, alienation, propagation of an extremist worldview, and of systems of education (madrasas). In summing up the possible root causes of the anger, the paper clarified the puzzling reference to alienation of youngsters in foreign countries in the ESS. This did indeed refer to youngsters both inside and outside Europe:

> Within Europe, young Muslims may often feel themselves to be subject to discrimination and participate relatively little in mainstream politics and public life. In this context of sometimes real grievances, a lack of any real opportunities to effect change or vent frustration and a consequent sense of anger and helplessness, the unambiguous messages of extremist propaganda can become very attractive, particularly to the youth population.[14]

The report was largely inspired by recent intelligence assessments (originating from the United Kingdom, Belgium, the Netherlands and a limited number of Member States). It warned that the 'processes by which individuals are drawn into terrorism [were] very complex.... Accordingly, generalizations must be viewed with great caution'.

The 'radicalization process' was accordingly represented as the ultimate stage of recruitment to terrorism for a minority of radical Muslims:

Recruitment to terrorist organizations is preceded, in many cases, by a process of radicalization, where an individual may become attracted to extremist ideologies. There are a number of factors that may contribute to this, although the specific process of radicalization can vary from individual to individual.[15]

This recruitment was understood as a wide-ranging and strategically planned endeavour by 'Islamist terrorist organizations' who were 'looking for and identifying potential recruits and then monitoring and manipulating these people to achieve an internalized radical political-Islamic conviction, with the final purpose of having them participate in the jihad in one way or another'.[16]

But in its concluding paragraphs, the May 2004 assessment also mentioned the new bottom-up trend, reported earlier by police and intelligence services, of 'self-motivated young radicals . . . who have had no physical contact with recruiters and who have been mobilized by extremist ideological messages encountered over the internet'.

At the end of 2004, the Dutch AIVD was the first Western intelligence service to state publicly that radicalization could indeed be a process of 'autonomous' recruitment (through self-initiated radicalization), without the mediation of a 'real' recruiter.[17] The murders of the libertarian Dutch politician Pim Fortuyn by an environmental and animal rights activist in 2002 and, still more so, of the movie director Theo van Gogh in 2004 by a young member of a loose grouping of radicals of Moroccan descent who had been born or raised in the Netherlands (with the exception of one or two converts to Islam), turned the spotlight on home-grown terrorism.

Moreover, this report for the first time attempted to define 'radicalism' (distinguishing it from extremism) and 'radicalization'. Radicalism was defined as:

> The (active) pursuit of and/or support to far-reaching changes in society which may constitute a danger to (the continued existence of) the democratic legal order (aim), which may involve the use of undemocratic methods (means) that may harm the functioning of the democratic legal order (effect). In line with this, radicalization can be interpreted as a person's (growing) willingness to pursue and/or support such changes himself (in an undemocratic way or otherwise), or his encouraging others to do so.[18]

In contrast to the earlier internal EU assessment, the AIVD privileged an essentially ideological understanding of the process of radicalization, disconnected from the potential political, social and economic causes of radicalization originally understood as 'anger'. It did acknowledge that the causes of the emergence of 'radical-political Islamic movements are diverse', including the national context. But it left the domestic context essentially out of the equation, and instead focused on the 'purely religious ideological component of radical-political Islam, which plays an increasingly important role in many countries (including the Netherlands) both on a national level and on an international level'.[19] What was originally, in the May 2004 EU assessment, only one of the possible root causes of radicalization now became a major prism through which to examine the process. Even if inside the EU some Member States – including the Irish Presidency at that time – warned against the pitfalls of involving Islam as a religion in the debate (in a classified EU-wide message on 4 February 2004), the ideological and religious prism nevertheless became a major factor in the emerging consensus on radicalization as the core approach to understanding contemporary terrorism.

The AIVD went to great lengths to distinguish between different forms of 'radical Islam', only to conclude that all of its forms – religious, apolitical or violent – constituted a threat, albeit of different natures, and were thus a matter for follow-up and investigation by intelligence services.

This turn to a religious and ideological prism produced a new set of competing paradigms, with important policy consequences. Even fifteen years on, this still bedevils and obscures the issue of radicalization, making it a source of persistent ambiguity. If radicalization is decontextualized and primarily considered an ideology-driven process, whereby ideas function as a conveyor belt to action, then a counter-narrative (instilling individuals with so-called moderate ideas) is an appropriate way of blocking its spread. But if the context or the conducive environment is the key structural driver behind the emergence of radicalization, then proposing a counter-narrative will be irrelevant or of only limited use. Moreover, the latter approach makes a suitable counter-strategy much harder to conceive, since it implies taking a hard look at structural drivers within one's own domestic environment and dealing with an extraordinarily broad range of issues.

Alongside the evolving thinking within the intelligence community and the European Commission, the Madrid bombings clearly acted as a milestone, not only for enhancing European coordination in counterterrorism, but also for pursuing the inquiry into root causes.

Within the European Commission, officials were, however, reluctant to use the concept of 'root causes'. They feared that it could be hijacked by radicals in the Basque region or Northern Ireland to justify their terrorist tactics. But they were also convinced of the need to address the underlying factors and thus to go beyond the mere law enforcement that constituted the traditional core of European counter-terrorism. Without tackling upstream the context that had engendered the current wave of 'Islamic terrorism', they feared that the European polity would be undermined by a growing polarization between Muslims and non-Muslims and between natives and migrant communities. They thus seized the opportunity offered by this emerging concept of 'radicalization', judging it to be more neutral than 'root causes'.

They were nonetheless aware of the inherent dangers in advancing this concept. Not only did they realize that it was an oversimplification of an extremely complex phenomenon at the intersection of individual pathways and a societal context, but they also comprehended that radicalization was not to be criminalized, lest freedom of speech and the very essence of liberal democracy were endangered. The concept must also not be hijacked by anti-migrant and anti-Islam pundits and movements, thus endangering the social fabric of the EU.

In October 2004, the European Commission released its first public paper on 'radicalization', accompanied by the qualification 'violent'.[20] Speaking of 'disrupting the conditions facilitating the recruitment of terrorists', it evidently echoed the May 2004 report and the intelligence assessments. The Commission announced its intention to draw upon 'the expertise of the European Monitoring Centre on Racism and Xenophobia, experts and researchers', with the aim of identifying 'where European policies and instruments can play a preventive role against violent radicalization'. The Commission also made plain that it intended to boost intra-European cooperation in this field and thus to enhance its role in a policy domain that was still largely dominated by intergovernmental decision making.

The two EU counterterrorism working groups drew up a second joint report in November 2004. It now zoomed in on the personal trajectories of individuals and evidently privileged ideological factors over the contextual factors that had been prominent in their first report as the sources of eventual anger. The Netherlands now held the rotating EU presidency. This partly helps to explain the shift from context to ideology, since it reflected the stance taken by the Dutch intelligence service. But one might also consider this to be the result of a common-sense process of narrowing down a complex phenomenon into an operational approach. A strategy that intended to dry up all the possible root causes of anger among youngsters was doomed to be a whole-of-government approach, extremely wide-ranging, complex, time-consuming and spanning virtually all imaginable policy domains, far beyond the classical realm of counterterrorism. Concentrating upon individual pathways seemed, on the contrary, to have the benefit of simplicity. Focusing on the process an individual undergoes from his or her original 'normal' status to becoming a terrorist seemed a lot easier than addressing the environment that made him or her vulnerable to the siren song of extremism.

Accordingly, this November report identified a number of particular 'hot spots' where radicalization processes were likely to occur (certain mosques, schools, ghettos, the internet). But the report now also insisted that it tended to take place via loosely connected networks and individuals rather than through specific organizations dedicated to the task. This unmistakably indicated that the original idea of an external recruiter actively taking the lead in the process of radicalization had given way to bottom-up dynamics. The report mentioned that while 'exogenous factors' (i.e. the role of al-Qaeda as a leading factor in radicalization) had somewhat diminished, 'endogenous factors have an increasing influence on radicalization'.

The report now clearly leaned towards the ideological paradigm, like the Dutch AIVD reports. While contextual factors were not entirely neglected – underlying factors such as social deprivation or lack of integration were indeed mentioned – the emphasis was nevertheless clearly on the ideological process of the individual:

A univocal definition of radicalization cannot be given. At the same time, it is clear that individuals can move from mainstream Muslim beliefs and practices towards Islamist extremism. This may be motivated by a potential confrontation with Western society, though other factors also can play a role here such as justification of criminal activities, peer pressure, the appeal for 'justified' violent behaviour.[21]

2005: The institutionalization of competing paradigms

In December 2004, the European heads of state and government decided to elaborate a strategy and action plan to address radicalization and recruitment to terrorism. It had now become agreed standard language within the EU that in the long run the Union's response to terrorism had to address the 'root causes of terrorism', as this Council decision stated. It called on the Council to establish a long-term strategy and action plan on both radicalization and recruitment by June 2005.[22]

Alongside the ongoing work that had started within the Commission after the March train bombings, the EU Council secretariat also initiated a comprehensive effort of consultation and information gathering on radicalization under the guidance of Gilles de Kerchove, then director for Justice and Home Affairs.

The July 2005 bombings in London acted as a further booster for counterterrorism work and thinking at EU level. While holding the EU presidency in the second half of 2005, the United Kingdom proposed streamlining into a single overall framework the wide variety of ad hoc measures that had been undertaken since 9/11. This would mirror the structure of its own recently adopted counterterrorism strategy (which itself had been influenced by the ongoing work within the European Commission on a counterterrorism strategy).

Radicalization as prism for understanding and countering terrorism was now rapidly gaining traction within EU counterterrorism thinking. The Commission announced in September 2005 that it was establishing 'a network of experts for the sharing of research and policy ideas which will submit a preliminary contribution on the state of knowledge on violent radicalization in the beginning of 2016'.[23] This document defined violent radicalization as 'the phenomenon of people embracing opinions, views and ideas which could lead to acts of terrorism . . .'. The document once again stressed that this was 'a very complex question with no simple answers and which requires a cautious, modest and well-thought approach'. It was also adamant in warning against the use of the words 'Islamic terrorism'. Stating that no religion tolerates, let alone justifies, terrorism, the document emphasized:

> The fact that some individuals unscrupulously attempt to justify their crimes in the name of a religion ... cannot be allowed in any way and to any extent whatsoever to cast a shadow upon such a religion. ... Stating this fact clearly is, in the Commission's view, the first requirement for the Union in the fight against violent radicalization.[24]

The emerging consensus on the concept of 'violent radicalization' should not, however, be overstated. Quite the contrary. Most EU Member States were of the opinion that the emphasis should rather be on preparedness and protecting the public from the immediate threat of terrorist attacks. Moreover, in the absence of a univocally agreed definition of radicalization, elusiveness was the dominant characteristic of the discussions that followed. Some Member States increasingly identified ideology as the major driving force of radicalization. But a small number of Member States, together with the Commission and the Council Secretariat, were adamant about addressing contextual factors in view of long-term sustainable results in counterterrorism efforts.[25]

The European Commission itself was firmly in favour of maintaining a broad approach to upstream prevention at the heart of European counterterrorism efforts. One of the motivations behind Commission officials' desire to gather together the aforementioned Expert Group was the hope of building a critical mass to sustain this approach. It wanted to pool existing academic knowledge on different types of radicalization in order to identify the core characteristics of the process as a necessary basis for devising adequate counterstrategies.

The EU Counter-Terrorism Strategy adopted by the heads of state and government in their December 2005 Council meeting, while still defining terrorism as an external phenomenon ('much of the terrorist threat to Europe originates outside the EU'), now also endorsed the home-grown radicalization challenge that needed to be addressed.[26] It took some discussion among the Member States, but by identifying 'Prevent' ('preventing people turning to terrorism by tackling the factors or root causes which can lead to radicalization and recruitment, in Europe and internationally') as the first of the four strategic objectives, the EU clearly stressed the preventive work that needed to be undertaken to combat terrorism in the long term.

The other strategic objectives were the following: 'Protect' (sheltering citizens and infrastructure from attacks), 'Pursue' (pursue and investigate terrorists and their networks across EU borders), and finally 'Respond' (enhancing consequence management mechanisms and capabilities used in case of an attack in one of the Member States).

As part and parcel of this new overall strategy, the European Council simultaneously adopted the *Strategy for Combating Radicalization and Recruitment to Terrorism*, thus confirming that radicalization had become one of the central threads in Europe's 'root cause' approach to counterterrorism. This document called for a better understanding of the 'motives behind such a decision [i.e. to become involved in terrorism]' and for a way to 'identify and counter the ways, propaganda and conditions through which people are drawn into terrorism and consider it a legitimate course of action'.[27] The strategy recognized that radicalization was rooted in the domestic context of the Member States: Within the Union, too, structural factors existed that might create disaffection and susceptibility to the overtures of extremists, such as social and economic inequalities among relevant minority groups.

This was plainly spelled out in the accompanying (classified) Action Plan, which almost exclusively dealt with factors in the domestic realm. In an attempt to operationalize the complex mosaic of root causes that had been identified since 2004, the Action Plan defined three venues for specific action: 'facilitational factors' (disrupting the activities of terrorist networks), 'motivational factors' ('ensuring that voices of moderation prevail over those of extremism') and 'structural factors' ('promoting yet more vigorously security, justice, democracy and opportunity for all'). In the last dimension, EU Member States were exhorted to 'combat those who exacerbate division by inciting racism, xenophobia and specifically Islamophobia' and to target resources to reduce existing inequalities. Member States should consequently 'develop and promote full and active engagements of all citizens in their communities'.

By the end of 2005, radicalization had become the holy grail of European counterterrorism. But under this apparent unanimity, major ambiguities existed as a result of competing paradigms. Firstly, while the political discourse still very much emphasized the external realm, the home-grown dynamics advanced by the practitioners had by now become the essence of the threat. Secondly, even if 'root causes' were increasingly embraced as an idiom, the focus was split between insistence on the context and the seemingly more practical approach of looking into individual pathways, with ideology as the privileged culprit. But even to those officials who were involved in these discussions on a daily basis, the distinction between both paradigms was not wholly clear, nor the dissimilar policies that would flow from them.

A comet in the EU counterterrorism sky: The EC Expert Group on violent radicalization

Commission officials who had been energetically advancing the need for upstream prevention nevertheless realized that not much was known about what happened in the black box labelled 'radicalization' and what exactly made the environment conducive to radicalization. They also acknowledged that the relationship between ideas and action, between radicalization and terrorism, was poorly understood. Past studies on why, how and when individuals became involved in terrorism had indeed never produced definite answers.

In a landmark 1981 contribution on 'The Causes of Terrorism',[28] Martha Crenshaw already acknowledged that answering the question of why specific individuals engage in political violence was a complicated problem. Context, Crenshaw urged, is of the essence in understanding terrorism. Its causes lie in a facilitative or conducive environment that permits its emergence *and* in direct motivating factors that propel people to violence. Together with colleagues such as Ted Gurr, Crenshaw thereby insisted early on upon the need to look into the interplay between this societal context, psychological considerations and group dynamics to understand terrorism. Even in 1981, Crenshaw had insisted that terrorism had never been an automatic reaction to given conditions, but also that terrorists only represented a small minority of people who experienced the same conditions. But answering the question of why specific individuals engaged in political violence was a complicated problem, 'and the question of why they engage in terrorism is still more difficult'.[29]

Fraught with methodological difficulties and confronted with a seemingly endless stream of factors to be taken into consideration, the why-terrorism-occurs research failed to gain traction. Instead, the focus shifted to more practical policy-oriented studies and crisis management analyses.

Beyond academia, individual trajectories were not an essential part of the counterterrorism toolbox of law enforcement or intelligence services either. The context being considered a sufficient explanation of why individuals chose terrorism, looking into individual pathways never played much of a role in assessing and countering the threat: 'No one talked of the IRA being radicalized, or Shining Path, or Black September or the Red Brigades. Though all of these older groups certainly were by our modern understanding.'[30]

Commission officials were evidently aware of the intricate, interlinked and complex nature of the issues involved, and the absence of satisfying answers. How and why do individuals embrace radical ideas? How do ideas (ideology, religion) translate into action? Are psychological or socio-familial profiles a way forward in identifying potential terrorists? What is the interaction between context and individual pathways? What is the role of systemic factors? And how can all this be operationalized in policy? The endeavour was thought to be rewarding, though if one could succeed in understanding how these sequences worked, it was assumed, it might be possible to devise adequate strategies to extract individuals (or groups, for that matter) from radicalization and thus turn them away from terrorism.

As previously mentioned, Commission officials started to screen leading authors in several fields that might be helpful in deepening the concept of violent radicalization. Experts with different academic backgrounds ranging from Islamic studies to deviant behaviours (studying subcultures like skinheads, radical rightists and leftists, those who enacted political violence, gang members) to international politics were invited to join the group. Fernando Reinares from the Universidad Rey Juan Carlos in Madrid was appointed as its chair.[31] This policy advisory group was tasked with preparing a synthesis report on the existing knowledge in the field of violent radicalization. Originally planned for June 2006, it was only by 15 May 2008 that the final report was submitted to the Commission, as a result of a series of personal and practical difficulties that had hampered the group from the start (by mid-2007, one of its members even thought the group was dead).

In its report, the group re-stated that the concepts of 'radicalization' and 'violent radicalization' had originated in EU policy circles after the 2004 Madrid bombing, and that they had not been widely used in social science as a concept. They cautioned against the ambiguity of these concepts, since no uniform usage existed in social sciences and humanities. Moreover, 'radicalization' in connection with terrorism was qualified as inherently confusing as a result of its relationship to 'radicalism' as an expression of legitimate political thought.

The Expert Group thus suggested an alternative to the concept of 'radicalization':

> While radicalism can pose a threat, it is extremism, and particularly terrorism, that ought to be our main concern since it involves the active subversion of democratic values and the rule of law. In this sense violent radicalization is to be understood as socialization to extremism which manifests itself in terrorism.[32]

Drawing on their pooled expertise, the experts explicitly rejected any exclusive link with a specific religion, for example, Islam. They noted on the contrary that 'remarkable similarities [exist] between radicalization to current Islamist or jihadist terrorism and radicalization associated with left-wing, right-wing or ethnonationalist terrorism in Western Europe since the 1960s'. It is probably useful to quote this assessment in full:

> Past and present waves of violent radicalization which lead to terrorism among mainly young people share certain structural features:
>
> (i)   Firstly, radicalization thrives in an enabling environment that is characterized by a more widely shared sense of injustice, exclusion and humiliation (real or perceived) among the constituencies the terrorists claim to represent. . . . Nothing creates so fertile a breeding ground for political radicalization than the feeling of belonging to the camp of those left behind in the progress of mankind but at the same time upholding potent and aspirational symbols of empowerment.
>
> (ii) Secondly, radicalization always takes place at the intersection of that enabling social environment and individual trajectories towards greater militancy.
>
> (iii) Thirdly, terrorist violence . . . stands only at the far end of a wide repertoire of possible radical expressions and only a small number of radicals become terrorist extremists. Indeed, even radicalization into violence short of terrorism is not a prevalent phenomenon among the vast majority of citizens of the European Union and only a tiny minority of newcomers succumb to it.[33]

To make clear their point that 'radicalization' was an exceptionally complex, gradual and phased process, they noted that:

> One of the most significant understandings gained from academic research over recent years is that individuals involved in terrorist activities exhibit a diversity of social backgrounds, undergo rather different processes of violent radicalization and are influenced by various combinations of motivations. This is relevant not only with respect to the more recent expressions of Islamist terrorism but also as regards right-wing, left-wing and ethnonationalist manifestations of such violence previously experienced in a number of European countries.[34]

And insisted that:

> There is not any single root cause for radicalization leading to terrorism but a number of factors may contribute to it. Precipitant ('trigger') factors vary according to individual experience and personal pathways to radicalization. For instance, historical antecedents of political violence, excessive repression by state authorities in the recent past and profound social changes (in Europe or in the

country of origin) may, under certain conditions, contribute to a polarized social climate in which confrontation rather than conflict resolution becomes the preferred option. Yet personal experiences, kinship and bonds of friendship, as well as group dynamics are critical in triggering the actual process of radicalization escalating to engagement in acts of terrorism against civilians.

What then was the role of ideology (and religion, for that matter) in the processes leading to terrorism? The group clearly distanced itself from the burgeoning trend in the United Kingdom and other Member States of considering ideology as a primary driver. Ideology acted as a vehicle to reduce potential moral inhibitors and as a justification of the resort to extreme actions such as terrorism, but not really as a driver, according to the authors.

Finally, since it was asked to provide policy advice, the Expert Group expressed scepticism about the efficiency of one-size-fits-all deradicalization programmes. As a result of the wide variations observed in processes of radicalization into violence, it judged it 'futile to try to develop strategies for preventing these processes as no such measures will be able to fit them all'.

But in their concluding remarks, the group recommended examining past and current individual, tailor-made exit strategies in, for example, Scandinavia and Germany, in which they emphasized as particularly relevant the conceptual distinction between deradicalization as a cognitive process and disengagement as a behavioural process that implies discontinuing involvement in terrorism (the former being extremely challenging). Since they realized that the Member States would undoubtedly embark on devising deradicalization programmes, they insisted these should be evaluated in order to provide evidence on what worked and what did not.

For reasons that were never made wholly clear to the group, but were rooted in turf wars within the Commission, after it completed its first study in May 2008, the EC Expert Group on Violent Radicalization was de facto discontinued by the French Commissioner, Jacques Barrot. Even if Commission officials and public Commission documents sometimes still referred to the report, it went largely unnoticed for many years before receiving renewed attention long after its official submission.

Pull and limits of a concept

It would require a huge leap of faith to imagine that if the report had been made public it would have made any difference. Radicalization proved irresistible as a concept. Because of its apparent simplicity, but also its inherent ambiguity, it got embroiled in the concerns over immigration and integration that had developed since the 1980s, and with the unease over Islam and Muslims boosted by the 9/11 attacks. The concept was all the more tantalizing because of the pre-existing popular idiom of 'radical Islam' and the ubiquity of the 'clash of civilizations' paradigm since 9/11. Both reinforced one another by lumping together disparate violent and non-violent groups into a unified global insurgency. Radicalization made it possible to speak about these issues in a way that seemingly differed from the anti-Islam rhetoric of right-wing pundits and movements.

In 2004, the head of Scotland Yard's counterterrorism command, Peter Clarke, was probably among the first officials to warn the media against labelling today's main terrorist threat as 'Islamic', since this was 'both offensive and misleading'.[35] But this is exactly what happened. Radicalization came to be seen as a unique and contemporary process linked almost exclusively to Muslim-related phenomena – exactly what the Council Secretariat, the Commission and its Expert Group had hoped to avoid.

The respected terrorism scholar Alex Schmid, former Officer-in-Charge of the Terrorism Prevention Branch of the UN and member of the Expert Group, explains in one the most comprehensive reviews of the state of knowledge on (de-) radicalization to date:

> We have to admit that in the final analysis, 'radicalization' is not just a socio-psychological scientific concept but also a political construct, introduced into the public and academic debate mainly by national security establishments faced with political Islam in general and Salafist Jihadism in particular. The concept was 'pushed' to highlight a relatively narrow, micro-level set of problems related to the causes of terrorism that Western governments faced in their efforts to counter predominantly 'home-grown' terrorism from second and third generation members of Muslim diasporas.[36]

University of Exeter scholar Jonathan Githens-Mazer makes a similar point:

> When applied to Islam and Muslims, the term radical is often being used interchangeably and opaquely with terms such as fundamentalist, Islamist, Jihadist and neo-Salafist or Wahabbist with little regard for what these terms actually mean, and instead indicate signals about political Islam that these members of the media and politicians wish to transmit.[37]

To be fair, the myriad radicalization studies produced since 2004 have nevertheless yielded useful and intriguing results. Radicalization studies have furthered our understanding of what happens to individuals once they get involved in a process that can ultimately result in terrorism. Radicalization is indeed first and foremost a socialization process in which group dynamics (kinship and friendship) are more important than ideology. These studies have provided us with a more detailed understanding of the stages in the process, which is similar to other forms of deviant behaviour, like gangs or delinquency.[38] The process of socialization into extremism and, eventually, into terrorism, happens gradually and requires a more or less prolonged group process. Feelings of frustration and inequity first have to be interiorized and then lead to a mental separation from society (which is considered responsible for those feelings). Individuals then reach out to others who share the same feelings and create an 'in-group'. Within such a group, personal feelings get politicized ('what are we going to do about it?'). Groupthink gradually solidifies into an unquestioned belief system and attitude, with alternative pathways gradually being pushed aside. In this process, ideology helps to dehumanize the outside-group and transforms innocents (who bear no responsibility for the original feelings of frustration and inequity) into guilty accomplices.

As years went by, the concept of radicalization secured its key position in counterterrorism in policies, law enforcement and academia. But this apparent consensus has obscured the limits of the concept as well as its enduring ambiguities and significant controversies. Radicalization is relentlessly thrown around in various contexts, with diverging meanings and competing policy recommendations.

In at least three respects, the concept has run into its own limitations:

(i) Firstly, contrary to the expectations of its advocates fifteen years ago, we're no closer to identifying what exactly triggers an individual to perpetrate a terrorist attack. Identifying him as 'radicalized' is not very helpful, since many others sharing the same ideas never go beyond this point. Unpacking the black box has thus not resulted in anything close to a prospective instrument for assessing individual behaviour.

(ii) Secondly, and contrary to what some early radicalization studies had initially imagined, personal trajectories or pathways are murky processes that are neither fixed nor predetermined but highly 'individualised and nonlinear, with a number of common "push" and "pull" factors but no single determining feature'.[39] For that reason, Mohammed Hafez and Chreighton Mullins came up with an alternative metaphor of radicalization as a 'puzzle' composed of four factors that come together to produce violent radicalization: personal and collective grievances, networks and interpersonal ties, political and religious ideologies, and enabling environments and support structures.[40]

(iii) Finally, jihadi plots from 2015 onwards by organized hubs and so-called lone actors alike have challenged earlier assumptions that the socialization process needed time to mature into action, that it required a more or less prolonged group process, whereby ideology solidified the cohesiveness of the in-group. All kinds of people have been involved in these plots, but a number of them literally jumped from drug trafficking and petty criminality or living a normal life into a jihadi plot, without any protracted process and with only a limited acquaintance with religious thought compared to the early jihadi generations:

> Information on foreigners joining the ranks of IS suggests that recruitment can take place very quickly, without necessarily requiring a long radicalization process. Age plays a role: younger people are found to be more impressionable and radicalize quicker than older candidates.[41]

In fact, before these individuals decided to act or to join ISIS, there was not much of a 'radicalization process' going on, at least not as earlier understood. To describe this novel phenomenon, a new concept was even coined: 'flash' or 'instant' radicalization. Few observers realized that it was strikingly different from what radicalization was once thought to be.

Beyond these limits to the concept, radicalization also still grapples with the same ambiguities as when it was conceived. A first enduring ambiguity concerns the identification of the key drivers behind radicalization. Is it ideology or context? In fact, this controversy is as old as the study of terrorism. Should one focus on the ideology that drives an individual to embrace terrorism or should the focus be on the conducive environment that lures individuals into a journey that ultimately ends in terrorist violence?

The former approach typically reduces the multi-faceted interaction between context, individual trajectories and group processes to a question of ideology. While radical-right pundits and politicians have tried to make Islam itself the core issue, others referred to a 'distorted interpretation of Islam' as the culprit. According to this paradigm, jihadi terrorism is essentially the result of an ideology-driven process. The key vector in addressing radicalization is subsequently a war on ideas through the promotion of a 'moderate Islam' (whatever that may mean) to combat the negative influence of 'radical Islam'. As a corollary, society is considered to play no significant role in radicalization. Concluding a comprehensive discussion on radicalization in the wake of a failed terrorist plot in Verviers (Belgium) in January 2015, the president of the Flemish nationalist group in the Flemish parliament thus asserted that 'society can never be blamed for radicalization'.[42]

The latter approach however considers radicalization to be primarily a context-driven process. Radicalization is to a context what fever is to illness – a symptom. Sometimes, medicine for fever will alleviate suffering, but as long as the triggering illness is not cured, fever will continue to haunt the patient. The ensuing policy recommendation is then to concentrate on the conducive environment that permits the emergence of radicalization and provides for motivating factors that can propel people to violence. This position was taken by the Belgian federal prosecutor in charge of terrorism, Frédéric Van Leeuw, who readily admitted that 'our Western society is part of the problem' when explaining the departure of so many foreign fighters.[43] A similar assessment was made by Belgium's highest police official (and the new Europol director), Catherine De Bolle:

> What really shocked me, before the attacks and with all that has happened since, is that society has failed to include people. There are many who live with us for years, even decades. We didn't succeed in devising a common denominator. They do not really feel as if they are being included, as if they are part of our society, of Belgium.[44]

These competing paradigms can be easily perceived in the wide-ranging report by the Belgian Parliamentary Commission established after the terrorist attacks in Brussels in March 2016. In its assessment of the relationship between radicalism and the terrorist attacks, the competing paradigms are simply juxtaposed. The report starts by zooming in on the religious dimension and concludes that religion, and its fundamentalist currents in particular, has been of paramount influence in the rise of radicalism. This fundamentalist radicalism moreover is seen as the precursor to violent radicalism.[45] However, the last part of the report reflects on discussions with first-line practitioners and prevention officials, concluding that radicalization has many causes, depending on the paradigm, that it is more important to deal with the (societal) roots of radicalization, rather than with its manifestations, and that discriminations have an important, if not determinant, role in the emergence of radicalism/violent radicalism.[46]

The persistence of these competing paradigms helps to explain why deradicalization programmes often constitute a potpourri of objectives from inclusiveness and prevention of all kinds to repression and counter-narratives. As a result, assessing what works and what doesn't remains as difficult as it has always been.

The second enduring ambiguity directly flows from the first. It remains impossible to measure radicalization. Even if simply viewed as personal trajectories towards violence, 'radicalization' has essentially remained a catch-all. Many different expressions of an individual's ideas and behaviour are mixed together as 'signs of radicalization', and these range from the increased presence of girls and women wearing the hijab, to men dressed in Salafi trousers, orthodox and hate preachers, radical ideas and the terrorist acts themselves. Putting these disparate signs together into a box labelled 'indicators of radicalization' empties the concept of all explanatory meaning, turning it into a container concept.

No satisfying metrics have therefore ever been developed to quantify radicalization. One should thus not take at face value sweeping statements, by authorities or by observers, that radicalization is increasing. Such statements mostly lack robust fundamentals and merely reflect mainstream thinking. An example of this is provided by the policy declaration of the incoming Belgian government in October 2014. It stated that 'The preservation of the democratic system and the safety of our citizens are for the government an absolute priority. Today, it is under pressure from a growing threat of radicalization and terrorism.' On what indicators – beyond the number of foreign fighters from Belgium (and even this criterion was not made explicit) – the assessment of 'growing threat of radicalization' was based, was never made clear.

A third and last area of controversy that has accompanied the concept of radicalization from its adoption in 2004, concerns its relationship to Islam. Early on, many have warned against its exclusive focus on Muslims and Islam. This nevertheless occurred and has continued to do so ever since. It thus unwittingly helped to consolidate the popular Western image of Muslim minorities as suspect communities. It reinforced the existing image of Islam as an imported and threatening value system and Muslim minorities in the West as a potentially disloyal 'fifth column'.[47]

The sloppy use of the concept and its inherent ambiguities contributed to move the once quintessentially radical-right stance against Islam into mainstream politics and discourse. The 2000s witnessed a fierce anti-Islamic *Kulturkampf*, propelling a polarizing debate on the compatibility of Islam with Western values, portraying a global ideological insurgency against Western Enlightenment akin to the clash of civilizations in the 1990s. In the second half of the 2010s, the argument moved beyond this caricature and instead started to focus specifically on the impact of Saudi Wahhabi proselytism on Muslim minorities in the West. Saudi Arabia was accused of being the primary funder of Islamist extremism in the West.[48] Its multi-billion-dollar efforts to promote a newly coined 'Salafi-Wahhabism' was now said to be preparing the ground for radicalization and thus providing a stepping stone to jihadism. In a number of European countries, a growing discussion surfaced about the foreign funding of Islamic institutions, in particular in Germany, Austria, Belgium, Italy and France. In Belgium, the aforementioned Belgian Parliamentary Commission specifically targeted the Saudi-financed Grand Mosque in the centre of Brussels as the vanguard of radicalization in Belgium.

This anti-Salafism stance gained a broad political and media audience in Europe, ranging from Islamic reformers to radical secularists and mainstream politicians. But it remains nevertheless impossible 'to prove beyond doubt a direct causal link between militancy and Saudi-inspired ultra-conservative forms of Sunni Muslim Islam'.[49] Moreover, the argument that Salafi-Wahhabism increasingly contributes to shaping an environment conducive to social isolation and therefore ultimately to jihadi mobilization turns the true sequence of events upside down. In itself, an ideology is sterile. It only takes root if it corresponds to a demand and a need. Salafism is gaining ground precisely because social isolation is real. Salafism offers sense and meaning to those who experience social exclusion. Combating Salafism while ignoring the effects of social exclusion of minority groups is thus likely to fail.

The anti-Salafism campaign brings the state into a position of deciding what kind of Islam is acceptable to European societies. This is at odds with the constitutionally guaranteed freedom of religion. And, perhaps most importantly, instead of helping endeavours to anchor Islam naturally in local environments, this campaign risks backfiring. It runs the risk of hardening positions and furthering polarization by inadvertently reinforcing the distorted jihadi narrative that there is no place for Muslims in the West. Discussion about Islam in Europe has to be a common endeavour of Muslims and society as a whole, but with Muslims determining how to practise their faith. Authorities have to tread lightly when promoting this debate within the framework of combating radicalization.

Conclusion

The concept of radicalization has been less helpful or adequate at explaining and countering terrorism than its early advocates envisaged fifteen years ago. Yet, since it has become a household concept, we can't escape its use. In order to minimize its drawbacks, it is useful to remember its intricacies and its multiple layers. Alex Schmid summed it up neatly: 'Radicalization, like terrorism, too often means different things to different people, sometimes based also on different political interests.'[50]

A comparison with another terrorist campaign (where the concept of radicalization has not been en vogue) might help recalibrate our understanding and reaction to jihadi terrorism. Andrew Parker, the head of the British MI5, made the following comment on Northern Irish terrorism:

> We . . . detect and disrupt the vast majority of their attempts. But occasionally we are all stung with the tragedy of wanton murder, as we saw most recently with the shooting of David Black last November. Rejecting the political process in Northern Ireland, these ragged remnants of a bygone age are in a cul-de-sac of pointless violence and crime with little community support. We will continue to work with the police to put these thugs and killers in front of the Courts.[51]

A 2016 social survey of the Brussels district of Molenbeek indicated that jihadi 'radicals' enjoy as little community-level support as the Irish 'radicals' to whom Andrew Parker referred.[52] This time too, most plots are detected in time, but sometimes security services are unsuccessful in stopping human tragedies. Comparing both terrorist campaigns from the same standpoint helps to avoid overblowing the jihadi threat and thus deprives jihadi terrorists of their capacity to further tear apart the social fabric of societies by enhancing anxiety over migration and Islam.

Another reminder of bygone times might serve as a welcome lesson too. Now largely forgotten, a similar widespread mania about a 'pan-Islamist' threat to European civilization emerged in the 1930s. When assessing this frenzy, the renowned Dutch historian and gifted writer Jan Romein (1893–1962) perceptively concluded, in no uncertain terms: such representations survive not because they're true, but because they're useful.[53]

Notes

1 This chapter is adapted and updated from 'All Radicalisation is Local: The Genesis and Drawbacks of an Elusive Concept', *Egmont Papers* 84, June (2016/b): 1–48.
2 AIVD, *The Transformation of Jihadism in the Netherlands: Swarm Dynamics and New Strength* (The Hague: AIVD, September 2014), p. 52.
3 Europol, *Terrorist Activity in the European Union: Situation and Trends Report* (TE-SAT) (The Hague: Europol, 2 December 2004), p. 5.
4 Council of the European Union, 'Conclusions and Plan of Action of the Extraordinary European Council Meeting', SN 140/01, 21 September 2001.
5 Europol, TE-SAT, p. 30.
6 AIVD, *Recruitment for the Jihad in the Netherlands* (The Hague: AIVD, December 2002), pp. 10–11.
7 *Verslag van de Vaste Commissie voor de Inlichtingen- en veiligheidsdiensten over haar werkzaamheden (juli 1990–juli 1991).* Letter from the Minister of the Interior to the President of the House of Representatives, 12 February 1992, p. 19. Available at http://resolver.kb.nl/resolve?urn=sgd%3Ampeg21%3A19911992%3A0006610.
8 Martijn de Koning, Ineke Roex, Carmen Becker and Pim Aarns, *Eilanden in een zee van ongeloof: Het verzet van activistische da'wa-netwerken in België, Nederland en Duitsland* (Nijmegen and Amsterdam: IMES Report Series, Radboud University, 2014).

9   BVD, *Jaarverslag 2001 [2001 Annual Report]* (The Hague: BVD, 2002), p. 10 and p. 18. Available at https://english.aivd.nl/publications/annual-report/2002/09/06/annual-report-2001.

10 Ibid., p. 6 and p. 27.

11 Remarks by President George W. Bush at Victory 2004 Rally in Oshkosh, Wisconsin, 16 October 2004. Available at www.prnewswire.com/news-releases/remarks-by-the-president-at-victory-2004-rally-74343082.html.

12 Council of the European Union, 'A Secure Europe in a Better World' (Brussels: European Security Strategy, 12 December 2003).

13 Barton Gellman, 'In U.S., Terrorism's Peril Undiminished', *Washington Post*, 24 December 2002.

14 COTER, 'Thematic Assessment on Recruitment to Terrorism', DUB COREU, CFSP/PRES/DUB/1167/04. Dublin, 26 May 2004.

15 Ibid.

16 Ibid.

17 AIVD, *From Dawa to Jihad* (The Hague: AIVD, December 2004), p. 40; AIVD, *Jaarverslag 2004 [2004 Annual Report]* (The Hague: AIVD, 2005), p. 16.

18 Ibid., pp. 13–14.

19 Ibid., p. 23.

20 European Commission, Communication from the Commission to the Council and the European Parliament entitled 'Prevention, Preparedness and Response to Terrorist Attacks', COM(2004) 698, 20 October 2004.

21 Joint COTER/TWG, *Report on Recruitment*, HAG COREU, CFSP/PRES/HAG/1565/04. The Hague, 18 November 2014.

22 Brussels European Council, Presidency Conclusions, 16238/1/04 Rev 1, 16–17 December 2004.

23 European Commission, Communication from the Commission to the Council and the European Parliament entitled 'Terrorist Recruitment: Addressing the Factors Contributing to Violent Radicalization', COM(2005) 313, 21 September 2005.

24 Ibid., Annex, p. 11.

25 Paul Rietjens, 'België, de EU en het jihadi-terrorisme', *Studia Diplomatica*, VX (2007), Supplement 1.

26 Council of the European Union, 'The European Union Counter-Terrorism Strategy', 14469/4/05 REV 4, 30 November 2005.

27 Council of the European Union, 'The European Union Strategy for Combating Radicalization and Recruitment to Terrorism', 14781/1/05 REV 1, 24 November 2005.

28 Martha Crenshaw, 'The Causes of Terrorism', *Comparative Politics* 13, no. 4 (1981): 379–99.

29 Ibid., p. 390.

30 Andrew Silke and Katherine Brown, '"Radicalisation": The Transformation of Modern Understanding of Terrorist Origins, Psychology and Motivation', in *State, Society, and National Security: Challenges and Opportunities in the 21st Century* (Singapore: World Scientific Publishing, 2016).

31 The list of members and their affiliation, as well as the text of the report is available at www.clingendael.nl/sites/default/files/20080500_cscp_report_vries.pdf.

32 Expert Group on Violent Radicalisation, *Radicalisation Processes Leading to Acts of Terrorism*. A concise report submitted to European Commission, 15 May 2008. See note 31.

33 Ibid.

34 Ibid.

35 Campbell and Cowan, 'Profile: Peter Clarke', the *Guardian*, 29 July 2005.

36 Schmid, 'Radicalisation, De-Radicalisation', p. 19.

37 Jonathan Githens-Mazer, 'Rethinking the Causal Concept of Islamic Radicalisation', *Political Concepts: Committee of Concepts and Methods Working Paper Series* 42 (2010): 8.

38 Scott H. Decker and David C. Pyrooz, 'How 100 Years of Gang Research Can Inform the Study of Terrorism, Radicalization and Extremism', *Perspectives on Terrorism* 9, no. 1 (2015): 104–12.

39 Ben Emmerson, *Report of the Special Rapporteur on the Promotion and Protection of Human Rights and Fundamental Freedoms while Countering Terrorism* (Geneva: Human Rights Council, UN, 22 February 2016) (A/HRC/31/95).

40 Mohammed Hafez and Chreighton Mullins, 'The Radicalization Puzzle: A Theoretical Synthesis of Empirical Approaches to Homegrown Extremism', *Studies in Conflict & Terrorism* 38, no. 11 (2015): 958–75.

41 Europol, 'Changes in Modus Operandi of Islamic State Terrorist Attacks'. Review held by experts from Member States and Europol on 29 November and 1 December 2015 (The Hague: Europol, 18 January 2016). Available at www.europol.europa.eu/content/ectc.

42 Available at www.matthiasdiependaele.be/nieuws/samenleving-nooit-schuldig-aan-radicalisering.

43 Quoted in *De Morgen* (Belgian Dutch-language daily newspaper), 16 December 2016.

44 Quoted in *Le Soir* (Belgian French-language daily newspaper), 5 August 2017.

45 *Vierde tussentijds verslag over het onderdeel 'radicalisme'*. Parlementair onderzoek belast met het onderzoek naar de omstandigheden die geleid hebben tot de terroristische aanslagen van 22 maart 2016 (Brussels: House of Representatives, DOC 54-1752/009, 23 October 2017), p. 37. Available at http://www.dekamer.be/FLWB/PDF/54/1752/54K1752009.pdf.

46 Ibid., p. 178, p. 183 and p. 158.

47 Githens-Mazer, 'Rethinking the Causal Concept of Islamic Radicalisation', p. 14.

48 Tom Wilson, 'Foreign Funded Islamist Extremism in the UK', *The Henry Jackson Society, Centre for the Response to Radicalization and Terrorism*, Research Paper no. 9 (July, 2017).

49 James M. Dorsey, 'Did They or Didn't They? The Battle for Control of Brussels' Grand Mosque', 17 November 2017. Available at https://www.tremr.com/jmdorsey/did-they-or-didnt-they.

50 Schmid, 'Radicalisation, De-Radicalisation', p. 19.

51 Address by the Director General of the Security Service, Andrew Parker, to the Royal United Services Institute (RUSI), Whitehall, 8 October 2013. Available at www.mi5.gov.uk/home/about-us/who-we-are/staff-and-management/director-general/speeches-by-the-director-general/director-generals-speech-at-rusi-2013.html.

52 European Institute of Peace, 'Molenbeek and Violent Radicalization: A "Social Mapping"' (Brussels: European Institute of Peace, May 2017), p. 10. Available at https://view.publitas.com/eip/eip-molenbeek-report-16-06/page/1.

53 Jan Romein, *Machten van dezen tijd* (Amsterdam: Wereldbibliotheek, 1932).

Chapter 2

TURNING 'RADICALIZATION' INTO SCIENCE: AMBIVALENT TRANSLATIONS INTO THE DUTCH (SPEAKING) ACADEMIC FIELD

Nadia Fadil and Martijn de Koning

The relationship between the scientific field and political life has been a recurrent source of preoccupation for scholars, especially for those working on issues related to migration, Islam and security.[1] Commenting on the state of the art of the literature on Islam in Europe, Dutch anthropologist Thijl Sunier notes that 'the increased emphasis, since 9/11, on the presence of Muslims as a potential risk for society has not only increased the entanglement of policy priorities and research agendas, it has also resulted in a gradual narrowing down of the research focus to the governance of security, deviant behaviour, cultural clash and the ways in which nation states deal with the challenges of an increasingly vocal and transnational religious constituency'.[2] The prominence and growing scholarly interest into the question of radicalization can be seen as one of the latest examples of such a convergence. Since its introduction in the Netherlands in 2001 by the Dutch intelligence services, the concept of radicalization has undergone a number of significant transformations in its definition and appropriations that reach well beyond the Dutch context. As has been suggested by a number of scholars, we now live in an 'era of radicalization',[3] as the term has become one of the most influential concepts to address the relationship between international conflicts and domestic conflicts. Yet the prominence of this term, also in the scientific field,[4] is remarkable considering the large number of studies that have challenged the scientific validity of this term. Several scholars have taken issue with its conceptual flaws and its selective problematization of certain forms of activism – especially coming from Muslims.[5]

In her sociological study of the terrorism studies in the US, Lisa Stampnitzky observed a similar contradiction in how 'terrorism experts' (who often worked for think tanks and are at the periphery of the scientific field) relate to their own object of study: although the term 'terrorism' was largely criticized as an ill-defined concept and for lacking a proper object of study, it nevertheless led to a flourishing field of studies that gathers a large range of actors – academic and non-academic.[6]

Following the work of Thomas Medvetz,[7] she describes the field of terrorism studies as an interstitial space of knowledge production, which she defines as 'a space of knowledge production' which is 'oriented between and towards multiple arenas of knowledge production, consumption, and legitimation, including academia, the media and the state'.[8] While its hybridity can be partially explained through the juvenile nature of this kind of expertise, it is the structure of the field, i.e. the coming together of different actors (scientific and non-scientific) around one shared object (i.e. terrorism), Stampnitzky argues, that explains its inability to operate as a properly 'disciplined' field.[9] Studies like those of Stampnitzky have made important advances in furthering the comprehension of the unruly characteristic of terrorism studies and how terrorism studies have given rise to interstitial fields which challenge the idea of clearly delineated fields – in the Bourdieusian sense of the word.[10]

This chapter seeks to account for the ways in which radicalization has emerged as an epistemological object of inquiry in the Dutch-speaking context. Building upon the previous observations, we seek to understand how the field of 'radicalization studies' can similarly be understood as an interstitial field, which gathers scholars, policymakers and consultants around a commonly shared problem. Yet instead of considering this emergence of a shared concern around 'radicalization' among scholars and policymakers as typical or unique for such kinds of inquiries, we want to show how – in the context of the Netherlands – such convergences are embedded in an older and strongly established tradition of policy research whereby frequent exchange of money and expertise occurs between the universities and the public authorities, also termed *beleidsonderzoek*. This research consists of investigations into particular social problems that have been jointly identified by scholars and policymakers and which are published as reports.[11] The idea of a clearly delineated academic field seems, hence, to hold less stringently when it comes to the Netherlands, as there is an old and well-established tradition of collaboration between the university world and policymakers in the realm of social sciences. The different studies that have attended to the emergence of such interstitial fields have, however, often taken the US as a case study, and situated this growing interdependence in light of a privatization and neo-liberalization of the knowledge economy (through the emergence of think tanks and others). Whereas such developments can also be witnessed in the Netherlands, many of the most influential studies on radicalization that were published in the country were the result of collaborations between governmental agencies and (tenured) academics affiliated with some of the most prestigious Dutch universities.

Rather than assuming a clear juxtaposition between the field of security actors and the scientific field, or a simple co-optation by scientists of the concept, the case of the Netherlands thus forces us to situate how the emergence of this term occurs through a series of *translations*. In using the notion of translation, we rely on Michel Callon's[12] conceptualization of the term.[13] He developed this concept to understand how the idea of the 'social' becomes constructed through a complex assemblage of different actors who arrive at a commonly shared understanding (and construction) of social life. This idea was further extended to understanding how social scientists, natural scientists, farmers and non-human artefacts join forces in the identification and the construction of a 'social problem'. Such alliances, or translations, are however never stable but occur through processes of enrolments, or co-optations, which might also be destabilized through rebellion. Building upon these insights, we will be interested in understanding how Dutch-speaking social scientists, who can be understood as one of the participating actors in the construction of the 'problem of radicalization', have recuperated this concept – which was in this particular context initially proposed by the Dutch state – and re-signified it in their own terms in the early period of its conceptualization (most notably between 2005–9). Four mechanisms will be identified: the first one is the turning of radicalization into a 'process', the second one is the number of attempts at 're-politicizing' the question, the third one is the attempt to avoid stigmatization of Muslim communities by focusing on 'Salafism', and the fourth one is the desire to develop the concept into something that extends into other fields besides solely Muslim forms of activism. One of the central characteristics of this scientific translation, we will argue, consists of a continuous attempt at re-conceptualizing the idea of radicalization into general and abstract terms. Whereas in the reports by the AIVD the term radicalization was initially coined explicitly with reference to Islamic forms of militancy, we witness a subsequent attempt at translating this term into broader terms as to avoid stigmatization of Muslims. Yet despite these attempts at 'clarification' or 'purification', ambiguity nevertheless persists in the usage of the term, ensuring that the concept is primarily geared towards Muslim actors. Are processes of radicalization unique to Muslim forms of activism, or can we speak of a general process of radicalization that affects the society as a whole and implicates non-Muslim actors as well? A central aim of this chapter is to examine this continuous *va-et-vient* between specificity and generality that seems to be at the heart of its scientific translation.

The organization of this chapter will be as follows. The first section will offer a short historical overview of how this concept was used by the AIVD, and the direct relationship with Muslim activism that informs its use. It is only after 2003 that a more general conceptualization of the term will be deployed. Yet despite these attempts at generality, one can observe a consistent connection with Islam. The following sections of this chapter will therefore examine how this connection has been challenged by the academic literature in two ways: firstly, by conceptualizing radicalization as a *generic*, rather than a Muslim-specific process and then, secondly, by challenging the central role given to Islam, yet also limiting the conceptualization of radicalization as driven by the so-called Salafism phenomenon. In the last part of this paper, a number of concluding remarks will be made regarding how the term manages to travel between 'expert' and 'scientific' knowledge fields through this process of (selective) appropriation, contestation and re-signification.

Radicalization and the BVD/AIVD: An overview

The introduction of the term radicalization by the Dutch intelligence services in 2002 occurs at a moment when the former BVD (*Binnenlandse Veiligheidsdiensten/*

Domestic Intelligence Services) becomes rebranded as AIVD (Algemene Inlichtingen en Veiligheidsdiensten/General Intelligence and Security Services). This follows the regrouping of international and domestic intelligence services under one office. This period also coincides with the moment where the focus on international terrorism prevails in the international agenda, which spurs the need for new forms of data gathering.[14] In the newly rebranded AIVD, the necessity of gathering information was no longer restricted to networks and actors who were considered potentially dangerous and/or implicated in possible acts of political violence, but was also located at a meta-level, as the necessity of anticipating potentially violent acts became a more important task for security services.[15] This will be at the heart of the comprehensive approach (*brede benadering*) that will be introduced in the *2001 Annual Report* and also converges with a new diagnosis of what was understood as a new threat in a post-Cold War context, i.e. (Islamic) terrorism. The latter was understood as an intrinsically unpredictable hazard with potentially devastating effects, also at a local level, but could be prevented if properly anticipated. Information that was gathered should therefore not only consist of networks or actors, but also a meta-analysis of the changing social dynamics that would be at the heart of the work of the intelligence service.[16] The development of the concept of radicalization figured as one of the key indicators of this new turn. At the time of its introduction, this term was seen to enable a unique convergence between (international) security concerns and (domestic) concerns with integration. Such convergences occurred for the first time in 1996, but would be expanded further after that period.

The securitization of 'integration' (1991–2003)

When examining the first reports published online since 1991, the attention to Islamic organizations is cursory and occurs primarily through an international lens. The presence of the spectre of Islamic fundamentalism was already there,[17] and a clear trans-Atlantic agenda predominates the early reports. Yet this category was used to designate both the Baathist regime of Saddam Hussein (following the Iraq–Iran war) and the 'revolutionary state fundamentalism' of the Iranian regime (following the revolution in 1979 and the call to kill anyone associated with Rushdie's book *The Satanic Verses*).[18] The term 'politically violent radicalism' (*politiek gewelddadig radicalisme*) will, on the other hand, be used without any specific ideological signature as left-wing and other groups are similarly branded as such. This will change after 1993 when a gradual differentiation is introduced between *activist* movements (left-wing movements) and *radical Islamic organizations*. The emergence of the Armed Islamic Group (*Groupe Islamique Armé*, GIA) in Algeria and the attacks in France in 1995 will provide the context for these changes. Yet also here an internationalist lens prevails: acts of violence perpetrated by the GIA will be primarily linked and connected with the Algerian civil war and read as retaliation to the French support of the Algerian state. The local articulations of this international threat of 'political Islam' and the domestic context were therefore only considered to the extent that a certain form of 'logistic 'support' was provided for these networks, but they were not seen as a local threat. It is only in the second half of the nineties that such local articulations will increasingly come to the fore. In the *1996 Annual Report*, an important section will be devoted to 'Islamic organizations' (*islamitische organisaties*). Yet differing from the earlier reports, these organizations will from now on be understood as a potential danger for the national context. In the report they are depicted as potential promoters of 'anti-western and anti-integration tendencies' that play into the 'socio-economic malaise and lack of perspectives in which large groups of allochthons find themselves'.[19] This concern with the presence of Islamist groups in the Netherlands will culminate with a special report published in 1998, which explicitly addresses the presence of Islamist networks in the country (*De Politieke Islam in Nederland*).

In order to understand this attention accorded to the Islamist movements and the ways in which this spectre of fundamentalism has been translated into the Dutch context, it is important to connect it with another significant social and political change that was occurring around the same period, i.e. the growing politicization of the question of integration of socio-cultural minorities, which is explicitly mentioned in the BVD reports of 1999 and 2000.[20] It is indeed in these reports that we can find an explicit reference to this concern with 'integration'. This follows upon the official instalment of an integration policy in 1998 (*integratiebeleid*), where the cultural specificity of ethnic minorities will increasingly be viewed as a potential social hazard.[21] An organicist view is promoted in this analysis, which considers society to be composed of heterogeneous sets of groups and entities that need to be kept together through a common reference to shared norms and values.[22] The BVD will build upon this diagnosis, but with a clearly different outlook on its priorities. In its *1999 Annual Report*, it redefines its tasks and functions as follows: 'signal and (help) counter threats to the integration process at an early stage'.[23] This renewed focus comes to support the new integration *dispositif*[24] that has been installed around that period, yet with a very specific, security-oriented specialization. The main task of the BVD will not be to examine the failing 'process' of integration (which belongs to the competence of the integration policy), but rather to identify and monitor the *carriers* who are understood to potentially hinder this integration process. It is in this specific context that Islamist groups emerge as promoters of such anti-integrationist stands and are perceived as potential threats from that perspective. Attention will therefore centre on documenting, reporting and identifying actors or groups who could potentially be perceived as threatening or limiting a successful integration process.

This perspective will be further developed in the subsequent reports. In the *2000 Annual Report*, we find a new subheading entitled *Forces Opposing Integration* (*Tegenkrachten van integratie*) that will replace the previous section *Violation of Primary Rights* (*Aantasting van grondrechten*). In that report a mix of actors will be listed. But the adopted perspective is explicitly cultural and religious, for all actors listed can be qualified as Muslim (the Moroccan Community, Turkish networks and Muslim schools), with the exception of right-wing organizations. A particular analytical model seems thus to inform this correlation between the 'problem of integration' and the security threat. Firstly, the problem of integration of ethnic-cultural minorities is understood as something that could potentially lead to and result in social segregation and a gradual alienation from the existing structures. Secondly, (mostly) Islamist groups are identified as the main agents that mobilize around these questions and could potentially hinder a smooth integration process by ideologically manipulating a disenfranchised youth. This indirect connection, which starts from a perceived problem of integration, upon which Islamist groups are then seen to act, will be at the heart of the further expansion and development of the radicalization narrative after 2001. The term radicalization, when introduced in 2001, thus comes to expand the already existing link between security and integration; this idea has been at the heart of the analysis made by the AIVD since 1996. It is through this concept of *radicalization* that this connection will be further deepened and expanded after 2001. The events in New York City will provide a new context where this correlation between failed integration and a potential security threat will be further explored.

Yet in the further expansion of this term, a clear ambivalence will traverse this use of radicalization, namely: should radicalization be seen as a particular concern to the Muslim community, or should it be understood as resulting from a *generic process* of alienation. An example of this ambivalence can be found in the first use and introduction of the concept in the *2001 Annual Report*. The term radicalization is announced here at the very outset of this report as one of the hallmarks of this new integral approach (*brede benadering*).[25] At the same time, however, defining this term will occur in a section that deals with the Moroccan community and addresses potentially hazardous tendencies within this community.[26] This clear connection between the term radicalization and the Muslim and/or Moroccan community will continue to inform the subsequent reports, until it becomes presented and treated as a distinctive phenomenon in 2003. In the *2003 Annual Report*, a generic definition will indeed be given to the term radicalization that is not directly tied with any particular religious or cultural community. Radicalization, rather, becomes defined as the growing ability to strive for 'deep changes' in a way that conflicts with a democratic order and with the possible use of non-democratic means, such as violence.

> *Radicalisering*, as examined by the AIVD, is understood as the growing ability to pursue and support deep changes in society, which stand in conflict with or pose a threat to the democratic order. Undemocratic means are also often used to this end (for instance, violence). In the research of the AIVD there is an attention to the processes of radicalization among the autochthonous population (such as right-wing movements) as well as ethnic minorities (such as Islamic radicalism or ethnic nationalism).[27]

The definition explicitly mentions 'autochthonous populations' and 'ethnic minorities' as to avoid a particular stereotypical characterization of this concept. Furthermore, a *multi-dimensional* analysis is added in the definition, for radicalization is understood to have religious, political and ethnic roots and it is not only restricted to the ability to use violence. It is, rather, expanded to entail the stimulation of hatred and isolation through, for instance, the promotion of a 'separate legal system'.[28]

From 'radicalization' to 'Salafism' (2003–15)

While the earlier attempt was to expand the use of the term radicalization to *all* segments of the population, this question of radicalization will continue to entertain a particular relationship with Islam, and more explicitly so in the later reports. In the *2004 Annual Report*, for instance, a more specific use of the term radicalization in connection to Muslim activism will prevail and become more dominant. This period follows the Madrid bombings, the murder of Theo van Gogh and the growing focus on *Salafi-jihadi* networks, of which *de Hofstad network* was regarded by authorities as the most threatening example.[29] The Madrid bombings of 2004 were a first important explanation behind this shift. For the Netherlands, 9/11 was geographically far away (over the Atlantic), symbolically close (part of Western civilization) and to a certain extent made sense (given the American role in the Middle East), although by no means justified as the casualties were innocent citizens. The plight of two young men from the south of the Netherlands who in 2002 left for Kashmir to join the military struggle against India but got shot by Indian border police, also shook the country being that it involved two young men from the Netherlands. However, they did not attempt to fight in the Netherlands, but 'somewhere far away'. Madrid was qualitatively different in the minds of the Dutch intelligence community: it meant that Europe had become the battlefield. The Madrid bombings created a sense of urgency of countering and preventing political violence, which was not present before. After the Madrid bombings, a coordinator of counterterrorism (NCTb) was appointed to map the Dutch counterterrorism efforts and a year later the NCTb organization was established (in 2008 it was renamed the National Coordinator for Security and Counterterrorism, NCTV). A second major event was the murder of Theo van Gogh in November 2004. The perpetrator, Mohammed Bouyeri, was known to visit the *As Soennah* mosque in The Hague and the *Tawheed* mosque in Amsterdam; both regarded as 'Salafi' by academics and experts. This would increase the attention for Salafism as a dangerous precursor for violence. After the murder of Dutch writer and movie director Theo van Gogh in 2004, 'Salafism' became the focus of Dutch counter-radicalization policies, and was regarded as a threat to social cohesion, integration, the democratic order and national security.

This shift will also characterize the further conceptualization of this concern with radicalization. From 2004 until 2009, a clear distinction will be drawn between 'radicalization' that will become exclusively tied with Muslims (with the exception of Moluccans who will also be included under this label) and 'activism' (in 2004) or 'extremism' (from 2005 until 2009) that will be linked with left-wing and right-wing groups. The publication of the influential AIVD report in December 2004 entitled *Van dawa tot jihad: De diverse dreigingen van de radicale islam tegen de democratische rechtsorde* (*From Dawa to Jihad: The Various Threats of Radical Islam against the Democratic Legal Order*) represents an important illustration of the further limitations of this concept to Muslim forms of activism, both through the conceptual development it offers of the term radicalization as well as for the typology that is introduced of different forms of Muslim radicalism. This report builds upon a previous attempt to identify 'carriers' of radicalization, of which Salafism is considered as an important player. In June 2004, a special note was drafted that targeted particularly the 'Saudi influences': *Saudi invloeden in Nederland: Verbanden tussen salafitische missie, radicaliseringsprocessen en islamitisch terrorrisme (Saudi Influences in the Netherlands: The Relationship between Salafi Missioning, Radicalization Processes and Islamic Terrorism)*. Differing from the earlier report of 1998 (*De Politieke Islam in Nederland*) that concluded that only a small minority of Muslim organizations potentially stood in the way of a smooth integration, this report focused on how radicalization hinges upon the spread and dissemination of Salafism. This analysis is furthermore accompanied by an extended conceptual development of the term radicalization. Two dimensions are now distinguished in this process: an anti-integrative dimension (*radicalisering in de anti-integratieve zin*) and a potential-use-of-violence dimension (*actieve strijd tegen de omgeving*).[30] This distinction will be recuperated in the subsequent special report of the same year. But the focus will here be primarily on Salafism and the dimensions rebranded as the horizontal (*horizontale verhoudingen*) and the vertical dimension (*vertical verhouding*) of radicalization,[31] as can also be seen in Figure 2.1.

On the basis of this distinction, a typology is constructed between the types of Muslim radicalism, depending on how they relate to this horizontal and vertical axis (radical political Islam, radical Islamic puritanism and radical Muslim nationalism). Islamic puritanism, which promotes a return to Islam, is considered central to the radicalization process. While the AIVD itself asserts that there is no direct relationship between Islamic puritanism and the use of violence, it nevertheless presupposes a continuum between the idea of *da'wah* (missionizing), the Manichaean views that are promoted through these ideologies and jihad.[32] This idea of a continuum, which considers *da'wah* a recruiting mechanism that can eventually result in forms of violence, will be at the heart of the subsequent analysis of radicalization to such an extent that one can almost speak of a synchrony between *da'wah*, Muslim puritanism and radicalization. The 2006 special report on violent jihadism (*De Gewelddadige Jihad in Nederland: Actuele trends in de islamistisch-terrorristsiche dreiging/ Violent Jihad in the Netherlands: Contemporary Trends in the Islamic-Terrorist Threat*) builds further on this idea of continuity between *da'wah* and jihad and considers the important role of Salafi centres as a main trigger in this process.[33]

In their counter-radicalization work, the AIVD has taken a very clear and explicit position against 'Salafism': as a threat to security, social cohesion and integration. As also noted by Sedgwick, the AIVD thereby sets itself apart from other European security and intelligence services at that time (around 2007).[34] But this focus on Salafism was also part of a basic trend that in the last few years became more prominent in countries such as Germany, France and Belgium as well. The notion of Salafism had not yet been conceptualized in the publications of

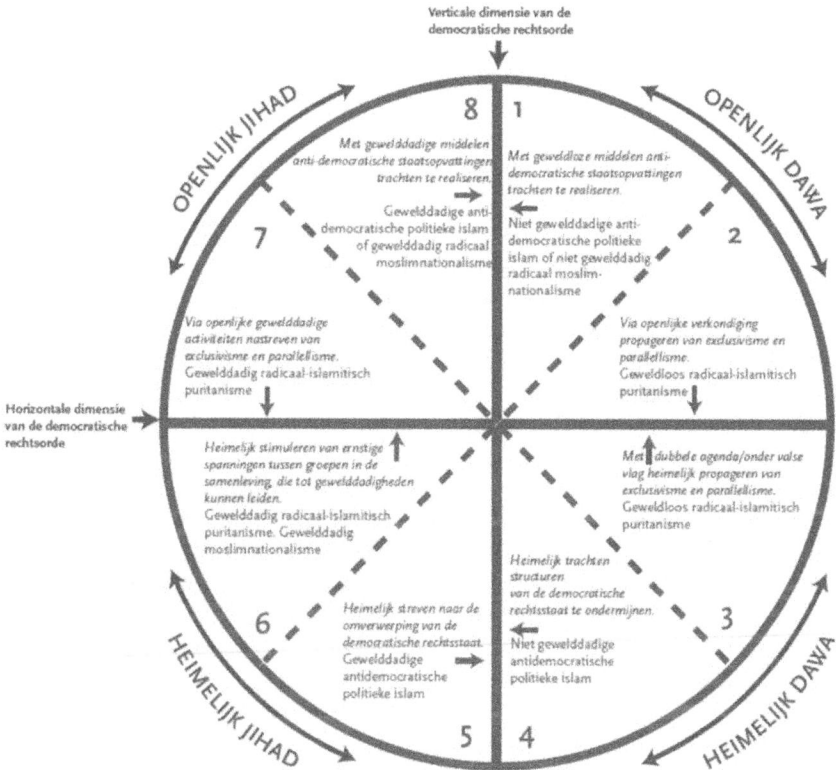

Figure 2.1 AIVD report, *Van dawa tot jihad* (2004)

Source: AIVD, *Van dawa tot jihad: De diverse dreigingen van de radicale islam tegen de democratische rechtsorde* (Den Haag: AIVD, 2004), p. 40.

the BVD (and later AIVD) in 2001 and 2002. This changed, however, in 2004, when the report on Saudi influences in the Netherlands is published. This report refers to Salafism as a global current of Islam with ancient and strong roots in Saudi Arabia, though not exclusively. According to the report, Salafism is a puritan form of Islam that calls people to return to 'the pure Islam': the Islam from the time of the Prophet Muhammad. The report distinguishes between two main currents: *salafiyya ilmiyya* (recognizing the authority of scholars who are loyal to the Saudi regime and at the same time anti-Western) and the *salafiyya jihadiyya* (which does not recognize that authority and calls for a global jihad against the West and the Saudi monarchy).[35] The latter is called 'jihadism' throughout the report. The report connects the 'Salafite mission' with the process of radicalization. It does so in several ways. First of all, it claims that Salafism is a solution for the identity crisis among Muslim youth. Secondly, according to the report Salafism seeks to ban and counter everything that is considered non-Islamic from one's life. It is only by doing so that one can become a 'true Muslim'. Thirdly, the Salafi ideology may lead to radical convictions when its puritanical character becomes combined with other visions about society. Fourthly, this radicalization can occur in different ways: anti-integration (with a hostile isolationism, rejecting state authority and promoting vigilantism), or an active struggle against society. This may ultimately lead to direct or indirect involvement in 'radical Islamic violent activities'. Fifthly, and lastly, recruiters who are active in and near Salafi mosques try to isolate and prepare young Muslims for the violent jihad.

After 2009, the tone of the debate and the AIVD's publications seemed to become less alarmist, although specific anti-radicalization training programmes and information campaigns still focused mainly on Salafism, and the restrictive measures against several people who were suspected of planning to go to Somalia and Chechnya to take part in the military jihad remained in force. From 2010 onwards, a new target came into focus for the AIVD, media and politicians. In March that year, Sharia4Belgium appeared on the scene in Belgium under the leadership of Fouad Belkacem (alias Abu Imran). In 2012, the AIVD issued a publication that dealt specifically with 'jihadist networks'. According to the AIVD, the term 'jihadism' refers to an 'extremist ideology', based on the glorification of violent jihad. In the same AIVD glossary, 'violent jihad' was defined as 'Armed struggle against the perceived enemies of Islam, legitimated by invoking Islamic jurisprudence'. The ideology of Sharia4Belgium did indeed contain elements of jihadism as the AIVD defined it, but the group did not engage in armed struggle. Rather, it engaged in a provocative and aggressive struggle against those whom they considered enemies of Islam in Belgium and the Netherlands, but at the time this did not include armed violence, although many perceived the behaviour as aggressive. However, the idea that actual violence might occur, and that the *da'wa* of Sharia4Belgium (and its Dutch branch, Sharia4Holland) was a precursor to this, regularly surfaced in our conversations with policymakers during that period.

There was a fear that Salafists might resort to unbridled violence and that they and their religious beliefs would exert considerable pressure on others, particularly women. Furthermore, their attempts to participate in society were put down to infiltration. The view was not so much that Salafists were likely to resort to violence, but that they were a threat to social cohesion and in particular to freedom that would come under threat because of the Salafists' rejection (hatred) of the West. In more recent publications, however, the AIVD has stated that, in the case of the Dutch foreign fighters in Syria, Salafism constitutes the breeding ground for violent radicalization and that Salafist doctrines may lead to intolerance, societal tensions and activities that are incompatible with Dutch democracy and the rule of law.[36]

Academic translations of radicalization

The academic translations of radicalization occur in different ways. In this section we will focus mostly on the publications by academics but we can think of other types of interactions as well. For example, the NCTV, besides being an important initiator and funder of many of the academic publications, also regularly hosts expert and consultancy meetings in which they invite academic researchers. Conversely, when academics hold conferences and seminars in the Netherlands, civil servants from a wide variety of local and national state institutions are present as well. Furthermore, the field of radicalization studies also accommodates a number of consultancy agencies, who regularly invite both academics and civil servants to speak at their (often quite expensive) seminars.[37] Although these more formal and informal networks are beyond the scope of this chapter, we think it is important to note how the question of radicalization is a good example of an interstitial space of knowledge production[38] which brings together the academic field, experts and consultants and the field of policymaking.[39]

When examining the existing studies from Dutch-speaking countries on radicalization, one can notice a clear increase in the focus on this term from 2005 onwards.[40] This period signals the publication of two reports that explicitly address the question of radicalization. The first empirical study that can be found is by Visser and Slot,[41] a policy research effectuated by the service Research and Statistics of the city of Amsterdam and commissioned by the Teachers' Union (*Algemene onderwijsbond*). In this survey, 239 teachers were asked to fill in a questionnaire wherein they assessed the degree of extremism and radicalization at schools.[42] This study followed news coverage and AIVD reports about new forms of anti-Semitism among Muslim youth and growing concerns of extremism. Also in 2005 a special issue of the journal *Justitiële Verkenningen* of the Research and Documentation Centre of the Ministry of Justice was published, which features articles by Coolsaet and Roy and others.[43] And in 2006 two major studies were published, coordinated by IMES (Institute for Migration and Ethnic Studies at the University of Amsterdam) on the processes of radicalization among Muslim youth.[44] The murder of the controversial movie director Theo van Gogh in the streets of Amsterdam in the fall of 2004 will figure as important context against which these studies will be conducted. His murder sent shockwaves throughout the country and triggered a nationwide debate on the danger of radical Islam and, more importantly, the failed integration of Muslim youth. The perpetrator, Mohammed Bouyeri, was indeed known as 'one of our guys', and 'well integrated'.[45] What causes the sudden switch from someone who seems apparently well integrated, into someone who no longer identifies with this society and even openly calls for the use of violence against non-believers will figure as a guiding question throughout these studies. Or, to paraphrase Slootman and Tillie: what happens in the phase *prior* to radicalization will be of interest to many of these studies.[46] In so focusing, the concerned studies frame and situate the term 'radicalization' as a preventive concept that seeks to attend to the steps that precede the possible use of violence. In what follows, we seek to examine how the scientific translation of this concept ensued. Whereas it is clear from the outset that the conceptualization offered by the AIVD figures as an important source and reference in this initial stage, we will also attend to the ways in which this concept will become recuperated in a way that fits the sociological language and the need to attend for 'root causes' of radicalization.[47] As such, we suggest that the perspective offered in the scientific narratives partially deviates from the AIVD template in two ways: first, by re-conceptualizing radicalization into a complex and multi-layered *process* and second, by trying to dislodge the term from its privileged connection with Islam by problematizing the link with Salafism and expanding it into other forms of activism.

Radicalization as a process

A first point of demarcation between the scientific studies and the AIVD reports lies in the focus made on 'carriers' in general, and *Salafism* in particular. As stated earlier, in the reports by the AIVD, identifying the 'carriers of radicalization' figured as one of the main targets in their surveillance policies. Important attention was thus accorded to identifying the patterns and practices of recruitment (*rekruteringsactiviteiten*) and support (*ondersteuningsactiviteiten*) that could help in understanding why someone would suddenly turn to the use and/or legitimation of violence.[48] *Da'wah* practices were understood – from within this perspective – as a recruiting mechanism through which disenfranchised youth could be manipulated into radical views. Islamist groups, or what the AIVD describes as 'radical Islam' (further sub-divided into different typologies), figured as one of the principal targets in these preventive policies. Monitoring Salafi groups became, thus, a means to attend to what they considered to be one of the principal vectors into violence. In the social scientific literature, a more nuanced perspective will prevail on this question. This is not only tied with a different assessment of Salafism, in which some analysts will instead highlight their potentially pacifying effect. But it also – and more importantly – follows from a different conceptual model, which challenges the importance of recruiters by considering the agency of the youngsters. In contrast to the AIVD, a larger emphasis will be accorded to understanding *why* certain individuals are prone to 'radicalize' and attracted to certain recruiters, thus displacing the focus from the 'recruiters' to the individual subjects themselves. In the study of Buijs, Demant and Hamdy,[49] for instance, the theory of recruiters will even be explicitly challenged.[50] Although they acknowledge the presence of fighters who migrated to Western Europe in the nineties and participated in the jihad in Afghanistan, their role, as recruiters, will be minimized and they will be portrayed as 'catalysts'. The central focus will rather be on the 'lost youngsters' who 'recruit their own leaders'.[51] One thus seems to observe an explicit attempt at bolstering the agency of the concerned youth, which critically challenges claims of 'false consciousness' or the idea that these youngsters are simply 'manipulated' or 'deprived'. This idea of an active agency is also substantiated through biographical accounts of youngsters where we learn how they gradually come to embrace 'radical' worldviews as an active and voluntary choice. Several studies will also highlight the importance of existential crises (which Buijs, Demant and Hamdy consider to be a fundamental starting point in understanding processes of radicalization). A double set of theological beliefs (a Manichaean worldview, the refusal of democracy or a utopian worldview) that guide these individual's actions and psychological traits are also considered as main characteristics of these 'radicalized subjects'.[52] The radicalized subject thus appears as a *hyper-individualized* subject, who ventures into unclear destinations and breaks with the tradition in which she/he was raised. A similar finding also emerges in a study by the anthropologist Frank van Gemert who specialized in youth delinquency among Dutch-Moroccan youth. In a short paper on this question, he argues against the hypothesis that radicalization is comparable to processes of delinquency, suggesting that radicalized subjects are much more ideologically driven and less the consequences of their social condition.[53]

Yet in addition to this micro-focus, a macro-sociological perspective will also prevail in these academic developments. In the different definitions offered, radicalization will indeed be primarily understood as a slow and multi-layered *process* that is tied to the loss of legitimacy of a particular order.[54] Slootman and Tillie, for instance, put this view at the heart of their definition as they equate the 'process of radicalization' with 'a growing loss of legitimacy of the democratic order'.[55] The focus on alienation that is offered by this definition differs markedly from the one given by the AIVD who instead underlined 'the growing desire to pursue and support deep changes within society that stand in conflict with or represent a threat to the democratic order'.[56] Here, it is the active pursuit of change that opposes a democratic order that will prevail. This desire for change is furthermore de-contextualized as it is tied with the intrinsic motivation of the concerned youth. The definition offered by the Dutch researchers shows, for instance, a more Weberian understanding of power. In this definition, a particular order can only sustain itself to the extent that it maintains a degree of legitimacy in the eyes of its followers.[57] A more interactional account on power is thus presented, which not only places the attention upon the individual actors, but also accounts for the context and circumstances under which a particular authority is considered legitimate. Differing from some of the critiques expressed elsewhere, which challenged the psychologizing and depoliticizing aspects of some terrorism and radicalization theories,[58] a conceptual model is hence offered which accords a considerable importance to the contextual and political circumstances that may trigger a loss of confidence in the ruling democratic order. Building upon the model of Sprinzak,[59] Buijs, Demant and Hamdy will for instance indicate that radicalization is provoked by experiences of exclusion and a sense of poor political representativeness.[60] Slootman and Tillie also highlight the experience of exclusion and marginalization that they consider as one of the central drivers of this process.[61] The different reports will furthermore also consistently highlight this importance of restoring trust, enabling social participation and fighting discrimination. The international dimension will, on the other hand, be omitted.[62] One of the few exceptions to the latter is the study by Feddes, Nickolson and Doosje who identify so-called 'trigger factors' of radicalization: particular events that initiate a process of radicalization.[63] Besides micro-factors (such as experiencing discrimination, death of a loved-one) and meso-factors (marriages, meeting a radical person, propaganda), they also identify macro-factors such as calls to violence, government policies and illicit attacks against one's own group.[64]

A double move seems thus to inform the studies at hand: whereas the sociological dimension of this question – where the individual is recognized as a social being that is spurred by a number of sociological and political dynamics – is central in the social scientific theories, a 'micro' understanding – which highlights the individual agency of the youth and which also enumerates a set of traits and hallmarks of 'radicalized subjects' – will also be understood as an independent and competing dimension. Slootman and Tillie speak for instance of a set of 'ideas' (*denkbeelden*),[65] while in the study of Buijs, Demant and Hamdy, the idea of 'beliefs' prevails.[66] This constant move between contextualization and politicization (in the sociological and political sense) and de-contextualization and individualization (which ultimately results in a de-politicization) can be partially understood by a consistent effort by the scholars to account for the individual agency while at the same time acknowledging the structuring role of the social and political circumstances. But it also needs to be understood, we want to argue, as a continuation of the security agenda that has sought to conceptualize the notion of 'radicalization' primarily as a preventive concept that can be used to anticipate risky behaviour by offering tools to design and implement preventive policies.

Radicalization and Islam

A second series of ambivalences concern the 'Muslim-specific' nature of this process: does radicalization only pertain to Muslims and/or to a specific group of Muslims? As noted earlier, the term radicalization had been introduced by the AIVD to primarily account for Muslim forms of activism, although subsequent reports will remain quite ambivalent about the more general reach of this term. A similar ambivalence can be observed in the social scientific adoption of the term. Whereas most early studies will primarily use this term with reference to Muslim forms of activism, later studies will increasingly problematize the term. The introduction of this concept within Dutch-speaking academia shows a use of the term radicalization that primarily concerns Muslim tendencies. The conceptual framing of radicalization will depict the latter as a generic phenomenon that can occur in any political formation, yet in its operationalization and usage it will be most often mobilized to study tendencies deemed problematic within Muslim communities. In several cases, this specific focus will not necessarily be explained, but simply assumed.[67] But in the two main studies mentioned earlier, a clear justification will be given by either referring to the funders (for instance, the city of Amsterdam in the case of Slootman and Tillie) or by giving more substantial arguments. Buijs, Demant and Hamdy, for instance, consider a generic approach on radicalization that equally includes other forms of extremism or radicalism to be too broad. They argue that radicalism is too much of a 'large container term that covers a large spectrum from democracy to extremism.[68] They will therefore restrict their focus to what they describe as 'Islamic radicalism', which is understood here as a particular school of thought within Islam which has been theorized by a number of Muslim thinkers (i.e. Qutb and Mawdudi) and which is characterized by certain features.[69] In doing so, the researchers seem to share the AIVD concern which views 'Muslim radicalism' or Salafism as one of the main threats for Dutch society. However, nuances will be offered in their study which distinguish the 'good' from the 'bad' variants of Muslim political activism.

The suggested – or even explicit – link made between 'radicalism' and 'Islam' will, however, be challenged by several authors in the Dutch-speaking scientific field. A first set of critiques will be formulated by anthropologists and religious studies scholars who have worked with Muslims considered as 'orthodox' or Salafi. They will tackle, on the basis of their empirical work, what they view as a series of secular presuppositions and biases on religious orthodoxy as well as the suggested link between Salafism, religious orthodoxy and violence. The work of Martijn de Koning, who conducted six years of anthropological fieldwork among Salafi-oriented Dutch-Moroccans in Gouda, offers a good example of such a critique.[70] Instead of considering the orthodox religious turn among his Dutch-Moroccan informants as a deviation, the author rather sees it as an attempt to formulate answers to the questions that confront them and that are fundamentally modern (i.e. individualization, fractured social relationships, globalization, etc.). By drawing on the religious tradition, these youngsters emulate the examples as set by the Prophet and seek to construct forms of belonging that enable them to address the challenges of modernity and at times also engage with it in a critical fashion.[71] Furthermore, the *da'wah* advocated by his informants must primarily be read as an invitation to engage with Islamic spirituality on a personal basis – thus excluding the tacit (or in some cases even explicit) links drawn between Salafism and jihadism.[72] Other studies on Dutch Salafis have looked at how young people consume, (re)produce and transform religious knowledge and negotiate different Salafi authorities. De Koning's work was also part of the research programme 'Salafism as a Transnational Movement' of the Institute for the Study of the Modern World (ISIM) and (after 2009) Radboud University Nijmegen which included the researchers Becker, Wagemakers and Meijer.[73] Although none of these projects directly engage with the question of radicalization, a concern with this question appears in some of these studies – most notably in the work of De Koning who suggests that there might be possible links between jihadism, Salafism and violence. Hence, where the automatic link between Salafism and radicalization is problematized, a possible, indirect relationship is assumed.[74] A similar critique can be found in the work of Welmoet Boender, who equally challenges this idea that religious orthodoxy is analogous with Muslim radicalization on the basis of her fieldwork with imams in the Netherlands.[75] Furthermore, both the work of Boender and De Koning have been discussed in public debates about radicalization, often in relation to the question of how dangerous Salafism is.[76]

A final example of a study that shows attempts at deconstructing the link between Salafism and radicalization, albeit assuming and confirming the idea that there exists a tacit link between the two, can be found in the report by Roex, Van Stiphout and Tillie.[77] In 2009, the Research and Documentation Centre of the Ministry of Security and Justice (*Wetenschappelijk Onderzoek- en Documentatie Centrum* or WODC) commissioned research about the nature, size and potential threat from Salafism in the Netherlands. Meijer and De Koning (who were already conducting their own research on Salafism in Europe and the Middle East together with Joas Wagemakers and Carmen Becker) were initially consulted by the WODC about potential research questions. The research was granted to Ineke Roex, Sjef van Stiphout and Jean Tillie.[78] The publication by Roex, Van Stiphout and Tillie is one of the first studies exclusively focusing on Dutch Salafism, although the research by Buijs, Demant and Hamdy[79] equally attended to the question of whether 'political Salafism' could provide a threshold against 'jihadism'. This particular question, set against the background of the AIVD and Dutch politicians questioning the double agendas of 'Salafist' preachers propagating an anti-integration, anti-democracy and isolationist message, framed the research by Tillie, Roex and Van Stiphout.[80] The elaborate research focused on analysing the moral revival work of Salafi mosques through an account of 'Salafi' organizations and a survey among Dutch Muslims. In this survey, they tried to measure the degree of commitment towards orthodox Islamic thought, assuming that the extent to which people were inclined to it may equally reflect Salafi thought. One of their conclusions was that political radicalization takes place outside 'Salafist' organizations, and that so-called orthodox Muslims are relatively older, less educated and more often unemployed. However, they also noted that sensitivity to radicalism and violent extremism is higher among these 'orthodox' Dutch Muslims, which would be evidence of a correlation between orthodoxy and political radicalism.

The research was influential on a national policy level and in the media for its nuanced approach. The study was able to show how most of these organizations had distanced themselves from political violence (or 'jihadism'). The study also enabled local policymakers to remain wary of 'Salafist tendencies' among Muslim communities, while at the same time encouraging them to establish collaborations with some organizations claiming to follow a Salafi method of Islam. In particular, the fieldwork done by Roex was reportedly of significance in influencing local policymakers into having a more nuanced and differentiated view on what they regarded as Salafi mosques.[81] This produced a complicated relationship between the Dutch state and Muslim organizations. While attempts have been made to curb the influence of so-called Salafism when engaging with those Muslim initiatives deemed liberal enough for the state agencies, on the local level, municipalities have been and still are working with Salafi networks and individuals, or at least with some. The broad security gaze that is the result of the counter-radicalization efforts remains dominant nevertheless.

From (Muslim) specific to general

Whereas the first series of critiques explicitly challenged the assumed link between Muslim orthodoxy, Salafism and radicalization by drawing on an ethnographic study of this group, a second set of studies will instead problematize the exclusive focus on Islam by expanding this term to include other sociological groups. The ostensible aim here is to understand (and scientifically construct) 'radicalization' as a distinctive sociological phenomenon, which cuts across distinct political ideologies and cultural groups. Some subsequent studies will do so by broadening their lens to other groups.[82] The study of J. A. Moors, E. van den Reek Vermeulen and M. Siesling provides an interesting case due to its desire to expand the reach of the concept to 'other' (ethnic) communities besides the Moroccan (and to a lesser extent, Turkish) one.[83] The report, which was commissioned by the Dutch authorities, states quite explicitly that it wants to demarcate itself from the prevalent focus on Moroccan minorities and the importance given to Islam in the existing literature.[84] By including other ethnic minorities, i.e. the Somali, Pakistani, Kurdish and Moluccans, the report aims to offer a deeper understanding of the processes of radicalization. But whereas the report critically challenges the prevailing AIVD understanding of radicalization by equally addressing contextual elements, it nevertheless ends up restricting this question to a problem of integration through its exclusive inclusion of racialized minorities, which also happen to be Muslim. Indeed, large parts of the report seem to be geared towards understanding the recruiting potential of orthodox and fundamentalist Islamic groups among the concerned communities. Furthermore, the presence of antagonistic views towards the Dutch state is also framed as one of the worrying trends. Although the authors conclude that there is no urgent threat coming from the concerned communities, they nevertheless forewarn the presence of a breeding ground for radicalization.[85] Despite its attempts at broadening the term radicalization to other communities and groups, the specific targeting and restriction of the researchers' lens to racialized minorities who happen to be Muslim ends up confirming the presupposition that radicalization is of particular concern to Islam alone.

A different approach is adopted in other reports that do not restrict the focus to religious or ethnic minorities but expand the term radicalization to different political formations. Such an extension was already observable in some of the AIVD reports, whereby right-wing movements – and in a later stage, left-wing and animal rights movements – will be included in this concern with radicalization. Here, it is useful to refer to the study of De Ruyver et al.[86] on the one hand, and that of Hans Moors et al.[87] on the other hand, as they represent two distinct ways of assessing (and constructing) the problem. The master thesis of Amy-Jane Gielen, *Radicalisering en Identiteit* forms a particularly good example of the way in which radicalization became reconceptualized as an identity question that prevails within distinct political currents that could be branded as 'extreme'.[88] Her research also had a large impact in the Netherlands and Belgium because of her active role as a consultant on this question, which is indicative of the semi-professionalization and commercialization of this question. Drawing on an empirical study among right-wing sympathizers and a review of the literature on Muslim forms of activism, Gielen attempts to offer a conceptual model that understands radicalization as a distinctive phenomenon – which is not necessarily tied with a particular religious orientation. Although she acknowledges the formative role of particular religious ideologies in the case of Muslims, her main emphasis is put on the notion of 'identity', which she considers central to this process.[89] In contrast to the studies discussed earlier, the conceptual model developed in Gielen's work considers the authoritarian personality structure of the individual as one of the key elements to understanding how radicalization processes occur. Drawing on the work of Theodore Adorno and her own interviews with young Dutch sympathizers of right-wing groups, Gielen considers the absence of a 'multiple identity' that can accommodate the different aspects of their identity as one of the hallmarks of this process.[90] This is also something she considers to be characteristic for Islamic movements based upon her review of the literature.[91] By highlighting the 'personality traits' throughout her work, Gielen thus contradicts the idea that radicalization is an outcome of particular religious tendencies or contextual developments, connecting it instead to one's identity development that can be overcome through proper training. A similar perspective, that primarily links radicalization with identity, will also be at the heart of the Belgian report by De Ruyver et al., who will include left-wing, right-wing and animal rights activists in their study.[92] A double aim seems to inform their report: Firstly, to offer a conceptual model to understand radicalization – which is here also understood as a complex process, but which additionally accords a large degree of importance to recruiters.[93] Secondly, to assess the degree of threat that emanates from these groups. Through interviews conducted with a series of experts on the danger posed by the distinct groups, they come to the conclusion that the problem of Islamic radicalism figures as one of the main challenges. This, they argue, also highlights the importance of 'integration' as well as the need to assess the identity construction among these youth.[94]

Like the previously mentioned reports, the study by Moors et al. is an attempt to expand the notion of radicalization by taking it away from the realm of Islam and linking it with other political formations, i.e. left-wing, right-wing and animal rights activism.[95] Yet differing from the previously cited reports, the suggested and assumed links between Islamic orthodoxy and radicalization are explicitly problematized. Furthermore, there is an explicit attempt to move away from an exclusive focus on radicalization through the introduction of another concept – i.e. 'polarization'. This concern with polarization was initially formulated by the Dutch government in its *Actieplan tegen Polarisatie en Radicalisering* (2007–11) and set itself the task of addressing societal tensions that endanger social cohesion.[96] The Action Plan was explicitly derived from the diagnosis set by the AIVD which argued in its *2005 Annual Report* that the tensions connected with the 'multicultural society' were one of the major challenges facing Dutch society.[97] The report by Moors et al. is the second in a series of reports that seek to assess this relationship between 'polarization' and 'radicalization',[98] the first report being *Trendanalyse Polarisatie en Radicalisering*, published by de Ministerie van Binnenlandse Zaken en Koninkrijksrelaties in 2008. Yet differing from the influential *Trendanalyse* published in 2008, this report presents itself as an explicitly *scientific* re-investment of this question.[99]

An important section of the report (written by the Dutch legal scholar and security expert Bob de Graaff) is also devoted to defining the notion of radicalization and understanding the indirect links that might exist between 'polarization' and 'radicalization'. The report pays significant attention to the rapidly changing social dynamics and the escalating media debates on Islam and migration, and argues that these developments enhance the experience of marginalization and persecution among the different segments of the Dutch population.[100] The subsequent chapters will continue to examine this question, yet the notion of 'radicalization' will be readjusted in its definition to the distinct political formations (i.e. Muslim radicalism, (new) right-wing radicalism, left-wing radicalism and animal rights activism). Rather than identifying a generic series of characteristics, a more case-oriented approach is thus preferred which tries to identify and understand how such processes might ensue according to a series of questions and problems that are specific for each tradition. Yet this ostensible attempt at demarcating the question of radicalization from Islam nevertheless results in a position whereby all political formations and actions that fall outside of liberal democracy will be seen as potentially threatening. In so doing, the report is in line with the approach suggested by the AIVD, which considers attempts at establishing 'deep change' as a potential security hazard. This report thus provides a good example of how the attempts at moving the term radicalization from its exclusive focus on Islam to other forms of political actions result in the demarcation and problematization of forms of political action that are not neatly captured by the contours of the institutionalized political process.[101] This introduction of 'polarization' as an addition to radicalization has, however, also triggered a number of critical essays which were published in a report edited by Raad voor Maatschappelijke Ontwikkeling[102] and who have challenged this concept by arguing that the term polarization assumes a 'consensus model' which is not only a fiction, but might stimulate new forms of polarization and conflict.[103]

Conclusion

This chapter has sought to account for the emergence of 'radicalization' as an interstitial field of study, which gathers the Dutch intelligence services and scientific actors in defining a particular problem. The first part of this chapter sought to offer a historical review of the introduction of the concept of radicalization by the Dutch intelligence services by documenting how this term came to be introduced in the framework of larger discussions on integration. We have tried to show how the term radicalization was partially built on an internal reorganization of the Dutch intelligence services, which also relied on a renewed risk-assessment of the surrounding dangers that considered the danger of terrorism to be potentially linked with the problem of integration. A second aim of this paper was to account for the ways in which Dutch academics have related to this term and how they came to adopt it through government-funded research on this question in the tradition of policy-oriented research (*beleidsonderzoek*). In this investigation into how the concept of radicalization came to travel into the Dutch academic field, we have also paid particular attention to the critical conversation that ensued concerning the diagnosis set by the AIVD. This focus related to the general analytical question that informed this chapter, which is to understand how 'radicalization' research emerges as an interstitial space which gathers together both security agencies and scholars. We have tried to show, throughout this chapter, that the enrolment of scholars[104] into this deradicalization field of study is far more complex than that of a simple co-optation into the analytical framework proposed by the AIVD, but that it occurred through an active re-appropriation by scholars and contestation of some of the premises of the term.

Our review shows how researchers have actively sought to demarcate themselves from the definition proposed by the Dutch intelligence services, by 'scientizing' the language – i.e. turning radicalization into a 'multi-dimensional' *process* – and by challenging the assumed link between certain Islamic ideologies (*Salafism*) and radicalization. The latter figured as an especially important source of contention, as scholars have explicitly challenged this link through empirical data and/or by actively opening up this notion of radicalization to other, non-Muslim phenomena. Yet despite these different critical demarcations, a shared series of assumptions about the supposed link between security (which is already often a racialized concept), migration, Islam and integration, continues to inform these studies. The different studies we have looked at adopted these pre-formed models of radicalization of Muslims as a lens through which they examined other modes of radicalization. Hence, the assumed link between Islam and security operates as the default template through which other phenomena become assessed. This results in a particular analytical model whereby attempts to contextualize radicalization (by accounting for the structural factors within Dutch society, or in some cases internationally) become combined with a strong focus on the individual, which often psychologizes so-called trigger factors. In line with the security gaze, political grievances, structures of inequality and injustice are thus turned into signals of potential risks to national security.

This overview should, however, not be taken to suggest that the relation between academia and the state's security gaze is only about the former responding to the latter (although the emphasis of this review was on the scientific field). Indeed, the security services have also on numerous occasions been inspired by scholarship produced by academics for their conceptualizations of the problem. In the AIVD report *From Dawa to Jihad*,[105] for instance, 'Salafism' (or 'Wahhabism' which is used here as a synonym) is regarded as 'radical puritanism': a type of 'radical Islam' that emphasizes resistance against Western domination, and particularly against a '"pernicious" Western lifestyle that is regarded as a threat to the "pure Islam"'. As an alternative, the Salafis espouse a societal order based upon 'Islamic morals' rather than an Islamic state. This characterization is, among others, based upon the work of Olivier Roy's *L' Islam Mondialisé*,[106] which labelled such Islamic currents as neo-fundamentalist. In the same AIVD report a distinction is made between those who focus on *da'wah* (and often implicitly condone the 'violent jihad' yet are careful not to call for jihad or to be associated with recruiting) and those who actively support and choose 'violent jihad'. It is important to consider how such characterizations were also made by scholars such as Wiktorowicz who have warned against the alleged double speak of the 'dawa Salafists'.[107] *Da'wah* in this report refers to 're-Islamising' Muslim minorities in the West working from 'extreme-puritan, intolerant and strong anti-Western frames of thought' and aiming to remain aloof from Western society and 'propagating exclusivism and parallelism'. In particular Wiktorowicz' article from 2006 is important here.[108] In this article he distinguishes between three different types of Salafism based upon different understandings of the sociopolitical context they are in: the purists, the politicos and the jihadists. The function of this division is, as becomes clear in his conclusion, how to empower the 'purists' at the expense of the 'jihadists'.[109] Such categorizations haven proven to be very useful for translating academic knowledge into bureaucratic knowledge, and this accounts for their political and policy-oriented usability and accountability.[110] Hence, rather than assuming a clearly delineated juxtaposition between the academic field and the policy field, the case of the Netherlands (and of Belgium) remains a good example of how the legitimization, production and circulation of knowledge about radicalization consists of different spaces which inform and shape, but also oppose, each other.

Notes

1 See, for instance, Valérie Amiraux, 'Academic Discourses on Islam(s) in France and Germany: Producing Knowledge or Reproducing Norms?', in *Islam and the West: Judgement, Prejudices, Political Perspectives*, ed. Werner Ruf (Münster: Agenda Verlag, 2002); Nadia Marzouki, 'De l'endiguement à l'engagement: Le discours des think tanks américains sur l'islam depuis 2001', *Archives des Sciences Sociales des Religions* 155 (2011): 21–38; and Stampnitzky, *Disciplining Terror*.

2 Thijl Sunier, 'Domesticating Islam: Exploring Academic Knowledge Production on Islam and Muslims in European Societies', *Ethnic and Racial Studies* 37, no. 6 (2014): 1142.

3 Baker-Beall, Heath-Kelly and Jarvis, eds., *Counter-Radicalisation*.

4 Right after the attacks of 13 November 2015, the French National Centre for Scientific Research (*Centre national de la recherche scientifique*, CNRS) launched a call among the 115,000 researchers to investigate the root causes of these forms of violence. The concern with 'violent radicalization' figured as a recurrent topic in several calls launched under the Horizon 2020 framework, or national frameworks such as the Belgian Federal Research Agency (BELSPO).

5 See Kundnani, 'Radicalisation: The Journey of a Concept'; and Kundnani, *The Muslims Are Coming!* See also, Gabe Mythen, Sandra Walklate and Elizabeth-Jane Peatfield, 'Assembling and Deconstructing Radicalisation in PREVENT: A Case of Policy-Based Evidence Making?', *Critical Social Policy* 37, no. 2 (2017): 180–201; Mark Sedgwick, 'The Concept of Radicalization as a Source of Confusion', *Terrorism and Political Violence* 22, no. 4 (2010): 479–94; and Paul Thomas, 'Divorced but Still Co-Habiting? Britain's Prevent/Community Cohesion Policy Tension', *British Politics* 9, no. 4 (2014): 472–93.

6 Lisa Stampnitzky, 'Disciplining an Unruly Field: Terrorism Experts and Theories of Scientific/Intellectual Production', *Qualitative Sociology* 34, no. 1 (2010): 1–19.

7 Thomas Medvetz, *Think Tanks in America* (Chicago, IL: University of Chicago Press, 2008).

8 Stampnitzky, 'Disciplining an Unruly Field', p. 3.

9 Stampnitzky, *Disciplining Terror*.

10 Lisa Stampnitzky, 'Experts, États et théories des champs: Sociologie de l'expertise en matière de terrorisme', *Critique Internationale* 59, no. 2 (2013): 89–104.

11 *Beleidsonderzoek* (policy research) is an old tradition in the Netherlands, which stems from the Second World War, and the idea of social engineering has also flourished

since then. There are a few research agencies that fall directly under the Dutch government's control, such as the Netherlands Institute for Social Research (*Sociaal en Cultureel Planbureau*, SCP), Statistics Netherlands (*Centraal Bureau voor de Statistiek*, CBS) and the Research and Documentation Centre (*Wetenschappelijk Onderzoek- en Documentatie Centrum*, WODC), but often such knowledge is the result of a collaboration between the universities and the government. Several academics who hold tenured positions at Dutch universities also serve in some of these public institutions (such as Christianne de Poot, scientific fellow at WODC and chair in criminology at VU University, and SCP Director Kim Putters who is also chair of health management at the Institute of Health Policy and Management of the Erasmus University, Rotterdam). For a further account, see P. H. M. van Hoesel, F. L. Leeuw and J. Mevissen, *Beleidsonderzoek in Nederland: Kennis voor beleid; Ontwikkeling van Een Professie* (Assen: Van Gorcum).

12 Michel Callon, 'Some Elements of a Sociology of Translation: Domestication of the Scallops and the Fishermen of St. Brieuc Bay', in *Technoscience: The Politics of Intervention*, eds. Kristin Asdal, Brita Brenna and Ingunn Moser (Oslo: Unipub, 2007 [1986]).

13 See Asdal, Brenna and Moser, eds., *Technoscience*; and Michel Callon and Bruno Latour, *La science telle qu'elle se fait: Anthologie de la sociologie des sciences de langue anglaise* (Paris: La Découverte, 1991).

14 See Didier Bigo, 'Globalized (In)Security: The Field and the Ban-Opticon', in *Terror, Insecurity and Liberty: Illiberal Practices of Liberal Regimes after 9/11*, eds. Didier Bigo and Anastassia Tsoukala (Abingdon: Routledge, 2008); and Didier Bigo, Laurent Bonelli and Thomas Deltombe, *Au nom du 11 Septembre. . .Les démocraties à l'épreuve de l'antiterrorisme* (Paris: La Découverte, 2008).

15 See Paul Abels, 'Inlichtingen- en veiligheidsdiensten en terrorismebestrijding', in *Inlichtingen- en Veiligheidsdiensten*, eds. Beatrice de Graaf, E. R. Muller and J. A. van Reijn (Brussels: Wolters Kluwer, 2010); and D. Engelen, 'Mars door de tijd van een institutie: Een beknopte geschiedenis van de AIVD', in *Inlichtingen- en Veiligheidsdiensten*, eds. De Graaf, Muller and Van Reijn (Brussels: Wolters Kluwer, 2010).

16 Maartje van der Woude, 'Brede benadering terrorismebestrijding', *Openbaar Bestuur* 11, no. 19 (2009): 2–5.

17 Edward W. Said, *Orientalism: Western Conceptions of the Orient* (London: Penguin, 1995 [1978]); and Bobby S. Sayyid, *A Fundamental Fear: Eurocentrism and the Emergence of Islamism* (London: Zed Books, 1997).

18 Although the Palestinian liberation movements are also mentioned in, for example, the *1991 Annual Report*. Rushdie nor his book are mentioned in this report, but it does allude to the writer by referring to the 'liquidation of "the enemies of Islam"' (p. 20).

19 BVD, *Jaarverslag 1996* [*1996 Annual Report*] (The Hague: BVD, 1997), p. 18.

20 See De Koning, Becker, Roex and Aarns, *Eilanden in een zee van ongeloof*; see also Introduction to this volume by Fadil, De Koning and Ragazzi.

21 Brief Minister, Grote Steden, en Integratiebeleid, December 1999; Tweede Kamer der Staten-Generaal, 1999–2002, 26333. In 1994 the policy for incorporating migrants was changed from a minority policy to an integration policy. Ministerie van Binnenlandse Zaken (1994) Integratiebeleid etnische minderheden, contourennota. Tweede Kamer 1993–4, 23684, nr. 1, 2 (Den Haag: SDU).

22 Jan Blommaert and Jef Verschueren, *Het Belgische Migrantendebat: De pragmatiek van de Abnormalisering* (Antwerp: IPrA Research Center, 1992); Jan Rath, *Minorisering: de*

Sociale Constructie van 'Etnische Minderheden' (Amsterdam: Sua, 1991); and Willem Schinkel, *Denken in Een Tijd van Sociale Hypochondrie: Aanzet tot Een Theorie Voorbij de Maatschappij* (Kampen: Klement, 2007).

23 BVD, *Jaarverslag 1999 [1999 Annual Report]* (The Hague: BVD, 2000), p. 15.

24 Michel Foucault, 'Lecture Two: 14 January 1976', in *Power/Knowledge: Selected Interviews and Other Writings, 1972-1977*, ed. Colin Gordon (New York: Pantheon Books, 1980).

25 AIVD, *Jaarverslag 2001 [2001 Annual Report]* (The Hague: AIVD, 2002), p. 18.

26 Ibid., p. 30.

27 AIVD, *Jaarverslag 2003 [2003 Annual Report]* (The Hague: AIVD, 2004), p. 33.

28 Ibid., p. 33.

29 De Koning, Becker, Roex and Aarns, *Eilanden in een zee van ongeloof*.

30 AIVD, *Saoedische invloeden in Nederland: Verbanden tussen salafitische missie, radicaliseringsprocessen en islamistisch terrorisme* (Den Haag: AIVD, 2004), p. 6.

31 AIVD, *Van dawa tot jihad: De diverse dreigingen van de radicale islam tegen de democratische rechtsorde* (Den Haag: AIVD, 2004), pp. 15–17.

32 Ibid., pp. 33–4.

33 AIVD, *De Gewelddadige Jihad in Nederland. Actuele trends in de islamistisch-terorristsiche dreiging* (Den Haag: AIVD, 2006), p. 40.

34 Sedgwick, 'The Concept of Radicalization as a Source of Confusion'.

35 AIVD, *Saoedische invloeden in Nederland*, p. 2

36 AIVD, *Jaarverslag 2014 [2014 Annual Report]* (The Hague: AIVD, 2015).

37 Recent examples of 'for profit' initiatives are Saha Communications (which organized a meeting for social workers and local civil servants, with academics such as Bertjan Doosje and Martijn de Koning) and Radar Advies that established and coordinates the European Radicalization Awareness Network (RAN) with academics and professionals.

38 Medvetz, *Think Tanks in America*.

39 See also Marzouki, 'De l'endiguement à l'engagement'.

40 A few studies exist on radicalization prior to the 2000s; however, they often do not focus on the process of becoming radical but rather on radicalism from the viewpoint of bringing about a desired change in society through the use of militant strategies, with a clear identity and an evil opponent. These studies focused on left-wing and right-wing radicalism (see, for example, Kroes, *Conflict en Radicalisme* (Meppel: Boom), or looked at processes of alienation to account for non-conformist attitudes (see E. H. Bax, 'Oriëntaties van lager geschoolde werkloze en werkende mannelijke jongeren: Een vergelijkend onderzoek', *Mens en Maatschappij* 54, no. 4 (1979): 361–84). But in using the concept of radicalization, most studies we have been able to identify, relate it with the political hardening of confessional groups in the framework of the reformation and counterreformation (see L. C. J. J. Bogaers, 'Politieke en religieuze radicalisering', in *Geschiedenis van de provincie Utrecht II*, ed. Cornelis Dekker (Utrecht: Utrecht Historische Reeks, 1997); and Annemieke Klijn and Jeroen Winkel, 'Münster, Amsterdam en de Wederdopers', *Groniek* 23, no. 2 (1978): 12–16.

41 Marian Visser and Jeroen Slot, *Extremisme en Radicalisering in het Amsterdamse Voortgezet Onderwijs* (Amsterdam: Gemeente, 2005).

42 Another report was published in the same year by Paul Emmelkamp, Jan Henk Kamphuis and A. Reinders, *Radicalisering van jongeren: Een literatuurstudie naar de ontvankelijkheid voor radicalisering* (Amsterdam: Psychology Research Institute, Universiteit van Amsterdam, 2005).

43 Rik Coolsaet, 'Het islamitisch terrorisme: Percepties wieden en kweedvijvers dreggen', *Justitiële Verkenningen* 31, no. 2 (2005): 9–27; Olivier Roy, 'Euro-islam: De jihad van binnenuit?', *Justitiële Verkenningen* 31, no. 2 (2005): 28–46.
44 Frank J. Buijs, Froukje Demant and Atef Hamdy, *Strijders van Eigen Bodem: Radicale en Democratische Moslims in Nederland* (Amsterdam: Amsterdam University Press, 2006); and Marieke Slootman and Jean Tillie, 'Processen van radicalisering: Waarom sommige Amsterdamse moslims radicaal worden', *Instituut voor Migratie- en Etnische Studies* (Amsterdam: IMES, 2006).
45 Buijs, Demant and Hamdy, *Strijders van Eigen Bodem*, p. 8.
46 Slootman and Tillie, 'Processen van radicalisering', p. 10.
47 Martha Crenshaw, 'The Psychology of Terrorism: An Agenda for the 21st Century', *Political Psychology* 21, no. 2 (2000): 405–20.
48 AIVD, *Jaarverslag 2001 [2001 Annual Report]* (The Hague: AIVD, 2002), p. 22.
49 Buijs, Demant and Hamdy, *Strijders van Eigen Bodem*.
50 Although they will recognise the importance of former jihadists and fighters who participated in the wars in Afghanistan and migrated to Western Europe, they will downplay the importance these actors may have in recruiting youngsters to join a military fight. They rather see these recruiters as 'catalysts' whose role is secondary. What is important, to them, are the 'lost youngsters' who are searching for 'leaders' (see Buijs, Demant and Hamdy, *Strijders van Eigen Bodem*, p. 42).
51 Ibid., p. 42.
52 Ibid., p. 245; see also Slootman and Tillie, 'Processen van radicalisering', p. 103.
53 Frank van Gemert, 'Radicaliseren de criminele Marokkaanse jongeren van weleer? Socialecontroletheorie toegepast op twee case studies', *Proces* 2 (2006): 51.
54 See Buijs, Demant and Hamdy, *Strijders van Eigen Bodem*, pp. 41–2; Slootman and Tillie, 'Processen van radicalisering'; and also Tinka Veldhuis and Edwin Bakker, 'Causale factoren van radicalisering en hun onderlinge samenhang', *Vrede en Veiligheid* 36, no. 4 (2007): 447–70.
55 Slootman and Tillie, 'Processen van radicalisering', p. 17. See also Buijs, Demant and Hamdy, *Strijders van Eigen Bodem*, p. 16; and J. A. Moors, E. van den Reek Vermeulen and M. Siesling, *Voedingsbodem voor Radicalisering Bij Kleine Etnische Groepen: Een Verkennend Onderzoek in de Somalisch, Pakistaanse, Koerdische en Molukse Gemeenschappen* (Tilburg: IVA, 2009), p. 15.
56 AIVD, *Jaarverslag 2002 [2002 Annual Report]* (The Hague: AIVD, 2003), p. 33.
57 In his seminal essay, 'The Types of Legitimate Rule', *Economy and Society* (Berkeley, CA: University of California Press, 1978 [1922]), Max Weber offers a complex account of how authority is maintained, which challenges the prevailing Marxist conception that connects the latter with a matter of domination. In this essay, Weber highlights the interactional dimension of power by stating that an authority can only sustain itself to the extent that it is considered legitimate in the eyes of its followers.
58 Crenshaw, 'The Psychology of Terrorism'. See also, for a similar critique, Kundnani, *The Muslims Are Coming!* p. 120; and Mythen, Walklate and Peatfield, 'Assembling and Deconstructing Radicalisation in PREVENT'.
59 Ehud Sprinzak, 'The Process of Delegitimation: Towards a Linkage Theory of Political Terrorism', *Terrorism and Political Violence* 3, no. 1 (1991): 50–68.
60 Buijs, Demant and Hamdy, *Strijders van Eigen Bodem*, p. 237.
61 Slootman and Tillie, 'Processen van radicalisering', p. 44.

62 See also Kundnani, 'Radicalization: The Journey of a Concept'.
63 Allard R. Feddes, Lars Nickolson and Bertjan Doosje, *Triggerfactoren in het Radicaliseringsproces* (Amsterdam: Expertise-unit Sociale Stabiliteit, Universiteit van Amsterdam, 2015).
64 Ibid., pp. 65–8.
65 Slootman and Tillie, 'Processen van radicalisering', p. 3.
66 Buijs, Demant and Hamdy, *Strijders van Eigen Bodem*, p. 15.
67 See, for instance, Veldhuis and Bakker, 'Causale factoren van radicalisering', p. 449.
68 Buijs, Demant, and Hamdy, *Strijders van Eigen Bodem*, p. 14.
69 They consist of the following elements: (a) the idea that Islam is being marginalized, (b) distrust towards the established order, (c) recovering the foundations of Islamic faith, (d) the superiority of one's religion and (e) the active role of the believer in defending his faith. For the more 'extremist' variants of Muslim radicalism, they also add (f) the belief in the supreme rule of Allah, (g) a strong us versus them discourse which is seen as a war between Good and Evil and (h) jihad as a religious duty (see Buijs, Demant and Hamdy, *Strijders van Eigen Bodem*, p. 15).
70 Martijn de Koning, *Zoeken Naar Een 'Zuivere' Islam: Geloofsbeleving en Identiteitsvorming van Jonge Marokkaans-Nederlandse Moslims* (Amsterdam: Bert Bakker, 2008).
71 Ibid., p. 316.
72 Ibid., p. 317.
73 Martijn de Koning, Joas Wagemakers and Carmen Becker, *Salafisme: Utopische Idealen in Een Weerbarstige Praktijk* (Almere: Parthenon, 2014).
74 A similar mode of reasoning can be found in the international literature on Islamism which seeks to de-essentialize the idea of Salafism by distinguishing between 'good' and 'bad' forms of neo-fundamentalism. See especially the work of Farhad Khosrokhavar, *L'islam des jeunes* (Paris: Flammarion, 1997); Olivier Roy, *L'islam mondialisé* (Paris: Seuil, 2002).
75 Welmoet Boender, *Imam in Nederland: Rol, Gezag en Binding in Een Geseculariseerde Samenleving* (Amsterdam: Bert Bakker, 2007).
76 Much of the research on 'Salafism' employs a social movement perspective trying to explain what 'Salafism' is and why people are attracted to it. See, for example, Roel Meijer, *Global Salafism: Islam's New Religious Movement* (London: Hurst, 2009). Fiore Geelhoed tries to answer similar questions in *Purification and Resistance: Glocal Meanings of Islamic Fundamentalism in the Netherlands* (Rotterdam: Erasmus Universiteit Rotterdam, 2011), but through a fundamentalism perspective. Like Quintan Wiktorowicz in 'Anatomy of the Salafi Movement', *Studies in Conflict & Terrorism* 29, no. 3 (2006): 207–39, the emphasis is on the rational choices people make in order to explain their fascination with particular circles of Muslim thought and practice, often presenting the individual as a relatively homogenous, unified and coherent subject. Finally, De Koning, Wagemakers and Becker's, *Salafisme* is more concerned with the struggles of maintaining a correct Islamic practice in daily life and the institutionalization of circles of teaching and preaching in the Netherlands.
77 Ineke Roex, Sjef van Stiphout and Jean Tillie, *Salafisme in Nederland: Aard, Omvang en Dreiging* (Amsterdam: IMES, Universiteit van Amsterdam, 2010).
78 Ibid.
79 Buijs, Demant and Hamdy, *Strijders van Eigen Bodem*.
80 Roex, Van Stiphout and Tillie, *Salafisme in Nederland*, p. 1.

81   See also Ineke Roex, *Leven als de profeet in Nederland: Over de Salafi-beweging en democratie* (Amsterdam: Amsterdam University Press, 2013).

82   See Brice De Ruyver, Marleen Easton, Jannie Noppe, Paul Ponsaers and Antoinette Verhage, *Preventie van radicalisering in België [Onderzoeksapport]* (Antwerp: Maklu, 2011); Amy-Jane Gielen, *Radicalisering en Identiteit: Radicale Rechtse en Moslimjongeren Vergeleken* (Amsterdam: Aksant, 2008); and Moors, Van den Reek Vermeulen and Siesling, *Voedingsbodem voor Radicalisering Bij Kleine Etnische Groepen.*

83   Moors, Van den Reek Vermeulen and Siesling, *Voedingsbodem voor Radicalisering Bij Kleine Etnische Groepen.*

84   Ibid., p. 5.

85   Ibid., p. 113.

86   De Ruyver, Easton, Noppe, Ponsaers and Verhage, *Preventie van radicalisering in België.*

87   Hans Moors, Lenke Balogh, Jaap van Donselaar and Bob de Graaff, *Polarisatie en Radicalisering in Nederland: Een Verkenning van de Stand van Zaken* in 2009 (Tilburg: IVA, 2009).

88   Gielen, *Radicalisering en Identiteit.*

89   For a critique, see Crenshaw, 'The Psychology of Terrorism'; Kundnani, 'Radicalisation: The Journey of a Concept'; Mythen, Walklate and Peatfield, 'Assembling and Deconstructing Radicalisation in PREVENT'.

90   Gielen, *Radicalisering en Identiteit.*

91   Ibid., p. 66.

92   De Ruyver, Easton, Noppe, Ponsaers and Verhage, *Preventie van radicalisering in België.*

93   Ibid., p. 38.

94   Ibid., p. 183.

95   Moors, Balogh, Van Donselaar and De Graaff, *Polarisatie en Radicalisering in Nederland.*

96   Ministerie van Binnenlandse Zaken en Koninkrijksrelaties, *Actieplan Polarisatie en Radicalisering, 2007–2011* (Den Haag, 2007).

97   Ibid., p. 4.

98   Moors, Balogh, Van Donselaar and De Graaff, *Polarisatie en Radicalisering in Nederland.*

99   Ibid., p. 7.

100   Ibid., p. 56.

101   A clear example is the way in which 'left-wing radicalism' is treated in this report. The addition of this category must be read as a corrective to the trend report published a year earlier, and which didn't include left-wing groups but only attended to right-wing, Islamic and animal rights groups. The focus on 'extreme-left' groups (*extreemlinks*) is thus characterized by any activity that is 'extreme', i.e. organized 'outside of the parliament and outside of the law' (ibid., p. 110).

102   Raad voor Maatschappelijke Ontwikkeling, *Polarisatie: Essays Over Oorzaken en Gevolgen van Verscherpte Tegenstellingen* (Amsterdam: BV Uitgeverji SWP, 2009).

103   Willem Schinkel and Marguerite van den Berg, 'Polariserend en moraliserend: Burgerschap in de inburgering', in *Polarisatie: Essays Over Oorzaken en Gevolgen van Verscherpte Tegenstellingen*, ed. Raad voor Maatschappelijke Ontwikkeling (Amsterdam: BV Uitgeverji SWP, 2009), p. 170.

104   Callon, 'Some Elements of a Sociology of Translation'.

105 AIVD, *Jaarverslag 2004* [*2004 Annual Report*] (The Hague: AIVD, 2005).
106 Roy, *L'islam mondialisé*.
107 Wiktorowicz, 'Anatomy of the Salafi Movement'.
108 Ibid.
109 Ibid., p. 234.
110 Werner Schiffauer, 'Vor Dem Gesetz: Der staatliche umgang mit dem legalistischen Islamismus', in *Subjektbildung: Interdiziplinäre Analysen Der Migrationsgesellschaft*, ed. Paul Mecheril (Bielefeld: transcript Verlag, 2014), p. 201.

Chapter 3

CONSIDERING INTERNAL DEBATES ON 'RADICALISM' WITHIN THE BRUSSELS' ISLAMIC COMMUNITY

Mieke Groeninck

The material for this chapter is based upon ethnographic fieldwork that goes back to May 2013, conducted in the Brussels' Islamic scene.[1] However, it draws on the developments after the Paris (13 November 2015) and Brussels (22 March 2016) attacks, and the debates that intensified. In the days after the tragic events, a lot of Islamic authorities and representative organs in Belgium and elsewhere condemned the attacks. But the attacks also brought momentum to a number of underlying internal discussions on the origin and meaning of 'radicalism' that have been going on during the last couple of years, and which also seem to build upon even longer theological and juridical divergence. One of the most articulated matters of 'contestation'[2] in these debates is the presence of 'Salafism' and its presumed ideological links to 'extremism', 'radicalism' and terrorism.[3] Only one of the two positions described in this chapter underlines this causal relation,[4] but both nonetheless articulate a problem of 'radicalism' within their community. A discourse analysis of the discussions on audiovisual and social media after the attacks, together with fieldwork and interviews conducted between 2013–16, will unravel these differences expressed by central authority figures in the Brussels' Islamic scene.

The aim of this chapter is to give an illustration of how the mainstream discourse on radicalization, which currently refers to notions of 'acceptable' and 'non-acceptable' forms of Islam articulated around the concept of 'Salafism', also induces intra-Muslim contestation on what is correct Islamic teaching and understanding. Discussions such as these are inherent to the Islamic discursive tradition 'that includes and relates itself to the founding texts of the Qur'an and the Hadith'.[5] According to Talal Asad, Islam is not a stable entity, but a 'living tradition' constituting 'an historically extended, socially embodied argument'.[6] Knowledge of what constitutes correct, orthodox Islam is related to questions of power that aim to 'regulate, uphold, require or adjust correct practices, and to condemn, exclude, undermine or replace incorrect ones'.[7] The current debates among Islamic authorities described here in the context of radicalism, could also be seen as aiming for 'a (re)ordering of knowledge that governs the "correct" form of Islamic practices' and understanding.[8] This is driven by an attempt 'at achieving discursive coherence, at representing the present within an authoritative narrative that includes positive evaluations of past events and persons'.[9] According to Asad, such an attempt implicates a 'collaborative achievement' between authority and a public that subscribes itself within this same Islamic tradition. Hence, for authorities' arguments to be persuasive, there are consecutive 'conceptual and institutional conditions that must be attended to'.[10] This explains the need to unravel 'internal debates' according to their own 'ways of reasoning',[11] for instance, in order to understand how concepts like 'radicalization' and 'Salafism' are translated, but also to reconfigure the Islamic tradition in a certain time and place.

In what follows, I will describe two positions in this debate through the discourses of two Islamic authorities, Youssouf and Adam.[12] The first position doesn't *ipso facto* identify radicalism as a form of 'Salafism' that exists within the current Islamic community in Brussels; for Youssouf the problem is grounded in social and political issues, exclusivism and human ignorance about the Islamic tradition itself with its prescribed ethical conduct. This position does not consider radicalism as an inherent possibility to certain methodological and reformist branches within the longer Islamic tradition. The second position, however, disagrees on this point. For Adam, what leads people to radicalism is the hermeneutic methodology used to interpret the Texts according to what he calls 'a Salafi way of thinking'. This position argues that the problem is directly connected to this branch within the Islamic tradition, giving way to the necessity of reform. Ultimately, the first position centres on a lack of education, knowledge and ethical conduct, while the second shifts the problem towards hermeneutics as well. By focusing on the discourse of these prominent figures, it will become clear how each position's 'pedagogy of persuasion',[13] while responding to recent events, is simultaneously and strongly embedded in the Islamic tradition's past evaluation and future aspirations.

A united Islamic ummah *against a not-so-Islamic-problem*

The problem of radicalism is individual

The first position will be analysed through the discourse of a well-known Brussels' Islamic teacher and preacher, here under the name of Youssouf. His reactions after the Paris attacks in November 2015 and the Brussels attacks in 2016 were similar, and voiced what the majority of my respondents could to a certain extent adhere to. He condemned the attacks firmly on his Facebook page blaming the 'extremist group of Daesh' for these murderous attacks, as well as for the chaos, fear and general mistrust they create. But in both reactions, he also took a stand against those discourses – from Muslims and non-Muslims – that attempted to depict 'certain tendencies of Islamic thinking [that he referred to as "orthodox"] as dangerous and as being the basis of the murderous excesses of these youngsters'.

'If they would only know,' he wrote after the Paris attacks, 'that these adolescents are the victims of their own ignorance. Most of the time, they don't even know how to read or write Arabic and their religious culture is disconcertingly mediocre.' Therefore, 'their ignorance has to be remediated urgently by advisory lectures and discussions with competent persons,' he remarked after the Brussels attacks.

In both of his reactions, he placed the roots of radicalization not within the established and firmly based tradition of Islam, but in what he felt was a superficial and unsubstantiated misuse of it by some people in order to trick youngsters (according to him often already with a problematic social background) to sympathize with their black-or-white propaganda that allows them to 'legitimize' violence against the 'other', Muslims and non-Muslims. Therefore, Youssouf believed that although traditional centres of authority such as mosques are not relevant to radicalization, they nonetheless might offer a part of the preventive solution. Apart from parents and peers, he also called on mosques to recognize their responsibility to provide a safe-haven for this group of youngsters, and to make efforts to address their specific issues. He feels that they should organize debates and discussion groups that help their sons and daughters [to] be less vulnerable, better equipped with funded knowledge of Islam, and more critical towards pseudo-discourses and authorities that [are] built upon a longer tradition of so-called 'takfirism' and 'kharijism'.[14] 'But', he added, 'to succeed in this endeavour, we first of all have to reach these youngsters who are radicalized and the majority of whom hardly ever visit the mosques. I was able to come to this conclusion after the discussions I've had with some of them.'

Ethics of divergence

Youssouf claims that, besides national, societal, communal and familial measures against radicalism, what is needed now is a 'united Islamic community' instead of 'internal *fitna*'. *Fitna* (unrest or rebellion) dramatizes the religious divergence that exists and that he says has become a popular topic among scholars and 'regular' Muslims alike. He emphasizes what he calls an 'ethics of divergence' (the name of a course he had delivered during that year's Ramadan), which aims for mutual respect among the different strains of Islamic understanding that currently exist and, according to him, should be granted the right to exist because they have *always* existed within the Islamic tradition. Divergence is not a problem, he says; it only becomes problematic when it evolves towards *exclusivism* (takfirism in the worst case) which promotes the idea that, as Youssouf explains, 'They are better Muslims than we are, that such and such are "unbelievers" (*kāfir*), or that only they can make a claim for certain knowledge of the truth and of salvation.' He feels that exclusivism is first of all a problem of misconduct due to ignorance of, and alienation from, the authentic Islamic tradition, which he perceives as offering numerous examples of ethical conduct with a variety of different opinions.

Youssouf's emphasis on an ethics of divergence should be placed within a long tradition of Muslims' efforts to ethically deal with internal differences in mostly juridical issues (*ikhtilāf*), which takes the first generations of followers after the

Prophet as an example.[15] As authors tend to conclude from historical sources, the most well-known *mujtahids* (legal authorities) from the first centuries after the Prophet (for example, Imam Shafi'i, Abu Hanifa, Imam Malik, Ahmad ibn Hanbal) were generally in favour and respectful of juridical divergence based on differences in either local usages or juridical methodology.[16] It was not until the tenth century (fourth century after the Prophet) that 'their' *madhāhib* evolved into doctrinal schools, on the basis of which sectarian violence would later have an opportunity to take place.[17] In his book published in 1986, titled *Adāb al-ikhtilāf fī al-islām* (Ethics of divergence in Islam), the contemporary scholar Taha Jabir al-Alwani (d. 2016),[18] declared that such internal and intolerant disagreement that has led to juridical stagnation (*taqlīd*),[19] has caused the Islamic *ummah* the most harm throughout its history.[20] 'Currently, our *ummah* is in a very bad state,' al-Alwani writes. Therefore, what he believes is needed now is

> a return to the roots of the problem and a reform of the ways of thinking, in order to reestablish the lost order of priorities and install a model for the next generations to come. Thereto, a return to the sources is necessary. . . . Muslims need to stay true to the Qur'ān and the Sunna of the Prophet. They have to decide on rules and principles of *qiyās*[21] and deduction, in order to normalize the interpretation of the Texts and guarantee the evolution of intellectualism in the right way.[22]

Youssouf's remedies seem to echo the ideas of al-Alwani, both in method and scope. The first important element is the relation to the Qur'ān and the Sunna, that should remain 'true' and within the boundaries of what he calls 'classical Sunni orthodoxy'. As we will return to later on, this has implications on the kind of divergence that this position encourages to respect. As a teacher who enjoyed a traditional schooling in Islamic sciences at an Islamic university, and someone who can be seen as a bridge between the grassroots level and the established *'ulamā* (Muslim scholars or religious leaders) in Europe, Youssouf has a fairly clear view on possible points of internal divergence. For him, divergence happens mostly over 'details', whereas the essence and finality of practices and beliefs (as in, for example, 'the categorical and fundamental elements of prayer') are the same for every Muslim. Similar to what has been argued by Talal Asad in *Genealogies of Religion*, this presupposes the concept of an underlying essence and an aspired finality, knowable through (the equally presupposed concept of) an orthodox Islam.[23] Hence, for Youssouf, an ethics of divergence is incumbent upon the distinction he makes between essence and details. Radicalization occurs when this distinction isn't made, or is, in Youssouf's conception, wrongly made. This clearly indicates how the travelling concept of radicalization is here translated and reconfigured along the lines of how power and authority structures define what constitutes (the essence of) Islamic orthodoxy. However, in order for such '(re)ordering of knowledge' to be persuasive for the audience concerned, an attempt must be made 'at achieving discursive coherence, at representing the present within an authoritative narrative that includes positive evaluations of past events and persons'.[24]

Therefore, in his course on 'ethics of divergence', Youssouf attempts to explain where juridical divergence among the four Sunni schools of law comes from, by referring to certain nuances in *usūl al-fiqh* (methods of jurisprudence). This is done with the aim of showing that 'the divergence those youngsters do *fitna* over these days, are but mere details!' Hence, Youssouf regrets that in this search for correctness, personal appeasement and conformity, the right balance between the spiritual dimension and the attention to the rules of conformity is lost. And like al-Alwani, Youssouf proposes a remedy in which intellectual investment and a return to the priorities should result in specific ethical conduct in the face of juridical divergence; a 'model for the next generations to come'. In other words, for Youssouf, the '(re)ordering of knowledge' aspires to a change in practices, here understood as the believing subject performing efforts on the self out of a reasoned insight into the contingent sources of juridical divergence. To think again along the lines of Talal Asad, such a change in behaviour engaged in by Youssouf's audience 'involves an elaborate work of re-conceptualizing the context itself [here, the context of juridical divergence which might lead to radicalization] in ways that aim to be *plausible* to a Muslim audience'.[25] A concrete example of such is given when Youssouf discusses the debate over the position of the hands during prayer:

> This is of second order, whether you put your hands this way or that way. The categorical and fundamental elements of prayer are the same everywhere. Only small details may differ. But these youngsters should not give too much importance to it. They should busy themselves with what is really important.... Divergence has always existed, but that doesn't lead to an annulment of Islam. It just shows there's a flexibility. ... They act as true technicians of the *Sharīʿa*: people who think that the heart is absent, that it's only a matter of techniques. 'That's halal, that's haram, that is permissible, that isn't, you are a good Muslim, you aren't.' This leads to excesses! Some were even completely discouraged to continue in Islam, others flirted with takfirism.

Hence, 'appropriate knowledge'[26] of this 'zone of coherence and discursive space'[27] should be brought to the attention of young Muslims, so that permitted (mostly juridical) divergence (*ikhtilāf*) is no longer seen by them as problematic, but as 'a facility provided by Islam'. In such a case, they would be able to rise to a level on which 'divergence no longer threatens their *imān* (faith)'. As Youssouf explains, 'they would again focus on what is truly important within Islam (namely good conduct and spirituality) and the existence of other opinions would no longer be a cause of *fitna*'. Such a return to the essence thus implies a specific ethical conduct in the face of, in this case, juridical divergence on how to perform the act of prayer. By unravelling to what extent these 'practical details' and their internal differences are contingent as compared to the underlying essence which is shared by everyone in Youssouf's audience, he attempts to divert *fitna* and re-install internal coherence. According to this discourse, exclusivism is most of all a problem of ethics due to ignorance. In his discourse, Youssouf conceptualizes it as a form of contestation not only of orthodox authority, but also of what is considered a correct understanding of the (history of the) Islamic orthodox tradition in itself: 'Rather than fighting each other over such small details and acting like *Sharī'a*-technicians who claim someone is astray because he holds a different opinion, we have to come back to what is essential.' However, the aftermath of the attacks revitalized the discussions about what exactly is essential, where the 'permitted' boundaries of divergence lie and whether a change in ethics is all that is needed.

'Salafism' is radical

The second position develops in relation to standpoints taken by contemporary European reformist thinkers like Rachid Benzine (*l'Observatoire du Religieux*), and Tareq Oubrou (head imam Bordeaux).[28] Although the scope of their arguments differs, one of the central points is nonetheless the idea that there's an inherent problem in Islam that is inscribed in 'Salafism', which is believed to provide a possible basis for radicalization. They acknowledge that the offenders of recent terrorist attacks weren't recruited in Salafi-inspired mosques but nonetheless, they believe what they describe as 'Salafism' to facilitate extreme exclusivism or takfirism, which in some cases may result in a legitimization of jihadism.[29] According to these thinkers, both jihadis and traditional orthodoxy in general (of which Salafism is one branch), share a similar hermeneutic methodology towards the Qur'an and the Sunna, which allows for the possibility of degrading 'the other' (which in the worst case may lead to dehumanization). However, this is contrary to universal human rights, which are proclaimed as the starting point in the contemporary religious reform they aspire to. Thus, their common point with the previous position is that sectarian exclusivism is one of the major risks, because it ends all forms of meaningful communication and leads to stagnation and social divisions between 'us' and 'them' (regardless of who may constitute these categories). But rather than linking this to a lack of ethics of divergence, they claim that a fundamentally problematic way of reading and interpreting both the Qur'ān and the Sunna lies at the basis of this stagnation and degrading of 'the other'. Hence, instead of aspiring to work on the self by acquiring additional knowledge, according to this position what the *ummah* needs is an awakening out of this pathologized state of false understanding of the Texts. The focus thus shifts from ethics to reading; from *usūl* to hermeneutics.

Problem is inherent to 'Salafism'

I will analyse this point of view through the position of a Belgian Islamic reformist theologian, here under the name of Adam. Like Youssouf, he acknowledges the same problems within the contemporary Muslim community, such as a lack of tolerance for divergence, a tendency towards takfirism and a reversal of priorities. But unlike Youssouf, he doesn't think that education in ethics of divergence is the remedy for it. In reaction to the Paris attacks, he stated in an online article that these events should bring the discussion on 'Salafism' that has been lingering on for years, back to the front. He called for self-critical debates among Belgian Muslims; debates that he believed 'have been avoided for too long for fear of *fitna*, or out of convenience and a lack of self-criticism, even though such profound debates are part and parcel of our Islamic tradition'.

The object of these debates, however, should not be limited to the education of ethics of divergence, as he argues that a real respect for religious divergence (not only with regards to what Youssouf would consider 'details', but also to 'essence') is antithetical to the 'Salafi-inspired binary vision of the world'. Adam writes that, inherent to their specific hermeneutic methodology, based on what he calls 'a literalist reading of the Qur'an and the Sunna', are particular theological conceptions that make a division between 'us and them' (the latter being other Muslims and non-Muslims). This division is based on the theological conviction that 'they have a certain understanding of the Divine Will because of their literalist reading of the Qur'an'. And although 'the majority of people following the *salafi minhaj* (Salafi way) are apolitical', he argues that this dichotomous worldview based upon a concept of hierarchical understanding of the Divine Will, 'provides nonetheless the frame within which jihadi families subscribe themselves'.

Adam feels that especially in Belgium, the influence of 'Salafism' has had an opportunity to spread due to the historical specificities of the institutionalization of Islam on Belgian soil. Since the official recognition of Islam in Belgium (1974), Saudi Arabia has played a particular role through the Muslim World League's presence in Brussels. The latter had an office based in the Islamic and Cultural Centre (ICC) of Belgium. The Brussels' Great Mosque was responsible for the appointment of the very first Belgian Islamic teachers and functioned as an informal representative organ for the Muslim community in its relation to the Belgian government.[30] In line with Adam's argument, there's a strong discourse especially in francophone Belgium claiming that from then on, the Saudi presence through the ICC as well as via other means, has played a key role in the continuous spread of 'Wahhabi-inspired Salafism' in the Belgian Muslim community up until today. According to Adam, this is recognizable in a number of 'problematizations', like for example the strong emphasis on 'traditional practices based on a literal interpretation of the Sunna' in which, 'externalized orthopraxy has gained the upper hand over more spiritually inspired ways of Islam'. This point was equally denounced by Youssouf. Another site of problematization, however, is what Adam describes as 'a reduction of the divergence in opinions in matters of religion (*ikhtilāf*) to a bare minimum'. Whereas for Youssouf, divergence or *ikhtilāf* concerned practical 'details', Adam claims that this already excludes a large field of divergent opinions (also regarding 'categorical and fundamental elements', as Youssouf called them) based upon a different reading and interpretation of the Texts. And it is the latter that Adam, together with other reformist thinkers, deems necessary in order to provide a sustainable answer to 'Salafi-inspired radicalism': not an ethics of divergence, but a rethinking of hermeneutic paradigms.

Hermeneutics and change of paradigm

Adam's argument for a rethinking of the Islamic textual paradigms stands partly in line with Tareq Oubrou's *Coran: Clés de lecture*[31] and Rachid Benzine's *Les nouveaux penseurs de l'islam.*[32] In the latter publication, Benzine exposes the work of twentieth- and twenty-first-century reformers in Islam who, despite their internal differences, all share the desire to:

> Re-examine the ways in which Islam was able to construct itself historically. To 'revisit' the successive interpretations of the Qur'anic message and the other foundational texts (Hadiths, Sunna, the corpus of the juridical schools, . . . and to approach them critically. They wish to expose every aspect of the lived reality of Islam to scientific research.[33]

The central emphasis in this position is a complete hermeneutical deconstruction of the Texts in order to historicize and analyse them 'in the context of the cultural, political and ideological domain of the period in which it was first revealed and then later interpreted and put into practice.'[34] Because, as Adam writes in one of his online articles, this hermeneutical exercise will necessarily also have to deal with 'a metaphysical and theological reflection on God, the legislator (*Shari'*) and the potential goals of His interference', it is out of this exercise that contemporary religious meaningfulness might be reconstructed. The means therefore are:

> Using every classical and contemporary method that is at our disposal: linguistics, semiotics, anthropology, epigraphy, historical critique . . . It's only by using these scientific methods that we will be able to regain access to the Qur'ānic imagery and to unravel what could have been the Prophet's intention while addressing him to his surroundings. That means we have to re-read the Text from the position of the historical world that surrounded it, instead of making contemporary projections unto the Text. That is the difference between ideology and history. This approach will allow us to reformulate contemporary theology(ies) on a sound basis. A basis upon which no absolute destruction by its enemies is possible, and upon which no opposition between believers and unbelievers can be made, since these categories did not exist in the first ages of Islam. . . . During the time of the Prophet, there was no 'they' and 'we', nor denials of humanity for theological opponents.[35]

In other words, whereas Youssouf, like al-Alwani, believed that an ethics of divergence, a change in practical attitude, would follow once believers' ignorance about where the mainly juridical divergence came from would be tackled, for Adam and other contemporary reformists, the ethics of divergence is not the focus of emphasis. According to them, this limited understanding of *ikhtilāf* (or divergence) is already grounded in what it is they want to rethink: namely human's relation to the Hadiths and the Qur'an, in terms of hermeneutic methodology. Regarding the former, these reformist thinkers argue that Hadith collections should be re-approached from a historical anthropological point of view. Regarding the latter, Benzine writes that for reformists, the Qur'an is still considered to be 'the revealed Parole of God for men, even if they may wonder what is covered by our notions of Parole of God and Revelation'.[36] One example is Oubrou's *Clés de lecture*, in which he states that in order to come out of the eternal tension between spirituality and temporality, between God's sacral essence and the material form of the Qur'an, through which He communicated to people in a specific time and place,

> Textual research should comprise a search to understand the *signs of God* [which Oubrou clearly differentiates from the sacral itself]. The ontological access (*ta'wîl*) to God remains for the hermeneutical scholar an inevitably incomplete task, because his work but consists out of hermeneutics of the trace, all the while bearing in mind that there's always a semiological and semantic margin between the internal Parole of God (*al-kalâm al-nafsî*), the Intention of God, and the Parole of God as it is expressed in Arabic in the Qur'ānic text.[37]

Hence, like Youssouf, a return to the textual sources is propagated by these Muslim reformists as well, though from a different, historical and hermeneutical approach. This requires an adjustment towards what is here considered a more *apt* reading and interpretation of the Texts as opposed to 'Salafi' ways of understanding them. As explained by Asad and as also indicated in the case of Youssouf, such an attempt by authorities to re-order knowledge 'that governs the "correct" form of Islamic practices' and understanding, requires a 'collaborative achievement' between authority and a public for which this seems plausible.[38] It is therefore significant that the majority of my respondents who self-identify as 'practising Muslims' were generally not in favour of Adam's position, whereas (and sometimes also *because*) it was often adopted into the mainstream deradicalization models by Belgian and other government officials.[39]

Conclusion

This chapter attempts to outline two different positions concerning 'radicalism' that were discerned in the Brussels' Muslim community in the aftermath of the Paris and Brussels attacks. They both link 'radicalism' to a lack of tolerance for internal divergence, a tendency towards takfirism and a reversal of priorities. But they differ in the discernment of the respective causes and remedies for what they perceive as this problematic situation. While the first position places the roots of the problem in ignorance about the reasons for internal divergence within the current comprehension of Sunni orthodoxy, the second questions the hermeneutic paradigm of orthodoxy itself. While the first believes education by the traditional Islamic authorities in ethics of divergence is what is needed now, the second feels that a hermeneutic rethinking in reading the Texts from a '(post)modern and scientific perspective' should be conducted by a diverse range of specialists. While the first believes that radicalism cannot but unfold due to a lack of ethics and to ignorance of the Islamic tradition itself, the second perceives it as an inherent possibility resulting from a certain reading of the tradition. And finally, while the first position is criticized by others (among its critics are Muslims and non-Muslims alike) for not 'recognizing that the truth of Qur'anic scripture is grounded not in its theological claims but in culture and history',[40] the second position is cautiously promoted by, among others, a Flemish politician of Muslim descent for its fight against 'religious analphabetism or blind faith that questions nothing and remains uncritical'[41] instead offering ways to construct a 'Belgian Islam'.[42]

To conclude, the aim of this chapter was to illustrate how the concept of 'radicalization' travels and directs intra-Muslim debates on correct Islamic teaching, knowledge and understanding. Both positions can be seen as attempts to re-order knowledge that governs the 'correct' form of Islamic practice and understanding in a context of contest and problematization.[43] Each position focused on the need to work on the self based on ethical examples in the past, or on the need to apply a different reading of the Texts from a hermeneutic point of view. In order to be persuasive, both positions require a collaborative understanding between the narrator and audience, which explains their success with different publics. On frequent occasions, such intra-Muslim debates and arguments affect deradicalization policy (see Chapter 2 in this volume). As Fadil, De Koning and Ragazzi mention in the introduction to this book, this exemplifies how discourses on (de)radicalization 'provide a site of interaction (or even collusion) between state-led attempts at regulating (and securitizing) the Muslim field and intra-Muslim discussions and debates on "acceptable" forms of Islam'.[44] Unravelling both in an inter-traditional context, yet according to their own 'ways of reasoning',[45] which is the attempt of this book, allows us to understand their scope, plausibility, relevance and impact for a variety of publics.

Notes

1   For my doctoral dissertation, I monitored participant observation (between 2013–15) in three mosques and three Islamic institutes with a Moroccan background in the region of Brussels, which – despite their internal differences – can all be seen as belonging to the Islamic revivalist movement in Europe (see Jeanette S. Jouili, *Pious Practices and Secular Constraints: Women in the Islamic Revival in Europe* (Stanford, CA: Stanford University Press, 2015)). I have been particularly interested in the transmission of Islamic knowledge, as well as its influence in daily lives, questions of pious becoming and the maintenance of a tangible Islamic worldview. See Mieke Groeninck, 'Reforming the Self, Unveiling the World: Islamic Religious Knowledge Transmission for Women in Brussels' Mosques and Institutes from a Moroccan Background' (PhD diss., KU Leuven, 2017).
2   I understand 'contestation' here in a Foucauldian way, inspired by Blanchot, as 'the testing of the limit'. 'For Foucault, the idea of contestation is the negating of a limit in order to exit to an outside or exteriority that is truly outside' (see Leonard Lawlor, 'Contestation', in *The Cambridge Foucault Lexicon*, eds. L. Lawlor and J. Nale (Cambridge: Cambridge University Press, 2014)).

3   For more information on the Salafi doctrine, see, among others, Samir Amghar, 'Salafism and Radicalization of Young European Muslims', in *European Islam: Challenges for Public Policy and Society*, eds. S. Amghar, A. Boubekeur and M. Emerson (Brussels: Centre for European Policy Studies, 2007); De Koning, *Zoeken naar een 'Zuivere' Islam*; De Koning, Wagemakers and Becker, *Salafisme*; Frank Griffel, 'What Do We Mean by Salafi? Connecting Muhammad Abduh with Egypt's Nur Party in Islam's Contemporary Intellectual History', *Die Welt des Islams* 55, no. 2 (2015): 186–220; Bernard Haykel, 'On the Nature of Salafi Thought and Action', in *Global Salafism: Islam's New Religious Movement*, ed. R. Meijer (London: Hurst, 2009); Henri Lauzière, 'The Construction of *Salafiyya*: Reconsidering Salafism from the Perspective of Conceptual History', *International Journal of Middle Eastern Studies* 42, no. 3 (2010): 369–89; Henri Lauzière, *The Making of Salafism: Islamic Reform in the Twentieth Century* (New York: Columbia University Press, 2015); and Wiktorowicz, 'Anatomy of the Salafi Movement'.

4   For more on the concept of radicalization and how it presumes this link to Islamic theology and terrorist violence, see Kundnani, 'Radicalisation: The Journey of a Concept'.

5   Talal Asad, *The Idea of an Anthropology of Islam*, Occasional Papers Series (Washington, DC: Georgetown University Center for Contemporary Arab Studies, 1986), p. 14.

6   Alisdair MacIntyre, *After Virtue* (Notre Dame, IN: University of Notre Dame Press, 1981), p. 222.

7   Asad, *The Idea of an Anthropology of Islam*, p. 15.

8   Talal Asad, *Genealogies of Religion: Discipline and Reasons of Power in Christianity and Islam* (Baltimore, MD: Johns Hopkins University Press, 1993), p. 210.

9   Ibid.

10 Ibid.

11 Ibid., p. 200.

12 Both are important actors in my doctoral research, in which all my respondents are kept anonymous.

13 Saba Mahmood, *Politics of Piety: The Islamic Revival and the Feminist Subject* (Princeton, NJ: Princeton University Press, 2005), p. 79.

14 *Takfir* is the act of declaring someone an unbeliever (*kufr*). For more on Takfirism, see Camilla Adang, Hassan Ansari, Maribel Fierro and Sabine Schmidtke, eds., *Accusations of Unbelief in Islam: A Diachronic Perspective on Takfir* (Leiden and Boston, MA: Brill, 2015). The *Khārijītes* were those who rebelled against the Umayyad caliph Marwān II (AH 127–132/AD 744–750) and declared him an unbeliever who would go to Hell. This is considered historically to be an extremist point of view in comparison to Sunni traditionalism in which a distinction is made between believing and sinning, as well as an emphasis laid on the idea that only God knows who'll go to Heaven or Hell. See Cornelia Schöck, 'Belief and Unbelief in Classical Sunnī Theology', in *Encyclopaedia of Islam, THREE*, eds. K. Fleet, G. Krämer, D. Matringe, J. Nawas and E. Rowson (Brill Online, 2007).

15 As Muhammad Khalid Masud writes, the first books on the matter of juridical *ikhtilāf* were published in the eighth century (second century after the Prophet); and publications dealing with it have never disappeared ever since, illustrating 'the continuous interest of Muslim jurists in the subject'. See Muhammad K. Masud, 'Ikhtilaf al-Fuqaha: Diversity in Fiqh as a Social Construction', in *Wanted: Equality and Justice in the Muslim Family*, ed. Z. Anwar (Selangor: Musawah, 2009), p. 70.

16 Ibid., p. 66 and p. 71. See also, Wael B. Hallaq, *The Origins and Evolution of Islamic Law* (Cambridge: Cambridge University Press, 2005); Taha Jabir Al-Alwani, *Islam: Conflit d'opinions – Pour une éthique du désaccord* (Paris: Éditions Al-Qalam, 2010 [1986]).

17 Masud, 'Ikhtilaf al-Fuqaha'; Hallaq, *The Origins and Evolution of Islamic Law*.

18 Translated into French by Ihlam Benmahdjoub and Michèle Messaoudi under the title *Islam: Conflit d'opinions – Pour une éthique de désaccord*. This book is widely available in Brussels and in online Islamic book shops.

19 *Taqlīd* is generally translated as 'the act of following', which is often positioned as the antidote of *ijtihād*, or the effort in original thinking and reasoning based on knowledge. However, *taqlīd* has since the beginning of Islamic jurisprudence been a permitted legal tool for those jurists who did not (yet) have the qualities to perform an *ijtihād* themselves. It was not until later centuries that the act of stagnation, through *taqlīd*, was perceived in a predominantly negative way. See Hallaq, *The Origins and Evolution of Islamic Law*, p. 147.

20 Al-Alwani, *Islam: Conflit d'opinions*, p. 18.

21 *Qiyās* is a juridical term in Islam that can be translated as 'inferential reasoning' in case of a lack of consensus or an entirely new juridical problem. The most often used methods of *qiyās* or thinking through analogy is deduction (*istinbāt*) or induction (*istidlāl*). See Hallaq, *The Origins and Evolution of Islamic Law*, pp. 140–4; Marie Bernand and Gerard Troupeau, 'Kiyās', in *Encyclopaedia of Islam, Second Edition*, eds. P. Bearman, Th. Bianquis, C. E. Bosworth, E. van Donzel and W. P. Heinrichts (Brill Online, 2012).

22 Al-Alwani, *Islam: Conflit d'opinions*, p. 23 (my translation from French into English).

23 Asad, *Genealogies of Religion*, p. 210.

24 Ibid.

25 Ibid., p. 212.

26 Asad, *The Idea of an Anthropology of Islam*, p. 7.

27 Ebrahim Moosa, *Ghazali and the Poetics of Imagination* (Chapel Hill, NC, and London: University of North Carolina Press, 2005), p. 53.

28 Important international thinkers in this stream of thought are, among others, Mohammed Arkoun, Nasr Hamid Abu Zayd, Muhammad Shahrur, Fazlur Rahman, Abdul Karim Soroush, Ebrahim Moosa and Amina Wadud, to quote but a few (see also Michaël Privot, 'Réflexions sur la "légitimité" islamique dans l'espace francophone européen', *Les cahiers de l'islam* (25 January 2016) http://www.lescahiersdelislam.fr/ Reflexions-sur-la-legitimite-islamique-dans-l-espace-francophone-europeen_a1242. html (accessed 3 August 2016).

29 After the 13/11 Paris attacks, a number of Salafi-inspired authorities and mosques have spoken against this presumption. See, for example, Imam Abou Ismail on the website of a Dutch 'Da'wah institute', Al-Yaqeen http://al-yaqeen.com/bibliotheek/artikel.php?id= 1631 (accessed 26 December 2015).

30 For more on this specific history of the institutionalization of Islam in Belgium, see Pierre Blaise and Vincent de Coorebyter, 'L'islam et l'état Belge', *Res Publica* 35, no. 1 (1993): 223–37; Felice Dassetto and Albert Bastenier, *L'islam transplanté: Vie et organisation des minorités musulmanes de Belgique* (Antwerpen: EPO, 1984); Meryem Kanmaz and Mohamed El Battiui, *Moskeeën, Imams en Islamleerkrachten in België* (Brussel: Koning Boudewijnstichting, 2004); Johan Leman and Monique Renaerts, 'Dialogues at Different Institutional Levels among Authorities and Muslims in Belgium', in *Muslims in the Margin: Political Responses to the Presence of Islam in Western Europe*, eds. W. A. R. Shadid and P. S. Van Koningsveld (Kampen: Klement, 1996); and Laurent

Panafit, *Quand le droit écrit l'islam: L'intégration juridisuqe de l'islam en Belgique* (Bruxelles: Bruylant, 1999).

31 Tareq Oubrou, *Coran : Clés de lecture* (Paris: Fondation pour l'innovation politique, 2015). Available at http://www.fondapol.org/etude/tareq-oubrou-coran-cles-de-lecture/ (accessed 10 July 2016). Translated from French into English.

32 Rachid Benzine, *Les nouveaux penseurs de l'islam* (Paris: Albin Michel, 2004).

33 Ibid., p. 7.

34 Saba Mahmood, 'Secularism, Hermeneutics, and Empire: The Politics of Islamic Reformation', *Public Culture* 18, no. 2 (2006): 323–47.

35 Rachid Benzine and Michaël Privot, 'Islam, Coran, djihadisme . . . et la théologie dans tout ça?' *BibliObs*, 20 December 2015. Available at http://bibliobs.nouvelobs.com/idees/20151207.OBS0872/islam-coran-djihadisme-et-la-theologie-dans-tout-ca.html (accessed 10 July 2016).

36 Benzine, *Les nouveaux penseurs de l'islam*, p. 7.

37 Oubrou, *Coran: Clés de lecture.*

38 Asad, *Genealogies of Religion*, p. 210.

39 For instance, the deradicalization project announced in January 2016 by the Brussels' politician Rudi Vervoort (from the francophone socialist party in Belgium). However, this project was terminated at an early stage because of political and communal tensions and pressure on the reformist thinkers Ismael Saïdi, Rachid Benzine and Michaël Privot, which were part of the project. In 2006, Saba Mahmood wrote an article on a similar strategy by the US State Department through its project *Muslim World Outreach*, launched in 2003, in which the reformist branch within Islam was promoted in the fight against 'traditionalism' (see Mahmood, 'Secularism, Hermeneutics and Empire').

40 Ibid., p. 336.

41 This is a citation from the introduction given by the Flemish parlementarian Yamila Idrissi (from the Flemish socialist party in Belgium), concerning a lecture of Rachid Benzine on a modern reading of the Qur'an in Brussels, October 2015.

42 Michaël Privot and Radouane Attiya, 'Dans les mosquées, pas de prières pour les mécréants?' *Le Soir* (25 March 2016). Available at http://plus.lesoir.be/32528/article/2016-03-25/dans-les-mosquees-pas-de-prieres-pour-les-mecreants#_ga=1.97592543.1989293524.1452006835 (accessed 3 August 2016). Their call is an elaboration of the debate on a 'European Islam', which originated at the end of the 1990s/beginning of the 2000s when some voices within the Muslim community called for such a move (for instance, see Tariq Ramadan, *Être musulman européen: Études des sources islamiques à la lumière du contexte européen* (Lyon: Tawhid, 1999)). For more on this discussion about a European Islam, see Shirin Amir-Moazami and Armando Salvatore, 'Gender, Generation and the Reform of Tradition: From Muslim Majority Societies to Western Europe', in *Muslim Networks and Transnational Communities in and across Europe*, eds. S. Allievi and J. Nielsen (Leiden and Boston, MA: Brill, 2003); Nadia Fadil, 'Submitting to God, Submitting to the Self: Secular and Religious Trajectories of Second Generation Maghrebi in Belgium' (PhD diss., KU Leuven, 2008).

43 Asad, *Genealogies of Religion*, p. 210.

44 See Nadia Fadil, Martijn de Koning and Francesco Ragazzi, 'Radicalization: Tracing the Trajectory of an "Empty Signifier" in the Low Lands' (Introduction to this volume).

45 Asad, *Genealogies of Religion*, p. 200.

Part II

DE/RADICALIZATION POLICIES ON THE GROUND

Chapter 4

FOREIGN FIGHTERS ON TRIAL: SENTENCING RISK, 2013–17[1]

Beatrice de Graaf

'The youngest terror suspect ever', the Dutch yellow press journal *De Telegraaf* was titled on 16 September 2015. Rahma E., a Dutch-Somali born girl, 15 years of age, living with her mother in Maastricht was arrested for preparing to emigrate to the Caliphate in Libya and wanting to join international jihad. She was arrested in possession of a new phone with Syrian telephone numbers, travel itinerary, and after having chatted extensively about her plans with a sister in arms and having sent a gold ring as payment for her trip. Interestingly, in the verdict the judge made a sharp distinction between the different stages of preparatory actions. Rahma E. had carried out preparatory acts with respect to planning her trip to Syria to join Islamic State (IS) (see annex 1, below, nr. 31), hence preparing for committing a crime (joining a terrorist organization), but since she had not actually started her trip, she was acquitted from concrete executive actions, such as initiating the travel. This verdict implied that had she left the country for her trip, this would indeed have been considered an executive act of trying to join a terrorist organization – a departure from previous rulings that acquitted passport-carrying Dutch suspects from the same crime who were caught as far as Turkey.

The argument in this chapter is that trials against alleged foreign fighters demonstrate how the turn towards precautionary or actuarial justice[2] has progressed increasingly further in the field of preparatory acts ('left from the bang'). This transformation of terrorism law into a means of risk management with its corresponding challenges (see the above attempts to classify different kinds of preparatory acts) has been facilitated and instantiated by means of terrorism trials. Within the confines of the courtroom, scholarly models and schemes of radicalization processes are invoked to visualize linear and deterministic trajectories that inform the prosecution's attempts to prevent acquittals. The courtroom becomes a theatre of – rather crudely applied – counter-radicalization theories and solutions. Thus, criminal law in terrorism cases has come to infringe upon the existence of rehabilitative models since the objective of the legal proceedings has shifted towards control and deterrence rather than focusing on re-integration, rehabilitation and transformation of the convicted offender.

The underlying intellectual argument builds on the theory laid out in the *Terrorists on Trial* volume,[3] and on a previous journal paper.[4] It draws out the argument of performativity and actuarial justice and adapts it to recent court cases against foreign fighters. Through zooming in on cases of foreign fighters, it becomes clear that terrorism trials increasingly serve as an instrument to imagine trajectories of radicalization. The courtroom has become the place to gauge and unequivocally establish how far along this trajectory the suspect has ventured, and to draft a corresponding conviction to reverse-engineer this envisaged process of radicalization. Thus, the nature of a trial has been transformed, rendering it an instrument of counter-radicalization and risk management in itself.

The precautionary turn in criminal law

Elsewhere, we have explained how, since '9/11', through instances of 'anticipatory prosecution'[5] and by means of a series of new laws, acts increasingly further in advance of actual attacks are brought within the remit of criminal law. This transformation of criminal law has since then been studied extensively, from legal, criminological and political perspectives.[6] The so-called precautionary turn in criminal law is not strictly a post-9/11 development.[7] Since the 1980s a 'new penology' has emerged, with the objective of 'managing' dangerous populations through techniques of classification and prediction – while the traditional penal objectives of rehabilitation and normalization were simultaneously lost out of sight.[8] Simultaneously, religious orthodoxy, most notably Islamic orthodoxy (Salafism) has been securitized since the 1990s.[9] There is thus some continuity in the manifestation of the risk paradigm in criminal law,[10] but we argued that post-9/11 terrorism law and legal practice, especially with respect to ancillary and preparatory acts, depart in important ways from the new penology.

Since 2001, the adoption of new laws and corresponding jurisprudence has resulted in substantial legal changes, initiated to enable the successful prosecution of terrorism suspects in initial stages of planning and to reduce the risk of acquittals of terrorist suspects. In Europe, the cornerstone in this new legal edifice of precautionary criminal law has been the 2002 *EU Framework Decision on Combating Terrorism*, which obliges Member States to render punishable a broadly defined set of facilitating actions, including 'participating in the activities of a terrorist group by supplying information or material resources'. The Framework states that terrorist groups do not 'need to have formally defined roles for its members . . . or a developed structure'.[11] In 2008, three further activities were included in the Framework Decision: the public provocation to commit a terrorist offence, recruitment and training for terrorism. Since then, individual states have amended their own penal codes and other administrative regulations correspondingly.

In 2004, Dutch Parliament adopted its first antiterrorism laws – before that year, no specific antiterrorist act or judicial definition of a terrorist crime had existed – criminalizing various types and sorts of terrorist crimes and preparatory acts. Legal paragraphs 83/83a have introduced the concept of terrorism crime into Dutch penal law; paragraph 140a concerns membership in a terrorist organization, 205 involves recruitment, 96 deals with conspiracy and preparatory acts, while 134 criminalizes training and preparing for training. In 2006 more competences within criminal procedure were facilitated in cases of terrorist offences (closed hearing of witnesses, use of intelligence, Stb 580).[12]

Since 2013, under the influence of the threat of (returning) 'foreign fighters'[13] moreover, existing legal paragraphs have been amended to encapsulate an even broader range of possible offences (see Table 4.1). Each subsequent paragraph has enabled the prosecution to prove purpose of travel and intent of preparatory acts committed increasingly prior to or more detached from actual travel; the collection of evidence on a broader, even associative base, the use of social media postings, or other internet-based information as admissible evidence, and the use of intelligence as admissible evidence. Even without actual involvement in plots or conspiracies to carry out concrete attacks, or having been in the country of destination or having actually joined a terrorist group or moved to the so-called 'Caliphate' in the Middle East, these laws enable prosecutors to charge suspects based on acts that can be seen as incitement, recruitment, glorification or facilitation and preparation for or on behalf of terrorist acts and groups.

This transformation of criminal law in the wake of the fight against terrorism has shifted the burden of proof and evidence into the realm of virtual threats and possible violent futures, that might be inaugurated by the defendants.[14] In this sense, the classical goals of criminal justice – retribution, deterrence, incapacitation, and rehabilitation[15] – are giving way to the executive-oriented goal of security and risk management. Security has taken over the rule of law and has come to dominate it in an increasingly pervasive, and inconspicuous manner.[16]

This trend has been intensified since 2013, with the emergence of the phenomenon of so-called 'foreign fighters', people who travel to fight in conflicts and war zones outside their country. The war in Syria and Iraq has motivated thousands of young men and some women to join rebels, opposition groups and also jihadi organizations in their struggle. Since the declaration of the Caliphate in June 2014 by the terrorist group IS, the number of individuals that decided to participate in international jihad has steeply increased. Estimates suggest that around 30,000 foreign fighters joined terrorist organizations in Syria and Iraq, among them an estimated 4,000 fighters from Europe. With attacks staged, carried out, steered or inspired by IS in Europe, the Middle East and Africa, since then governments all over the world (Brussels, Beirut, Paris, Tunis, Istanbul, London) have adopted multifarious plans, programmes and measures to counter that threat. These measures range from military action, financial tracking and tracing of 'terrorist' monies, and legal measures to deter, prevent, and to criminalize other actions within the remit of joining IS/the Caliphate to programmes in the field of 'social engineering', such as exit programmes to facilitate and nudge people into deradicalization, disengagement, rehabilitation and re-integration projects.[17]

The security risk involving these foreign fighters has both an external and an internal component: they might reinforce the battle and conflict situation in Syria and Iraq and/or might return to their countries of residence and carry out attacks there – as has become manifest to a series of attacks in Paris, Brussels, Berlin and Munich between 2013 and 2017. The United Nations Counter-Terrorism Committee Executive Directorate (CTED) formulated the risk in these words:

> Many fighters leave their homes with no intention of returning, and instead do so with the intention of starting a new life, building a new 'state' or dying as martyrs. Not all return as terrorists, and many return precisely because they have become disillusioned and no longer wish to participate in armed conflict. However, those who do return may have been exposed to extreme violence, sophisticated training and battlefield experience. A small number of returning foreign terrorist fighters therefore pose a very significant threat to international peace and security'.[18]

Since 2013, international and national governmental organizations alike have underscored the importance of expanding the legal apparatus to bridge the gap between radicalization processes at home, travelling to join IS or other terrorist groups in Syria/Iraq or recruitment and facilitation efforts to support preparation for terrorist attacks (possibly by returning or thwarted foreign fighters) in Europe. This geographical and virtual span of potential criminal offences has been translated into attempts to draw up additional criminal paragraphs to help the prosecution of those men and women, foreign fighters or supporters, who are suspected of recruitment, incitement to hatred or terrorism, of joining terrorist organizations, preparing activities for committing terrorism and the actual participation in carrying out terrorist attacks. In September 2014, the UN adopted resolution 2178 that obliges states to develop and adopt legal measures to criminalize travel or attempt to travel for the purpose of planning, training or perpetration of terrorist acts, 'or the wilful provision or receipt of terrorist training, the provision or collection of funds to finance the travel of individuals to participate in these acts, and the wilful organization or facilitation (including acts of recruitment) of the travel of individuals to participate in these activities'.[19] Hence, new and extensive legal changes were called into existence in already extensive juridical provisions to anticipate and pre-empt terrorists.

Trials as a performative space

Notwithstanding this range of new legal paragraphs, the act of translating precautionary law in practice is not an easy undertaking. Given this difficulty, I have argued elsewhere that terrorism trials are important, even necessary, performative spaces where this precautionary turn in criminal law needs to become manifest. Terrorism trials are the place where potential future terror is imagined, invoked, contested and made real, in the proceedings and verdict, as well as through its wider media- and societal echoes.[20] Trials highlight the 'productive power of legal arguments' and the ways in which 'legal arguments are embedded in and reproduce deeper-lying social and symbolic structures'.[21] The courtroom is the place where the performative dimension of precautionary law becomes palpable. Through closely following terrorism trials, we can identify and map how the chain of translating the fear of terrorism and the suspicious behaviour of alleged foreign fighters in concrete convictions plays out and evolves over time.

Therefore it can be stated that terrorism trials often hinge on techniques of 'premediation'. Premediation denotes the post-9/11 media logic geared towards the mediation of multiple potential futures. For Grusin, premediation is not the same as prediction – it does not involve actuarial or statistical calculations of possible risks.[22] Instead, premediation refers to the cultural fantasies of how risk scenarios may play out, and the concomitant mobilizations of collective anxieties and political possibilities in the present. This is exactly the process that unfolds in the courtroom. The act of convicting terrorism suspects caught in the stage of preparation requires not only evidence, but also imagination, images and associations to tie together inchoate bits and pieces of indices – especially if the concrete execution of the trip or participation in the international jihad abroad or at home has not (yet) taken place.[23]

This paper builds on this debate by inquiring specifically into the way in which uncertain and potentially violent futures are configured into terrorism trials and their public mediation in cases built against 'foreign fighters'. In these trials, present criminal offences involving the *aims* and *intent* of alleged 'foreign fighters' are constituted through the appeal to potential future violences that they may engage in or facilitate. In most trials against foreign fighters, offences and potential plots were adjudicated that were 'more aspirational than operational'.[24] In these trials, the premediation appeal is frequently made by appropriating, citing and presenting (visual) schemes and models of radicalization, as furnished by the growing body of radicalization literature since 2001.

Criminal law meets radicalization theories

A few words must be spent on the increasing use of radicalization theories by the prosecution and in the courtroom in cases against terrorism suspects and alleged 'foreign fighters'.

In presenting the legal argument against the terrorist defendants in cases of preparatory activities (rather than actual attacks), the prosecution needs to tie inchoate facts and events together to prove the actual criminal offence. Moreover, it needs to prove terrorist intent. Underlying these attempts of interpellating and premediating a violent future evidence through notions of intent is the suggestion that this particular act is one step in the chain of an ongoing radicalization process.

Frequently, radicalization theories from the academic and scholarly domain are borrowed, appropriated and applied to underpin this legal argument.

Interestingly enough, parallel to the extension of the body of criminal law with the abovementioned paragraphs on terrorist related offences, since 2001 a whole corpus of radicalization studies has been developed. With the accession of (social) psychologists to the 'invisible college of terrorism researchers' – Pape, Horgan, Stern, Moghaddam and others[25] – terrorist and radical behaviour and belief systems, motives and intentions, were identified and charted. The existing field of terrorism studies (mostly historians, focusing on actual terrorist groups and attacks) expanded into the field of radicalization studies. According to most researchers, radicalization denotes 'to be extreme relative to something that is defined or accepted as normative, traditional, or valued as the status quo'.[26] They furthermore stress the important difference between extremism and terrorism: 'nearly all terrorists are extremists, but most extremists are not terrorists'.[27] This field also taps into the '*Extremismusforschung*' from the Scandinavian countries, Germany and Italy (dealing with right- and left-wing extremism)[28]; it makes use of research into political violence in Italy and the US,[29] and has broadened its scope with Social Network Analysis, discerning between multifarious roles of activists, radicals and facilitators in a given network.[30] As contested and open as the field still is, a few dominant radicalization theories (or scholarly narratives) have surfaced.

These narratives mostly ascribe to a linear process, as exemplified in the words of terrorism expert Neumann: 'violent radicalization is a process of changes in attitude that lead towards sanctioning and ultimately the involvement in the use of violence for a political aim'.[31] Although Neumann and other radicalization researchers will acknowledge that radicalization trajectories are unpredictable and hardly ever follow a generic path, such theories and models do implicitly assume such a linear trajectory. Neumann's definition has achieved a received status as a commonly accepted definition of non-legal and non-admissible political violent activism; as such, it has been integrated into EU and Dutch criminal law.

The most commonly used model for mapping and understanding radicalization processes – as well as understanding the phenomena of deradicalization and disengagement – is the metaphor of the 'staircase'. According to Moghaddam, radicalization is a psychological process, including cognitive, affective and behavioural components, starting with (1) perceived injustices and (2) perceived options to fight these injustices and unfair treatment, followed by (3) displacement of aggression and (4) moral engagement with violent activities, resulting in the sidestepping of final inhibitions and entering into radical violent behaviour. In this psychological model, not all that tread the first step will climb all the way up. Nor is descending the staircase impossible, although deradicalization can and should not be considered a straight reversal of the same order in which the steps were ascended. Counter-radicalization, then, has as its goal the 'transformation of the psychological citizen, [and] the psychological characteristics citizens need to have in order to participate effectively in and sustain a particular political system'.[32]

Within academia, such models are highly contested, since they leave open what exactly prompts the elevation to the next step (religious praxis or dogmas, peer group pressure or disturbing personal events), who is entitled to discern between legal and non-legal radical activities (incitement to hatred, discrimination, glorification, enabling and supporting, etc.), or where exactly the fine line between radical convictions and violence should be drawn.[33] Are the Muslim Brotherhood, AEL or the Ku Klux Clan criminalized, or designated terrorist organizations, or is that epitaph only attributed to groups such as al-Qaeda and IS?[34] Radicalization can also be considered a mere 'tendency to see one's own perspective representing the absolute truth and pure virtue, while other perspectives represent falsehoods or evils and can free one to believe that any sort of action that supports the dominance of that perspective within society is itself a virtuous act'.[35] Others hold that radicalization should not (only) be studied from a security perspective (and inevitably leading towards terrorism) but should be considered more a stage in a developmental psychological trajectory, an expression of adults discovering their identities.[36] Not every radical turns into a terrorist, and not every terrorist neatly climbs Moghaddam's radicalization steps. The perpetrator of the Nice attacks, on 14 July 2016, Mohammed Lahouaiej Bouhlel, did not develop ties to fundamentalist networks (Moghaddam's transition towards the second floor), nor had he become alienated or entrenched in rigid us-versus-them thinking within some sort of isolated sect (the third floor).[37] He most probably had not visited a mosque and had not been a devout Muslim at all, and turned to terrorism only a few weeks in advance of his deed.

Notwithstanding these academic quavers and quarrels regarding the use of radicalization schemes and models, a whole industry emerged providing training in the field of exit programmes (be they directed towards deradicalization, disengagement or desistance strategies[38]), some of them with quite promising results.[39] However, such schemes have become so much engrained in the debate on terrorism, that they have pervaded jurisprudence as well, as we will demonstrate below – and in a far more simplified way than the original theories purport.

Since 2013, the increasing gap between ancillary acts committed here and the purported plans to join IS far away, has driven the system of criminal law into the domain of radicalization theories, as a means of offering the connection between these disparate acts and the end goal of terrorism. The consequence of this encounter of criminal law and radicalization theories since 2013 has been substantial: the boundaries between criminal law and counter-radicalization efforts (in the non-legal, social, political and pedagogical sphere) has become fuzzy. We could argue that the 'soft' and 'hard' ways of counterterrorism are meeting each other here. Counter-radicalization programmes are often considered a 'soft', community-based mode of fighting terrorism – as opposed to court processes which belong to the 'hard' way. But in the courtroom, the two approaches are increasingly connected and overlapping.

If trials serve to adjudicate defendants based on their perceived stage of radicalization, the judge's sentence and the suspect's conviction are brought into the remit of counter-radicalization efforts, albeit in a highly obfuscated way.

Whereas counter-radicalization measures are in theory intended to map and chart radical patterns and trajectories of engaging in violence, and to prevent future terrorist crimes from occurring[40], criminal law has always been the 'ultimum remedium', the meting out of sanctions after counter-radicalization has failed and the radical individual has overstepped the legal boundaries. However, through precautionary logics informed by radicalization theories, politics of counter-radicalization and legal counterterrorism become increasingly entangled. Criminal law not only absorbs notions of risk management, but it also acquires the social engineering dimension intrinsic to counter-radicalization programmes. In this light, terrorism trials morph into instruments of counter-radicalization – markedly without the stated end goal of re-integration and rehabilitation[41] that are intrinsically part of the deradicalization paradigm. They become entrepreneurs in Moghaddam's 'transformation of the psychological citizen', the process in which radicalized youngsters are being guided back towards the state of possessing 'the cognitive and behavioral characteristics people need in order to function effectively as part of, and to sustain, a sociopolitical order'.[42]

Terrorism trials under scrutiny

By focusing in depth on some relevant case studies of terrorism trials against suspected foreign fighters, we seek to address the following questions: How are techniques of premediation tied to new scholarly insights on radicalization trajectories? Or, in other words, how are academic theories and models of radicalization processes invoked to visualize these possible terrorist futures, and the purported stage of the defendant's radicalization trajectory? And how are these premediated futures and stages of radicalization incorporated into actual sentencing?

Since 2013, most terrorism trials involved suspects indicted for crimes connected to their (attempts of) travelling abroad to join terrorist organizations, most notably those in Syria and Iraq. Of the forty-two persons that have been indicted between 2013 and 2016, and who have stood trial in that period, a simple database has been created to identify the indictment, the conviction (in first instance, for some in appeal as well), the sentence and the legal paragraphs that have been invoked. As follows from this table, the legal paragraphs involving preparatory activities have increased. Recruitment is one of the most frequent charges brought against the suspects, as are the charges of 'public abetment' to commit terrorist felonies, or attempting to 'acquire knowledge' in preparation for attacks or preparing to take part in a terrorist organization. Remarkably, as compared to earlier trials and sentences (e.g. against the Hofstad group), even the attempt to travel abroad can now, after 2013, be seen and used to indict the suspect for the 'preparation of murder/manslaughter with terrorist intent'. Since Islamic State is considered a terrorist organization, and the Caliphate is under the rule of this group, every attempt to travel to that area can and has been used to indict a suspect for the attempt to join this organization and hence to participate in its activities, for example manslaughter and murder with terrorist intent.[43]

Since 2013, the prosecution has been able to operate a series of new legal instruments to penalize preparatory actions. For this transformation and expansion of the legal instruments, see Table 4.1.

To illustrate this broadening of legal paragraphs and instruments that are adopted in cases against terrorism suspects where an actual attack has not yet taken place, but attempts to travel abroad have been made, we will offer a detailed reading of three case studies. These cases comprise recent trials in the Netherlands, where alleged 'foreign fighters' were involved between 2013 and 2017. We have selected three prominent cases, involving inchoate plots and very low levels of actual past physical harm. The cases attracted a large amount of media attention, and were subsequently subject to political debate and public contestation over the legal and legitimate approach to risk and danger in relation to the contemporary terrorist threat. To what extent is the law allowed to

Table 4.1 Transformation of Dutch material law, regarding terrorism related legal paragraphs since 2013

Criminal code of procedure	Content of the crime	Transformation that has taken place through this law
Art. 83	Law defining terrorist crimes	Heavier punishments have been introduced; terrorist crimes will receive aggravated sentences.
Art. 46	Expansion of the description of preparatory actions	'Monies' replaced by 'objects', bringing every object in the remit of evidence for preparatory acts.
Art. 140a	Taking part in a terrorist organization	Definition of 'organization' has been expanded; not just participation in an attack, but links to the organization itself is now a felony.
Art. 96	Conspiring against the state	The article on conspiracy has now also been linked to terrorism related offences.
Art. 205	Recruitment with terrorist intent	Not the success of the recruitment, but the attempt is considered an offence as well.
Art. 134a	Preparing for terrorist related actions	Every action, including the ones not resulting in a terrorist attack are included. This paragraph provides a safety net function for the authorities.
Art. 135, 136	Legal paragraphs penalizing the omission to inform the authorities of a (pending) crime	These paragraphs are specifically linked to terrorism.
Art. 189	Obfuscating a crime or the perpetrator of a crime	This is specifically linked to terrorism.
Art. 132	Paragraph regarding the initiation of a criminal investigation	Removal of the obligatory notion of 'suspicion'. Indication is now enough to start a criminal investigation, and to deploy special competences.

Source: Author composition based on scrutiny of legal records on terrorism trials.

prevent 'persons of risk' from carrying out their movements in the Netherlands and abroad?

Mohammed G.

The first trial involves Mohammed G., an Iraqi-born Dutch national living in Maastricht (see annex 1, nr. 1, 42, 43). In 2013 he was arrested, together with Omar H., for preparing for departure to Syria in order to join the 'international jihad'. This case was the first in the dozen or so to come involving apprehended individuals that were caught before they had left the country. Mohammed G. was charged with executing activities ('*uitvoerende handelingen*') with respect to committing a terrorist crime, in particular visiting websites on which violent jihad and martyrdom were glorified, booking reservations for tickets to Turkey, possessing large sums of money and a suitcase, and stating in chats and e-mails how he wanted to fight alongside the *mujahideen*. Moreover, the defendant was charged with engaging in chat sessions with the other suspects over the purchase of specific goods (waterproof wind and rain jacket, jungle boots, laptops, maps, cameras), the sale of other possessions that they no longer needed (computers, lounge suit and other household effects) and discussing to denounce their rent.[44]

In the verdict, the judge concluded that Omar H. and Mohammed G. did not go to Syria after all, but carried out activities to prepare for their departure. These actions (the chats and the website visits) were therefore considered preparatory actions for the commitment of murder and the causing of explosions. With this verdict, the judge turned actions that – taken on their own, isolated account – could still be considered relatively innocent, into a coherent set of steps leading towards participating in the violent jihad in Syria. Moreover, contrary to the defence's argument that these actions could also be viewed as 'training to prepare for terrorist crimes' (another penal paragraph, with a lower maximum sentence of eight years), the judge ruled that H. and G. were 'far beyond' mere training activities. According to the judge their actions were taken with the intent of really carrying out the crimes, and should therefore be assessed in a 'terrorist perspective': 'In her [the court's] eyes, their behaviour and utterances point to the fact that they adhered to the jihadist creed. Within this context she takes into consideration that terrorism is considered one of the most serious infractions of the rule of law and the democratic principle and hence takes account of this in her decision'.[45] However, Mohammed G. was discharged from prosecution and committed to a psychiatric hospital due to severe mental disturbances (psychosis and schizophrenia).

Three years later, Mohammed G. had been out of jail for almost two years when he was arrested and put on trial again, this time charged with 'the attempt to participate in a terrorist organization'. As the judge ruled: 'Attempt is illegal, when the perpetrator's intent has been revealed/laid bare though a beginning of an execution [executive act]'.[46] In August 2016, Mohammed G. was convicted on the combined evidence of the purchase of a false passport, the attempt to marry a female compatriot to accompany him to Syria (who turned out to be a police informer), tied together with a series of utterances, that according to the judge, put the other leads into a terrorist perspective. Mohammed G. was recorded saying 'I want to fight, I want to kill, I want to be'. According to his defence lawyer, Andrée Seebregts, G. was a 'vulnerable man', highly impressionable, with a low mental age or even retarded, who in a 'childlike fashion' wanted to achieve appreciation and recognition and had 'grandiose thoughts'. Seebregts urged the judges to take this into consideration in studying the produced 'evidence'. He even went further, attacking the court on the grounds that it blurred the lines between 'socially undesirable attitudes' and 'criminal behaviour'. He suggested that instead of sentencing G. for his actions, the court and the public prosecutor were judging his (feeble minded) convictions by putting them in a linear scheme of steps onto a radicalization ladder. G. had not collected information on bombs, attacks or weapons, but merely visited jihadist websites. Moreover, Seebregts – on behalf of his defendant – indignantly rejected the demand voiced by the prosecutor to ordain compulsory psychiatric treatment, explained by a mere 'just to be sure'. He exclaimed, 'We are not such a country, I would say'.[47]

Again, as in other cases of failed foreign fighters, the defence kept reiterating the dichotomy between 'beliefs and behaviour', between 'actions or convictions'. But for the prosecution and the judges this dichotomy was highly irrelevant, since the mere criminal act itself as a construction, was made up by the combination of mundane acts and projections of future violences as invoked by the defendants' jihadist utterances. Such utterances were in themselves not criminal, as the judges repeatedly stressed, but taken together with the other incidents, and embedded within the context of the envisaged radicalization process (as a combination of convictions, beliefs, attitudes and activities) they substantiated the suspicion of preparing to join international jihad. Not truth finding, but the establishing of possible future truths in order to manage the potential risk by means of invoking radicalization steps towards a premediated violent future was central to the attempts of the prosecution. Therefore, the sentence was not intended to criminalize jihadist statements as such, but designed to prevent and manage future risks as invoked and premediated through the offender's activities.

The judge corroborated this line of reasoning and sentenced G. to three years of prison, with a suspended sentence of entrustment (*Terbeschikkingstelling*, 'TBS'), although the forensic experts had ruled G. 'mentally responsible' and 'sane' this time. TBS entails a provision in the Dutch criminal code that allows for a period of inpatient treatment (within a detention centre) following a prison sentence for mentally disordered offenders. Therefore, after having served his prison sentence of three years, Mohammed G. will have to submit himself to psychiatric treatment. And although ambulatory in his case, this treatment is compulsory, implying that if he doesn't comply, he can be ordered back inside the detention centre for further treatment. In sum, this verdict produced two instances where risk averse reasoning supplanted old fashioned truth finding by the judge and raised serious questions: First of all, as the defence lawyer repeatedly stressed, what had Mohammed G. actually done 'wrong' apart from buying a false passport and attempting to marry – and even that could not be considered such a serious crime? And secondly, why was he sentenced to psychiatric treatment following prison without experts testifying to a problem of insanity?[48] The sentence was neither retributive nor particularly conducive to truth finding – it was conceived as a particular design of risk management, intended to limit recidivist behaviour by controlling and treating the defendant's alleged unstable mental state. Thus, the sentence resembled more of a human engineering project – to render this specific individual less radical and thus less of a threat – than an instance of classical adjudication.

Rahma E.

In this verdict (see annex 1, nr. 31), again, projected violent futures were interpellated to connect the bits and pieces of evidence into a clear-cut security threat and criminal case. As described above, the 15-year-old Somali-Dutch girl was indicted for having chatted extensively with 'sisters' in the Netherlands and Syria and for allegedly preparing for *hijra* (emigration) to Libya, in order to join the local IS branch there. She had also sent a ring as a first deposit to pay for her trip. The judge ruled that since she had been apprehended at home, without actually having purchased tickets or having left for Libya, she could not be convicted for actually having committed a terrorist crime (joining a terrorist organization). Her sentence was therefore based on preparatory acts rather than on executive ones. However, these preparatory acts were again projected into a linear future of radicalization and violent jihad: by citing Rahma's radical beliefs, her increasing turn towards other radical friends, her dissemination of texts and images from IS websites and by linking this behaviour to the intentions and propaganda of IS as an organization.

Interestingly, the content of Rahma's religious beliefs as such were not considered illegal – it was rather her social behaviour that prompted the court to qualify her as 'radicalized'. The defendant adhered to a 'fundamentalist' interpretation of the Qur'an, but the prosecution had 'not encountered ideas that show the desire to violently overthrow democracy'. What was held against the defendant was the fact that she had immersed herself in the study of the Qur'an, was neglecting school, displayed a 'tunnel vision' and was out of reach for her parents. Without invoking Kruglanski or Moghaddam by name, the verdict cites forensic researchers and experts who used the 'staircase' metaphor to 'visualize the process of racialization'. This staircase comprised 'an edifice with five floors, that narrows down with each subsequent step, making it harder to descend again'. According to the forensic experts, the defendant had very likely reached the 'third floor' (of forming a sect-like organization – in correspondence with Moghaddam's third floor), 'but factual radicalization had been averted on time by outside interference'. 'The possibility that the suspect would still take the stairs further up is not ruled out'.[49] Again, with this premediation of a staircase, winding upwards, with increasingly less possibilities of descending again, the defendant was squarely framed into a linear model, in which reversals or U-turns were considered highly unlikely (without outside interventions). The direction of the vector was thus pointing to a terrorist future, only disrupted by the act of her arrest. Thus, the prosecution effectively incorporated and straightened out the 'logic of radical uncertainty in legal reasoning'.[50] The court followed along and seemed to accept the claim to know where the radicalization trajectory would have ended up. Thus, the linear narrative of the radicalization model transformed the radical uncertainty into a certain legal narrative.

The sentence mirrored this analysis and diagnosis. For managing the risk of taking the escalator once again, Rahma E. was sentenced to eight months in a juvenile detention centre (plus a suspended sentence of seven months) and ordered to attend sessions with a theologian (to re-assess her interpretation of Islam). Moreover, for the first six months of her probation period, she was prohibited to contact her five 'sisters', and for twelve months, she was to stay away from international airports and wear a GPS bracelet.

Remarkable in this case, as in Mohammed G.'s case, were the 'creative' attempts by the judges to come up with restrictions that were designed to facilitate Rahma's re-integration: she was tasked to have obligatory discussions with a theologian, and was also held to start some kind of education and find a part-time job – intended to expand her 'tunnel vision', to break through her isolation by means of finding new friends and contacts outside her Islamic network, facilitate a 'healthy identity development' and improve her 'resilience'. Rather than putting her away for three years, as in other cases, the judge used the instrument of restrictions to steer the offender in the direction of a 'normal life', to hold off her descent of the staircase of radicalization, and to transform her isolated and insulated engagement into more outgoing behaviour.[51] As in Mohammed G.'s case, the sentence was informed by risk management techniques geared towards 'human engineering' and re-programming the individual's potential violent attitude.

Context Case

One of the last major cases in the Netherlands, involving several male and one female jihadist suspects (see annex 1, the Context Case includes the nrs 6, 7, 11–20, 37–40), pertained to a The Hague-based network of alleged recruiters, who supported international jihad by disseminating violent footage, inciting others to hatred and terrorism, recruiting for the violent jihad and even participating in that jihad themselves (for some of the group members). The file comprises 17,000 pages (plus 6,500 additional pages on methods and requestrations); fifty witnesses in the Netherlands and the UK were heard, and hundreds of shreds of evidence were bundled together to evoke and (re)construct the real or virtual crimes perpetrated.[52] Six male suspects were convicted for membership in a terrorist organization, and received sentences ranging from three to six years imprisonment. Two of the male suspects were considered 'hangers-on' (*meelopers*), and merely received sentences for incitement (forty-three days). One suspect, who did participate in a jihadist training camp in Syria received a sentence of 155 days' imprisonment and six months on probation. The single female suspect was acquitted of the membership charges, only convicted for retweeting an inciting tweet and sentenced to seven days' imprisonment.

As in the above, and almost all other foreign fighter cases, the court addressed and rejected the frequently voiced criticism that only acts and not convictions should be the subject of adjudication. No '*Gesinnungsstrafrecht*' [which penalizes thought and intent rather than material deeds and actions] had prevailed, according to the judges. The trial was – from a procedural point of view – a 'normal trial', as stated in paragraph 1.11 in the verdict.

After ten weeks of hearings, from September until mid-December 2015, the judges sided with the prosecution in confirming the charge that the suspects effectively had created a 'The Hague-based recruitment organization'. Some of them had participated in BehindBars/StreetDawah,[53] mobilizing support for imprisoned terrorist convicts or suspects and disseminating jihadist thought. Notwithstanding the fact that utterances and statements are in themselves legal, the judge concluded with the prosecution that the purpose of the 'The Hague-based network' had been to transcend 'mere' propaganda and to really set out to incite, recruit, finance and facilitate youngsters to travel to Syria and join the international jihad. Indeed, from the six suspects indicted, two were still waging jihad in Syria as of the day of the verdict. A third suspect had returned to his home town again. The judge admitted that 'no clue whatsoever' had been uncovered which pointed to the intent or preparation of a concrete terrorist attack in the Netherlands, nor to attempts to incite such an attack. However, and this was a central argument in all the cases under adjudication since 2013, 'the Netherlands are under obligation to fight terrorism wherever it occurs, and [to] take steps to stem the flow of Dutch (young) Muslims that want to participate in violent jihad in Syria'.[54] Moreover, 'Terrorism is considered internationally as one of the most heinous crimes and compels all states to fight this transgression. In this, it is the function of the criminal justice system to, as much as possible, both prevent acts of terrorism and prosecute and adjudicate them'.[55]

The process of compiling the legal evidence, as in the other cases, relied heavily on the premediation of the above stated acts of terrorism by connecting a multifarious and vast body of documents, statements and social media postings – with the argument that taken together, these (sometimes totally legal) acts 'reinforced' each other and prepared the hearts and minds of the targeted recruits for the violent jihad.[56] To ice the cake, the testimony of expert Martijn de Koning – who had been called as first witness for the defence to contextualize the activities undertaken by the defendants and to underline their theological nature – was appropriated by the prosecution and the judges instead. His two days' testimony was used to substantiate the indictment's claim that the defendants had indeed constituted a recruitment organization. Instead of relieving the defendants of that severe indictment, De Koning's remarks on the communication within the group and the defendants' jihadist beliefs were appropriated to underpin this claim.[57]

Taken together with the other cases since 2013 (see Annex 1), these three cases are exemplary of and delineate some trends and development in the transformation of turning penal law into an instrument of risk management: for example, preventing youngsters from climbing the radicalization staircase, and ending up either as a 'foreign fighter' or recruiting others to become one. In this, the end goal in previous years (preventing people from carrying out attacks) had been moved forward to the objective of preventing them from preparing to travel abroad to terrorist territories at all.

First of all, in almost all cases a whole series of legal paragraphs were used to construct an indictment and arrive at a verdict based on evidence pointing predominantly to preparatory actions only (save four actual foreign fighters who left for Syria in the Context Case) and not to attacks that had been actually committed. As can be seen from the last column in Annex 1, sentences invoking more than ten criminal paragraphs were no exception.

Second, as follows from the verdicts, judges came to different conclusions and assessments in similar cases, rendering an element of wilfulness and arbitrary rule to the criminal justice system.

Third, as a first intuitive remark and without further empirical research, premediation and anticipation of violent futures seem to have been applied in the cases of male defendants in a more negative manner than in those of the female defendants – evidence in cases of female (alleged) foreign fighters seems to have been discarded quicker by the judges, acquitting them from recruitment or incitement in most of the cases, leading to smaller or no sentences at all. This ties in with findings that point to the non-neutral character of actuarial justice, in which gender biases seem to be ingrained more than we think.

Fourthly, the process of gathering and presenting evidence in every case relied heavily on techniques of assemblage:[58] combining associative reasoning and premediation (invoking virtual violent futures) was used to build a unified body of evidence out of a disparate and inchoate set of activities and acts (social media postings, legal acts such as marriages, utterances, leafleting, possession of IS flags). This assemblage was then forged together by suggesting a 'reinforcement' and cumulation of a series of illegal and legal activities alike. Thus, taken together, the disparate activities and incidents were – by means of a wide array of legal paragraphs – forged to construct a veritable criminal 'act'.

Sentencing as risk management

Three conclusions can be drawn from this short oversight of foreign fighter cases:

First of all, with trials against suspected foreign fighters that have been caught before actually joining the jihad, premediation as a risk management technique has gained increasing importance in securing a verdict. The trial as such has become the disruptive moment to thwart risky youths in climbing further up the staircase, as was the explicitly formulated goal in the Rahma E. verdict. Here, the court used a 'thin' reading of a classic radicalization model, in doing so discarding all the caveat and nuances that radicalization research (sometimes) offers, and simply reproduced a linear narrative in sentencing. This trend towards appropriating the trial as a counter-radicalization tool might result in pushing other classical goals to be obtained by the sword of justice (such as rehabilitation or re-integration) further aside, as became clear in the Context Case. Given the context of fear and terror as well as frequently invoked international 'obligations', judges may have limited room for manoeuvre to issue milder verdicts or even acquittals, and are in danger of incurring substantial (international) public and political critique.[59] While overseeing the verdicts and sentences, it became clear that judges do differ in their interpretation of and in the premediation of anticipated violent futures. However, they all combined an increasing amount of novel and different legal paragraphs to assemble a cumulation of criminal offences leading to longer sentences (see table 1).

In the second place, these cases underscore the importance of reading and understanding terrorism trials as a performative space; as existing literatures have established, one distinguishing aspect of terrorism trials is that, for suspects as well as for security forces, the public presentation and contestation of narratives of justice and injustice are especially important.[60] This performative aspect is most salient in the battle between prosecution and defence over the dividing line between beliefs and behaviour, convictions and acts. In many of the verdicts, the judges have tried to overcome this divide in sticking to the criminalization of preparatory acts of travelling abroad, as well as combining this with more mundane legal actions cast in an incriminating light. At the same time, however, the judges tried to draw a stricter line between preparatory actions and executive activities. In the case of Rahma E., for example, the court tried to flesh out different stages of anticipated risks, dividing the risk in two categories, making it more tangible to convict the defendants on minor charges. In concentrating on such preparatory *acts*, the mere *convictions* of the defendant became less important than in previous trials. Rahma's interpretations of the Qur'an were considered 'fundamentalist' but not 'violent'; it was rather her use of IS texts, flags and images, her inclination to isolate herself from school and her family, and her turn towards 'sisters' already abroad, that prompted the prosecution and the judge to qualify her as having transgressed towards the 'third step' along the radicalization staircase.

In the third place, the trial becomes a theatre of counter-radicalization, a 'disruptive moment' in the process of risk management. The trial simultaneously serves to produce criminal acts through premediated violences, largely based on radicalization theories, and functions as the disruptive moment to bring the radicalization process to a halt. The verdict, subsequently, aims to reverse that process by issuing concrete attempts to transform the defendant into a 'psychological citizen'. In this, criminal law has transformed into a means of legal and enforced counter-radicalization – a transformation informed by models and theories developed by academics and scholars in the field of terrorism and radicalization studies. Their 'radicalization models' (such as Moghaddam's staircase), and even their testimonies (De Koning's in the Context Case), are appropriated for actuarial purposes, thereby rendering academia an instrument in the hand of criminal justice.

With this transformation of a trial and a verdict as an instrument of counter-radicalization, penal law has acquired a managerial function. Hence, the addition of various restrictions to the sentence, intended to facilitate controlling and monitoring the offender even after his release, and to submit the suspect to attempts of human engineering. If this managerial goal of the criminal justice system is taken seriously, the question that arises next is how these risk management techniques in preventing defendants from ascending the staircase of radicalization further, actually work out in practice. With an increasing number of young Muslims being sentenced based on an expanding body of legal paragraphs (see table 1), the number of convicts with relatively short sentences has grown as well. This prompts us to the next question of what to do with these convicts after their release.[61]

Inasmuch as terrorism convicts are increasingly sentenced – by means of a plethora of legal paragraphs – to relatively short periods of imprisonment, society will soon find itself confronted with the even bigger challenge of helping all these former inmates in finding their way back into society. The precautionary and actuarial turn in criminal law therefore requires a much stronger emphasis on the rehabilitative and re-integrative responsibilities that also belong to the classical goals of criminal justice. Rather than relying on simplistic interpretations of linear radicalization models, terrorism trials could and should draw on much more fine-grained, sophisticated theories on desistance and disengagement.

Notes

1　The author wishes to thank Hannah Joosse, Céline Mureau and Eva van de Kimmenade for assisting with the table and list of terrorist trials; and Martijn de Koning and Marieke de Goede for their helpful comments and suggestions.

2　Dominique Robert, 'Actuarial Justice', in *Encyclopedia of Prisons and Correctional Facilities*, ed. M. Bosworth (Thousand Oaks, CA: Sage, 2005), pp. 11–14.

3　Beatrice de Graaf and Alex P. Schmid, eds., *Terrorists on Trial: A Performative Perspective* (Leiden: Leiden University Press, 2016).

4　Marieke de Goede and Beatrice de Graaf, 'Sentencing Risk: Temporality and Precaution in Terrorism Trials', *International Political Sociology* 7, no. 3 (2013): 313–31.

5　Robert M. Chesney, 'Beyond Conspiracy: Anticipatory Prosecution and the Challenge of Unaffiliated Terrorism', *Southern California Law Review* 80, no. 3 (2007): 425–502.

6　For legal perspectives, see Robert M. Chesney, 'The Sleeper Scenario: Terrorism-Support Laws and the Demands of Prevention', *Harvard Journal on Legislation* 42, no. 1 (2005): 1–90; Maartje van der Woude, *Wetgeving in een veiligheidscultuur: Totstandkoming van antiterrorismewetgeving in Nederland bezien vanuit maatschappelijke en (rechts) politieke context* (Den Haag: Boom Juridische Uitgevers, 2010). For criminological perspectives, see Lucia Zedner, 'Pre-Crime and Post-Criminology?', *Theoretical Criminology* 11, no. 2 (2007): 261–81; Jude McCulloch and Sharon Pickering, 'Pre-Crime and Counter-Terrorism: Imagining Future Crime in the "War on Terror"', *British Journal of Criminology* 49, no. 5 (2009): 628–45. For political perspectives, see Oliver Kessler, 'Is Risk Changing the Politics of Legal Argumentation?', *Leiden Journal of International Law* 21, no. 4 (2008): 863–84; Sven Opitz and Ute Tellmann, 'Katastrophale Szenarien – Gegenwärtige Zukunft in Recht und Ökonomie', *Leviathan Sonderhefte*, 25 (2010): *Sichtbarkeitsregime. Überwachung, Sicherheit und Privatheit im 21. Jahrhundert*, S. 27–52.

7　See also, Clifford Shearing, 'Punishment and the Changing Face of the Governance', *Punishment & Society* 3, no. 2 (2001): 203–20; Tom Baker and Jonathan Simon,

Embracing Risk: The Changing Culture of Insurance and Responsibility (Chicago, IL: University of Chicago Press, 2002); Jonathan Simon, 'Choosing Our Wars, Transforming Governance: Crime, Cancer, Terror', in *Risk and the War on Terror*, eds. Louise Amoore and Marieke de Goede (London: Routledge, 2008); Richard V. Ericson, *Crime in an Insecure World* (Cambridge: Polity Press, 2007); Zedner, 'Pre-Crime and Post-Criminology?'

8 Malcolm M. Feeley and Jonathan Simon, 'The New Penology: Notes on the Emerging Strategy of Corrections and Its Implications', *Criminology* 30, no. 4 (1992): 449–74.

9 De Graaf, 'Religion Bites'; De Koning, Wagemakers and Becker, *Salafisme*.

10 See also, Anastassia Tsoukala, 'Security, Risk and Human Rights: A Vanishing Relationship?', *CEPS Special Report* (Brussels: CEPS, 2008).

11 Council of the European Union, Council Framework Decision of 13 June 2002 on Combating Terrorism, 2002/475/JHA.

12 Maartje van der Woude, 'De erfenis van tien jaar strafrechtelijke terrorismebestrijding in Nederland', *Strafblad* 10, no. 1 (2012): 9–18; Maartje van der Woude, 'Dutch Counterterrorism: An Exceptional Body of Legislation or Just an Inevitable Product of the Culture of Control?', in *The State of Exception and Militant Democracy in a Time of Terror*, eds. A. Ellian and G. Molier (Dordrecht: Republic of Letters Publishing, 2012).

13 The majority of Dutch 'foreign fighters' – estimated at 280 – joined IS. A small group went to al-Qaeda affiliate Tahrir al-Sham (previously called Jabhat al-Nusra). See AIVD, *Terugkeerders in beeld*, p. 2.

14 Louise Amoore, 'Risk before Justice: When the Law Contests Its Own Suspension', *Leiden Journal of International Law* 21, no. 4 (2008): 847–61, especially p. 850.

15 Misty Kifer, Craig Hemmens and Mary K. Stohr, 'The Goals of Corrections: Perspectives from the Line', *Criminal Justice Review* 28, no. 1 (2003): 47–69.

16 Susanne Krasmann, 'Law's Knowledge: On the Susceptibility and Resistance of Legal Practices to Security Matters', *Theoretical Criminology* 16, no. 4 (2012): 379–94, especially p. 381.

17 Bibi van Ginkel, 'Prosecuting Foreign Terrorist Fighters: What Role for the Military?', *ICCT Policy Brief* (The Hague: ICCT, May 2016).

18 CTED, 'Guiding Principles on Foreign Terrorist Fighters'. Detailed outcome of the special meeting of the Counter-Terrorism Committee with Member States and relevant international and regional organizations on 'Stemming the Flow of Foreign Terrorist Fighters', Madrid 27–28 July 2015, S/2015/939, 23 December 2015, Annex II, p. 6. Quoted in Van Ginkel, 'Prosecuting Foreign Terrorist Fighters', p. 4.

19 Ibid., p. 6.

20 De Graaf and Schmid, eds., *Terrorists on Trial*; De Graaf and De Goede, 'Sentencing Risk'.

21 Wouter Werner, 'The Use of Law in International Political Sociology', *International Political Sociology* 4, no. 3 (2010): 304–7, especially p. 305. See also, Oliver Kessler, ed., 'Forum: International Law and International Political Sociology', *International Political Sociology* 3, no. 4 (2010): 303–21.

22 Richard A. Grusin, 'Premediation', *Criticism* 46, no. 1 (2004): 17–39; Richard A. Grusin, *Premediation: Affect and Mediality after 9/11* (New York: Palgrave Macmillan, 2010).

23 Matthias J. Borgers and Elies van Sliedregt, 'The Meaning of the Precautionary Principle for the Assessment of Criminal Measures in the Fight against Terrorism, *Erasmus Law Review* 2, no. 2 (2009): 171–95, especially pp. 187–88.

24 Chesney, 'Beyond Conspiracy', p. 426.

25 Robert A. Pape, *Dying to Win: The Strategic Logic of Suicide Terrorism* (New York: Random House, 2006); John Horgan, *The Psychology of Terrorism* (London and New York: Routledge, 2014); John Horgan, 'Deradicalization or Disengagement? A Process in Need of Clarity and a Counterterrorism Initiative in Need of Evaluation', *Perspectives on Terrorism* 2, no. 4 (2008): 3–8; Jessica Stern, *Terror in the Name of God: Why Religious Militants Kill* (New York: HarperCollins, 2004); Fathali M. Moghaddam and A. J. Marsella, eds., *Understanding Terrorism: Psychosocial Roots, Consequences and Intervention* (Washington, DC: American Psychological Association, 2003).

26 David R. Mandel, 'Radicalization: What Does It Mean?', in *Home-Grown Terrorism: Understanding and Addressing the Root Causes of Radicalisation among Groups with an Immigrant Heritage in Europe*, eds. T. Pick, A. Speckhard and B. Jacuh (Amsterdam: IOS Press, 2010), p. 9.

27 Randy Borum, *Psychology of Terrorism* (Tampa, FL: University of South Florida, 2004).

28 German extremism research originated in the 1970s with Manfred Funke, 'Extremismus und offene Gesellschaft, Anmerkungen zur Gefährdung und Selbstgefährdung des demokratischen Rechtsstaates', in *Extremismus im demokratischen Rechtsstaat*, ed. M. Funke (Düsseldorf: Droste, 1978); Uwe Backes, *Politischer Extremismus in demokratischen Verfassungsstaaten: Elemente einer normativen Rahmentheorie* (Opladen: Westdeutscher Verlag, 1989); Uwe Backes and Eckhard Jesse, eds., *Vergleichende Extremismusforschung* (Baden-Baden: Nomos, 2005); In Scandinavia, mainly Tore Bjørgo, Magnus Ranstorp and Leena Malkki are active. See, Tore Bjørgo, *Racist and Right-Wing Violence in Scandinavia: Patterns, Perpetrators and Responses* (Oslo: Tano Aschehoug, 1997); Tore Bjørgo and John Horgan, eds., *Leaving Terrorism Behind: Individual and Collective Disengagement* (London: Routledge, 2009); Magnus Ranstorp, *Understanding Violent Radicalisation* (London and New York, 2010); Leena Malkki, *How Terrorist Campaigns End: The Campaigns of the Rode Jeugd in the Netherlands and the Symbionese Liberation Army in the United States* (Helsinki: University of Helsinki, 2010).

29 See also Donatella Della Porta, *Social Movements, Political Violence and the State: A Comparative Analysis of Italy and Germany* (Cambridge: Cambridge University Press, 1995). And in the US, see the founding father of research in post-war political violence, Ted Robert Gurr, *Why Men Rebel* (Princeton, NJ: Princeton University Press, 1970).

30 Marc Sageman, *Understanding Terror Networks* (Philadelphia, PA: University of Pennsylvania Press, 2004); Marc Sageman, *Leaderless Jihad: Terror Networks in the Twenty-First Century* (Philadelphia, PA: University of Pennsylvania Press, 2008).

31 Peter R. Neumann, B. Rogers, R. Alonso and L. Martinez, 'Recruitment and Mobilisation for the Islamist Militant Movement in Europe, *ICSR* 251, no. 1 (2007).

32 Fathali M. Moghaddam, 'De-Radicalization and the Staircase from Terrorism', in *The Faces of Terrorism: Multidisciplinary Perspectives*, ed. David Canter (Chichester: John Wiley & Sons, 2009): 277–92, especially p. 280.

33 Marieke de Goede and Stephanie Simon, 'Governing Future Radicals in Europe', *Antipode* 45, no. 2 (2013): 315–35, especially pp. 321–3.

34 See, for example, the discussion on the Brookings platform by Benjamin Wittes and William McCant, 'Should the Muslim Brotherhood Be Designated a Terrorist Organization?', *Brookings*, 30 January 2017, https://www.brookings.edu/blog/markaz/2017/01/30/should-the-muslim-brotherhood-be-designated-a-terrorist-organization/; and Dirk Jacobs, 'Arab European League (AEL): The Rapid Rise of a Radical Immigrant Movement', *Journal of Muslim Minority Affairs* 25, no. 1 (2005): 97–115.

35 Mandel, 'Radicalization: What Does It Mean?'

36 Marion van San, Stijn Sieckelinck and Micha de Winter, *Idealen op drift: Een pedagogische kijk op radicaliserende jongeren* (Den Haag: Boom, 2010).

37 Fathali M. Moghaddam, 'The Staircase to Terrorism: A Psychological Exploration', *American Psychologist* 60, no. 2 (2005): 161–69, especially pp. 163–65.

38 Gary LaFree and Erin Miller, 'Desistance from Terrorism: What Can We Learn from Criminology?', *Dynamics of Asymmetric Conflict* 1, no. 3 (2008): 203–30; Horgan, 'Deradicalization or Disengagement?', p. 4; Audrey Kurth Cronin, *How Terrorism Ends: Understanding the Decline and Demise of Terrorist Campagins* (Princeton, NJ: Princeton University Press, 2009).

39 See also Birgit Rommelspacher, *'Der Hass hat uns geeint': Junge Rechtsextreme und ihr Ausstieg aus der Szene* (Frankfurt am Main: Campus Verlag, 2006).

40 See also Froukje Demant, Marieke Slootman, Frank Buijs and Jean Tillie, *Teruggang en uittrede: Processen van deradicalisering ontleed* (Amsterdam: IMES, 2008). Translated into *Decline and Disengagement: An Analysis of Processes of Deradicalization* (Amsterdam: IMES, 2008).

41 See Tinka M. Veldhuis, *Prisoner Radicalization and Terrorism Detention Policy: Institutionalized Fear or Evidence-Based Policy Making?* (London: Routledge, 2016); Daan Weggemans and Beatrice de Graaf, *Na de vrijlating: Een exploratieve studie naar recidive en re-integratie van jihadistische ex-gedetineerden* (Amsterdam: Reed Business, 2015).

42 Fathali M. Moghaddam, 'The Psychological Citizen and the Two Concepts of Social Contract: A Preliminary Analysis', *Political Psychology* 29, no. 6 (2008): 881–901, especially p. 881.

43 See Annex 1: Table of Dutch terrorism verdicts, 2013–16.

44 Court of Rotterdam, Verdict against Mohammed G., 10/960233-12, 23 October 2013.

45 Anouk van Kampen, 'Eerste Syriëgangers veroordeeld voor voorbereiding jihad', *NRC Handelsblad*, 23 October 2013.

46 Court of Rotterdam, Verdict against Mohammed G., 10/660329-14, 4 August 2016.

47 Folkert Jensma, 'Weer bestraft voor terreurplannen', *NRC Handelsblad*, 30 August 2016; Court of Rotterdam, Verdict against Mohammed G., 10/960138-5, 29 August 2016.

48 See also questions raised by Folkert Jensma, 'Terug van weggeweest: strafbare gedachten', *NRC Handelsblad*, 3–4 September 2016.

49 Court of Roermond, Limburg, Verdict against Rahma E., 03/700456-15, 16 August 2016.

50 See Oliver Kessler and Wouter Werner, 'Extrajudicial Killing as Risk Management', *Security Dialogue* 39, no. 2–3 (2008): 290; Louise Amoore, *The Politics of Possibility: Risk and Security Beyond Probability* (Durham, NC, and London: Duke University Press, 2013); and Marieke de Goede, 'The Politics of Preemption and the War on Terror in Europe', *European Journal of International Relations* 14, no. 1 (2008): 161–85.

51 Court of Roermond, Limburg, Verdict against Rahma E., 03/700456-15, 16 August 2016, paragraph 7.

52 Context Case, Court of The Hague, Verdict, 10 December 2015, 09/842489-14, 09/767038-14, 09/767313-14, 09/767174-13, 09/765004-15, 09/767146-14, 09/767256-14, 09767238-14, 09/827053-15, 09/767237-14, 09/765002-15, and 09/767077-14.

53 AIVD, *The Transformation of Jihadism in the Netherlands*, p. 12.

54 Verdict Context Case, paragraph 1.12.

55 Verdict Context Case, paragraph 1.8.

56 Verdict Context Case, paragraph 18.87.

57 For example, see Verdict Context Case, paragraphs 10.5, 10.6, 10.7, 10.9, and 18.8.
58 For an elaboration on mosaic logic, see Louise Amoore, 'Data Derivatives: On the Emergence of a Security Risk Calculus for Our Times', *Theory, Culture & Society* 28, no. 6 (2011): 24–43; Amoore, *The Politics of Possibility*.
59 Gabriel Weimann, 'The Theater of Terror: Effects of Press Coverage', *Journal of Communication* 33, no. 1 (1983): 38–45; Brigitte L. Nacos and Oscar Torres-Reyna, *Fueling Our Fears: Stereotyping, Media Coverage, and Public Opinion of Muslim Americans* (Lanham, MD: Rowman & Littlefield, 2007).
60 Otto Kirchheimer, *Political Justice: The Use of Legal Procedure for Political Ends* (Princeton, NJ: Princeton University Press, 1961); Awol Kassim Allo, 'The "Show" in the "Show Trial": Contextualizing the Politicization of the Courtroom', *Barry Law Review* 15, no. 1 (2010): 41–72; Beatrice de Graaf, *Evaluating Counterterrorism Performance: A Comparative Study* (London and New York: Routledge, 2011); De Graaf and Schmid, eds., *Terrorists on Trial*.
61 Weggemans and De Graaf, *Na de vrijlating*.

Annex 1 Table of Dutch terrorism verdicts, 2013–18

No.	Name	Date	Conviction	Sentence	Law article
1	Mohammed G.*	23/10/13	Dismissal of charges and placed in a psychiatric hospital due to insanity.	–	–
2	Omar H.	23/10/13	Sentenced for purchasing materials capable of causing an explosion and spreading writings/pictures with intent of abetting.	12 months	Art. 14a, 14b, 14c, 33, 33a, 46, 57, 132 and 157 of the Dutch Criminal Code
3	Soumaya S.	25/03/14	Sentenced for taking part in a criminal organization and the possession of weaponry with terrorist intent.	3 years	Art. 33, 33a, 36b, 36d, 47, 55, 57 and 140a of the Dutch Criminal Code and Art. 26 and 55 of the Law on Weaponry and Ammunition
4	Hannan S.	25/03/14	Sentenced for the possession of a machine gun with ammunition and silencer.	74 days	Art. 26 and 55 of the Law on Weaponry and Ammunition
5	Labbib B.	25/03/14	Sentenced for taking part in a criminal organization that intends to commit terrorist felonies and the possession of weaponry, both with terrorist intent.	104 days	Art. 47, 57, 140 and 140a of the Dutch Criminal Code and Art. 26 and 55 of the Law on Weaponry and Ammunition
6	Shukri F.	01/12/14	Indicted for: 1. Recruiting for armed conflict; 2. Public abetment to commit terrorist felonies and the spreading of and being in possession of magazines, imagery and files in which terrorist felony is abetted. Finally, subpoena partially annulled. Indictments 1 and 2 are not considered as lawful/convincing and the suspect is acquitted.	–	–
7	Maher H.	01/12/14	Sentenced for the preparation of murder/manslaughter with terrorist intent and to acquire the opportunity, means and intelligence for it. Also sentenced for spreading writing and imagery that abet a terrorist felony.	3 years	Art. 57, 83, 83a, 96 lid 2, 132 paragraph 3, 288a, 289 and 289a paragraph 2 of the Dutch Criminal Code
8	Hakim B.	09/02/15 15/03/16	Declared innocent of all charges. Declared innocent of all charges.	–	–

#	Name	Date	Charges / Decision	Sentence	Legal basis
9	Mohammed el A.	09/02/15	Indicted for preparation of common crimes, preparation of terrorist crimes, conspiration to commit terrorist crimes – acquitted, declared innocent.	18 months	Art. 14a, 14b, 14c, 46, 140 and 140a of the Dutch Criminal Code
		15/03/16	Appeal: 1. Preparation/promotion of going to Syria to commit murder/manslaughter with terrorist intent; 2. A. Preparation/promotion of a terrorist crime (murder/manslaughter); B. Preparation of participation in a terrorist organization; 3. Participation in a terrorist organization; 4. Conspiracy to commit murder/manslaughter with terrorist intent. Acquitted of indictments 1, 2A, 3 and 4. Sentenced for indictment 2B.	Decided the case should be examined again	Art. 57, 96 and 289a of the Dutch Criminal Code
		14/03/17	Cassation		
		19/12/17	Appeal Finally sentenced for preparation/ promotion of going to Syria to commit murder/manslaughter with terrorist intent and for preparation/promotion of a terrorist crime (murder/manslaughter).	8 months	
10	Burcu T.	22/07/15	Indicted for raising finances and transferring money to intermediaries in Turkey who transferred these finances to terrorist organizations. Thus, indicted for: 1. Taking part in an organization that has the intent to commit terrorist felonies; 2. Assisting the continuation of a forbidden organization; 3. Violating the Sanctions Act 1977. Finally, acquitted of indictments 1 and 2. Sentenced for indictment 3.	6 months	Art. 57 of the Dutch Criminal Code Art. 1, 2 and 6 of the Law on Economic Offences Art. 2 and 3 of the Sanction Act 1977 Art. 2 of the Sanction Regulation Osama Bin Laden Art. 2 and 4 of the Regulation no. 881/2002 of the Council of the European Union of 27 May 2002 Art. 1 of the Regulation 198/2008 of the Commission of the European Communities of March 3, 2008

No.	Name	Date	Conviction	Sentence	Law article
11	Soufiane Z.	22/10/15	The suspect is supposedly deceased. Therefore according to Art. 69, the prosecutor is inadmissible to prosecute.	–	–
12	Imane B.	10/12/15	She did not take part in a terrorist organization, but is convicted for one abetted retweet.	7 days	Art. 83, 83a and 132 of the Dutch Criminal Code
13	Oussama C.	10/12/15	Sentenced for taking part in a criminal organization with terrorist intent.	3 years	Art. 14a, 14b, 14c, 14d, 57, 77b, 83, 83a, 131, 132, 140, 140a and 205 of the Dutch Criminal Code
14	Azzedine C.	10/12/15	Sentenced for taking part in a criminal organization with terrorist intent.	6 years	Art. 57, 83, 83a, 131, 132, 137c, 137d, 140, 140a, 261 and 267 of the Dutch Criminal Code
15	Rudolph H.	10/12/15	Sentenced for taking part in a criminal organization with terrorist intent.	3 years	Art. 14a, 14b, 14c, 14d, 57, 83, 83a, 131, 132, 140 and140a of the Dutch Criminal Code
16	Jordi de J.	10/12/15	Sentenced for participation in a Syrian training camp.	155 days detention	Art. 14a, 14b, 14c, 14d, 83, 83a and 134a of the Dutch Criminal Code
17	Moussa L.	10/12/15	Sentenced for abetting.	43 days detention	Art. 14a, 14b, 14c, 14d, 57, 83, 83a, 131, 132, 266, 267 and 285 of the Dutch Criminal Code
18	Hicham el O.	10/12/15	Sentenced for taking part in a criminal organization with terrorist intent.	5 years	Art. 57, 83, 83a, 96, 134a, 140, 140a, 157, 176b, 288a, 289 and 289a of the Dutch Criminal Code
19	Hatim R.	10/12/15	Sentenced for taking part in a criminal organization with terrorist intent.	6 years and repeal of Dutch citizenship	Art. 57, 83, 83a, 96, 131, 132, 140, 140a, 157, 176b, 288a, 289 and 289a of the Dutch Criminal Code
20	Anis Z.	10/12/15	Sentenced for taking part in a criminal organization with terrorist intent.	6 years and repeal of Dutch citizenship	Art. 57, 83, 83a, 96, 134a, 140, 140a, 157, 176b, 288a, 289 and 289a of the Dutch Criminal Code

No.	Name	Date	Description	Sentence	Legal basis
21	Salim S.	18/02/16	Case number 02/800190-15: Sentenced for recruiting persons for armed terrorist conflict. Case number 02/665539-15: Sentenced for: 1. Raising finances (with knowledge about criminal goal); 2. Withholding information about personal financial situation.	24 months	Art. 10, 14a, 14b, 14c, 14d, 27, 33, 33a, 57, 205, 227b and 420bis of the Dutch Criminal Code
		17/02/17	In appeal sentences confirmed.	12 months	
22	Seyed H.	18/02/16	Sentenced for: 1. Preparation of: – intentional arson – murder/manslaughter with terrorist intent – causing others to commit crimes – providing the opportunity to commit crimes 2. Taking part in an organization that has the intent to commit terrorist felonies; 3. Membership of an organization that has the intent to commit terrorist felonies; 4. Preparation of a crime with terrorist intent, including intentional arson, murder/manslaughter.	42 months	Art. 14a, 14b, 14c, 14e, 47, 55, 57, 96, 140a, 157, 176b, 288a, 289a and 421 of the Dutch Criminal Code
		06/10/17	In appeal, sentenced for: 1. Preparation of: – intentional arson – murder/manslaughter with terrorist intent – causing others to commit crimes – providing the opportunity to commit crimes 2. Preparation/promotion of terrorist crimes by joining IS; 3. Participation in a terrorist organization; 4. Financing terrorism.	42 months	Art. 14a, 14b, 14c, 47, 57, 96, 140a, 157, 176b, 288a, 289a and 421 of the Dutch Criminal Code
23	Adil C.	18/02/16	Indicted for: 1. Membership of a terrorist organization; 2. Raising finances for the jihad; 3. Having knowledge about the provision of financial support used to commit a crime (or preparation of a crime) with terrorist intent. Sentenced for indictment 2.	12 months	Art. 14a, 14b, 14c, 14e, 47 and 421 of the Dutch Criminal Code

No.	Name	Date	Conviction	Sentence	Law article
24	Hardi N.	18/02/16	Indicted for: 1. Preparation/promotion of terrorist crimes (including arson, murder, manslaughter) and/or possession of means to commit a crime and/or convincing others to commit a crime; 2. Participation in a terrorist organization. Sentenced for indictment 1, but acquitted of indictment 2.	24 months	Art. 14a, 14b, 14c, 14e, 47, 95, 157, 176b, 288a, 289a of the Dutch Criminal Code
		6/10/17	In appeal, sentenced for indictment 1 and acquitted of indictment 2.	24 months	Art. 14a, 14b, 14c, 14e, 47, 95, 157, 176b, 288a, 289a of the Dutch Criminal Code
25	Suleymaan R.	15/03/16	Indicted for: 1. Financing of terrorism; 2. Intentionally breaking the Sanctions Act of 1977 and the Sanctions Regulation Al-Qa'ida 2011; 3. Intentionally breaking the Sanctions Act of 1977 and the Sanctions Regulation of Terrorism 2007-II; 4. Accomplice to forgery with intent to prepare a terrorist crime. Sentenced for indictments 1, 2 and 4.	24 months	Art. 14a, 14b, 14c, 14d, 47, 57, 225 and 421 of the Dutch Criminal Code
26	Mohammed A.	30/03/16	Acquitted of terrorist-related crimes. Sentenced for preparing an armed robbery.	30 months	Art. 14a, 14b, 14c, 36b, 36c, 46, 47, 57, 312 and 317 of the Dutch Criminal Code Art. 26 and 55 of the Law on Weaponry and Ammunition
27	Ilyas H.	26/05/16	Indicted and sentenced for: 1. Preparation of a terrorist crime (arson/murder/manslaughter); 2. Preparation of a terrorist crime (arson/murder/manslaughter) (different location); 3. Intention to take part in an organization with intent to commit terrorist crimes.	18 months	Art. 14a, 14b, 14c, 33, 33a, 45, 57, 96, 140, 140a, 288a, 289 and 289a of the Dutch Criminal Code
		27/07/17	Sentences in appeal upheld and penalty increased.	3 years	Art. 14a, 14b, 14c, 33, 33a, 45, 47, 57, 96, 140a, 157, 176b, 288a, 289, 289a of the Dutch Criminal Code
28	Rachid el J.	03/06/16	Indicted for: 1. Membership of an organization with terrorist intent; 2. Preparation to take part in an organization with terrorist intent; 3. Actions with intent to prepare for terrorist crimes. Acquitted of 1 and 3; sentenced for 2.	A custodial sentence of 9 months and 240 hours of community service	Art. 9, 14a, 14b, 14c, 22b, 22c, 33, 33a, 46, 140 and 140a of the Dutch Criminal Code

#	Name	Date	Sentence	Indicted for	Articles
29	Wail el A.†	15/06/16	2 years	Indicted for: 1. Preparation to become a member of an organization with terrorist intent; 2. Conspiring to commit arson/murder/manslaughter with terrorist intent. Acquitted of indictment 2; sentenced for indictment 1.	Art. 10, 27, 45, 47, 140 and 140a of the Dutch Criminal Code
30	Nadeem S.†	15/06/16	3 years	Indicted for: 1. Preparation to become a member of an organization with terrorist intent; 2. Conspiring to commit arson/murder/manslaughter with terrorist intent. Acquitted of indictment 2; sentenced for indictment 1.	Art. 10, 27, 45, 47, 140 and 140a of the Dutch Criminal Code
31	Rahma E.	16/06/16	8 months youth detention	Indicted for: 1. Attempt to take part in a terrorist organization; 2. Writing/imagery in which terrorist felonies are being abetted. Sentenced for 1.	Art. 27, 46, 77i, 77x, 77y, 77z, 77gg, 77za and 140a of the Dutch Criminal Code
32	Mohammed B.	20/06/16	12 months	Indicted for: 1. Preparation of felonies with terrorist intent (arson/murder/manslaughter); 2. Providing opportunity and/or information and/or acquiring the skills to commit a terrorist crime and/or preparing for a terrorist crime. Acquitted of indictment 1; sentenced for indictment 2 (acquiring knowledge to make explosives).	Art. 134a of the Dutch Criminal Code
33	Walid B.	05/07/16	27 months	Indicted for: 1. Co-perpetration of preparing murder/manslaughter with terrorist intent; 2. Co-perpetration training for terrorism; 3. Attempt at taking part in a terrorist organization. Acquitted of 1 and 2; sentenced for 3.	Art. 14a, 14b, 14c, 14d, 14e, 45, 47, 57, 134a and 140a of the Dutch Criminal Code
34	Alaa-Eddine B.	05/07/16	27 months	Indicted for: 1. Co-perpetration of preparing murder/manslaughter with terrorist intent; 2. Co-perpetration training for terrorism; 3. Attempt at taking part in a terrorist organization. Acquitted of 1; sentenced for 2 and 3.	Art. 14a, 14b, 14c, 14d, 14e, 45, 47, 57, 134a and 140a of the Dutch Criminal Code
35	Maher H.	07/07/16	4 years	Sentenced for the preparation of murder/manslaughter with terrorist intent, and the intentional familiarization of oneself with the skills needed to commit a terrorist felony, and the spreading of writing and imagery that abets to committing a terrorist felony.	Art. 14a, 14b, 14c, 14e, 57, 83, 83a, 96 lid 2, 132, 134a, 288a, 289 and 289a of the Dutch Criminal Code

No.	Name	Date	Conviction	Sentence	Law article
36	Shukri F.	07/07/16	Indicted for: 1. Recruiting for armed terrorist conflict; 2. Abetting criminal acts (preparation of terrorist felony); 3. Spreading of writing/imagery in which terrorist felonies are being abetted. Acquitted of 1 and 2. Sentenced for indictment 3: An image in which a terrorist felony is abetted and spread, while the suspect knows or has serious cause to suspect that the image contains such abetment to commit terrorist felonies.	6 months	Art. 14a, 14b, 14c, 57 and 132 of the Dutch Criminal Code
37	Driss D. In absentia	22/07/16	Indicted and sentenced for: 1. Membership of a terrorist organization; 2. Preparation of murder/manslaughter and/or causing an explosion with terrorist intent; 3. Abetting to commit terrorist felonies.	6 years and repeal of Dutch citizenship	Art. 47, 57, 83, 96, 131, 140a, 157, 176a, 176b, 288a, 289 and 289a of the Dutch Criminal Code
38	Abdellah R.	22/07/16	Found guilty of taking part in a criminal organization, preparation of terrorist attacks and abetting publicly via the written word and imagery to commit terrorist felonies.	6 years	Art. 47, 57, 83, 96, 131, 132, 140a, 157, 176a, 176b, 288a, 289 and 289a of the Dutch Criminal Code
39	Noureddin B.	22/07/16	Found guilty of taking part in a criminal organization, preparation of terrorist felonies and intentionally acquiring knowledge and skills in order to commit terrorist felonies.	6 years and repeal of Dutch citizenship	Art. 47, 57, 83, 96, 134a, 140a, 157, 176a, 176b, 288a, 289 and 289a of the Dutch Criminal Code
40	Thijs B.	22/07/16	Found guilty of taking part in a terrorist organization with the intent of causing manslaughter/murder, and causing an explosion with terrorist intent.	6 years	Art. 47, 57, 83, 96, 134a, 140a, 157, 176a, 176b, 288a, 289 and 289a of the Dutch Criminal Code
41	'Asylum seeker'	28/07/16	Indicted for: 1. Intentionally acquiring knowledge/ obtaining objects to provide financial support for committing a terrorist crime; 2. Membership of a terrorist organization; 3. Directly or indirectly providing finances for a terrorist organization. Acquitted of 2; sentenced for 1 and 3.	180 hours of community service	Art. 9, 14a, 14b, 14c, 22c, 22d, 36c, 57 and 421 of the Dutch Criminal Code Art. 1, 1°, 2 and 6 of the Economic Offences Act Art. 2 and 3 of the Sanctions Act 1977 Art. 2 and 2a of the Sanctions Regulation Al-Qa'ida 2011

#	Name	Date	Verdict	Sentence	Articles
42	Mohammed G.	04/08/16	Acquitted of training for terroristic actions (lack of evidence). Sentenced for the attempt to take part in an organization with terrorist intent.	Suspect declared guilty without imposition of penalty	Art. 45, 140 and 140a of the Dutch Criminal Code
43	Mohammed G.	29/08/16	Sentenced for preparing for migration to Syria or Iraq to join the jihad and Islamic State and for preparing to commit crimes with terrorist intent.	3 years plus sentence of entrustment (TBS, a provision in the Dutch Criminal Code that allows for a period of treatment following a prison sentence for mentally disordered offenders)	Art. 33, 33a, 37a, 38, 38a, 38b, 96, 157, 176a, 176b, 288a, 289 and 289a of the Dutch Criminal Code
		02/10/17	Sentenced for intentionally preparing for a crime described in articles 157 and/or 176a and/or 176b and/or 289(a) and/or 288a (arson/murder/manslaughter/explosion).		
44	Mohanned B.	29/08/16	Sentenced for participation in a terrorist organization.	10 months	Art. 140a of the Dutch Criminal Code
		12/12/17	In appeal acquitted of participation in a terrorist organization.	Acquitted in appeal	
45	A. 5144 (1997)	26/09/16	Acquitted of preparation/promotion of murder/manslaughter/arson/explosion with terrorist intent; acquitted of distribution/projection of seditious material. Sentenced for participation in a terrorist organization with intent to commit a crime.	12 months of youth detention	Art. 27, 33, 33a, 45, 77a, 77i, 77k, 77m, 77n, 77x, 77y, 77z, 77za and 140a of the Dutch Criminal Code
		19/07/17	Sentenced for preparation/promotion of murder/manslaughter/arson/explosion with terrorist intent. Sentenced for participation in a terrorist organization with intent to commit a crime. Acquitted of distribution/projection of seditious material.	15 months	Art. 14a, 14b, 14c, 14d, 14e, 33, 33a, 24, 45, 56, 77b, 96, 140 and 176b of the Dutch Criminal Code
46	N.n. 7126 (1991)	01/11/16	Sentenced for preparation/training. Acquitted of sedition.	14 months	Art. 14a, 14b, 14c, 14d, 14e, 33, 33a, 36b, 36c, 36d, 45, 55, 57, 96, 134a, 157, 170, 287, 288a, 289 and 289a of the Dutch Criminal Code

No.	Name	Date	Conviction	Sentence	Law article
47	Lieke S.[‡] (currently called Hayat S.)	10/8/17	Analysts did not find any mental disorder.	Preliminary imprisonment. Then released but obliged to wear a GPS ankle monitor and attend sessions with an Islamic theologian. She also lost custody of her daughter.	–
48	Martijn N.	22/02/17	Case number 09/767093-15: Indicted for: 1. Complicity in preparation/promotion of murder/manslaughter/arson/explosion with terrorist intent; 2. Complicity in attempting to participate in a terrorist organization. Acquitted for 1; sentenced for 2. Case number 09/767070-16: (Different time period.) Indicted for: 1. Attempting to participate in a terrorist organization; 2. Preparation/promotion of murder/manslaughter/arson/explosion with terrorist intent. Acquitted for 1; sentenced for 2.	31 months	Art. 14a, 14b, 14c, 14d, 14e, 36b, 36c, 45, 47, 57, 83, 96, 140a, 157, 176b, 288a, 289 and 289a of the Dutch Criminal Code
49	N.n. 2258	23/03/17	Sentenced for participation in a terrorist organization.	18 months	Art. 140a of the Dutch Criminal Code
50	Azziza A.	28/03/17	Declared innocent of all charges.	–	–
51	Mohammed A.	26/04/17	Indicted for: 1. Recruitment for armed conflict; 2. Possession/ distribution of pictures and audio files in which terrorist felonies are abetted; 3. Participation in a terrorist organization. Sentenced for indictments 1 and 3. Partly acquitted for indictment 2 (not proven that he distributed the files, but proven that he possessed them).	4 years	Art. 14a, 14b, 14c, 33, 33a, 55, 56, 132, 140a and 205 of the Dutch Criminal Code

No.	Name	Date	Charge/Outcome	Sentence	Articles
52	Behzad R.	24/05/17	Indicted for: 1. Performance of actions to prepare for or foster terrorist crimes; 2. Preparation for participation in a terrorist organization. Acquitted of indictment 1; sentenced for 2.	300 days	Art. 14a, 14b, 14c, 33, 33a, 46, 140 and 140a of the Dutch Criminal Code
53	N.n. 6924 (1993) In absentia	27/06/17	Sentenced for: 1. Participation in a terrorist organization; 2. Convincing somebody to commit (or possess the means to commit or provide the opportunity to commit) a terrorist crime.	6 years	Art. 47, 57, 83, 96, 134a, 140a, 157, 176a, 176b, 288a, 289 and 289a of the Dutch Criminal Code
54	N.n. 6922 (1981) In absentia	27/06/17	Sentenced for: 1. Preparation/promotion of murder/manslaughter/ arson/explosion; 2. Sedition to commit terrorist crimes.	6 years	Art. 57, 63, 83, 96, 131, 132, 157, 176a, 176b, 288a, 289 and 289a of the Dutch Criminal Code
55	N.n. 6927 (1993) In absentia	27/06/17	Sentenced for: 1. Complicity in participation in a terrorist organization; 2. Complicity in preparation/promotion of murder/ manslaughter/arson/explosion with terrorist intent and/or complicity in intentionally facilitating (preparing for) a terrorist crime.	6 years	Art. 47, 57, 83, 96, 134a, 140a, 157, 176a, 176b, 288a, 289 and 289a of the Dutch Criminal Code
56	Yusuf S.	11/07/17	Sentenced for: 1. Participation in a terrorist organization; 2. Preparation/promotion of murder/manslaughter/arson/explosion.	6 years	Art. 57, 83, 96, 140a, 157, 176a, 176b, 288a, 289 and 289a of the Dutch Criminal Code
57	Ahmet U.	11/07/17	Indicted for: 1. Complicity in attempting to participate in a terrorist organization; 2. Preparing to participate in a terrorist organization; 3. Complicity in preparation/promotion of murder/ manslaughter/arson/explosion with terrorist intent. Acquitted of indictment 1. Sentenced for 2 and 3.	18 months	Art. 14a, 14b, 14c, 14d, 45, 46, 47, 57, 83, 96, 140a, 157, 176a, 176b, 288a, 289 and 289a of the Dutch Criminal Code
58	N.n. 6394 (1994)	10/10/17	Declared innocent of all charges.	–	–
59	N.n. 7369 (1979)	10/10/17	Sentenced for an attempt to participate in a terrorist organization.	24 months	Art. 14a, 14b, 14c, 14d, 14e, 36b, 36c, 45 and 140a of the Dutch Criminal Code

No.	Name	Date	Conviction	Sentence	Law article
60	Jaouad A.	02/11/17	Indicted for: 1. Preparation of felonies with terrorist intent (including arson/murder/manslaughter); 2. Possession of weapons intended for a terrorist crime; 3. Money laundering (1,600 euros); 4. Possession of professional fireworks for personal use. Acquitted of 1, 3 and 4. Sentenced for 2.	4 years	Art. 33, 33a, 36b, 36c, 57, 83a, 96, 157, 176a, 288a, 289 and 289a of the Dutch Criminal Code Art. 26 and 55 of the Arms and Ammunition Act Art. 1a, 2 and 6 of the Economic Offences Act Art. 9.2.2.1. of the Environmental Management Act. Art. 1.2.2. and 1.2.4 of the Fireworks Decree
61	N.n. 8497	02/11/17	Sentenced for participation in a terrorist organization.	3 years	Art. 14a, 14b, 14c and 140a of the Dutch Criminal Code
62	Laura H.	13/11/17	Indicted for: 1. Complicity/participation in a terrorist organization; 2. A. Attempting to coerce another to commit a terrorist crime; B. Providing the opportunity to commit a terrorist crime; C. Having the means available which are destined for committing a terrorist crime. Acquitted of indictment 1; sentenced for indictment 2.	2 years	Art. 14a, 14b, 14c, 14e, 83, 83a, 96, 157, 176a, 288a, 289 and 289a of the Dutch Criminal Code
63	Marlon G.	30/11/17	Indicted for: 1. A. Abduction of a minor from his/her custodian; B. *Intentionally* causing serious physical injury; 2. Intentionally unlawful deprivation of freedom and continued withholding of freedom; 3. Preparation of terrorist crimes; 4. Preparation to participate in a terrorist organization. Sentenced for indictment 1A. Party acquitted of 1B (but sentenced for causing serious physical injury). Sentenced for indictment 2. Acquitted of indictments 3 and 4.	2 years and compensation to the victim	Art. 10, 24c, 27, 36f, 57, 279, 282 and 300 of the Dutch Criminal Code

	Name	Date	Sentenced for	Sentence	Legal articles
64	Hasan A.	01/12/17	Sentenced for: 1. Deliberately gathering information and acquiring knowledge to commit a terrorist crime; 2. Preparation of felonies with terrorist intent (including arson/murder/manslaughter); 3. Acting against article 26 (possession of (a) weapon(s)).	30 months plus TBS (a provision in the Dutch Criminal Code that allows for a period of treatment following a prison sentence for mentally disordered offenders)	Art. 36b, 36c, 36d, 37a, 38, 38a, 57, 83, 83a, 96, 134a, 157, 176a, 288a, 289 and 289a of the Dutch Criminal Code Art. 26 and 55 of the Arms and Ammunition Act
65	N.n. 9915	18/12/17	Sentenced for participation in a terrorist organization.	48 months	Art. 140a of the Dutch Criminal Code
66	18-year-old female	19/12/17	Case number 03/721031-16: Indicted for: 1. Attempting to participate in a terrorist organization; 2. Preparation of participation in terrorist organization. Acquitted. Case number 03/702658-17: Indicted for collusion to perform a terrorist felony (murder/arson). Acquitted.	270 days of youth detention	Art. 27, 47, 77a, 77h, 77i, 77x, 77y, 77z, 77gg and 140a of the Dutch Criminal Code

Source: Author composition from Dutch judicial files, verdicts and newspaper clippings.

Notes: * All Mohammed G.'s in this table refer to the same person.

† Appeal still pending.

‡ Court ruling has not yet taken place. The information about this case in the table is based on news articles, since there are no official published documents about this case.

Chapter 5

PRE-EMPTIVE MEASURES AGAINST RADICALIZATION AND LOCAL PARTNERSHIPS IN ANTWERP

Ineke Roex and Floris Vermeulen

Community engagement has become an important element in local approaches to counter violent radicalization.[1] One of the main instruments for local authorities in community engagement is setting up partnerships with community-based organizations, mosques, (self-appointed) community/religious leaders, and other key figures from the community. Questions about when, with, whom and how to engage with communities are often difficult for local authorities to answer. Little research is available to assess and analyse different forms of partnerships. Because of this, it is often unclear why specific forms of partnerships are chosen, what these partnerships entail and most importantly what the effects of these partnerships are. In this chapter we want to look into these questions by using some of the literature on pre-emption to further understand forms, function and effects of local partnerships. We take the city of Antwerp, the perceived threat of the radical Islamic group Sharia4Belgium and those who left to fight in Syria after 2012, as a case study to further assess the value of the framework we propose. The radical Islamic group Sharia4Belgium has its origins in a small group of Muslim youngsters in Antwerp and gained national attention in 2010 through a series of provocative and visible public protests. The ideology and style of activism of the group was inspired by radical British Muslim groups such as Islam4UK and Al-Muhajiroun. In 2012 the group was officially disbanded, but several activists remained active in the city and played, among other things, an important role in recruiting youngsters to leave for Syria. Since 2014 some of the core members have received long jail sentences or have been killed in the war in Syria. For this chapter we make use of two periods of fieldwork in Antwerp, in the summer of 2010[2] and from February 2013 until April 2014,[3] in which we conducted a dozen informal conversations with people involved with Sharia4Belgium (members, ex-members, sympathizers) and a few dozen formal interviews with people in the surroundings or people who were confronted with the activities of the group: imams, (board) members of Islamic organizations in the city, and local authorities (policymakers, police and other security officials).[4]

The concept of pre-emption is used in this framework in order to make a distinction between the different reasons for authorities to establish partnerships, and more importantly to distinguish between different types of partnerships. The concept allows us to better analyse the impact of the perceived threat of violent radicalism on the ideas and behaviour of local authorities in community engagement. Pre-emptive measures are taken when authorities perceive an imminent and catastrophic threat. The more that authorities perceive this to be the case, the more they will consider controversial measures in order to eliminate the perceived threat. Furthermore, in a pre-emptive approach, authorities will be less inclined to reconsider, debate and discuss their decisions beforehand. Both elements may lead authorities to select controversial partners for their programmes; partners that in other circumstances would not have been considered, thereby opening up new opportunities for them. Here we follow O'Toole et al., who argue for a more practice-based approach to analysing state–citizen relations within local policies against radicalization.[5] Such an approach can unexpectedly reveal the possibilities for citizens and community organizations to effect more autonomous agendas than those necessarily marked out for them by policymakers.

Pre-emption and prevention

A possible threat of an attack by violent Islamic radicals puts local authorities in a difficult position; they have to act on a potentially devastating event that has not occurred, and about which they often do not have a full understanding. In such a situation, authorities have to speculate what the future will bring and use this speculation to prevent such a future from happening.[6] Scholars have developed the concept of pre-emption to better understand the way in which authorities operate in such a context. Massumi explains how uncertainty plays a crucial role in the pre-emptive analyses of authorities.[7] This uncertainty is not due to a simple lack of knowledge of what the future will bring. It is more the nature of the uncertainty that authorities are dealing with that is important here. In a pre-emption approach, the nature of the threat itself cannot be specified. Authorities do not know exactly what kind of an attack will occur in their city, who will be responsible, and what the exact background of the attack, and those responsible for it, will be. Those working with a pre-emptive approach acknowledge that this lack of knowledge can never be overcome. The situation is objectively one in which the only certainty is that threat will emerge where it is least expected.[8]

De Goede, Simon and Hoijtink argue that pre-emption should be understood as a political act with very specific features and consequences.[9] The threat is imminent, unspecified and devastating. Authorities therefore feel the need to act immediately, as delay will accelerate the materialization of the expected threat. A failure by the authorities to act then becomes part of the problem. Thus, pre-emption has the capacity to generate its own benchmarks. Its consequences cannot be understood in terms of failure or success, because in a pre-emptive logic inaction is not an option. One of the consequences of this logic is that normal procedures of democratic politics such as deliberation, discussion and transparency do not function. If there were a better understanding of the nature of the threat, from whom the threat might be expected (target group), which factors could explain the threat and how we might intervene, a more preventive approach could be considered. In these cases, authorities have more time and knowledge to anticipate future problems and can therefore formulate a more informed and systematic approach.

Pre-emption and community engagement

De Goede, Simon and Hoijtink state that the way in which authorities mobilize civil society actors to intervene with 'problem youth' without a clear framework to understand radicalization, results in a pre-emptive policy approach where authorities foster their own benchmarks for success, including measures of money spent and civil society cooperation enacted, but not necessarily evidence of radical paths rerouted or attacks prevented.[10] O'Toole et al.[11] illustrate how a number of Foucauldian-inspired studies have focused on the pre-emptive ways in which governments have sought to instil discipline and 'self-governance' among Muslims by establishing partnerships with actors from Muslim communities.[12] Heath-Kelly for instance suggests that the UK government has adopted a pre-emptive approach within the counterterrorism paradigm in which Muslims and their organizations are constituted as simultaneously 'at risk' and 'risky'.[13] But at the same time communities are required to take responsibility themselves to target violence and radicalization in their own community. Communities are thus formulated as the battlegrounds for policy programmes to reject the ideology of violent extremism and to moderate themselves while they do so. This process entails a series of wide-ranging interventions in Muslim religious, social and civil structures, with the aim of reforming, managing, regulating and 'disciplining' Muslim conduct.[14] This often results in communities under suspicion, as the entire community is targeted and expected to participate in this self-disciplining process.[15]

This strategy is not specifically designed for controlling Islamic immigrant communities. It is a common pre-emptive strategy for authorities, confronted with potentially violent under-represented groups that threaten political stability, to pursue a broad institutional engagement with 'moderate' representatives in an attempt to 'normalize' communities,[16] to make them more similar to mainstream society. Warren states that governments, when facing violent, under-represented groups, often seek to deflect political problems and issues onto quasi-corporatist structures.[17] Governments will seek some sort of 'voluntary' self-regulation rather than a direct resolution of the issue of under-representation and social inequality itself in order to anticipate the threat that comes from these groups. This creates structures that would not develop 'voluntarily' without the attention of government. Akkerman, Hajer and Grin argue that there are good reasons to distrust such quasi-corporatist structures from above.[18] They believe that networks and associations involved in state-initiated policymaking will become dependent on state aid in order to function. The problem is not only that associations become vulnerable to shifts in public policy, but also that such networks become skewed excessively in the direction of the state.

Rose has observed that communities in general have become integrated into many social policy fields in order to anticipate possible social problems, such as crime, poverty, public health issues or radicalization.[19] Communities become policy categories to be investigated, mapped, classified, documented and controlled. He calls this 'government through community'. The community is governmentalized through cultivating, instrumentalizing and utilizing community allegiances and partnerships to regulate and reform.[20] Uitermark states that these approaches in which potentially dangerous groups whose self-regulating capacities can be enhanced constitute an alternative form of social control to segregation or repression.[21] He argues that the rationalities of such an approach are not centrally imposed but emerge through interactions, among others by establishing partnerships, among policymakers and the areas they seek to govern.

In such pre-emptive and 'government-through-community' approaches, there are few possibilities for agency among the actors and community organizations. O'Toole et al. call for a more practice-based approach here.[22] Partnerships and quasi-corporatist structures can theoretically also open up the possibility that actors within governance spaces may adapt or change formal rules of community governance. Such an approach recognizes the potential for the exercise of agency by different actors in reinterpreting, appropriating, contesting or resisting governance practices. In studying local approaches targeting violent radicalization they found significantly different possibilities open to community actors to interpret the rules applied and use the funds available to execute their own visions. Vermeulen,[23] studying local approaches in different European cities, also illustrates different examples in which Muslim actors in different circumstances attempt – sometimes relatively successfully – to negotiate the terms in which policies and programmes targeting violent extremism are implemented.

In sum, 'government through community' is a strategy often used by authorities when confronted with violence from under-represented groups. In such a strategy, authorities implement and establish partnerships with 'moderate' organizations from the community to regulate, control and change the community. We are interested in the extent to which authorities in Antwerp used similar pre-emptive strategies when confronted with groups like Sharia4Belgium and how this changed over time as they reinterpreted the threat coming from this group. In addition to that, we are interested in the reaction of the community itself to the strategy used by authorities and the extent to which community actors are able to use potential partnerships to their own advantage.

Different forms of pre-emptive community-based partnerships: Value-based and means-based

Before we finish the description of the proposed framework to understand pre-emptive partnerships, and then assess the strategies of authorities in Antwerp and the reactions of community actors, we want to introduce one final distinction in pre-emptive partnerships. Birt, studying engagement policies in the UK, identified two different approaches that are useful in distinguishing between different forms of partnerships and relating them to a pre-emptive or preventive approach.[24] The first approach, which Birt called the 'value-based' approach, sees violent radicalization as a gross theological error of which both violent and non-violent extremists are guilty. Religious Islamic values and their perceived incompatibility with Western values are central to this explanation of violent radicalization. The state should therefore focus on changing extremists' religious ideologies and values – hence the term 'value-based'. State-initiated engagement with the Muslim community should be implemented by engaging with moderate Islamic organizations to correct extremists' theological error, in line with the broader strategy of authorities to diffuse violent movements as described above and other studies of 'government through community'.

The second approach is what Birt terms 'means-based'. This largely sees violent radicalization as a sociopolitical movement in which only individual violent extremists are complicit. Personal, social, emotional and psychological factors attract young people to join violent Islamic extremist groups. Radicalization is not automatically seen as a religious process. In practice, the means-based approach opts for strong engagement with organizations and individuals who will prove to have the most credibility with extremists. Most salient here is how effective such individuals' style of personal engagement is and, specifically, their scholarly, religious or personal credibility, and their willingness to cooperate on the basis of shared interests – not shared values. This often means that controversial conservative or even extremist (non-violent) organizations are most suitable for such partnerships, as these organizations may have some legitimacy among the alienated target group (radicalized youngsters). Birt argues that means-based approaches tend to favour short-to-medium timescales in partnering with those who can reach out effectively to the target group, while value-based approaches work in the longer term with a much wider group (the entire community). In this sense the means-based approach relates better to a pre-emptive strategy, because it is less precise in its analysis of the threat, whereas the value-based approach targets the values of the entire community, as this is the breeding ground for violent radicalization, in order to prevent violence from happening in the future.

In the rest of this chapter we will study the case of Sharia4Belgium in Antwerp and look at how authorities dealt with the emerging threat of this group. We will argue that at first the threat of Sharia4Belgium was not considered imminent and was seen primarily as a security issue. In such a context, we would expect authorities to take a preventive approach in which a value-based understanding to the establishment of partnerships is most appropriate. Over the years, primarily because of the increasing numbers of youngsters leaving to fight in Syria in which (at the beginning) Sharia4Belgium played an important role, the threat of the group was perceived as increasingly imminent, but also increasingly unspecified (after 2012, when the group was disbanded, some of the activists of Sharia4Belgium were still active in Antwerp). In this changed context we would expect authorities to adapt a more pre-emptive approach in which new and more controversial actors become eligible for partnerships. We are also interested in the way in which the potential partners for a more pre-emptive approach (controversial radical organizations and actors) in Antwerp perceive these developments. This will be addressed at the end of the chapter.

Antwerp and its emerging threat: Sharia4Belgium

The radical Islamic group Sharia4Belgium and its aftermath can be easily classified as an example of a group that has been perceived by the media, the public and authorities as causing a serious threat to the city of Antwerp in recent years. The group gained national attention in 2010, when it rudely interrupted a lecture about political Islam at the University of Antwerp entitled 'Long Live God, Down with Allah' by Benno Barnard, a Dutch author who lives in Belgium. Soon after this event, Sharia4Belgium launched their website, which announced the group's intention to introduce Sharia law in Belgium, making them a specific threat for the security services. Sharia4Belgium viewed Sharia law as the purest and best form of government. According to the group, democracy does not make people free and equal. 'Democracy is oppression, Sharia is liberation. We reject your democracy because we believe our system is better.'

Sharia4Belgium was initiated by three young men: Fouad Belkacem (alias Abu Imran), Faisal Yamoun (Abu Faris) and Hicham Chaib (Abu Haniefa). Fouad Belkacem was the spokesman. They gathered a few dozen sympathizers around them, although the initiative counted just a few die-hard activists. Their ideology and style of activism was directly inspired by the radical British Muslim groups Islam4UK and Al-Muhajiroun, which we label as spectacle activism. This is a 'form of protest in which not only content, but also visual and auditory forms create a situation which a third party is almost bound to respond to'.[25] Anjem Choudary and Omar Bakri were the spokesmen of these UK networks. They inspired the adherents of several other Sharia4 groups. Anjem Choudary gave Sharia4Belgium ideological instruction both online and offline.[26]

The group were in the spotlight again in November 2010, when the Belgian police arrested several individuals suspected of preparing an assault in Belgium and recruiting for jihad in Chechnya. Several of the young men appeared to be Sharia4Belgium sympathizers. Sharia4Belgium denied they were members, but did not dissociate itself from what the young men were accused of planning.

From the beginning Sharia4Belgium was primarily perceived by the media, politicians, policymakers and security services as a security threat. Not only was the disruption of Benno Barnard's lecture perceived as a threat of violence towards the speaker (although the disruption was non-violent in nature), but the sympathy of Sharia4Belgium for jihadi ideologies was, for many, alarming. However, most disconcerting was the fact that this group, unlike other Salafi organizations, called for the implementation of Sharia law in Belgium itself. The activities and demonstrations of Sharia4Belgium were mostly non-violent, but many outsiders saw them as provocative. Indeed, their activism could be perceived as, directly or indirectly, violent in nature. For instance, sometimes they called for jihad in

Muslim countries and expressed sympathy for jihadists who committed violence in Europe, such as Mohammed Merah. Adherents of the similarly named and linked Sharia4Holland sometimes became aggressive, with support of Belgian members from Sharia4Belgium. The technique of disrupting public events came to be mimicked by Sharia4Holland and adherents of *StraatDawah* (street dawah).[27]

From 2010 to 2012 Sharia4Belgium held around ten so-called 'street dawah' events, mainly on the streets of Antwerp but also in Mechelen and Brussels. They also initiated a few demonstrations, produced about 500 videos on their YouTube channels and organized semi-public lectures in their office, which were attended by a few dozen young Muslim men and women. Due to growing media attention, and compelled by their message and style of activism, young Muslims from the Netherlands started following Sharia4Belgium online and attended their lectures in Antwerp too. These lectures were commonly broadcast on social media channels and internet video chat communities like Paltalk. Although the majority of the lectures were given by men, there was also a female branch of Sharia4Belgium, which produced a few of its own videos.[28] During their demonstrations in Borgerhout and Sint-Jans-Molenbeek, Sharia4Belgium were able to mobilize a few hundred people. In 2010, security services estimated that Sharia4Belgium had around six to twenty activists and about a hundred sympathizers. The activists were between twenty and thirty years old, but some sympathizers were younger.

After Fouad Belkacem and Hicham Chaib were arrested in the summer of 2012, the group Sharia4Belgium collapsed. On 7 October 2012, the group announced the end of the organization on their website. Also, Sharia4Holland ceased to be active. At that time, a few adherents left Belgium to join rebel groups against the regime of President Bashar al-Assad in Syria. In 2015, Fouad Belkacem received a twelve-year jail sentence as the leader of Sharia4Belgium, which was considered by the judge as a terrorist organization. Hicham Chaib, who had emigrated to Syria, was identified as the head of a violent Islamic State (IS) religious police unit in Raqqa. Faisal Yamoun died in 2014 during fights in Syria.

Although Sharia4Belgium's activism lasted for just two years and the group officially no longer exists, the journey of the majority of the group to Syria, joined by a few hundred others, came as a shock for many and resulted in large mainstream attention for Sharia4Belgium. A few online groups popped up after 2012 sympathizing with the fighters and arrested (former) Sharia4Belgium members. People leaving to fight in Syria also caused Sharia4Belgium to remain an eminent threat to the security of the city of Antwerp, which to some extent makes such pre-emptive measures acceptable to many politicians. The journey of these so-called jihadi fighters caused a growing alertness for radicalization processes and home-grown jihadism. European governments remain highly concerned about the people who return to their homelands after their experiences abroad. They could have built up military and ideological expertise in Syria, or at the very least returned traumatized. Coolsaet argues that especially at the start of the conflict in Syria, Sharia4Belgium played an important role in Belgium to emphasize the push and pull factors for potential Syria fighters.[29] The court in Antwerp stated in its verdict on Belkacem that since the foundation of Sharia4Belgium in 2010, the organization has attempted to make young people more willing to become involved in violent conflicts around the world, including Belgium, by formulating an aggressive discourse. Sharia4Belgium activism was meant to create a group identity among its followers in which violence and becoming a martyr played an important role.

Policy measures in Antwerp

The rise of Sharia4Belgium generated significant attention from the security services and local policymakers. In the beginning, the threat of the group was primarily perceived as just a security threat, important but not imminent, and did not lead to specific policies or the immediate establishment of partnerships. Local authorities in Antwerp were quick to define non-violent Islamic extremism as the enemy. Salafi groups were not seen in any way as legitimate partners for forms of cooperation to target violent radicalization; on the contrary, Salafi groups were mainly excluded and obstructed by authorities in Antwerp because of their radical and extremist views.[30] In addition to this, around 2010–11, the authorities in Antwerp attempted to bring together a set of 'representatives' from the local Muslim communities to engage with on issues concerning Islam or immigrants of a Muslim background. However, only 'moderate' Islamic organizations gained access to these institutionalized forms of engagement, whereas fundamentalist or extremist voices did not. The approach of local authorities in Antwerp was a selective one, and organizations were mainly viewed as being *acceptable* to the extent that they were *moderate* Islamic organizations. One of the consequences of the approach by local authorities in Antwerp, which shows strong resemblance to a value-based approach, was that the local Muslim communities felt stigmatized, excluded and victimized, which jeopardized any future forms of collaboration between authorities and Islamic organizations in that period.[31]

The policy framework of the Antwerp authorities changed significantly as more and more youngsters from Belgian cities left for Syria. From that moment onwards, the threat from Sharia4Belgium was perceived as much more imminent and alarming, even after the group itself had officially ended. Intelligence and security services kept the former adherents of Sharia4Belgium, their sympathizers and their successors (though not under the Sharia4Belgium flag) under high surveillance. National and local policies were designed and implemented and local Muslim communities set up several counter-initiatives. In 2013, several Belgian cities including Mechelen and Antwerp appointed a coordinator for the development of a deradicalization policy. The policy in Antwerp has two elements: one part focuses on individuals and the other has a collective character. The individual approach focuses on individual extremists and their families, wherein signals of their radicalization are provided to the local authorities. The collective approach includes new partnerships with Islamic organizations to reach out to Islamic communities and make them less vulnerable to extremist ideology. Such an approach was dismissed in 2010,[32] but became acceptable after 2012.

Possible Islamic partners for local authorities in Antwerp

In the new context after 2012 certain controversial imams became conceivable partners for some authorities in Antwerp. This was not openly communicated, but through certain examples of people and organizations we can provide a snapshot of this development. A good example of how the situation changed in this regard is the case of Nordine Taouil, a prominent and controversial imam in Antwerp.

In 2012, the question of whether Nordine Taouil could be a potential policy partner was perceived differently by policymakers than in 2009. At the time of protests against the headscarf ban in Antwerp's state schools (2009), Taouil suggested in a speech that schoolgirls should stay at home to express their opposition to the ban. The media interpreted this as fundamentalism. In a television programme called *Terzake* (To the Point), the head of the State Security Department called Nordine Taouil 'an extremist of the Salafist-Wahhabist school'. The Minister of Justice concurred. Shortly afterwards the imam's wife, who worked at a youth club, was fired because of her husband's alleged extremism. The Islamic community was furious. Her dismissal came as an enormous shock to the local Muslim community. They felt that orthodoxy and radicalism was unjustly criminalized and, in this case, the imam was unjustifiably presented as the enemy. But also back then a number of city officials felt the same. In their opinion, Taouil was very much the kind of man you could and should talk to.[33] One of the policymakers concerned with security issues stated the following in regards to a possible partnership with Taouil:

> The press has labelled Nordine Taouil as an extremist. It is true that he has studied in Saudi Arabia. But I think it is someone with whom you can really discuss things. We need to include him in our policymaking and collaborate with him. We should not criminalize radical people.
>
> interview with local policy maker, 2014

Slowly, over the course of recent years, other controversial networks and organizations that are perceived as (former) Salafi networks have become possible partners for local authorities in Antwerp although this is not explicitly stated anywhere. Particularly controversial and conservative organizations were supported by the local authorities to criticize members and activities related to Sharia4Belgium. At times, national authorities have taken an ambiguous position towards these organizations. For instance, one of these organizations was accused of supporting extremist ideologies and risked losing their recognition as an official mosque. At the same time other civil servants attempted to help this organization behind the scenes in their efforts to reach out to youngsters with extremist ideological ideas and to engage in discussion and dialogue with others about religious issues. Two people affiliated with this organization stated the following about this issue:

> Authorities find it difficult and problematic to acknowledge that the leader of our organization is a good partner for them. Behind the scenes the police admit

that they would love to work with him. I guess they do not want to say this in public because they are too proud to admit that they were wrong with their earlier accusations. The organization is not an extremist organization.

interview with board members of a local Islamic organization, 2010

Similar discussions have taken place about many other controversial organizations and partners, even Sharia4Belgium and its leaders. Some civil servants who we spoke to during our fieldwork felt that with Sharia4Belgium, and those affiliated with it, it is best to have some sort of conversation going on, to have and establish at least some contact. Most important in their view is not to isolate this group and the individuals around the organization further. Other civil servants felt that such conversations and contacts are useless, naïve and perhaps even dangerous. A dialogue with Sharia4Belgium for them was primarily undesirable because of the clearly anti-democratic stance of the group. Some suggested that it is necessary to exclude and isolate Sharia4Belgium as much as possible to prevent any public visibility for their actions and ideas. Yet some imams we spoke to argued that this complete exclusion might make Sharia4Belgium and their members even more dangerous:

I feel it is better to keep some sort of contact with him [Abu Imran] in case he changes his mind. In that case he will be able to speak with someone. If he is not able to do that, he will become more dangerous.

interview with local imam, 2010

This position was supported by certain people we spoke to in the police. Members of a particular unit responsible for targeting radicalization tried to get in contact with people affiliated with the Sharia4Belgium network, though without success. They are of the opinion that some contact is better than no contact.

Reactions by other 'radical' Islamic groups in Antwerp towards Sharia4Belgium, and first steps in starting programmes

In order to understand potential but controversial partners for the authorities in Antwerp we want to briefly discuss the reactions of some actors towards Sharia4Belgium and how this is possibly related to their willingness to collaborate with local authorities. For instance, Hizb ut-Tahrir recently took a strong stance against IS, while some Sharia4Belgium adherents sympathize with IS.[34] Hizb ut-Tahrir purports to reach their goals through intellectual and political debate and education. They set themselves apart from the violence involved in some of Sharia4Belgium's actions and, in particular, their call to implement Sharia law in Western Europe. They only advocate the implementation of Sharia in countries where Muslims form the majority population. The call to implement Sharia law in Europe is also a breaking point for Salafi groups, who think Sharia4Belgium's dawah style is the wrong way of doing dawah. Both the content of their message and the way it is propagated is viewed by Salafi groups as un-Islamic. A leader of another Salafi organization in Antwerp had a similar opinion. In one of the interviews she noted that:

> It is impossible to suddenly implement Sharia or the Caliphate. I wish we could do this, but the change would be too much. People might not want to be here anymore. To be a real Muslim one should not live in a Western country. There is a clear war here against Muslims. . . . They [Sharia4Belgium] are my brothers, but they should not formulate their opinions so hard. The Prophet taught us to stay soft . . . One should not state that there is only one way: to convert or go to hell.
> Interview with president of non-jihadi Salafi organization, July 2013

Salafi groups think the call for implementation of Sharia law is above all not realistic.[35] Sharia4Belgium adherents are also criticized by other Salafi groups because of their perceived ignorance about Islam and their religious youthfulness.

> Especially Muslims who speak in public and post movies on the internet like Sharia4Belgium have no religious knowledge. The other Muslims who speak in public through the media are mediocre. If you are a real Muslim in Belgium, you will stay silent, because you know that if you do not you will end in jail. People are too afraid to talk.
> Interview with president of non-Jihadi Salafi organization, July 2013

Official Salafi organizations and prominent Salafi preachers, including the Madkhali mosque in Antwerp, and several Salafi imams, including the afore-mentioned Nordine Taouil, have spoken out against Sharia4Belgium. Some smaller Salafi groups sometimes expressed their sympathy although they do not agree with everything. In particular, Sharia4Belgium's practice of *takfir* (declaring fellow believers to be infidels) is highly criticized.

> I need to work on myself before I can accuse others. I would not make any judgements on Arabic Kings. They [Sharia4Belgium] call them *taghut* [denoting a focus of worship other than Allah]; I would not dare to say such a thing. To do *takfir* is just not right!
> Interview with president of non-jihadi Salafi organization, July 2013

Other Muslim groups criticize Sharia4Belgium not only from an Islamic perspective but a democratic perspective as well. Several Muslim organizations from Antwerp brought out a joint press release against Sharia4Belgium shortly after their first disruption in 2010. They distanced themselves from the opinions and behaviour of the group, and stressed that Sharia4Belgium is not representative of the whole Muslim community and that their behaviour should not be associated with Muslim communities in general. National Muslim organizations also took a stance against Sharia4Belgium. In a press release these actors pointed the finger at Islamophobia as a fertile ground for radical groups. They called for the propagation of 'the universal value of freedom and pluralistic democracy'. A mosque organization in Antwerp published the following a press release:

> The Muslim community in Antwerp wants to disassociate from the behaviour of Sharia4Belgium. That kind of behaviour should be judged on an individual basis and not seen as illustrative of an entire community. Youngsters should be punished by the law and by their parents for the mistakes they make. Tolerance and respect for others should be honoured. Freedom of speech is very important for the continuity of a dialogue between communities.[36]

These reactions illustrate two things. First, it shows how the mindset of controversial local Islamic leaders has changed since 2010. Increasingly they have publicly proclaimed their discontent with Sharia4Belgium. This could be a result of the earlier-described 'government through community' in which local actors feel pressured by authorities to make moderate claims to counter the violent discourses of other groups. However, we feel this discontent is also fuelled by the perceived threat and urgency that is felt in the local Islamic communities and by many parents because of the increasing number of youngsters leaving for Syria. Second, these statements represent a changing and common belief that if groups like Sharia4Belgium and their discourse do present a serious problem for the community, these organizations and actors could become acceptable partners for local authorities as well. In that sense we see a two-fold development: local authorities increasingly perceive controversial actors as potential partners in their pre-emptive approach, whereas controversial local actors themselves become more interested and eligible in becoming part of a particular policy approach targeting violence.

Recently we have seen the emergence of several bottom-up Muslim initiatives in Antwerp from some of those controversial organizations and actors that were described above, to prevent Islamic youth from becoming radicalized. They do this by organizing religious lessons, Friday sermons, youth evenings, social activities, international trips and internet and media activities. These preachers and organizations frame the problem of radicalization in different perspectives. First of all, they see it as a problem of ideology and knowledge. They think Salafists dominate quickly available information about Islam and they incorrectly present themselves as the only true Islam. The groups want to create a middle way in this (virtual) religious market, teaching young Muslims about the diversity and heterogeneity of Islam, and showing them what they call 'moderate Islam'. They believe Sharia4Belgium's adherents have less knowledge about Islam and wrongly deny that there are differences of opinion within Islam. These actors show young Muslims interpretations of Islam more in keeping with contemporary times and claim that the jurisprudence of Islam is dynamic instead of static. Some claim that the lack of spirituality explains extremism and therefore they organize lectures about this topic. Their counter-initiatives are thus ideologically driven, which may cause a problem for authorities to support them, as in many people's eyes this is a violation of the separation between Church and State. Further research is needed to assess whether organizations and actors get the opportunity to frame and formulate these initiatives independently. One of the main research questions is whether these partnerships can be sustained over a longer period of time. During our interviews, respondents noted that they were frustrated by the ad hoc and short-term character of many of the contacts and partnerships. They did not feel that authorities took them seriously. If this is the case then pre-emptive partnerships can also have a negative effect and further isolate controversial organizations and actors in the city.

Conclusion

Sharia4Belgium was seen as a serious threat in Antwerp and authorities felt the need to act and do things that were seen as unacceptable until very recently. It is not clear to what extent we can really consider this a pre-emptive approach, characterized by the idea that authorities face an imminent unknown threat and that inactivity would lead to a catastrophe for which authorities would be partly responsible. Further research on the exact view of authorities on this matter is needed. However, it is clear that authorities in Antwerp are now more willing and able to consider partnerships with controversial figures from the Islamic community, especially compared to 2009–10. These new partnerships most often involve establishing contacts behind the scenes, which suggests a lack of democratic deliberation and debate. Such actions by the authorities seem to be guided at least partly by pre-emptive motives. In 2010, when the threat of Sharia4Belgium was primarily considered to be a security threat that should be dealt with by security forces, authorities in Antwerp considered a different type of partnerships, namely more value-based partnerships that targeted moderate Islamic organizations in the city with the aim of making the entire community more moderate.

Today, we also see more willingness and a sense of urgency by different controversial actors in the local Islamic community of Antwerp to become involved in a policy area, deradicalization, that they would have considered unacceptable in 2010. The relatively large numbers of youngsters that have gone to fight in Syria and the distress this has caused among family members is most likely the cause of this new sense of urgency. This also means that we have slowly witnessed more opportunities for controversial people to be involved in the public debate in Antwerp and the emergence of some programmes by Salafi organizations to target violent radicalization among youngsters.

The current situation in Antwerp seems to differ from the subsidized partnerships and support for moderate voices described by the literature on 'government through community'. These controversial actors are less dependent on authorities, and they risk their own position in the community as partnerships with local government are not always appreciated. However, the fact that they have often become more outspoken and negative towards groups like Sharia4Belgium and have slowly engaged in projects targeting radicalization shows that the situation in the city is changing. We interpret this as being partly due to pre-emptive measures and 'government through community', but due also to the threat felt in the community itself to act. The extent to which these new initiatives are really organized independently (so that actors/organizations can change/influence the structures/frames from above) and at the same time are supported broadly within the community will show the actual result of these developments.

Moreover, we need more research on what the effects of perceived threats on partnerships can be. In the aftermath of the attacks in Paris in November 2015, the Dutch Parliament took a measure *against* controversial partnerships with Salafi organizations. Further pre-emption should take this oppositional stance into account as well. What we need is a better understanding of the different engagement strategies of authorities, such as preventive, pre-emptive and precautionary strategies, and to study how these strategies change as the perception of the threat changes and how this then affects partnerships in different ways. This research should include the positions and perceptions of community actors as well, as these partnerships can only be understood sufficiently when both sides of the partnership are studied.

Notes

1 See Floris Vermeulen and Frank Bovenkerk, *Engaging with Violent Islamic Extremism: Local Policies in Western European Cities* (The Hague: Eleven International Publishing, 2012); and Adrian Cherney and Jason Hartley, 'Community Engagement to Tackle Terrorism and Violent Extremism: Challenges, Tensions and Pitfalls', *Policing and Society: An International Journal of Research and Policy* 27, no. 7 (2015): 1–14.

2 Vermeulen and Bovenkerk, *Engaging with Violent Islamic Extremism*.

3 De Koning, Roex, Becker and Aarns, *Eilanden in Een Zee van ongeloof*.

4 For more information about the fieldwork in Antwerp, see De Koning, Roex, Becker and Aarns, *Eilanden in Een Zee van ongeloof*.

5 Therese O'Toole, Nassar Meer, Daniel Nilsson DeHanas, Stephen Jones and Tariq Modood, 'Governing through Prevent? Regulation and Contested Practice in State–Muslim Engagement', *Sociology* 5, no. 1 (2015): 160–77.

6 Marieke de Goede, *Speculative Security: The Politics of Pursuing Terrorist Monies* (Minneapolis, MN: University of Minnesota Press, 2012).

7 Brian Massumi, 'Potential Politics and the Primacy of Preemption', *Theory and Event* 10, no. 2 (2007).

8 Ibid. See also Marieke de Goede, Stephanie Simon and Marijn Hoijtink, 'Performing Preemption', *Security Dialogue* 45, no. 5 (2014): 411–22.

9 Ibid.

10 Ibid.

11 O'Toole, Meer, Nilsson DeHanas, Jones and Modood, 'Governing through Prevent?'

12 Yahya Birt, 'Promoting Virulent Envy? Reconsidering the UK's Terrorist Prevention Strategy', *The RUSI Journal* 154, no. 4 (2009): 52–8; Heath Kelly, 'Counter Terrorism and the Counterfactual'; and Thomas Martin, 'Governing an Unknowable Future: The Politics of Britain's Prevent Policy'', *Critical Studies on Terrorism* 7, no. 1 (2014): 62–78.

13 Heath-Kelly, 'Counter Terrorism and the Counterfactual'.

14 O'Toole, Meer, Nilsson DeHanas, Jones and Modood, 'Governing through Prevent?'

15 Floris Vermeulen, 'Suspect Communities—Targeting Violent Extremism at the Local Level: Policies of Engagement in Amsterdam, Berlin, and London', *Terrorism and Political Violence* 26, no. 2 (2014): 286–306.

16 Jonathan Laurence, 'The Corporatist Antecedent of Contemporary State–Islam Relations', *European Political Science* 8, no. 3 (2009): 301–15.

17 Mark Warren, *Democracy and Association* (Princeton, NJ: Princeton University Press, 2001), p. 34.

18 Tjitske Akkerman, Maarten Hajer and John Grin, 'The Interactive State: Democratisation from above?', *Political Studies* 52, no. 1 (2004): 82–95.

19 Nikolas S. Rose, 'The Death of the Social? Re-Figuring the Territory of Government', *International Journal of Human Resource Management* 25, no. 3 (1996): 327–56.

20 See also Michael Marinetto, 'Who Wants to Be an Active Citizen? The Politics and Practice of Community Involvement', *Sociology* 37, no. 1 (2003): 103–20.

21 Justus Uitermark, 'Integration and Control: The Governing of Urban Marginality in Western Europe', *International Journal of Urban and Regional Research* 38, no. 4 (2014): 1418–36.

22 O'Toole, Meer, Nilsson DeHanas, Jones and Modood, 'Governing through Prevent?'

23 Vermeulen, 'Suspect Communities'.

24 Birt, 'Promoting Virulent Envy?'

25 De Koning, Roex, Becker and Aarns, *Eilanden in een zee van ongeloof*, p. 20.

26 Ineke Roex, *Leven als de profeet in Nederland*.

27 For instance, the disruption of a debate in December 2011 and an electoral meeting in 2012, both in Amsterdam.

28 De Koning, Roex, Becker and Aarns, *Eilanden in een zee van ongeloof*.

29 Rik Coolsaet, 'Wat drijft de Syriëstrijder?', *Samenleving en Politiek* 22, no. 2-15 (2015): 4–13.

30 Vermeulen and Bovenkerk, *Engaging with Violent Islamic Extremism*.

31 Ibid.

32 Ibid.

33 Ibid.

34 HizbutTahrirNL, 'Interview with Okay Pala: Together against Anti-Islam Policy' (In Dutch: *Interview met Okay Pala: Samen tegen anti-islambeleid*) [Video file]. Available at https://www.youtube.com/watch?v=-Pqk4fJ82gY, 12 September 2014.

35 See also Roex, *Leven als de profeet in Nederland*.

36 'Moslimgemeenschap distantieert zich van sharia4belgium', *Het Nieuwsblad*, 6 April 2010. Available at https://www.nieuwsblad.be/cnt/dmf20100406_137.

Chapter 6

COUNTERING RADICALIZATION: HIJACKING TRUST? DILEMMAS OF STREET-LEVEL BUREAUCRATS IN THE NETHERLANDS

Francesco Ragazzi and Lili-Anne de Jongh

How do policies aimed at preventing radicalization affect trust relations between Muslim communities and authorities in Europe? While such measures started without much controversy in the mid-2000s in the Netherlands and in the United Kingdom (UK), by 2016, they have come under increasing accusations of generating division, mistrust and suspicion within multicultural societies. As one imam from the London Borough of Newham put it in an open letter to the city council in January of 2016: UK's Counter-extremism strategy 'almost exclusively targets young Muslims for the views they hold on religion or issues such as government or foreign policy ... Schools and teachers are cast in the role of spies on our young people. This is leading to increasing division and to a breakdown of trust in schools and colleges'.[1]

The declarations made by this UK community leader stands in sharp contrast with the public objective of counter-radicalization policies across Europe. As the European Commission envisions it in its communication of January 2014, front-line workers, i.e. 'social workers, educators, healthcare workers, police, prison staff and probation staff' are expected to 'recognize and interpret signs of radicalization' in order to refer these individuals for 'interventions' ... 'these strategies require building trust within and between the communities, promoting a better understanding of each other's sensitivities and problems, engaging different sections of society, and much more. Bringing all these different aspects together diminishes the risk of radicalization, and results in a greater chance of stopping processes leading towards extremism and violence'.[2] According to the official view summarized in this EU document, it is therefore both possible and necessary to pursue two apparently contradictory logics: one of suspicion – searching for signs of radicalization, reporting individuals – and another of establishing trust and cooperation between the Muslim communities and the rest of society.

The counter-radicalization policy of the Netherlands has often been presented as a success in this regard. While being one of the first and most engaged European countries in developing these policies, it has done so with very little contestation. Is the dissatisfaction of Muslim and civil rights organizations in the UK based therefore on a poor implementation of these policies? Or is there something more problematic about this contradiction? The aim of this chapter is to explore this question by asking more broadly, the following questions: what is the effect of counter-radicalization policies on trust relations? And how do actors in charge of implementing them deal with the contradictory objective of both maintaining trust while applying a logic of suspicion?

While critical scholarship on counterterrorist and counter-radicalization policies has substantially grown over the past few years,[3] it has in a large part focused on discourse analysis of official policy documents and their rationalities.[4] The aim of this chapter is complementary to this approach in that it aims at recovering how, in practice, street-level bureaucrats[5] enact, appropriate and at times resist the imperatives that are imposed on them by the contradictory logics of counter-radicalization. As such, it builds on recent work that has been interested in analysing security politics from the point of view of everyday practices, whether in the study of counter-radicalization policies,[6] or critical security studies more broadly.[7]

We have chosen to analyse in detail actors from four municipalities in the Netherlands in order to observe the deployment of counter-radicalization strategies at the local level. We find that while the official discourse around counter-radicalization claims that it is interested in maintaining and nourishing trust relations between communities and the state – which in principle would therefore only be in accord with the professional ethics and objectives of the local actors engaged in implementing them – in practice these actors negotiate uneasily the imperatives of confidentiality and trust-building embedded in their professional habitus and the new functions of intelligence gathering and informal policing that is required from them. Faced with the contradiction between this imperative and the perspective of losing credibility in the community and with their 'clients', they respond with two distinct strategies that we term 'complicit compliance' and alternatively 'wilful ignorance'. In both cases, only one of the imperatives can be preserved: the logic of suspicion and intelligence gathering or the logic of community trust.

The chapter is grounded in ethnographic observation and eleven semi-structured interviews conducted between April 2015 till February 2016 in four municipalities in the Netherlands; two municipalities with a population of between 150,000 and 600,000 inhabitants and two municipalities with a population of between 40,000 and 60,000 inhabitants. The interviewees were four local policymakers specialized in counter-radicalization and safety, one mayor, three local social welfare consultants, two youth workers and one neighbourhood police officer. The respondents were all positioned in the areas of counter-radicalization policies at the municipal level and were thus considered to be key informants in describing the counter-radicalization work at the local level. The research also made use of primary sources including position papers, policy documents and evaluation papers of the Association of Dutch Municipalities (*Vereniging van Nederlandse Gemeenten*, VNG),[8] the Dutch Ministry of Security and Justice, the

Dutch National Coordinator for Security and Counterterrorism (*Nationaal Coördinator Terrorismebestrijding en Veiligheid*, NCTV)[9] and policy statements and counter-radicalization guidelines of the four municipalities. While the approach is inductive and case-specific, and more comparative research will be needed to confirm the findings, we claim that the conclusions of our study illuminate some of the key problems that counter-radicalization policies face in Europe and in other parts of the world.

The chapter is organized as follows: we first provide context to the evolution of counter-radicalization policies in the Netherlands, showing the municipal level has increasingly been designated as the key site of implementation of counter-radicalization policies, forcing local actors into the contradictory imperatives of maintaining relations of trust while enforcing practices of suspicion. In a second section, we specify our conceptualization of trust relations, highlighting how trust is not only a key building block of society, but functions also as a technique of anticipation and social control. In the third and main empirical section, we show (1) how local actors are encouraged by the national policy to maintain and work through trust relations; (2) how in practice they are required to use these relations to provide intelligence and enforce social control, and (3) how they develop strategies of reluctant yet complicit compliance or wilful ignorance in order to cope with the contradiction. In the conclusion, we highlight both the theoretical and policy relevance of our findings.

Development and implementation of counter-radicalization policies in the Netherlands

Following the attacks on the World Trade Center in New York in 2001, the assassination of politician Pim Fortuyn in Hilversum in 2002, and the attack on filmmaker Theo van Gogh in Amsterdam in 2004, the Netherlands has intensified its counterterrorism practices. From 2004 onwards, both the Dutch Ministry of Security and Justice and the National Coordinator for Security and Counterterrorism (NCTV) expressed their ambition to develop 'strong and comprehensive' measures in order to counter the executives of 'jihadist ideology' and the process of radicalization.[10] To reach this ambition, both actors agreed to include preventive measures alongside repressive measures within current counterterrorism policies. A combination of preventive and repressive measures is considered to be 'proportionate, effective and legitimate' in relation to current terrorism threats. As emphasized by the Ministry of Security and Justice, 'radicalization and terrorism are regarded as a complex whole, and therefore require a cohesive approach'.[11]

Counterterrorism policies in the Netherlands have not always included both preventive and repressive measures. Up until the early 2000s, the emphasis within national counterterrorism policies was still very much focused on repressive measures alone. Yet, the official inclusion of the Comprehensive Approach in the memorandum 'Terrorism and the Protection of Society' in 2003 gave room for the combination of preventive and repressive measures within national and local policies. The inclusion was formally finalized in 2007, and is now described extensively in the 'Integral Approach Jihadism' action programme. Solely focusing on repressive measures is therefore no longer considered to be a productive way of tackling terrorism.

Current counterterrorism measures consist of a combination of preventive and repressive measures and are executed through an intensified 'coordination, harmonization and cohesion between institutional bodies' dealing with counterterrorism practices.[12] 'Partnerships' were thus developed whereby both national and, particularly, local actors collaborate together. Dutch municipalities received 'a leading role' in making sure counterterrorism measures were acted out, especially against jihadism.[13] Since 'a terrorist attack will always take place within a municipality',[14] it is, according to the Dutch government, necessary to also integrate counter-radicalization programmes within the local policy domain. As a result of this, certain responsibilities and tasks regarding counterterrorism, which were once under the authority of the state, were transferred to the local government.[15] Emphasis was placed on the responsibility of the municipalities to prevent and repress radicalization acts linked to jihadism.[16]

The preventive and repressive measures to be deployed at the local level are defined under the 'Comprehensive Approach'.[17] Since the process of radicalization is not to be dealt with in isolation, the Comprehensive Approach functions as a toolbox in which different instruments can be used in combination or separately. According to the Ministry of Security and Justice, 'The Comprehensive Approach should be considered as the basis of Dutch counterterrorism policy'.[18]

Preventive measures are defined by the Comprehensive Approach as a process of 'identifying groups and individuals which appear to adhere to radical ideas and subsequently counter further radicalization, violent and otherwise, by means of intervention strategies'.[19] Preventive measures are acted out by the so-called community actors, being, among others, neighbourhood police officers, policy advisors and social welfare organizations. The Comprehensive Approach defines repressive measures as 'a diverse range of security actors that repress violent actors who are on the point of committing violent acts or who have already committed such acts'.[20]

With the development and implementation of the Comprehensive Approach, new challenges for the involved community actors rose to the surface. Where the tasks of municipalities were once mainly based on preventive approaches, which were seen as a major advantage to control crime and maintain trust, it was now decided by the state that they could also be held responsible for the enactment of repressive approaches. This mixture of 'hard' and 'soft' measures is viewed by the involved actors as both a 'problem' and a 'solution'. The policy measures are intertwined; incorporated but also challenged not only by those who counter them, but also by those who govern them. Although acknowledging that community policing must be incorporated to counter radicalization, several municipalities in the Netherlands state that they experience difficulties when it comes to dealing with these contradictory policies.[21] However, on the national level, the Dutch government proposes that this local approach is instead a 'solution' and necessary to be able to counter radicalization.[22] Therefore, different actors and institutions assign different meanings to this counterterrorism approach.

Trust and suspicion in countering radicalization

The literature on counterterrorism and counter-radicalization has analysed this development and implementation of counter-radicalization policies along two dominant interpretations. A first perspective, which we label the 'partnership thesis', has been to consider these initiatives as a 'soft' form of counterterrorism; a welcome addition to the 'hard' counterterrorism measures deployed after the September 11, 2001, attacks, which have been mostly focused on tough law enforcement legislation and practices.[23] Soft counterterrorism, known in the UK as 'Preventing Violent Extremism',[24] and in the Netherlands as the 'Comprehensive Approach',[25] should therefore been considered as a way to de-exceptionalize counterterrorism, to make it more transparent, democratic, inclusive and tuned in to the preoccupations of local communities. The policies first developed in the Netherlands and in the UK in the mid-2000s can be interpreted as pursuing a preventive objective while limiting discrimination against Muslim populations. According to the partnership thesis, trust is therefore both a *condition of possibility* and a *positive outcome* of preventive policies. Grounded in utilitarian thinking, it considers them in addition as a tool for more efficient 'intelligence sharing' between social, educational and community services and the police and intelligence services, a more efficient way of carrying out preventive work. Trust is necessary for this information to be shared and to circulate. From a moral and ethical point of view, and in contrast with 'hard counterterrorism', counter-radicalization policies are therefore considered as a way of maintaining pacified relations between authorities and Muslim communities in multicultural neighbourhoods. Trust is a positive outcome, and creating relations of trust through preventive counter-radicalization is therefore the 'right thing to do', both in ethical and practical terms.

In contrast to this line of analysis, others have considered these programmes rather as a continuation, by other means, of the 'hard' practices of counterterrorism.[26] Rooted implicitly in a Marxian notion of false consciousness, the participation of communities is considered illusory and tokenistic; mere propaganda used to better justify covert forms of spying and infiltration into Muslim communities. According to this view, there is nothing 'soft' to the approach; it functions as a covert form of intelligence gathering aimed at supporting the hard approach by manipulating consent. As such, it participates in the alienation of Muslims in Europe, relegated to the category of a 'suspect community'.[27] The 'suspect community' thesis therefore considers the breakdown or undermining of trust through the diffusion of suspicion as a *negative outcome*, namely as that which is sacrificed by counter-radicalization policies in the name of more pressing objectives: intelligence gathering, infiltration and surveillance.

In this chapter, we argue that both interpretations offer only a partial account of how counter-radicalization operates. Contrary to the partnership thesis, and in line with the scholarship on community partnerships,[28] we view counter-radicalization as the setting up of unequal relations of power in which trust is extracted as a specific modality of intelligence gathering and social control. Yet contrary to the false-consciousness thesis, we argue that trust relations are not a 'collateral damage' of counter-radicalization: they are specifically what is targeted and tapped into. Our argument is that the functions of partnership and trust on the one hand and surveillance and suspicion on the other are equally and contradictorily embedded in the practices of counter-radicalization policies. Central to their rationality is a project of bending, harnessing or hijacking existing or supposed relations of trust that form the basis of specific social settings as a specific form of anticipatory security. The project of hijacking trust is, however, built on a key contradiction; namely the assumption that the prevention of radicalization can be carried out by both requiring trust and enacting suspicion. But one inevitably necessarily undermines the other. The policies are therefore conceptualized on a logical fallacy that is bound to fail. Indeed, one of the main likely outcomes of these policies is a deeply entrenched mistrust of all institutions and individuals that collaborate with them. It is precisely to avoid this outcome that actors engage in several strategies of compliance or avoidance at the local level. In order to develop this point, we however first need to make explicit our understanding of the notion of trust.

Conceptualizing trust relations

While it forms part of the background of most theories of the social, surprisingly only a few authors have explicitly theorized the function and role that this specific type of relation performs in society.[29] Among those who have contributed to the recent debates, Möllering has highlighted the importance of Georg Simmel's thought in shaping contemporary thinking around this notion.[30] Simmel remarked that without 'the general trust that people have in each other, society itself would disintegrate'.[31] Simmel details in *Philosophie des Geldes* the different psychological and social operations required to transition from material money to credit money: the farmer's belief that the crops will grow, the trader's belief that his goods will be desired.[32] For Simmel, trust is as strong – if not stronger – than rational calculation; it is a 'psycho-sociological quasi-religious faith', based on a mix of knowledge and non-knowledge. As he puts it:

> To 'believe in someone', without adding or even conceiving what it is that one believes about him, is to employ a very subtle and profound idiom. It expresses the feeling that there exists between our idea of a being and the being itself a definite connection and unity, a certain consistency in our conception of it, an assurance and lack of resistance in the surrender of the Ego to this conception, which may rest upon particular reasons, but is not explained by them.[33]

Trust constitutes therefore the glue that holds society together, precisely because it creates a conduit of authorization of human relations that does not necessitate a constant rational assessment of costs, benefits, risks and advantages. Instead it relies on credentials to assume that a specific human interaction will go as anticipated.

Drawing on Simmel, Niklas Luhmann emphasizes a second key feature of trust relations, namely their anticipatory characteristic: 'to show trust is to anticipate the future. It is to behave as though the future were certain'.[34] Luhmann conceptualizes trust as a mechanism of 'reduction of complexity' that functions as a method of hedging bets and anticipating risks. To trust someone, explains Luhmann, is indeed a particular choice that combines the knowledge about this person with the absence of knowledge that is contained in the expectation of the future.[35] The third key feature of trust is that it functions as a particular form of social control, as highlighted by the strand of sociology inspired by Durkheim. The 'faith' outlined by Simmel to explain the leap one makes when trusting someone is understood by Durkheim as one of the features of solidarity, and in particular the mechanic solidarity of traditional communities – 'moral density' in Durkheimian terms.[36] In other words, trust is not only an individual decision, but it is also, very often, a moral obligation. In many social contexts, it is extremely costly not to trust – in particular if the person to be trusted is endowed, through cultural norms embedded in relations of power, with the capacity to command obedience. This can be the case either because trust is assumed to be the default appropriate behaviour (say, trust in the police force or in the courts) or because trust is the necessary precondition for certain professions to work. In sum, while trust is a necessary binding relation of society, it interestingly functions both as a technique of anticipation and a key component of social control.

Trust, suspicion and the 'helping professions'

It is therefore no wonder that states have always had a particular attention for relations of trust. The project of state formation, conceptualized canonically as the process of monopolization of relations of power pre-existing in society into a rationalized bureaucratic structure,[37] can indeed be equally read as a project of monopolization of relations of trust, albeit in an ambiguous way. On the one hand, state institutions require from populations that they forgo traditional relations of trust towards their traditional institutions, between for example members of families, clans, tribes or guilds, to the profit of an unmediated relation to the authorities, required for the provision of public services, justice, protection and later on welfare. On the other hand, state bureaucracies project a constant gaze of suspicion towards the populations they govern, in order to root out crime, sedition, waste, subversion and other 'social ills'. Institutionalized trust and suspicion are therefore at the core of the ambiguous nature of state power, which is always both protective and oppressive, empowering and dominating.[38]

As the bureaucratization of the state has progressively permeated the different spheres of society, it has however appeared with some salience that certain relations of trust within society must be preserved and kept out of the suspicious gaze of the state – through the conception of professional confidentiality or discretion – for the very system to be able to function. For some professions, this privilege of confidentiality has been embedded in their practice ever since they have existed. The principle of attorney-client confidentiality, for example, is considered the 'oldest and most widely recognized privilege'.[39] The hypothetical scenario in which a lawyer would have to tell his or her clients that 'anything they say could be used against them' and that they would have to testify against them if needed, is telling enough to understand the absurdity of such a proposition. Similar dispositions exist in democratic countries to protect doctor–patient relations, as encoded in the 'Hippocratic oath'.[40] Religious ministries, in many instances, are allowed to oppose, for a certain number of matters, a principle of exclusivity between them and their flock to state inquiries.[41]

As in the legal, medical or religious professions, social workers need to ensure a certain degree of confidentiality with their clients in order to carry out their professional duties. As Merton, Merton and Barber put it, 'A significant pair of professional–client norms is the professional's promise of confidentiality, on the one hand, and the client's duty to disclose, on the other. Confidentiality is usually justified as a matter of principle with the observation that in its absence, clients could not be expected, and would not be likely, to reveal intimate and sometimes shameful details of their lives.'[42] The confidential information obtained by social workers, teachers or professors, is shared with them precisely because the parties involved have established that this information should remain secret and that the relationship between them has the unique purpose of helping them. Confidentiality is therefore understood as the necessary condition for the function of assistance to work.[43] Yet here lies the core of the problem: the project of community policing and intelligence-led policing that underpins counter-radicalization policies aims precisely at undermining this 'disinterested' confidentiality.

Counter-radicalization and the incompatibility of trust and suspicion

As our research shows, the difficulty for educators, social workers or teachers to carry out counter-radicalization policies while preserving confidentiality and autonomy constitutes the core of the problem. Can such a policy work? As the following section shows (1) while the programme of counter-radicalization proclaims itself as a project based on trust-building, in practice (2) what is imposed on the local actors is precisely an imperative to use the trust relations they establish as a modality of intelligence gathering for anticipation and a tool of social control – undermining the trust they obtained in the first place. This (3) generates important concerns about the inability to reconcile relations of trust with obligations of suspicion and fear for the credibility and reputation of the institutions. Faced with an irreconcilable objective, local actors therefore (4) develop strategies of 'complicit compliance' or 'wilful ignorance'.

Partnerships and collaborations: Trust according to national policies

Based on the national guidelines attributed to the Comprehensive Approach, community actors (we mean by this: local authority representatives, social workers, youth workers, community police officers) are advised on how to detect radicalization and how to use the relations of trust in order to prevent it. By investing their time and effort in delivering training, intercultural dialogue sessions and social gatherings, these actors hope to increase the level of trust between them and the community members. These activities are part of the 'package of social, political, legal, educational and economic measures specifically designed to deter disaffected (and possibly already radicalized) individuals from crossing the line and becoming terrorists'.[44] These packages can include interfaith meetings, professional development seminars, development of tools/measures to better enable teachers and public authorities to address radical and negative opinions, establishment of a help desk to which public authorities and public actors can turn to for information on radicalization or to 'report' a possible suspect, the creation of mentoring systems for young people to establish face-to-face dialogue and the existence of 'resource' individuals and role models. By adopting these packages and by implementing them within the community, community actors are encouraged to maintain and work through trust relations.[45]

Trust, based on this perspective, is considered to be the key feature that will make the enactment of counter-radicalization measures possible and it is also expected to derive from executing the measures. Without trust, community actors argue that there can be no information sharing between community partners and members, no direct or indirect contact and dialogue and no cooperation and collaboration.

The way community actors understand and experience trust is formed through their direct engagement with community members and fellow local partners. According to them, trust can be defined, and is experienced as such, in multiple ways. Trust is according to them 'being approachable' towards community members and local partners. Trust is also understood as doing favours for community members, and thereby getting personally involved. As a policy advisor argues, 'Trust is just doing something, for example, when nobody else is doing something' (personal communication, 30 April 2015). Trust is not considered to be a static feature but a process that evolves over time. As a policy advisor on radicalization states,

> We stay with them for a couple of hours or sometimes the entire evening. From the moment of that first contact, we are building a relationship. Trustful and meaningful relationship. . . . Now I know some guys for four or five years.
> personal communication, 1 May 2015

Trust is extended by 'being open' and 'transparent' towards community members and local partners. This is considered to create the possibility to show the 'real' intentions of the community actors. As explained by a mayor, 'Just be open and transparent. You don't want to play a game; that is no use. . . . You will probably cause a lot more trouble if you are going to be suspicious about your intentions' (personal communication, 6 May 2015). Trust proves to be effective when it comes to sharing ideas, information and perceptions between community actors and members. Trust is considered to be an 'instrument' which community actors need for their work to function. On the one hand, it is considered to give individuals the feeling that they are part of a community; underlining the notion of partnership between community actors and members as described by the Comprehensive Approach. This is illustrated by a local policy advisor: 'It is important that citizens get the feeling that they are being heard ... we therefore have an open attitude' (personal communication, 1 May 2015).

Community actors argue that trust can give members of the community the opportunity to get acquainted with each other. It creates a comfortable atmosphere in order to discuss problems. As a mayor indicates,

> I find it important that they know me so that they can find me when something is going on.... As long as you know things about each other, you can try to understand each other. And when you understand each other, you can truly freely live side by side.
>
> personal communication, 6 May 2015

Although community actors state that by keeping in touch with members of communities, by showing their willingness to help out by doing something or being there, and by being open and transparent about their intentions, trust can be built and maintained; it is also considered as a feature of hope and desire about what could and should exist between actors, partners and members of society. According to the actual experiences of trust relations by community actors at the local level, trust is extremely difficult to build, let alone to maintain. As a local policy advisor states,

> Trust is extended by visiting the local mosque, and it is shown to us there. We visit the local community centre; we visit the community and tell something about what we do, and on the other hand we undermine it, unconsciously, maybe consciously but unintended, because we are of course working with repressive measures as well, where we also play a role and of which we are also aware.
>
> personal communication, 23 April 2015

In sum, community actors share the common belief that trust is necessary for the execution of the Comprehensive Approach and that by building partnerships and collaborations between members of society and national partners by means of social packages, that same trust can be maintained. Nevertheless, in practice it turns out to be a feature that's difficult to build and maintain.

Trust and the imperatives of anticipation and social control

The practices of community actors reveal, however, another dimension of trust relations in the implementation of these policies, underpinned by a logic of suspicion. These relations are used in order to produce intelligence about community members and partners. Trust is thus considered to be a relation that can be 'tapped', meaning using trustworthy relationships to collect information concerning radicalization issues, such as knowledge on networks and the social capital of certain community members. This relationship is therefore not just an instrument of partnership but also functions as a monitoring tool in order to regulate social life; making sure individuals behave according to group standards. As a local policy advisor on safety states, 'You stick to the monitoring tasks you get from the national level ... you are wary, especially of the police' (personal communication, 1 May 2015). Another local policy advisor on radicalization adds, 'I always pay attention to the way people are dressed ... just look at how people are living. If you see something special or different, then you can go a little further' (personal communication, 30 April 2015).

The national government plays an important part in setting up the agenda when it comes to the enactment of counter-radicalization measures at the local level.[46] The 'Integral Approach Jihadism' action programme and the 'Approach to Radicalization and Counter-Terrorism on a Local Level'[47] specify the terms of this policy. Both policies, grounded in a combination of preventive and repressive measures, provide guidelines for community actors on how to detect radicalization within their communities and how to counter it. Those guidelines include suggestions on how to go about preparation, prevention, countering terrorist activities, dealing with direct threats, what needs to be done when there is an actual attack and also what to monitor and report.[48]

Both the 'Integral Approach Jihadism' action programme and the 'Approach to Radicalization and Counter-Terrorism on a Local Level' are specifically focused on the countering and weakening of the 'jihadist movement' in the Netherlands.[49] Through these state practices, the national government creates a standard of what needs to be 'replaced'; namely the jihadist movement, meaning the 'networks, groups, cells and individuals who follow the ideology and strategy of jihadism'.[50] 'Jihadism', according to these policies, is

> [a]n ideological trend within political Islam which, on the basis of a specific description of the salafist doctrine and the thoughts of Sayyid Qutb, uses an armed battle [jihad] in order to reach a global domination of Islam and the reestablishment of the Caliphate.[51]

Community actors are, however, not required to strictly follow the national policies and can design their own 'package' of counter-radicalization measures suitable for the local situation. This is highly appreciated by community actors, as is illustrated by a local youth worker: 'We decide as a district and along with our partners what we are doing. There is some kind of toolbox [Toolbox Extremism developed by the NCTV, 2014 ed.] and from that toolbox we pick and choose what we want to use in our own community' (personal communication, 6 May 2015).

As community actors play a leading role in creating an 'accurate image' of radicalization within their own domain, it is up to the municipalities to gather as much information as possible about definitions and characteristics of radicalization and jihadism from different community actors.[52] In practice, it remains a challenge for community actors to produce a construction of radicalization that is suitable for the local situation, as the concept of radicalization and jihadism moves from one context to the other. This leads to confusion and a lack of clarity with the executors of the counter-radicalization policies. This is illustrated by a local policy advisor: 'I would call radicalization a very broad definition, with all kinds of different meanings. But is it the left group, is it the right group, or is it the middle group that we need to look at?' (personal communication, 1 May 2015). Several local policy advisors state that they will evaluate each possible indication of radicalization since 'interpretation is very situational' (personal communication, 30 April 2015). Furthermore, 'We have no standard characterization. If our partners think that it has something to do with radicalization, then they can come to us and we will examine the information' (personal communication, 23 April 2015).

Thus, the discourse of radicalization and the way it should be countered at the local level is formed through the interpretations of the community actors themselves and the national policies regarding radicalization and counter-radicalization. As a local policy advisor on safety states, 'We don't have strict policies, so we have our own guidelines which we use, which contain certain characteristics of the groups we could follow and signal' (personal communication, 1 May 2015). Community actors therefore decide for themselves where to look when they monitor and which group standards are applicable for community members. This presents new challenges at the local level when it comes to deciding which section of the population needs to be targeted and to which moral standards the community members should apply:

> Not all the partners know how to deal with it. Especially during that first part, that is something they struggle with. That monitoring and giving interpretation. That is the most important element. You could see that as something like separating groups. You see that in all kinds of organizations; with the municipality but also with the police. That is not right. In that way, we try not to cross the line. But I cannot say with certainty that we never cross that line.
>
> interview, 30 April 2015

The 'line' marks clearly the boundaries between legitimate community work and police work. Inevitably the Muslim population becomes a target of surveillance. As a local youth worker states, 'There will be judging; there will be someone on the bench getting the label jihadist' (interview, 7 May 2015). Individuals are monitored for their behaviour, and required to change it when not appropriate, as this incident at a school illustrates:

> So he could not pray at school, according to his director. Those are the ingredients which give such a guy the feeling of 'I am a Muslim, look at those Muslims; they are no good. The whole world should be a Muslim state'.
>
> interview, 7 May 2015

The link between radicalization and surveillance of the Muslim community is not limited to schools, it pervades all areas of the community: 'We are looking closer at the Muslim community when we hear something ... you will immediately link that to radicalization' (personal communication, 6 May 2015). One local mayor confirms in a direct way that she is more aware about the Muslim community due to the local responsibility of countering radicalization:

> Yes, I am more aware. If I am really honest, yes I am. That is definitely the case, especially of the Muslim community ... due to this toolbox [Toolbox Extremism, NCTV, 2014 ed.], we definitely saw the need to pay them a visit.
>
> interview, 6 May 2015

The consequence of the surveillance imperative is therefore a process in which community actors themselves decide when and where to look when executing monitoring and surveillance techniques. Since this is most of the time lacking in current prescribed policies, ultimately it leads to the construction of a deviant 'other' – in this case Muslims. Counter-radicalization measures therefore function as a political tool and a form of social control through which community actors therefore construct, through their practices a reality in which, mostly young, Dutch, Muslims are the 'risky' suspects of radicalization.

Trust as a capital that can be lost

According to our respondents, the credibility of local institutions and the relations of trust between community actors and the public is severely undermined because of the combination of preventive and repressive measures to counter radicalization. Because of this combination, community actors do not only need to build a relationship with community members, but also monitor them for possible signs of radicalization. This contradiction not only appears to undermine their credibility but also the more utilitarian functions of community policing, such as the collection of information from 'community partners'. Security actors therefore try to emphasize the preventive role of their activities. As a local policy advisor on safety states,

> 'We as a municipality really want to turn to those preventive measures instead of repression. We do not believe in repression' (interview, 30 April 2015). This is also illustrated by a policy advisor on radicalization: 'The most sustainable task or instrument for municipalities lies with prevention'.
>
> interview, 17 April 2015

A manager of a social welfare organization adds:

> When it comes to radicalization ... we are not the Muslim investigation bureau, as I would call it. We don't have the competencies for that and we don't want to be that! Because then you get a whole other role in the society and then you lose a lot of trust and then you aren't able anymore to do the things in which you are now successful.
>
> interview, 29 May 2015

A manager from a social welfare organization underlines the struggles community actors face when they are combining repressive and preventive measures in practice:

> All organizations are searching for how to talk about this subject, how they should combine prevention and repression. They need to wonder whether repression would still make prevention possible. You really need to think this through. Especially when we talk about prevention, trust is very important. If the youngsters do not trust you . . . you can try whatever you want . . . it will have little effect on those youngsters and parents because they do not trust you anymore.
>
> interview, 29 May 2015

Moreover,

> It is not our purpose to get people arrested. That is not our goal. So we need to balance that out and we need to be aware about it. . . . We are not committed to monitoring . . . This way you can lose trust and stop a conversation. That is the last thing we want. They could think like, 'this organization will monitor us'.
>
> interview, 29 May 2015

As a result of this new repressive role they are asked to carry out, local actors have become aware of the high risk of losing their credibility within the community. In order to cope with this, they deliberately amplify the role they believe best suits their intentions and actions. This is illustrated by a local policy advisor on radicalization:

> 'We are not an extension of the government. We have our own role. It is also a choice that we do not want to have that other role. That is our credit, our credibility. Like I said, trust is our biggest capital' (interview, 29 May 2015). And a youth worker states, 'Sometimes you need to seem real and sometimes you need to seem artificially real, but at the end of day you should always try to act as yourself'.
>
> interview, 29 January 2016

When they do not amplify their role, community actors believe there will be the risk of misplaced distrust in the institution, its credibility and therefore its function as an executor of counter-radicalization policies. This is illustrated by a local policy advisor:

> Trust is very important but that remains difficult. You see, the municipality and the police are part of the government and not everyone is willing to report a problem there. And that will remain, and therefore we try to get in touch with people in the districts who can make that connection. Furthermore, if people are being watched by the community as informants or police agents, then they no longer have a function. Then you are done!
>
> interview, 23 April 2015

A manager of a social welfare organization echoes these concerns:

> They have the idea that they cannot go to the municipality – often that is one step too high – sometimes it is because of a language barrier, otherwise they have the idea that their passport will be taken away from them if they go there. That is what they think.
>
> interview, 29 May 2015

Faced with the contradiction embedded within counter-radicalization policies, community and local actors are well aware of the fact of being seen as extensions of the police or the intelligence services. This not only makes their work difficult, it threatens to undermine their standing in the community entirely.

Coping with contradiction: Strategies of 'complicit compliance' and 'wilful ignorance'

In order to cope with this contradiction, community actors therefore develop at least two strategies to comply with their new task of detecting radicalization while maintaining their reputation. The first one could be termed as 'complicit compliance'. While the objective of intelligence gathering is what local actors are officially required to carry out, they are well aware that it cannot be made obvious to the public. A tight inter-agency cooperation – in this case, the process through which social workers, local authority civil servants and ultimately intelligence services will keep the community unaware of the fact that information is being collected about them and shared – becomes the condition of possibility for these local actors to keep the relations of trust intact.

In practice, 'complicit compliance' works through the cooperation between the local partners such as the municipality, neighbourhood police officers and social welfare organizations, and national partners such as the General Intelligence and Security Services of the Netherlands (AIVD), the Public Prosecution Service (OM), the Ministry of Security and Justice, and the National Coordinator for Security and Counterterrorism (NCTV). The notion of 'trust' in these circumstances, takes a different definition – it comes to refer to the trust that actors sharing information will not disclose to the public who reported it. In other words, that the betrayal of trust implied by the logic of suspicion will not be revealed. As one social welfare consultant states,

> When you do report something, and say 'we have done everything when it comes to prevention but it did not work out and I am really worried that something is going to happen'. You should then trust your partner that they will work with it adequately and in a confidential way and that they will not harm the trustful relation that you had built.
>
> interview, 29 May 2015

Yet complicit compliance does not go without challenges and hiccups, and the loss of credibility implied by the betrayal of trust is looming. As one local safety policy advisor underlines,

When you have a bad experience with someone and then the police talks to that person and then suddenly says that the municipality knows everything about the situation and that the person needs to talk to the municipality. Then that person thinks, 'well, I will have a little chat with the municipality tomorrow'.

interview, 30 April 2015

For this reason, not all workers decide to play the part of the compliant civil servant, and in order to keep their reputation intact, choose a second strategy that we label 'wilful ignorance'. It consists, for local actors, in making their public aware that they are in the position to report specific information. Like a youth worker emphasizes, 'Guys, you can tell me everything but I cannot promise that everything you tell me stays within this group. And then it is up to them to share information or not' (interview, 29 January 2016).

Afraid of losing their credibility, community actors see a constant need to explain their intentions and their role:

'You have to have a purpose in order to deal with this tension. You have to make choices, know that you are not always doing it right. You have to talk to them. Every time you have to explain what you are doing. . . . Explain, explain, explain, explain' (interview, 30 April 2015). A policy advisor on radicalization agrees, 'We must keep explaining and you need to be transparent'.

interview, 29 May 2015

Community actors are, however, aware that this might contradict the trust relations they once built. As a social welfare consultant argues,

You should not say to that specific youngster that you are going to report it. When that is out in the open, all the other youngsters will not listen to you.

interview, 30 April 2015

To prevent this, some community actors ask members (implicitly or explicitly) not to mention any fact or intention that might require reporting. A youth worker explains his desire and challenge of keeping his preventive role intact:

But if he says like, 'listen, I have made my decision: I am going to Syria'; well, yeah, then I have a problem. First of all, I say to him that I don't want anything to do with him – 'I cannot help you with anything' – and most importantly I say to him, 'you now tell me something with which I need to do something about'. . . . Before this, I always say, 'listen, whatever choice you make or no matter the path you choose to walk on, never say to me what you are going to do'. I don't want to know what they want to do, because I say this in all transparency to them, but this information is like a burden for me because I need to put it somewhere since I am a professional. But also as a regular citizen, it is your job to report such a thing.

interview, 7 May 2015

Community actors thus prevent getting into situations which might require reporting. This is also highlighted by a social worker, who states that she tries to avoid speaking to certain community members:

'I don't talk to the youngsters … if I do that, then there is something going on' (interview, 21 May 2015). Moreover, 'Most of the time the answer is to avoid the discussion'.

interview, 29 May 2015

In both instances, it therefore emerges that the street-level bureaucrats cannot comply with the contradiction without compromising at least one of the objectives of the policy: they must either misinform the public about the real practices of information sharing, and therefore betray their trust – or, in order to maintain this trust, paradoxically, prevent information from emerging in order to avoid reporting it.

Conclusion

From 2004 onwards, counterterrorism in the Netherlands has increasingly shifted its focus from the national to a local level. As a result, municipalities and other community actors have been responsible for the local delivery of counterterrorism measures, both 'hard' and 'soft'. The delegation of these seemingly contradictory policies to a local level created challenges for the actors involved, at the core of which lies the problematic status of relations of trust. Counter-radicalization requires them to establish and maintain relations of trust while at the same time enacting a logic of suspicion. Contrary to the main interpretations of role status of trust in the counter-radicalization literature, seen either as the basis of partnerships or as that which is sacrificed in order to carry out covert operations, we find that trust is precisely what is targeted by counter-radicalization. Trust is conceptualized as the best way to anticipate and 'feel' the community and therefore the best way to report possible 'weak signals' of a plot or an attack. But in practice it is also understood as a key instrument in the enforcement of social control. The local actors of the Dutch counter-radicalization policy are therefore stuck in a double bind: they must establish relations of trust, but in order to subvert them. As our research finds, while the project appears possible in principle, in reality local actors chose one of two options in order to resolve the contradiction. We termed the first 'complicit compliance', a strategy which consists in complying with the policy, sharing information with security professionals but abstaining from informing their public about it – and therefore betraying their trust. The second strategy, which we termed 'wilful ignorance' consists instead in making it clear to the public that, like during a police arrest, 'anything they say can be held against them', encouraging them therefore not to mention any sensitive information. This, of course, entirely defeats the idea that community actors can capture 'weak signals' or participate in the flow of 'community intelligence'.

In conclusion, we must ask, what then is the alternative? Should nothing be done? The solution offered to us by one of our respondents could highlight a possible way forward, namely to keep 'trust' and 'suspicion' separated. When asked about what could be told to the agents of law enforcement, he suggested the following:

> I would definitely give them the following advice: please let us fulfil our role, let us be the bridge to the street. That would be the only thing . . . let us do our job, let us stay in the role we have. We have common ground when it comes to our mutual concerns, but in the other circle you guys have your own profession. Please stay there and don't hand me anything from your profession which could bother me. The common ground is a place where we can cooperate. That is also . . . they must not obligate us to do something because then you blow those kids away and they will disappear in the underground . . . it will then stay in the underground for a very long time and when it does pop up again, then you have no idea of the consequences. Then you are in real trouble.
>
> interview, 1 May 2015

Notes

1. Phoebe Cooke, 'Newham Imams Oppose "Divisive" Counter-Terrorism Strategy', *Newham Recorder*, January 2016.
2. European Commission, *Preventing Radicalization to Terrorism and Violent Extremism: Strengthening the EU's Response* (Brussels, 2014), p. 6.
3. Baker-Beall, Heath-Kelly and Jarvis, eds., *Counter-Radicalisation*.
4. See, in this context, Heath-Kelly, 'Can We Laugh Yet?'; De Goede and Simon, 'Governing Future Radicals in Europe'; Christopher Baker-Beall, 'The European Union's Fight against Terrorism: A Critical Discourse Analysis' (PhD diss., Loughborough University, 2010); George Kassimeris and Leonie Jackson, 'British Muslims and the Discourses of Dysfunction: Community Cohesion and Counterterrorism in the West Midlands', *Critical Studies on Terrorism* 5, no. 2 (2012): 179–96; Richard Jackson, 'An Analysis of EU Counterterrorism Discourse Post-September 11', *Cambridge Review of International Affairs* 20, no. 2 (2007): 233–47; and Hakimeh Saghaye-Biria, 'American Muslims as Radicals? A Critical Discourse Analysis of the US Congressional Hearing on "The Extent of Radicalization in the American Muslim Community and that Community's Response"', *Discourse & Society* 23, no. 5 (2012): 508–24.
5. Michael Lipsky, *Street-Level Bureaucracy* (New York: Russell Sage Foundation, 1980).
6. See, for instance, Lasse Lindekilde, 'Value for Money? Problems of Impact Assessment of Counter-Radicalization Policies on End Target Groups: The Case of Denmark', *European Journal on Criminal Policy and Research* 18, no. 4 (2012): 385–402; Paul Thomas, *Responding to the Threat of Violent Extremism* (London: Bloomsbury Academic, 2012); Gabe Mythen and Palash Kamruzzaman, 'Counter-Terrorism and Community Relations: Anticipatory Risk, Regulation and Justice', in *Regulation and Criminal Justice: Innovations in Policy and Research*, eds. Hannah Quirk, Toby Seddon and Graham Smith (Cambridge: Cambridge University Press, 2014); and Lee Jarvis and

Michael Lister, 'Disconnected Citizenship? The Impacts of Anti-Terrorism Policy on Citizenship in the UK', *Political Studies* 61, no. 3 (2013): 656–75.

7   See Didier Bigo, 'The (In)Securitization Practices of the Three Universes of EU Border Control: Military/Navy – Border Guards/Police – Database Analysts', *Security Dialogue* 45, no. 3 (2014): 209–25; Federica Infantino, 'La frontière au guichet', *Champ Pénal/ Penal Field* 7 (2010). Available at http://journals.openedition.org/champpenal/7864 (accessed 8 March 2018); Karine Côté-Boucher, Federica Infantino and Mark B. Salter, 'Border Security as Practice: An Agenda for Research', *Security Dialogue* 45, no. 3 (2014): 195–208; and Julien Jeandesboz, 'Beyond the Tartar Steppe: EUROSUR and the Ethics of European Border Control Practices', in *Europe under Threat? Security, Migration and Integration*, eds. J. Peter Burgess and Serge Gutwirth (Brussels: VUB Press, 2011).

8   Association of Dutch Municipalities (*Vereniging van Nederlandse Gemeenten*, VNG), 'Aanpak radicalisering: samenspel tussen gemeenten en Rijk essentieel' (The Hague: VNG, 2014).

9   National Coordinator for Security and Counterterrorism (NCTV), *National Counterterrorism Strategy, 2011–2015* (The Hague: NCTV, 2011).

10 Marianne van Leeuwen, *Confronting Terrorism: European Experiences, Threat Perceptions and Policies* (The Hague: Kluwer Law International, 2003), p. 147.

11 Ministry of Security and Justice, 'Counterterrorism Measures in the Netherlands in the First Decade of the 21st Century: On the Cause, Application, and Amendment of Counterterrorism Measures in the Netherlands 2001–2010', *Council of Europe Counter-Terrorism* (2010). Available at http://www.coe.int/t/dlapil/codexter/Source/ Working_Documents/2011/CT_Measures_Netherlands.pdf (accessed 8 March 2018), p. 44.

12 NCTV, *National Counterterrorism Strategy, 2011–2015*.

13 VNG, 'Aanpak radicalisering: samenspel tussen gemeenten en Rijk essentieel'.

14 Dick Schoof, 'We zijn niet naïef', *Binnenlands Bestuur* (2014). Available at http://www. binnenlandsbestuur.nl/bestuur-en-organisatie/achtergrond/achtergrond/we-zijn-niet-naief.9456951.lynkx (accessed 8 March 2018).

15 Tapio Juntunen and Ari-Elmeri Hyvönen, 'Resilience, Security and the Politics of Processes', *Resilience: International Policies, Practices and Discourses* 2, no. 3 (2014): 195–209; and Markus Crepaz, *Trust Beyond Borders: Immigration, the Welfare State, and Identity in Modern Societies* (Ann Arbor, MI: University of Michigan Press, 2008).

16 Ibid.

17 Van Leeuwen, *Confronting Terrorism*, p. 148; and Ministry of Security and Justice, 'Counterterrorism measures in the Netherlands', p. 13.

18 Ibid.

19 Ibid., p. 43.

20 Ibid., p. 44.

21 VNG, 'Aanpak radicalisering', p. 1.

22 NCTV, *National Counterterrorism Strategy, 2011–2015*, p. 8.

23 Spalek and Lambert, 'Muslim Communities, Counter-Terrorism and Counter-Radicalisation'; Basia Spalek, 'Community Policing, Trust, and Muslim Communities in Relation to "New Terrorism"', *Politics & Policy* 38, no. 4 (2010): 789–815; Robert Lambert, *Countering Al-Qaeda in London: Police and Muslims in Partnership* (London: Hurst, 2011); Basia Spalek and Laura Zahra McDonald, 'Terrorism and Counterterrorism: Spotlight on Strategies and Approaches', *Arches Quarterly* 5, no. 9

(2012): 20–8; and Debbie A. Ramirez, Sasha Cohen O'Connell and Rabia Zafar, *Developing Partnerships between Law Enforcement and American Muslim, Arab, and Sikh Communities: A Promising Practices Guide* (Boston, MA: Northeastern University, 2004).

24 Thomas, *Responding to the Threat of Violent Extremism.*

25 Monica den Boer, 'Wake-Up Call for the Lowlands: Dutch Counterterrorism from a Comparative Perspective', *Cambridge Review of International Affairs* 20, no. 2 (2007): 285–302.

26 See Arun Kundnani, *Spooked! How Not to Prevent Violent Extremism* (London: Institute of Race Relations, 2009); and Kundnani, *The Muslims Are Coming!*

27 See Christina Pantazis and Simon Pemberton, 'From the "Old" to the "New" Suspect Community: Examining the Impacts of Recent UK Counter-Terrorist Legislation', *The British Journal of Criminology* 49, no. 5 (2009): 646–66; and David Miller and Rizwaan Sabir, 'Counter-Terrorism as Counterinsurgency in the UK "War on Terror"', in *Counter-Terrorism and State Political Violence: The 'War on Terror' as Terror*, eds. Scott Poynting and David Whyte (London: Routledge, 2013).

28 Adam Crawford, *The Local Governance of Crime: Appeals to Community and Partnerships* (Oxford: Oxford University Press, 1999).

29 For key texts on trust, see, among others, Barbara A. Misztal, *Trust in Modern Societies: The Search for the Bases of Social Order* (Cambridge: Polity Press, 1996); Seligman, *The Problem of Trust* (Princeton, NJ: Princeton University Press, 1997); Sztompka, *Trust: A Sociological Theory* (Cambridge: Cambridge University Press, 2000); Geschiere, *Witchcraft, Intimacy, and Trust: Africa in Comparison* (Chicago, IL: University of Chicago Press, 2013).

30 Guido Möllering, 'The Nature of Trust: From Georg Simmel to a Theory of Expectation, Interpretation and Suspension', *Sociology* 35, no. 2 (2001): 403–20.

31 Georg Simmel, *The Philosophy of Money* (London: Routledge, 1990), p. 178.

32 Möllering, 'The Nature of Trust', p. 405.

33 Georg Simmel, *The Philosophy of Money*, p. 179.

34 Niklas Luhmann, *Trust and Power: Two Works* (Chichester and New York: John Wiley & Sons, 1979), p. 10.

35 Ibid., p. 10.

36 Émile Durkheim, *The Division of Labor in Society* (New York: Free Press, 1997).

37 Max Weber, *Economy and Society*; and Michael Mann, *The Sources of Social Power* (Cambridge: Cambridge University Press, 1986).

38 On this ambivalent relation, see Michel Foucault, *Discipline & Punish: The Birth of the Prison* (New York: Vintage Books, 1975); and authors who have pursued his main lines of investigation such as Jacques Donzelot, *The Policing of Families* (New York: Pantheon Books, 1979); David Garland, *The Culture of Control: Crime and Social Order in Contemporary Society* (Oxford: Oxford University Press, 2001); Stanley Cohen, *Visions of Social Control: Crime, Punishment and Classification* (Cambridge: Polity Press, 1985); John Muncie, *Youth and Crime* (London: Sage, 2004); Adam Crawford, *Crime Prevention Policies in Comparative Perspective* (Cullompton: Willan, 2009).

39 Stephen A. Saltzburg, 'Privileges and Professionals: Lawyers and Psychiatrists', *Virginia Law Review* 66, no. 3 (1980), p. 603.

40 M. A. Rothstein, 'Privacy and Confidentiality', in *Routledge Handbook of Medical Law and Ethics*, eds. Y. Joly and B. M. Knoppers (Oxon and New York: Routledge, 2014).

41 J. Wright, 'Priestly Silence: A Study of the Ministerial Experience of Confidentiality' (PhD diss., Princeton University, 2000).

42 Robert K. Merton, Vanessa Merton and Elinor Barber, 'Client Ambivalence in Professional Relationships: The Problem of Seeking Help from Strangers', in *New Directions in Helping*, Vol. 2, ed. Bella M. DePaulo (New York: Academic Press, 1983), p. 34.

43 Cynthia Bisman, 'Personal Information and the Professional Relationship: Issues of Trust, Privacy and Welfare', in *Private and Confidential? Handling Personal Information in Social and Health Services*, eds. Chris Clark and Janice McGhee (Bristol: Policy Press, 2008), p. 24.

44 Schmid, 'Radicalization, Counter-Radicalization', p. 50.

45 Institute for Strategic Dialogue (ISD), *European Counter-Radicalization and De-Radicalization: A Comparative Evaluation of Approaches in the Netherlands, Sweden, Denmark and Germany* (London: ISD, 2014).

46 Ibid., p. 4.

47 National Coordinator for Security and Counterterrorism (NCTV), *Actieprogramma Integrale Aanpak Jihadisme: overzicht maatregelen en acties* (Den Haag, 2014a); and National Coordinator for Security and Counterterrorism (NCTV), *Handreiking aanpak van radicalisering en terrorismebestrijding op local niveau* (Den Haag, 2014b).

48 NCTV, *Actieprogramma Integrale Aanpak Jihadisme*; NCTV, *Handreiking aanpak van radicalisering*.

49 NCTV, *Actieprogramma Integrale Aanpak Jihadisme*, p. 2.

50 Ibid., p. 32.

51 Ibid., p. 31.

52 NCTV, *Handreiking aanpak van radicalisering*, p. 38.

Chapter 7

(DE-)RADICALIZATION AS A NEGOTIATED PRACTICE: AN ETHNOGRAPHIC CASE STUDY IN FLANDERS

Silke Jaminé and Nadia Fadil[1]

In the spring of 2013, several Belgian media outlets started covering the stories of Jejoen Bontinck and Brian de Mulder, two Flemish converts who had left the country to join the Islamic revolutionary forces in Syria in their jihad against Bashar al-Assad. These two young men had converted to Islam as teenagers and became members of the controversial movement Sharia4Belgium. By the end of 2012, the two boys had left for Syria to join the battle against Assad together with other Sharia4Belgium members. The moving testimonies of the (grand-)parents of the two boys in the national press and Bontinck's father's desperate attempts to bring his son back home (in which he succeeded) provoked a large debate on Islamic radicalization in Flanders – Belgium's largest and most prosperous region. The phenomenon of the Syria foreign fighters or 'Syria warriors' – as they were called in the Flemish-Belgian media – had already started garnering public attention in the autumn of 2012. Yet the media coverage of this new development had been cursory, owing to the fact that at the time the reach of this phenomenon was still unknown and, furthermore, several analysts were still dubious in relating to the idea of foreign fighters in Syria. But with the publication of the stories of Jejoen Bontinck and Brian de Mulder, a large societal debate ensued concerning the problem of 'radicalization', which also brought the reality of Syria foreign fighters 'close to home'. The story of these two young, 'average', Flemish boys turned them into iconic symbols – representing the idea that the danger of 'radicalization' could happen to 'any of us'. The idea that the threat of radicalism was far away, or only a concern of 'immigrants', could no longer be maintained.

With its approximately 500 'foreign terrorist fighters' in Syria,[2] Belgium figured as the number one Western European sending country between 2012 and 2016.[3] This produced an onslaught of national, and international, attention and various analysts have speculated about the reasons behind it. The killing of four people in the Jewish Museum in Brussels on 24 May 2014 and the direct implication of Belgian-Maghrebi in the attacks on Paris on 13 November 2015 and on Brussels on 22 March 2016 have furthermore spurred the idea that there is a problem of 'jihadism' and 'Islamic radicalism' in the country that has been neglected by local authorities. The reputation of Belgium, and especially Brussels, as a logistical platform for terrorism and a hotbed of Islamic radicalism is not new. The small size of the country, which is bordered by the North Sea, France, the Netherlands, Luxemburg and Germany, renders it a strategic location and easy zone of transit for all kinds of activities. The idea that the country serves as a logistical platform for terrorist and illegal actions towards France by Islamist groups was put forward by analysts already in the nineties.[4] This reputation of Brussels furthermore also builds on to older dystopian imaginaries that have prevailed over the city, not least in the relationship to Islamism.[5] Since the late eighties, several local politicians have routinely warned that Muslim fundamentalists were extending their reach into the city: the demonstrations in Brussels in 1986, attended by a large crowd of Muslims who supported the Libyan leader Muammar Qaddafi in opposition to the American attacks, is a case in point. This event, which was reported by the Belgian media with a sense of alarm, triggered worrisome comments by politicians and analysts.[6] But with the phenomenon of the so-called 'Syria foreign fighters', a renewed sense of urgency on the need for effective measures was heightened, which translated into to the deployment and adoption of counter-radicalization policies. These measures were initially developed at a local level. The city of Antwerp was pioneering in this respect, as it initiated the first series of activities in 2012.[7] Soon after, the need for more adequate measures started spreading to other Flemish and Belgian cities as they became increasingly confronted with a relatively important departure of youngsters to Syria (especially from the city of Vilvoorde).

This chapter examines the ways in which deradicalization policies are implemented and negotiated at a local level in a specific organization, *Naamloos*, located in a Flemish town we will call here *the City*.[8] Existing research on counter-radicalization policies has generally tended to examine the ways in which such policies have resulted in a growing securitization of cultural diversity,[9] the creation of 'suspect communities',[10] and/or the co-optation and implication of Muslim and non-Muslim actors in a top-down seated policy.[11] Lesser attention has, however, been accorded to how these practices are negotiated and implemented by policymakers and community workers on the ground.[12] Drawing on one year of anthropological fieldwork among city officials and social workers between 2014 and 2015, this chapter seeks to show how the politics of deradicalization need to be approached as a negotiated practice, where its implementation occurs through the constant interrogation of its object, methods and aims.

The chapter will be organized as follows. In the first part we will offer a brief review of the literature, paying particular attention to the kind of research that has been conducted on similar public policies elsewhere in Europe (most notably in the UK). In this first part, we will also introduce the broader political-anthropological framework that will guide us throughout this chapter and argue that the heightened emphasis on autonomy is a key instance through which state-based initiatives become implemented on the ground. The second part of this chapter will, in turn, offer a brief sketch of the history of Belgian deradicalization policies, with an emphasis on the region of Flanders, where the discussed case study is situated. The third and fourth part of this chapter will offer some ethnographic insights into the practices of negotiation that are at the heart of the local agency of the social workers on the ground. One of the central observations that runs through these different descriptions is the persistent attempt and desire by the youth workers to demarcate themselves from the state by asserting their autonomy. Most notably, our attention will be oriented towards the competing frameworks adopted on the ground (the 'harm' vs. the 'vulnerability' framework), as well as the self-techniques through which the social workers came to demarcate themselves as experts.

Deradicalization and the anthropology of 'the state'

Conventional views on policymaking and the state tend to imagine the latter as a hierarchical structure wherein local civil servants put the decisions that are adopted by policymakers into action. Such a perspective also draws on an understanding of the state that is viewed as a 'discrete entity' that exists through a series of bureaucratic procedures that are implemented in a fairly straightforward manner. This traditional conception is largely inspired by a Weberian model,[13] being that Weber was one of the first to conceptualize bureaucracy as the defining structure of modern liberal society.[14] Bureaucracy is then primarily characterized by its insistence on a-personal, abstract and routinized rules, which become implemented. The individuality of the person is seen to disappear while only their hierarchical role prevails. Such state-centric perspectives and top-down views on the workings of bureaucracy have however been challenged over the years. An important reference in this respect is Lipsky's study *Street-Level Bureaucracy*.[15] In this seminal work, the political scientist introduces the central role of discretion and low-level personnel in making the bureaucratic system tangible:

> Most citizens encounter government (if they encounter it at all) not through letters to congressmen or by attendance at school board meetings but through their teachers and their children's teachers and through the policeman on the corner or in the patrol car. Each encounter of this kind represents an instance of policy delivery.[16]

This view, which looks at local practices, does not consider the state as pre-given, but rather understands the latter as a series of discrete practices that are embodied by the civil servants. The lower-level bureaucrats become, thus, the emblematic and concrete manifestation of what the state is and, accordingly, research attends to the level of discretion of civil servants and how front-line workers practically negotiate decision making on the ground.[17]

Such a line of inquiry has also been adopted in the recent studies on de/radicalization. Several studies, especially in Britain, have examined the ways in which deradicalization policies are implemented on the ground. Much attention has been given to the programme PREVENT, one of the sub-programmes of

Britain's counterterrorism strategy CONTEST, which was implemented in 2003. An important aim of this programme is to anticipate the possible use of violence through the reinforcement of social cohesion programmes and community work, which at the same time act as intelligence gathering devices. This programme has been sharply critiqued by many scholars, not in the least because of the securitization it entails of social and community work and the (at times explicit) targeting of Muslims.[18] Whereas some studies, such as that from O'Toole, DeHanas Nilsson and Modood[19] and that from Thomas,[20] have attended to the various revisions of this programme (especially after 2010), and the subsequent attempts to separate security-related matters from social cohesion, the securitizing lens that informs the whole programme and the continuous suspicion of particular communities is considered as a structural hallmark of the programme.

Some of these studies have also attended to the ways in which civil servants and other front-line workers have implemented these programmes on the ground. One of them is the study by Husband and Alam,[21] who have examined the implementation of PREVENT by a number of local governments in five metropolitan cities. They note that despite the large degree of autonomy and discretion that initially characterized the adoption of this programme by the local authorities, there is a series of tensions that are created by the obligation to report that is entailed in these programmes, as the front-line workers are caught between that obligation and their desire to maintain relationships of trust with the local communities.[22] They also note how the initial refusal expressed by several local stakeholders to collaborate with these programmes was disregarded for a more pragmatic approach.[23] Overall, a complex picture is painted wherein the money awarded in the framework of PREVENT seems to be recuperated for a wide array of purposes, not least the reinforcement of various new forms of collaboration at a local level.[24] Similar insights also emerge from Paul Thomas's study, which argues that 'significant variations' exist 'in how local authorities have actually so far operationalized the programme and how they have actually allocated the PREVENT funding coming from central government'.[25] Thomas even stresses the ambivalent effects of these policies, as they often also result in the strengthening of local agency and the creation of 'new "governance spaces"' for Muslim community organizations.[26]

Whereas the focus on street-level bureaucrats does well in displacing the analytical lens onto the everyday practices of civil servants instead of simply assuming the direct application of these orders, it still presupposes the existence of the state as a reified entity and draws on the idea of a direct connection between the 'state' and the 'civil servants'. Such a perspective, however, does not entirely fit with the reality we encountered, nor the complex institutional character of Flemish public organizations. Most non-profit organizations that take up public tasks are VZW's (*Vereniging Zonder Winstoogmerk* – Non-Profit Organizations) but these cannot be compared to non-governmental organizations (NGO's). They do not work separately from the government since most of their funds come from governments on different levels and they are mandated to implement governmental policies. Yet this does not make them explicit agents of the state apparatus either.

Rather, these organizations draw on a combination of structural and project-based funds from the different governments to take up public tasks that are autonomously defined. In so doing, the ability to articulate their own orientation and act autonomously from 'the state' towards their clientele is a constitutive hallmark of the way in which the field is structured. Such an understanding of public policies comes close to the perspective proposed by Sharma and Gupta who consider the idea of the state as 'an effect of everyday practices, representational discourses and multiple modalities of power'.[27] In their work, the anthropologists propose an alternative view on the understanding of state politics by moving away from a state-centric approach in which the state is represented as a discrete entity. Rather, the state is seen here as an ensemble of relations between social actors, and therefore the challenge consists of understanding how this idea of the state – as a vertical and superseding actor – becomes constructed in everyday interactions.[28]

Such a decentred approach to the state, which attends to the multi-layered and complex articulations between various social actors (so-called state and non-state actors), has particularly been central in the body of literature on *governmentalization*.[29] This literature has been particularly prone to examining the gradual restructuring of the state into public/private partnerships[30] and the heightened focus on efficiency, responsibilization and autonomy of the 'civil society'.[31] Sharma and Gupta's work is equally located within these changing dynamics of transnationalism and neoliberalism whereby key tasks that were initially assigned to locally embedded administrations have become outsourced.[32] Yet an essential characteristic of their work is that this orientation also fits into a broader anthropological purpose of understanding 'how "the state" and its boundaries are culturally constructed'.[33] This anthropological shift unpacks the assumed existence of 'the state' by paying attention to the various ways in which this idea of the state becomes reiterated and enacted in everyday settings. This means looking at actors and tensions that are constitutive of the state, the cultural variations on this idea of the state (thus moving away from the normative dichotomy of 'weak' vs. 'strong' states), as well as an interest into how these boundaries between 'state' and 'non-state' actors are reproduced on the ground.[34] It is this latter focus on boundary drawing in particular that will be of crucial interest for the present chapter.[35] By applying this framework to public policies on deradicalization and attending to the ways in which they are being implemented, our chapter seeks to show how the idea of both partnership *and* difference was at the heart of *Naamloos'* adoption of these policies. Indeed, it was through a heightened awareness and insistence upon their local autonomy and agency that the team of *Naamloos* engaged with this question of radicalization – which occurred through an explicit demarcation from the state agents of *the City*. Yet instead of viewing these instances of demarcations simply as a subversion or overthrow of the deradicalization framework, we take them as the mechanism through which (state-subsidized) policies concerning deradicalization become enacted on the ground. In other words, the practices of negotiation were, in this context, the means through which the framework of radicalization became articulated.[36]

The ethnographic data gathered for this chapter draws upon participant observation of the staff meetings at *Naamloos*, interviews with their coordinators and the activities of a civil servant who served as head of the deradicalization programme in *the City*. During a period of one year, we participated in the activities organized by the team of *Naamloos* and were able to witness the different negotiations in which they assessed the different cases that were relegated to them by the city officials.[37] As an independent and well-established youth organization, with a specialization in intercultural affairs, the organization was awarded a budget to provide deradicalization training to youngsters who had been identified by the civil servants of *the City* as potentially 'radicalized'. One of the central aims in our analysis will be to understand how such negotiations were part of the routines performed by *Naamloos* in its implementation of deradicalization coaching trajectories. As we will try to show, a consistent manoeuvring of this 'independence' and 'autonomy' was at the heart of the daily operations of the organization. We want to argue that this independence was articulated on two levels. The first one was performed at a discursive level, i.e. by critically negotiating the framework of radicalization. A second point of demarcation occurred in their daily practices as 'professionals', 'experts' and trustworthy 'social workers' (that were not civil servants). By paying attention to these negotiations and demarcations, our aim is to understand how deradicalization gains its influence precisely through its capacity to enable a loose understanding between competing actors.

Deradicalization as a 'local affair'

The fear of radicalization, as a quickly spreading 'virus' among Muslim youngsters,[38] took off in Flanders in the autumn of 2012. On a sunny Saturday in September, which coincided with the yearly fair and *Reuzenstoet* (Giants' parade) in Borgerhout, text messages calling upon Muslims to publicly demonstrate against the movie *The Innocence of Muslims* were circulating. The movie was released on the internet earlier that summer and portrayed the life of Prophet Muhammad in a way that was seen as very controversial. Because of a resemblance to the Danish Cartoon controversy a few years earlier, many officials and commentators feared that the release of the movie would instigate new forms of violence. The text messages that circulated that day were known to originate from Sharia4Belgium, a controversial movement whose leader Fouad Belkacem (aka Abou Imraan) had been condemned a few months earlier for encouraging violence.[39] Several hundred youngsters showed up on that Saturday afternoon, which led to public confrontations with the police. About a hundred were arrested and fined, and several were also subjected to interviews by civil servants who had already been alarmed by the growing influence of Sharia4Belgium.[40] The stories that came out of the interviews confirmed the fears of the civil servants that, in their view, a significant number of Antwerp youth were prone to a 'radicalized' mindset. On the basis of these findings, the civil servants from the *Dienst 'Samenleving en Opbouw'* ('Society and Construction' Office) decided to act quickly and create a 'cell' devoted to the problem of radicalization. In so doing, they also created the first official public initiative on this question in the country.[41] Shortly after its creation, the information on the first departures of foreign fighters for Syria reached the city officials, which resulted in a further expansion of the initiative. Other cities like Vilvoorde would also follow the lead of Antwerp as the phenomenon grew in magnitude and reached other cities.

The example of Antwerp and the bottom-up approach of the first deradicalization initiatives is characteristic of the ways in which these policies took off in Belgium and continue to be organized and managed in the country. In contrast to the UK, the Netherlands or France, where deradicalization initiatives were implemented by central governments, the Belgian case is characterized by a complex patchwork of initiatives that involve both state and non-state actors and are organized at different governmental levels. This is partially due to the history of the first initiatives, but also due to the complex nature of the political and institutional landscape of the country. The cities and the local authorities have consistently been positioned as privileged and guiding actors (*regie*) on deradicalization, not least due to their proximity with the concerned communities.[42] A clear example of this is the publication of a brochure in July 2013 that was co-authored by four mayors – all from different political parties – from four different cities (Mechelen, Antwerp, Vilvoorde and Maaseik).[43] The publication of this brochure equally set the tone for a new series of collaborations implemented at a local level with the support of the federal Belgian authorities. The strong emphasis on the local level does not mean, however, that the other levels of competence were simply dismissed. In addition to these sets of local initiatives, the federal and regional authorities have both consistently sought to position themselves as players on the field, especially from 2013 onwards.

At the federal level, the first steps towards a policy on deradicalization were already initiated in 2002. The events of 9/11 and the growing concerns about terrorism figured as an important impetus behind the first national security plan entitled 'Plan M' (*Plan Mosquées*) in 2002. In 2005, a more expansive version of this plan was developed within the framework of new antiterrorism legislation and initiatives, which also included a series of preventive measures on radicalization (the first 'Plan R') and the creation of a coordinating agency on issues of security, the OCAD/OCAM (*Orgaan voor de Coordinatie en Analyse van Dreiging/Organ de Coordination pour l'Analyse de la Menace*)-Coordination Body for Threat Analysis in 2006.[44] These developments were partially instigated by the presence of local cells of the GICM (*Groupe Islamique Combatant Marocain*) in Brussels and Maaseik, a Moroccan branch of al-Qaeda that was also considered to be behind the attacks in Casablanca in May 2003 and Madrid in March 2004. Since its first introduction, in 2005, this 'Plan R' has been subjected to various revisions. In 2012, for instance, the issue of 'radical extremism' became more acute as new groupings such as Sharia4Belgium became a more prominent source of concern. Yet with the departure of foreign fighters for Syria in 2013, and the attacks of Paris in 2015 and Brussels in 2016, more visible and public measures were adopted which included subsidies given to local authorities and police forces (such as the 'Plan Canal' in Brussels, installed in 2016). This emphasis on collaboration and information exchange was at the heart of the governmental declaration of October 2014, entitled *Integral Approach Radicalism* (*Integrale Aanpak Radicalisering/Approche Intégrale Radicalisation*),[45] and was accentuated in the later revisions of Plan R in 2016.[46] A two-pronged approach informs the current federal policy on deradicalization. The first part consists of an intensified vertical collaboration between the local and federal police services in terms of information gathering and the follow-up of certain cases. This occurs through the *National Task Force* (NTF), which is officially designated as the general management and follow-up of Plan R and the *Local Task Forces* (LTF), who fall under the authority of the NTF and whose main function is to guarantee the implementation of these policies and to stimulate information exchange between the higher and the lower levels. The horizontal level consists, in turn, of the *Local Integral Security Cells* (*Locale Integrale Veiligheidscel* – LIVC/ *Cellule de Sécurité Intégrale Locale* – CSIL), local platforms of exchange between social workers, stakeholders, deradicalization officers and representatives from the mayor's office, or the mayors themselves. The creation of such a platform and its composition belongs to the discretion of the local authorities, but the main function is to facilitate communication and signal potentially problematic cases.

At the level of the regional governments in general, and Flanders in particular, a similar privileged attention is accorded to the local authorities, combined with more sustained efforts in coordinating the circulation of the available information and the interaction between the different stakeholders. The different measures adopted by the Flemish government are included in the plan *Actieplan ter preventie van radicaliseringsprocessen die kunnen leiden tot extremism en terrorisme* (Actionplan for the prevention of processes of radicalization that can lead to extremism and terrorism), launched in January 2015.[47] This plan consists firstly of an attempt to coordinate and reinforce the existing expertise and to stimulate the circulation of information between local, regional agencies (such as schools, youth organizations) and federal authorities (such as the OCAD and the police). This is to be done through the creation of platforms of exchanges and the reinforcement of the existing networks of collaboration. A second important part of the plan consists of subsidies for the local authorities, also aiming at reinforcing the collaboration between the regional and local authorities. A final part of the plan focuses more on the religious denominations (training of imams) and making links with the (Muslim) youth (such as through the creation of a Network of Islam experts for the schools).

Negotiating 'radicalization'

B: The evolution of radicalism in this case is unclear. The behaviour towards his parents might change, but he is growing a beard again.

A: His beard is not as long as mine. The fact that he is growing a beard again, that he is praying ... must be stimulated. He must feel accepted as a good Muslim.

> Heads-up by youth coach A and family coach B of a family
> coaching process to C, the coordinator of this deradicalization
> programme, 4 December 2014

In the aftermath of the Bontinck and De Mulder cases – and many cases publicized in the media that would follow – the need for programmes that catered to youth (and their families) who might want to leave for Syria became of urgent concern. Many believed that the departure for Syria indicated a process of radicalization that could be tackled if properly identified. According to this vision, radicalization figures as a stairway process wherein different phases or steps will eventually lead to violent extremism.[48] The departure for Syria was understood by many as an extreme expression of radicalization, and the conviction grew that it would become much harder to turn the process back once these youngsters had been introduced to the violence in Syria. The civil servants thus considered the implementation of preventive coaching programmes that could prevent any further escalation, and even bring youngsters a few steps back in the process of radicalization, as important.

Naamloos was one of the first organizations in Flanders to benefit from subsidies given explicitly for work on radicalization – and as such, their coaching trajectories were a test case that was monitored closely by city officials and other stakeholders in the field of youth work. Their main task was very clear: they should stop youngsters from leaving and relieve the stress on their families. To reach this aim, they worked together with the city officials who received the calls from parents and teachers and then forwarded the ones they deemed eligible to *Naamloos*. Yet this relegation from the city officials to the social workers was far from straightforward, as is shown in the introductory quote to this section. In their everyday practices, the team of *Naamloos* maintained a critical distance from the (de-)radicalization framework by questioning whether the cases they had in front of them could be understood as such. A critical engagement with the framework of radicalization thus informed their daily practices. They would, on the one hand, acknowledge the existence of 'common' signals – like an interest in Salafism or growing a beard. Yet on the other hand, the precise meaning of these particular signals or indicators would also constantly be questioned, or even ridiculed. The publication of the brochure by the four mayors in the spring of 2013,[49] for instance, triggered quite a few instances of mockery by the staff members of *Naamloos*. Team members of *Naamloos*, of whom many were Muslim, would, for instance, dispute some of the 'signs of radicalization' that were identified in the brochure by making reference to their own beards, jokingly commenting that theirs were longer. These negotiations of radicalization were very consciously made, and understood by the staff members themselves as a form of activism: they understood their political role as one of critically examining and, if possible, challenging the framework that was proposed. The ethnographic vignette below offers a good illustration of how these negotiations took place.

During one of the weekly meetings and intakes of *Naamloos*, a particular case was discussed and brought forward by one of the staff members. It concerned family M. They had approached the civil servant because the parents feared that their son, R., might leave for Syria.[50] The parents had indeed observed some changes in the behaviour of their son. He had started growing a beard, read a lot of Islamic and Salafi-inspired texts and became suspicious of his parents and siblings. One of the parents had reported their son to the civil servant once the boy had stopped attending school. The main reason he stopped going to school was because he had grown convinced that a good Muslim should not be in a class with girls and female teachers. When this case was presented to *Naamloos*, the team agreed that the programme would probably be a good fit for this family and could help them to overcome these conflicts. The family was known as respectable, they had no major social or psychological issues and the 'modern and open' approach of the parents stood in sharp contrast with the sudden religious turn of their son. They considered the parents' concerns thus reasonable and agreed to take up this particular case in their programme. The boy himself, however, was not too keen on being part of such a deradicalization programme. He believed he did not need any extra information on Islam and that there wasn't anything wrong with him. During the intake with the city services a civil servant had noticed a tablet on his bed with an Islamic site opened. This information was shared with the team members of *Naamloos* and one of the coaches used it during their first encounter to initiate a discussion on media and Islam with R., and inquire as to why he considered TV '*haram*' (illicit). During this first meeting the boy repeated he had no wish to leave for Syria. He also stressed that he had no time to follow a coaching programme, because he had started home schooling in order to attend university later.

> **A:** We agreed I would give him some time for reflection. Afterwards he could make his decision and tell me what he will do. At the agreed moment he indeed contacted me. He said he had no time for the coaching as he was preparing for his 'Middenjury' (central exam). I must say I respect his decision, it means that he still wants to graduate. I told him so too. Afterwards I sent him an SMS to reassure him that he could always count on me for help.[51]
> Youth coach A's report to coordinator C, 22 September 2014

A few weeks later, when the coordinator of *Naamloos* met with the civil servant of *the City* to discuss the ongoing cases and possible new intakes, the case of R. was raised. The coordinator reported the findings of coach A: he had met with R. and concluded that there were no grounds to think that there was a problem of radicalization. Rather, the case was framed as an example of a *rebellious* boy who used religion to challenge the authority of his parents. The fact that R. took his studies seriously and was working hard to get his secondary school diploma was also proof of his commitment and that he wouldn't risk leaving for Syria anytime soon. The civil servant listened to the arguments brought forward by the coordinator and agreed with their renewed assessment. They agreed that no further deradicalization was needed in this particular case, not even if the parents kept insisting. The risk that R. would leave or do any harm was seen as not big enough and being a worried parent of a rebellious teen wasn't a valid reason to keep a youngster in such a programme.

> **Civil servant:** If a youngster – who is no longer a minor – is rebellious and acts against his parents, this is not illegal, even if he uses this Salafism to express himself. Maybe we should help the parents cope with this.

Coordinator: They could go to an organization with these questions. Our programme cannot start without the consent of this youngster. This is essential for our programme to start.
Civil servant: Are you worried about him? That he might leave or do any harm?
Coordinator: I don't believe he might, he is very serious about his studies. He was quite open about this to coach A.
Coordinator C reporting to civil servant D, 9 December 2014

The description above, which shows the interactions between the staff of *Naamloos* and the civil servants handling a particular case, demonstrates how the general framing of radicalization given by the city officials and the parents is accepted but then refused through a counter-framing. The reason why the coaches initially accepted this framing was linked with the parents' reputation as caring, liberal and modern. But after meeting with the boy, the coaches concluded that R. didn't qualify for such a framing. An important key argument in this respect is the risk-assessment by the coaches and the conviction that R. wouldn't do any harm, but that his main drive was to gain his diploma and build a future. Whereas such perspectives are indicative of the gradual expansion of risk management within social work and youth work,[52] the example above also shows the presence of competing narratives on the agency of the youngster among the concerned social actors. The parents' (and the civil servant's) perspective initially framed the conduct of the boy in terms of *offence*. This, however, was challenged by the social workers who proposed an alternative framing, i.e. that of 'rebellion'. R. was viewed by coach A as an independent boy, with a solid will of his own, who 'uses religion' to challenge his parents' authority and who has a thirst for knowledge. In opposition to the parents' framing – which entails an idea of *danger*, pathology and wickedness – the notion of rebellion here situates the conduct and behaviour of the youngster within a normal and even healthy life trajectory.

The example above shows how the engagement with the radicalization framework was far from straightforward, but entailed active and complex negotiations on the ground.[53] Yet these negotiations do not mean that the idea of radicalization as a whole was ineffective in conditioning the actions or interpretations of the social workers. The general attitude adopted by the social workers towards the framework of radicalization comes closer, we want to argue, to what Ernesto Laclau and Chantal Mouffe describe as *articulation*. The term articulation was introduced by the two authors in their seminal work *Hegemony and Socialist Strategy*,[54] which laid out the groundwork of a theoretical understanding of hegemony, ideology or – as they prefer to use – 'discourse'.[55] Differing from essentialist perspectives that portray society as being constituted by pre-existing social relations and entities, the approach proposed by Laclau and Mouffe understands the social world as an ensemble of disassembled entities that can occasionally come together in a semblance of unity.[56] It is through *discourse* or ideology that the *articulation* of these heterogeneous elements occurs, or as Stuart Hall, citing Laclau, puts it: 'it succeeds to the extent that it articulates "different ideologies to its hegemonic project by an elimination of their antagonistic character"'.[57] We consider the concept of articulation here a fitting heuristic device to understand how the discourse of radicalization enables a complex assemblage between heterogeneous, and at times, contradictory frameworks and social actors that become centred on the question of risk.

Risk emerges here as a mediating factor that enables the coming together of a series of competing (or even contradictory) frameworks and practices, eventually resulting in the securitization of social work.[58] Imaginaries and languages that would otherwise be incompatible are able to come together because of this collectively shared concern around the radicalizing potential of this particular youngster. In the case of R., the framing of rebellion overturned that of harm. Yet both were articulated in relationship to the risk potentially posed by R. Rather than signalling an either/or, we want to suggest that the framework of radicalization enables a coming together of these perspectives that are no longer considered mutually exclusive but instead become *optional* and complementary. The passage below forms a good example of how such articulations occur and how competing narratives are turned into perspectives. In this case, it is the framing of *vulnerability* that will prevail in the assessment of the social workers.

S. had been reported to the civil servants of *the City* by teachers of his school, with the approval of his parents. Two of his older siblings had left for Syria and at school he had declared he wanted to leave as well. The parents were in bad shape: they not only worried about S., but they were also devastated by the absence of their older children. After a few meetings with the youth coach it appeared that the younger brother was rather heartbroken about the absence of his siblings and did not really wish to leave. Although the coaches had come to the conclusion that the boy wasn't 'radicalized', they nevertheless continued the coaching of this family for another four months. The vulnerability of this family as a whole and the direct help they got from the team (as people who did not judge them as a family of 'terrorists' and supported them in their contact with the older kids) was simply too important for the youth care organization to ignore.

> A: He said out loud he wanted to leave for Syria. But to me he admitted that it was mainly to see his older siblings. He felt like he could share his grief with me, things he could not talk about with others.
> B: Their departure broke his and his mother's heart.
> A: The radicalized mindset is absent in him. A therapeutic consultation could help him to cope.
> Youth coach A chatting to family coach B, 22 April 2014

This concrete case is telling because of the very pronounced presence of *risk* (i.e. a family where several siblings left for Syria), yet with a subsequent emphasis on vulnerability by the social workers. The framework of vulnerability figures as one of the main threads for youth work and other forms of aid-assistance or care that are organized in Western societies. Sharon Stephens argues that the narrative of 'children at risk' – which builds upon the nineteenth-century conceptualization of childhood as a distinct life-stage[59] – gained a particular prominence in the second half of the twentieth century.[60] Children were increasingly seen to be caught in a series of escalating conflicts which challenged an undercurrent theme that accompanied this idea of 'childhood at risk', i.e. the idea of childhood as a 'space of innocence'. In addition to this first articulation, a second would gradually emerge in which the children are not so much seen as being at risk, but rather *as a risk*.[61] This idea has also been captured by Barry Goldson,[62] who notes in his analysis of the evolution of the British youth criminal justice system and the discourse about juvenile delinquency, how the 'offence' perspective had come to prevail throughout the nineties.[63] In the context of Flanders, social work and youth work is largely understood and organized according the theory of *Maatschappelijke Kwetsbaarheid* (social vulnerability). Vulnerable social groups and individuals are, according to this perspective, approached as social groups and individuals who, in their everyday interactions with social institutions, are largely confronted with exclusion and discrimination.[64] The example above offers a good illustration of how a situation that was primarily understood as a potential risk situation becomes reframed into a vulnerability situation. For the youth workers it is not S. himself, but rather the actions of his siblings (who have left for Syria) that are understood to be a 'risk', and it is their influence upon S. that is understood as a potential problem. His desire to follow them is reframed as an expression of brotherly love rather than radicalization. Furthermore, the family of S. is also understood as a risk factor, for they too are seen as being affected by the departure of their children. But although the coaches agree that neither S. nor his family are 'radicalized', they nevertheless deem it necessary to continue their coaching trajectory under this rubric. The grief of the parents and of S. was indeed deemed too important to leave them to themselves. Furthermore, the coaches also insisted on the 'trust' that is given to them by S. and his family, which differs from the teachers and other officials, as S. and his family seemed to find comfort in the coaching process.

The negotiations above are thus illustrative of how this radicalization framework was systematically re-appropriated and expanded in order to include pre-existing accounts that centred on the idea of vulnerability. Time and again, the social workers of *Naamloos* refused a perspective that approached these youngsters simply as dangerous, privileging instead a more complex reading that highlights the multi-layered nature of the problem. It is important to note, though, that in these re-appropriations of the framework, the team members did not simply undo the potential risk factors that are tied to this question. Rather, this question of risk and harm became re-signified into a complex problem that cannot be restricted as a mere concern with religion or danger, but which rather entails the active interactions between a large succession of social problems. It is also in this direction that the coordinator of *Naamloos* concluded, when he stated at an evaluation meeting at the end of their first year, that six out of the seven families they had supervised were not exclusively cases of 'radicalization', but rather what they called 'multi-problem' families:

> When we hear their stories, really traumatic experiences show up. These youngsters feel like they have nothing to lose, radicalism is their last resort. And to be honest, if you hear all these problematic stories you would think 'we need

two years to resolve all of it'. In a phased approach this is not true, we can approach radicalism as an isolated problem and work on it.

Coordinator C, 8 January 2015

Distinguishing oneself as an expert: 'Our recipe to counter radicalization'

The organization *Naamloos* had a strong reputation in the field. Their decade-long experience in culturally-sensitive social work and youth work, had gained them much admiration and respect from their peers. The methods and tools they developed in helping vulnerable youth and families from ethnic-cultural minorities were often considered to be effective and innovative. The bid *Naamloos* won on radicalization, a topic considered highly controversial, was met with a lot of suspicion by fellow social workers, and was therefore challenging. A proper definition of the concept of radicalization was lacking, and the available methodological tools to coach youngsters and their families were still embryonic or unknown. In accepting the task of giving deradicalization training, *Naamloos* was thus faced with the challenge of maintaining its reputation by offering adequate training that would meet the needs of the concerned youth and their families.

This section attends to the various ways in which *Naamloos* sought to craft a sense of autonomy, and how an affirmed discourse of *expertise* was instrumental in this process. This discourse of expertise was a central component of how *Naamloos* presented itself to other actors, whether the civil servants of *the City*, the families or the youngsters. In using the term expertise, we draw on the definition offered by the French anthropologist Dominic Boyer: 'an actor who has developed skills in, semiotic-epistemic competence for, and attentional concern with, some sphere(s) of practical activity'.[65] Two important layers are implied in the definition given by Boyer: expertise pertains to a series of competences, but it also implies a particular attitude towards a specific theme. Building upon Boyer's definition, we seek to examine how the social workers of *Naamloos* positioned themselves as experts through claims of competence about and concern with the theme of radicalization. But our observations will also complement this definition by showing how this identity as 'experts' was never fully stable, but instead a constant concern. Their acceptance as trustworthy experts was indeed a recurring point of conversation among the team members, not least because of the sensitive nature of this topic. One of the key mechanisms or self-techniques[66] in constructing this self-understanding as 'experts', we want to argue, was the production of *distinction*[67] from other stakeholders, and in particular the civil servants. Although the members of *Naamloos* considered the civil servants from *the City* as key partners, they also repeatedly distinguished themselves from them in their rhetoric and everyday practices. In what follows, we will attend to some of these iterations of distinction that came about through a particular focus on time and methodology.

The first point of distinction concerns the way in which their understanding of expertise is mediated by a particular phenomenology of time. All cases of 'radicalization' treated by *Naamloos* had been assigned by *the City*, which was responsible for the intakes and for transferring cases to the organization. Whereas this reduced the agency of *Naamloos* in the selection process, their complaints related more often to the *rhythm* of the decision process of the civil servants. During the meetings, they would often complain about what they experienced as a 'slowness' on the part of *the City*. This pertained both to the assignation of particular cases as well as to the decision to extend the project for another year. The cases below describe a situation where organizations on a Weberian 'lower' – or 'street'[68] – level seem to display a more formal structure than 'higher' bureaucratic structures.

At one of the meetings of the steering committee, the members of *Naamloos* were addressing the rhythm of the intakes. The city structure was less organized than they expected and the transferral of cases wasn't always smooth. This raised questions and concerns.

> The follow-up between our meetings is too slow. By the time we meet again the issues we had are no longer relevant. The whole organization has become quite chaotic and nobody understands anymore what is going on. We don't see a clear connection anymore between the different signals we get . . . the communication is also too slow.
>
> Steering committee, 22 September 2014

> A: 'Why does it have to take so long?'
> C: 'They work slow . . .'
> B: 'And the families don't trust them. They are linked to the police.'
> A: 'They certainly do their job, but they have another role.'
> C: 'Their attitude is different. They have to make a judgement on every case, and the indicators they use are not sharp.'
>
> Youth coach A and family coach B reporting to coordinator C,
17 November 2014

In their year-long experiment, the team of *Naamloos* established a clear, set protocol on how to deal with vulnerable youth. Their ability to quickly respond to ongoing demands and situations of crisis, in combination with a solid structure, were what made them trustworthy and reliable to many. This contrasted with the image of the civil servants who were still in a phase of identifying and determining criteria (as noted by coordinator C). While the team members of the organization understood the institutional constraints of the civil servants, their identity as professionals was premised on the possibility of immediately responding to demands, following up cases quickly, having clarity on the methods used and being able to plan long term. For *Naamloos*, addressing the problem of radicalization implied being able to answer to the sense of 'urgency', act in the here and now and follow up certain cases depending on the existing needs. Conversely, although the civil servants were equally attuned to the sense of urgency that dominated in relation to this question, their agency rather consisted of trying to 'buy time' and avoid crystallizing these deradicalization initiatives into firm policies. Thus, time does not emerge here solely as an instrument, but figures as the basis upon which one's competence and expertise are constructed. Acting as a reliable partner meant, for the team of *Naamloos*, acting quickly and efficiently. Several social analysts have already pointed towards the relationship that exits between time, space and agency.[69] A similar temporal disjuncture appears to be at play here as *Naamloos'* professionalism seemed to be driven by an *interventionist* perspective on time, whereas the civil servants seem to draw instead on a *longer time-perspective*, which goes beyond specific cases. A constant dialogue with politicians, the police, social workers and the parents was at the heart of the civil servants' daily routine, which was also influenced by the ongoing public debates and the ruminations of their hierarchical superiors. Finding the right tools – even though they felt pressured to act more quickly – was therefore a deliberate tactic.[70] They were cautious not to achieve what Hajer describes as 'discursive closure',[71] but to leave the possibility for new interpretation open. For *Naamloos*, on the other hand, being present in the hour of need was what constituted a good social worker.

This concern with time, however, also intersected with the methods used by the different agents. One of the reasons it took 'so long' to decide was also because the civil servants of *the City* were still in the process of determining the correct indicators through which they could potentially identify youngsters as 'radicalized'. The team members of *Naamloos* felt, on the other hand, that the methods used by the civil servants were not sufficient: we see this explained above as coordinator C argues that the method used by the civil servants are 'not sharp enough'. Differentiating themselves, they felt that their year-long experience with vulnerable youth had given them enough expertise to properly and quickly address different cases, including those pertaining to radicalization. The meetings of the steering committee, where the coaches who worked on radicalization met with other team members from the organization, were an important moment where the previous methodological tools used by the team members were discussed and fine-tuned according to these different cases. Here they came to develop what they called their 'recipe' to radicalization. The starting point for the team members of *Naamloos* was the 'Radicx' tool, an instrument developed by the Dutch teaching consultants Verhagen, Reitsma and Spee,[72] and which had become widely popular among several other organizations in Flanders.[73] The tool consists of a grid where the actions of the youngsters are placed into four categories (behavioural, contact and relations, cultural and religious, and political and ideological) and reviewed as positive and supportive, neutral or threatening. Each action is placed within a context of 'normal' behaviour that is expected from youngsters (such as displaying rebellious actions in front of their parents). Yet in reviewing the different cases, the social workers would often also be invited to consider other methodologies, such as the *New Authority* approach.

The New Authority theory, developed by Haim Omer,[74] was a tool often used by the team members of *Naamloos* in their contact with the families of the youngsters in other cases. This tool stresses the importance of the parental role through non-violent resistance. It fits the view that vulnerable youngsters cannot find trust within their families or with their parents and therefore seeks to restore that. Although some were sceptical about the possible use of this tool, believing that it was hard to establish a stable and positive relationship within families wherein mistrust, grief and potential violence prevailed, they nevertheless sought to convince each other about the value of this method.

> After discussing a particular case with her colleagues, family coach B was advised to look into the *New Authority* approach, which challenges and invites parents and caretakers to properly deal with children who display self-destructive behaviour. Initially, she was quite sceptical about this possibility, because there were too many emotions involved in this family. Yet after a discussion with N., who was an expert in this method, she saw how the method fit: 'This New Authority approach could restore these parents back to their parental role. Especially the father needs this. He glorifies the middle son and places himself on a lower rank than his children.'
>
> Staff meeting, 6 May 2014

The example above shows a move away from a strict security-oriented focus that primarily revolves around the idea of the youngster as a potential risk, to a more general approach that attends to the different family dynamics.[75] By situating the cases of radicalization within a perspective that was already embedded in the structure of *Naamloos* and used by other team members to address other problems of social vulnerability and youth delinquency, the question of radicalization was not understood as something separate, but as positioned within the continuity of other cases they dealt with.

Establishing trust: Between formality and informality

The question of trust has often figured as one of the lynchpins in the discussions on radicalization. The anticipation that the civil servants would simultaneously inform state authorities is seen to create a number of major tensions and dilemmas that directly affect the capacity to establish and build a trusting relationship with the concerned communities.[76] In his study on deradicalization policies in Denmark, Lasse Lindekilde states that the latter might even result in what he calls 'iatrogenic effects': rather than enabling collaboration, the measures of deradicalization instil distrust towards the governing authorities, which could 'lead young Muslims to isolate from the majority of society and actively discredit authorities'.[77] For *Naamloos* too, this question of trust was understood as a vital question, but it played out quite differently. This first had to do with their structural embedding. As an independent organization, they were able to act with more autonomy than the civil servants. Whereas the civil servants were the ones who were in charge of identifying radicalized youngsters and remaining in contact with the police, this was not the case for the team members of *Naamloos*.[78] The team members of *Naamloos* were protected from such an obligation through a right to discretion, which enabled them to keep certain information to themselves. But in addition to these structural elements, their capacity to establish trust was also connected with what they would occasionally describe as their 'own recipe' and which refers to the capacity to maintain a large degree of proximity and trust. In what follows, we will attend to this social construction of trust,[79] and how references to cultural/ethnic proximity were a crucial mediator in this.

> **C:** It is important we make them understand how A and B rely on a relationship of trust, to show them our recipe for deradicalization.
> **B:** The efforts we bring, our personal network, as a Muslim, as a mother ... this trust and this link.
> **E:** But certainly our professionalism, our expertise in this field.... A random volunteer could not do this.
> **C:** This was the only way we could improve so much and achieve such an amount of work. Some cases need continued care, for the whole family, but that's something we can intercept internally, we can guarantee this happens.
>
> > Meeting between coaches A, B, E and coordinator C, preparing
> > an evaluation by city services[G131], 21 October 2014

The citation depicts an ongoing conversation between the team members of *Naamloos*, which followed from a suggestion by the civil servants to consider welcoming volunteers into their project. The workload related to the deradicalization project was indeed considerable, and at times the organization felt understaffed to properly address all incoming demands. Yet the suggestion to include volunteers to help them out in the contact with the families was not only unwelcome to the staff members, but even vehemently rejected: volunteers were indeed seen to lack the necessary qualifications to act as professionals. By suggesting that 'random volunteers' could do a similar kind of work, the staff members at *Naamloos* felt that their expertise was not taken seriously. Their approach drew on the ability to continually balance human expectations as well as a series of habitual practices and skills that revolve around the capacity to maintain a relationship of proximity while at the same time acting professionally. And in this coming together of professionalism and informality, their Muslim identity was seen to figure as a key asset.

> **C:** How did you enter the family; what made them open up to you?
> **B:** They could trust me. They said so themselves: you are a good Moslima, you'll really help us.... They were so grateful. They said we were like two guardian angels that fell from the sky.
>
> > Coordinator C chatting to family coach B, 22 September 2014

The staff members of *Naamloos* took pride in the highly diverse composition of their organization. The fact that most social workers and the coordinator were ethnic minorities and also Muslim was not only an element of distinction from the other NGO's, but it was also understood as one of the reasons behind their success.

Their ethnicity and religiosity enabled them to establish a degree of affinity and closeness that were understood to be more difficult to achieve if one did not share the same ethnic and/or religious background. This rationale was also transposed onto their understanding of radicalization, as explained in the passage above. In the citation above, we see how coach B's Muslimness is understood as an essential condition for being able to construct a relationship with the families. Her Muslimness is here more than simply a matter of origin: the two social workers are represented as 'guardian angels', as shepherds, whose ability to reach out to the concerned families was predicated on their ethical subjectivity. The absence of a moral ambivalence around these trust relationships, as observed by Ragazzi and De Jongh (see Chapter 6 in this volume), is also striking and can partially be explained through the clearly circumscribed position of the social workers: their relationship of trust was not cast in terms of being outsiders, but rather as 'insiders' who offer *help* and *support*. By framing their role primarily as that of being caretakers, and seeing their intervention towards the families and the youngsters as guided towards finding a solution that could take them away from the lurking dangers of radical Islam, a different professional role was performed that placed them between a relationship of formality and informality towards the concerned families.[80]

This observation adds an important nuance to the existing literature that is primarily geared towards the dilemmas experienced by front-line workers in implementing state-guided policies on radicalization and the 'otherizing' mechanisms towards Muslims. These tensions materialized in particular when the Muslimness of the concerned front-line workers was addressed. Husband and Alam note, for instance, the specific kind of stress that Muslim personnel are confronted with, as they were often expected to have easier access to the target groups or were branded as instant experts, yet at the same time had difficulties being taken seriously as professionals.[81] Here, however, the Muslimness of the social worker figured more as an asset than as a source of tension: it was both the condition as well as the means through which a trusting relationship with the families and the youngsters was achieved and their work could be done. This observation is analogous to Francesco Ragazzi's observation that deradicalization policies often operate through the selective co-optation of what he calls 'trusted Muslims': '"Trusted Muslims" are not only "good Muslims", they are the necessary articulations of a policy of community representation and infiltration in the Muslim population, which is why the institutions of policed multiculturalism invest in traineeships to increase their skills, such as leadership programmes, [and] insert them in national and international networks such as the Radicalization Awareness Network to increase their social capital and experience'.[82] Yet in this particular context, it is not so much the co-optation of Muslims that is at stake, but rather a pro-active investment by professional actors (i.e. social workers) into this deradicalization field and the explicit usage and reference of their Muslimness for a successful engagement with the youth. Highlighting their Muslim identity and orientation was indeed one of the means through which the *Naamloos* team sought to underscore its *difference* from the state and the police. Rather, by viewing their role as that of a good shepherd – i.e. 'the guardian angels' – they positioned their work as part of a more general common good that went far beyond the role of the state. A pastoral understanding of power thus seems to be deployed here, which understands the role of the social worker primarily in its caring function (the guardian angel) but with an explicit theological orientation. However, this doesn't mean the guidance of the team members of *Naamloos* can simply be dislocated from modern power. Rather, it functions as a distinct corollary of modern power, or – as suggested by Foucault – it can be understood as one of the articulations of the 'surveillance-correction' continuum.[83] Yet in this particular context, the theological dimension of this kind of pastoral care becomes explicit.[84] Even more, it is through the explicit acknowledgement of this theological substance that this guidance is understood to work. Such observations should invite us to consider the ways in which religion not only figures as an object of intervention in these deradicalization policies, but often becomes the substance through which such policies can become realized, ushering in a renewed presence of 'religion' in practices that were deemed 'secular' (see also Chapter 3 by Groeninck in this volume).

Conclusion

This chapter has sought to examine the ways in which deradicalization policies are adopted and implemented by a number of front-line workers in an organization we called *Naamloos* in Flanders, one of Belgium's first regions to adopt and develop deradicalization policies in the wake of the departure of youngsters to Syria. Differing from the other European countries, the deradicalization measures deployed and adopted in Flanders were initiated in 2012 through a bottom-up structure, whereby local agents played a pioneering role in the instalment of these policies. This bottom-up approach, which leaves much room for negotiation, was also characteristic of the ways in which the team members of *Naamloos* adopted this programme and implemented it. The different sections of this chapter showed how these negotiations extended into their understanding of particular cases, the adopted framework, their relationship with the public administrations as well as their engagement with the youngsters and the families. A clear desire to distinguish themselves from the state authorities, and maintain a sustained engagement with the youngsters and the families through a relationship of trust was equally at the heart of their everyday practices. But instead of seeing these negotiations as clear evidence of disruption or inefficacy of the proposed de/radicalization framework, we have taken them as examples of the operation of this very same framework. Building on the work of Sharma and Gupta,[85] we have argued that these negotiations around this idea of deradicalization and the insistence on one's autonomy from the state figure as the mechanism through which public policies concerning deradicalization become implemented on the ground. Attending to these negotiations and various mechanisms should allow us to move away from a state-centred logic which prevails throughout much of the literature, opting instead for a more sustained understanding of the everyday mechanisms and practices that turn the question of 'radicalization' into a widely adopted social concern.

Notes

1 We would like to thank Francesco Ragazzi and Maarten De Waele for their stimulating and helpful comments and suggestions on earlier drafts.
2 The term 'foreign terrorist fighters' is the official term used by the Belgian government, but needs to problematized here due to the mechanism of 'othering' it contains, considering the fact that the Belgian-born ethnic minorities are consistently framed as 'foreigners' by the Belgian press. Yet in the signification it holds, it refers to the ensemble of non-Syrian fighters who have joined Syrian fighting forces in the Middle East (of whom a large part have ended up joining ISIS). The term 'foreigner' does, thus, not refer to their representation as 'foreigners' in the Belgian or European press, but rather to their status as foreigners in the Syrian context.
3 Rik Coolsaet, 'Facing the Fourth Foreign Fighters Wave: What Drives Europeans to Syria, and to Islamic State? Insights from the Belgian Case'. *Egmont Papers* 81, March (2016/a): 1–52.
4 Alain Gignard, 'The Islamist Networks in Belgium', in *Jihadi Terrorism and the Radicalization Challenge in Europe*, ed. Rik Coolsaet (Aldershot and Burlington, VT: Ashgate, 2008).
5 Nadia Fadil, 'Brussels as a Landscape of Fear', in *Islamist Movements of Europe*, eds. Frank Peter and Raphael Ortega (London: I.B. Tauris, 2014).
6 Felice Dassetto and Albert Bastenier, *Medias u Akbar* (Louvain-la-Neuve: CIACO, 1987).
7 Vermeulen and Bovenkerk, *Engaging with Violent Islamic Extremism*.
8 We have decided, for reasons of confidentiality, to keep the name of the city where we conducted our ethnographic fieldwork anonymous. The references made to Flemish cities in this chapter draw on publicly available documents and expert interviews.
9 See Tufyal Choudhury, 'The Radicalisation of Citizenship Deprivation', *Critical Social Policy* 37, no. 2 (2017): 225–44; and Kundnani, *The Muslims Are Coming!*
10 Mary J. Hickman, Lyn Thomas, Henri C. Nickels and Sara Silvestri, 'Social Cohesion and the Notion of "Suspect Communities": A Study of the Experiences and Impacts of Being "Suspect" for Irish Communities and Muslim Communities in Britain', *Critical Studies on Terrorism* 5, no. 1 (2012): 89–106; Therese O'Toole, Daniel Nilsson DeHanas and Tariq Modood, 'Balancing Tolerance, Security and Muslim Engagement in the United Kingdom: The Impact of the "Prevent" Agenda', *Critical Studies on Terrorism* 5, no. 3 (2012): 373–89; Pantazis and Pemberton, 'From the "Old" to the "New" Suspect Community'; and Ragazzi, 'Suspect Community or Suspect Category?'
11 Ragazzi, 'Countering Terrorism and Radicalisation'.
12 Examples are Husband and Alam, *Social Cohesion and Counter-Terrorism*; Lindekilde, 'Value for Money?'; O'Toole, Nilsson DeHanas and Modood, 'Balancing Tolerance, Security and Muslim Engagement in the United Kingdom'; and Thomas, *Responding to the Threat of Violent Extremism*.
13 Max Weber, *Economy and Society*.
14 Sharma and Gupta, eds., *The Anthropology of the State*.
15 Michael Lipsky, *Street-Level Bureaucracy*.

16 Ibid., p. 3.
17 See Tony Evans and John Harris, 'Street-Level Bureaucracy, Social Work and the (Exaggerated) Death of Discretion', *The British Journal of Social Work* 34, no. 6 (2004): 871–95; Marcia Meyers and Susan Vorsanger, 'Street-Level Bureaucrats and the Implementation of Public Policy', in *Handbook of Public Administration: Concise Paperback Edition*, eds. Guy B. Peters and Jon Pierre (Thousand Oaks, CA: Sage, 2007); and Janet Vinzant Denhardt and Lane Crothers, *Street-Level Leadership: Discretion and Legitimacy in Front-Line Public Service* (Washington, DC: Georgetown University Press, 1998).
18 See Kundnani, *The Muslims Are Coming!*; and also Ragazzi, 'Countering Terrorism and Radicalisation'; and Baker-Beall, Heath-Kelly and Jarvis, eds., *Counter-Radicalisation*.
19 O'Toole, Nilsson DeHanas and Modood, 'Balancing Tolerance, Security and Muslim Engagement in the United Kingdom'.
20 Thomas, 'Divorced but Still Co-Habiting?'
21 Husband and Alam, *Social Cohesion and Counter-Terrorism*.
22 Ibid., p. 145.
23 Ibid., p. 157.
24 O'Toole, Nilsson DeHanas and Modood, 'Balancing Tolerance, Security and Muslim Engagement in the United Kingdom'.
25 Thomas, *Responding to the Threat of Violent Extremism*, p. 99.
26 Ibid., p. 103.
27 Sharma and Gupta, eds., *The Anthropology of the State*, p. 165.
28 Ibid., p. 9.
29 Michel Foucault, 'Governmentality', in *The Foucault Effect: Studies in Governmentality*, ed. Graham Burchell (Chicago, IL: University of Chicago Press, 1991).
30 See Béatrice Hibou, ed., *La privatisation des États* (Paris: Karthala, 1999); and Peter Geschiere, 'Witchcraft and the State: Cameroon and South Africa Ambiguities of "Reality" and "Superstition"', *Past and Present* 199, no. 3 (2008): 313–35.
31 This approach has been particularly influenced by the work of Michel Foucault. For a selective overview of relevant literature on this matter, see Foucault, *The Foucault Effect*; Mitchell Dean, *Governmentality: Power and Rule in Modern Society* (London: Sage, 1999); Mitchell Dean, *Governing Societies: Political Perspectives on Domestic and International Rule* (Berkshire: Open University Press, 2007); and Nikolas S. Rose, *Powers of Freedom: Reframing Political Thought* (Cambridge and New York: Cambridge University Press, 1999).
32 Sharma and Gupta, eds., *The Anthropology of the State*.
33 Ibid., p. 9; see also Michel-Rolph Trouillot, 'The Anthropology of the State in the Age of Globalization: Close Encounters of the Deceptive Kind', *Current Anthropology* 42, no. 1 (2001): 125–38.
34 Sharma and Gupta, eds., *The Anthropology of the State*, pp. 9–10.
35 Fredrik Barth, ed., *Ethnic Groups and Boundaries: The Social Organization of Culture Difference* (Long Grove, IL: Waveland Press, 1998).
36 Laclau and Mouffe, *Hegemony and Socialist Strategy*.
37 The empirical data upon which this chapter draws was largely gathered by Silke Jaminé, who effectuated this research for her Master's thesis. Nadia Fadil supervised this process and participated in a few meetings with local stakeholders. The chapter as a whole, and the analysis that informs it, was co-authored on an equal basis.
38 Kundnani, 'Radicalisation: The Journey of a Concept', p. 21.

39 The organization was created in 2010 and gained a small notoriety in Flanders and the Netherlands. Although the organization never really took off and was disbanded in 2012, it managed to catch the public eye through their public actions (such as sabotaging lectures or taking over demonstrations) and – especially – the large amount of YouTube videos they created and posted online. In these videos, which attracted a considerable amount of online viewers, they openly rejected Western democracy, called for the implementation of the *Sharia* throughout the world, criticized or ridiculed Belgian politicians and Muslim leaders and engaged in theological discussions on a range of topics such as the importance of the Caliphate. The movement was initially not taken seriously by most commentators, and they were viewed as a bunch of amateurs who didn't have any serious following. Yet with time, and as the attention for the movement grew, a more confrontational tone was adopted vis-à-vis the Belgian authorities. One of the key incidents concerned the arrest of a face-veiled woman by the police forces in Brussels in the spring of 2012, right after the instalment of a nationwide ban on the face veil. In a video, the leader of Sharia4Belgium, Fouad Belkacem (aka Abou Imraan), publicly denounced the use of violence against the woman by police forces, showing her *niqaab* torn into pieces as evidence. This incident also resulted in confrontations between youth and the police in Molenbeek/Brussels. This event was the final deathblow for the movement. Fouad Belkacem was arrested shortly after on accusations of instigating violence, and the movement was disbanded. In the months that followed, dozens of members of Sharia4Belgium left for Syria and the organization was officially considered a public enemy. The clear evidence of the links between the Syria foreign fighters and the movement also resulted in its condemnation as a terrorist organization in one of the largest terrorist trials in Belgian history in 2016. For a further account on the movement, see Pim Aarns and Ineke Roex, *'Als ik iemand beledigd heb, dan was dat mijn bedoeling': Sharia4Belgiums ideologie en humorgebruik* (Amsterdam: University of Amsterdam Press, 2017); De Koning, Roex, Becker and Aarns, *Eilanden in een zee van ongeloof.*

40 Maarten De Waele, Hans Moors, Aart Garssen and Jannie Noppe, eds., *Aanpak van gewelddadige radicalisering* (Antwerpen/Apeldoorn: Maklu, 2017), p. 12.

41 Interview with civil servant, 26 September 2014.

42 De Waele, Moors, Garssen and Noppe, eds., *Aanpak van gewelddadige radicalisering.* See also, Kato van Broeckhoven and Amy-Jane Gielen, *Handvatten voor een lokale aanpak van radicalisering* (Brussel: VVSG, 2015).

43 Somers, De Wever, Bonte and Creemers, *Beheersen van Moslimradicalisering.*

44 Paul van Tigchelt, *Het Plan R – Het Actieplan Radicalisme* (Brussel: OCAD, 2016).

45 Federale Regering België, 'Regeerakkoord/Accord de gouvernement' (Brussel: Belgian Federal Government, 2014).

46 Van Tigchelt, *Het Plan R.*

47 De Vlaamse minister van Binnenlands Bestuur, 'Actieplan ter preventie van gewelddadige radicalisering en polarisering: Overzicht acties en maatregelen', Inburgering, Wonen, Gelijke Kansen en Armoedebestrijding (2015). Available at http://www.vvsg.be/radicalisering/Documents/actieplan_radicalisering.pdf (accessed December 2018).

48 Coppock and McGovern, 'Dangerous Minds'; Paul Ponsaers, Brice De Ruyver, Marleen Easton, Antoinette Verhage, Jannie Noppe, Jo Hellinckx and Maarten Vandevelde, 'Onderzoeksrapport polarisering en radicalisering: een integrale preventieve aanpak' (Brussel: Governance of Security, 2010); Fathali M. Moghaddam, *From the Terrorists' Point of View: What They Experience and Why They Come to Destroy* (Westport, CT:

Praeger Security International, 2006); and Sophia Moskalenko and Clark McCauley, 'Measuring Political Mobilization: The Distinction between Activism and Radicalism', *Terrorism and Political Violence* 21, no. 2 (2009): 239–60.

49 Somers, De Wever, Bonte and Creemers, *Beheersen van Moslimradicalisering*.

50 The abbreviations used in this text are fictional and only used for practical purposes. They do not reflect the real names of the cases. The cases, on the other hand, are authentic.

51 All citations in italic are translations of conversations witnessed during research. In order to gain trust during meetings and to protect the privacy of youngsters and families, recordings were never made. The citations are based upon notes taken during the meetings and reviewed by respondents.

52 Muncie, *Youth and Crime*; and Ragazzi, 'Countering Terrorism and Radicalisation'.

53 See Husband and Alam, *Social Cohesion and Counter-Terrorism*; and Thomas, *Responding to the Threat of Violent Extremism*.

54 Laclau and Mouffe, *Hegemony and Socialist Strategy*.

55 Kevin DeLuca, 'Articulation Theory: A Discursive Grounding for Rhetorical Practice', *Philosophy & Rhetoric* 32, no. 4 (1999): 334–48; and Stuart Hall, 'Race, Articulation and Societies Structured in Dominance', in *Black British Cultural Studies: A Reader*, eds. Houston A. Baker Jr, Manthia Diawara and Ruth H. Lindeborg (Chicago, IL: University of Chicago Press, 1996).

56 Bruno Latour, *Reassembling the Social: An Introduction to Actor-Network-Theory* (Oxford: Oxford University Press, 2007).

57 Laclau cited in Hall, 'Race, Articulation and Societies Structured in Dominance', p. 335.

58 Ragazzi, 'Countering Terrorism and Radicalisation'.

59 Philippe Ariès, *Centuries of Childhood* (Harmondsworth: Penguin Books, 1962).

60 Sharon Stephens, ed., *Children and the Politics of Culture* (Princeton, NJ: Princeton University Press, 1995).

61 Ibid., p. 11.

62 Barry Goldson, '"Unsafe, Unjust and Harmful to Wider Society": Grounds for Raising the Minimum Age of Criminal Responsibility in England and Wales', *Youth Justice* 13, no. 2 (2013): 111–30.

63 Barry Goldson, '"Children in Need" or "Young Offenders"? Hardening Ideology, Organizational Change and New Challenges for Social Work with Children in Trouble', *Child & Family Social Work* 5, no. 3 (2000): 255–65; and Goldson, 'Unsafe, Unjust and Harmful to Wider Society'.

64 This theory was developed by the criminologists Nicole Vettenburg and Lode Walgrave throughout the eighties and still figures as an important starting point for most of the youth work organizations in Flanders. See Nicole Vettenburg, Lode Walgrave and Jaak Van Kerckvoorde, *Jeugdwerkloosheid, delinquentie en maatschappelijke kwetsbaarheid: een theoretisch en empririsch onderzoek naar de veronderstelde band tussen werkloosheid en delinquentie bij 17-19 jarigen* (Antwerpen: Kluwer, 1984).

65 Dominic Boyer, 'Thinking through the Anthropology of Experts', *Anthropology in Action* 15, no. 2 (2008): 39.

66 Hubert L. Dreyfus, ed., *Michel Foucault: Beyond Structuralism and Hermeneutics* (Chicago, IL: University of Chicago Press, 1982).

67 Pierre Bourdieu, *La distinction: Critique sociale du jugement* (Paris: Les Éditions de Minuit, 1979).

68 Lipsky, *Street-Level Bureaucracy*.

69 In a special issue devoted to this question, Laura Bear notes that dominant views on modernity too often draw on a linear and one-dimensional understanding of time, or

conversely assume a temporal landscape that is oversaturated by notions of insecurity and non-predictability (such as in neoliberalism). Several recent interventions have, on the other hand, sought to shed a more complex light on this question by showing how diachronic experiences of time are constitutive of modern structures. Capitalism, for instance, draws on a particular temporal structure (productivity) that is not uniformly shared by all participating actors, an observation that was from the very outset included in Marx' reflections. See Laura Bear, 'Doubt, Conflict, Mediation: The Anthropology of Modern Time', *Journal of the Royal Anthropological Institute* 20, no. 1 (2014): 3–30. See also the work of Simone Abram, 'The Time It Takes: Temporalities of Planning', *Journal of the Royal Anthropological Institute* 20, no. 1 (2014): 129–47, who describes how Norwegian and Swedish bureaucracies, and their attempts at planning the future, draw on a complex variety of 'games of temporality'.

70 Michel de Certeau, *The Practice of Everyday Life* (Berkeley, CA: University of California Press, 2013).

71 Maarten A. Hajer, *The Politics of Environmental Discourse: Ecological Modernization and the Policy Process* (Oxford: Oxford University Press, 1997).

72 Anniek Verhagen, Maartje Reitsma and Ine Spee, *Vroegtijdige signalering van radicalisering* (s-Hertogenbosch/Utrecht: KPC Groep & APS, 2010).

73 See, for instance, http://www.advlimburg.nl/media/89722/radicx-tool.pdf.

74 Haim Omer, *Nieuwe autoriteit: samen werken aan een krachtige opvoedingsstijl thuis, op school en in de samenleving* (Amsterdam: Hogrefe, 2011).

75 Ibid.

76 Husband and Alam, *Social Cohesion and Counter-Terrorism*; Thomas, *Responding to the Threat of Violent Extremism*; and Ragazzi and De Jongh (Chapter 6 in this volume).

77 Lindekilde, 'Value for Money?'

78 Although in the meantime *Naamloos* has also been invited to sit on the Local Information Councils. The material discussed here thus predates that period and pertains solely to the first year where they offered their coaching.

79 Linda R. Weber and Allison I. Carter, *The Social Construction of Trust* (New York: Kluwer/Plenum, 2003).

80 In her ethnography of social workers in Brussels, Maryam Kolly describes this delicate balance between 'formality' and 'informality' that professionals have to perform towards youth. Whereas social workers can only have access to the youngsters by virtue of not being seen as part of the establishment (which is described by the emic term *Flamanisé*), they simultaneously have to be careful to not be viewed as too easily manipulable (*enrôlable*) by these same youngsters, for the latter could equally jeopardize their capacity to be taken seriously. See Maryam Kolly, 'Introduire du possible dans les métiers impossibles?', in *Gestes spéculatifs*, eds. Isabelle Stengers and Didier Debaise (Paris: Les Presses du Réel, 2015).

81 Husband and Alam, *Social Cohesion and Counter-Terrorism*.

82 Ragazzi, 'Suspect Community or Suspect Category?', p. 734.

83 Michel Foucault, *The Archaeology of Knowledge* (New York: Pantheon Books, 1972), pp. 4–5.

84 Dreyfus, ed., *Michel Foucault*.

85 Sharma and Gupta, eds., *The Anthropology of the State*.

Part III

DE/RADICALIZATION AND ITS EFFECTS

Chapter 8

ROUTINIZATION AND MOBILIZATION OF INJUSTICE: HOW TO LIVE IN A REGIME OF SURVEILLANCE

Martijn de Koning

'And also a warm welcome to the people of the AIVD who are listening in.'
—AH

The above quote is taken from a speech made in 2012 at a meeting of a network of militant activists who called themselves *BehindBars*. While the remark is clearly made in jest, it illustrates the activists' suspicion that they were being monitored by the Dutch security and intelligence service, the AIVD. This particular activist network emerged around 2010 and presented the authorities with a problem: although clearly flirting with sympathy for al-Qaeda, they had not resorted to violence – although several had tried to go to Iraq, Somalia, Afghanistan and Chechnya to join the violent struggles in 2005 and 2008. Most of them failed, however. But should they be seen as a threat to the state and society or were they simply a 'bunch of idiots' as one public servant claimed?

All this changed in 2012 and 2013 when it became apparent that many of the activists had left for Syria to join the fight against the regime of Bashar al-Assad. As a result, they became the focus of media attention and the topic of questions in parliament. Additionally, the terrorism threat level was raised, and the activists became even more closely monitored by the intelligence and security services. The attraction this group held for young Muslims was a key consideration in governmental anti-radicalization policies. Our study of these militant activists focused on the nature and type of activism they employed and how this activism interacted with the media and state.[1] This chapter draws upon the empirical study I conducted in the Netherlands with Team Free Saddik/BehindBars/ StreetDawah activists. And more specifically upon the ways in which these activists anticipated that they were being monitored by Dutch intelligence and the AIVD, and the extent to which the police interfered with their private lives. But it wasn't only the state institutions that the activists felt scrutinized by, it was also the debates taking place about Islam and Muslims in general. On the one hand they felt that, as Muslims, they were marked out as a problem and, on the other, they noticed how particular themes from the public debates trickled down into the everyday conversations that they had with people, most noticeably after shocking events such as the violent attacks of 9/11 and the murder of Theo van Gogh, but also throughout the rise of Islamic State (IS). At the same time, counter-radicalization policies resulted in Muslims being monitored as potential security threats by police and security services.

The circle of people who worked together between 2010 and 2014 under the names Team Free Saddik/BehindBars/StreetDawah can best be described as a changing circle of friends and acquaintances who shared similar ideological references and gathered together from time to time to organize political campaigns and support rallies for prisoners (Muslims whom they regarded as political prisoners) through which they demonstrated their sympathy and support for al-Qaeda and IS (also known as ISIS). They frequently criticized Dutch politics in provocative and sometimes aggressive ways.

In this chapter I explore how militant activists experience the public and political debates about Islam and radicalization and the monitoring by police and intelligence services as forms of soft and hard surveillance. I focus in particular on two overlapping but also contradictory patterns of responses that I encountered most frequently: routinization and mobilization. Routinization and mobilization are both driven by a sense of injustice but relate to different types of reactions: the first is invoked by the desire to resist by not allowing the surveillance to affect one's daily life and the second by the need to speak out. First I explain how the radicalization discourse has its roots in the racialization of danger, which objectifies Muslims as a potential threat to security and social cohesion. I then argue that the workings of this security gaze in the media, politics and in the monitoring by police and security services, can be described as a regime of surveillance. This triggers the question: how does one live in a situation where one is categorized as a (potential) danger and a problem? I look particularly closely at how the activists managed to routinize the surveillance in their daily lives and how they used it to mobilize people by first analysing their responses to the soft surveillance, then the hard surveillance. Finally, I describe a particular event that marked the collapse of this regime of surveillance – a football game – and the police response.

The racialization of danger in the Netherlands

The idea of Muslims constituting a danger to society is not new. In this section I will address how Muslims are racialized as potential threats through the nexus of race, religion and security. Although the connection between (radical) Islam and threat is often seen as a result of the 9/11 attacks, the securitization of Islam and Muslims was already emerging in the Netherlands in the 1980s and 1990s.[2] The belief that migrants and their culture posed a danger to society was present from the earliest days of the Dutch minority policies and stemmed from the worry that migrant cultures were a potential threat to the Dutch rule of law.[3] Policymakers and government advisors were motivated by the belief that the Dutch rule of law was the result of the codification of 'cultural achievements'; something that had to be protected. It was, in particular, the 'compatibility of Islam and the rule of law' that was challenged, and it was believed that a 'conflict of values and norms' could emerge.[4]

Later, during the 1990s, political parties across a broad political spectrum questioned whether an increase in 'cultural diversity' would threaten social cohesion.[5] By the 1990s, developments had already taken place that involved migrants being categorized primarily on the basis of their culture and/or religion. After the Rushdie Affair, the Dutch security service presented a report making clear that it had shifted its focus from the 'communist threat' to migration and Islam, stating that one of the possible side effects of migration from South European and North African countries could be a 'progressive radicalization or fundamentalization of Muslim communities in foreign parts'. Concerns were raised that conflicts from the countries of origin could be transferred to the Netherlands with 'bloodshed, obstruction of the freedom of speech or other constitutional rights [and] severe disturbances of the public order' as a possible consequence (see Chapter 2 by Fadil and De Koning in this volume).[6] In debates and policies in the 1990s, Dutch values with regard to secular and sexual freedoms became the standard for measuring integration: the so-called culturalization of citizenship.[7] Both the culturalization of citizenship and the securitization of Islam have had profound impacts on Dutch integration policies, evidenced by the stronger emphasis placed on the value of assimilation.[8]

A second strand in the racialization of Muslims pertains to the distinction made in Dutch integration policies and debates between so-called autochthonous and allochthonous people. It has been difficult to determine the precise definition of these terms and to decide who is placed in the category of allochthonous. In general, this category refers to people who are considered to be non-native and a distinction is made between Westerners and non-Westerners. However, neither of these distinctions is applied in a consistent manner. As Yanow and Van der Haar show, people who are seen as having a large cultural distance from the autochtonized Dutch people, based upon ideas about birthplace and kinship, are categorized as non-Western allochthonous, as are children who have at least one parent born outside the Netherlands.[9] The opposition, therefore, not only pertains to birthplace but also to kinship, while the link with culture connects both birthplace and kinship to stereotypical explanations of perceived collective differences in attitudes and practices.

Although the process of allochtonization does not necessarily, or exclusively, refer to Muslims, they have nevertheless become exemplary 'allochthones'.[10] This does not mean that Christian migrants, by definition, become part of the Dutch moral community, as the quintessential autochtonized Dutch person is white and many allochtonized people (for example, Moroccan-Dutch) are referred to as having a little colour.[11]

A third strand of racialization occurred through what Tebble identified as the discourse of 'identity liberalism' which emerged in opposition to multiculturalism and is characterized by a strong focus placed on advocating a national culture based upon shared values, underpinned by appeals to the state to protect this national culture against allegedly intolerant forces so as to safeguard liberal democracy.[12] The emphasis in the pleas made by a few Dutch politicians was not only on having a people with a shared culture (which for them was liberal and secular) but also on building a strong defence of liberal principles in the face of an illiberal force that was increasingly exemplified by Islam. In particular, the visible presence of Islam, such as women wearing headscarves or face veils, the various mosques, plus the audible presence of the public call to prayer, were seen as actively opposing the so-called secular and/or Judeo-Christian tradition of the Netherlands.[13]

The regime of surveillance

The events of 9/11, the murder of Theo van Gogh in 2004, and the rise of anti-Islam politicians such as Wilders, have resulted in the growing securitization of Islam in the Netherlands; a process which has placed the focus in media, politics and integration policies almost entirely on Muslims and Islam and the alleged threat they present to democracy and social cohesion.[14] The debates about (radical) Islam and the counter-radicalization policies have influenced Muslims' lives severely, as Croft has shown to particular effect in the UK.[15] In his research Croft examines the performance of different identity formations and the categories of Otherness that are produced by securitization. He focuses in particular on the Radical Other (while acknowledging the existence of other categories as well, such as the Abject Other, the Oriental Other, and so on).[16] Elaborating on Croft's work, Eroukhmanoff argues that the securitization of Muslims produces a different category of Otherness as well: the *Remote Other*.[17] The Remote Other may be distant in a spatial or temporal sense but is even more so in an ontological sense: an Other who can be observed, defined and analysed from a distance in order to determine signals, indicators and triggers of radicalization which can then be responded to with the imposition of certain measures. Eroukhmanoff makes a plea for a more relational approach to the Remote Other who she describes as being unconnected and independent from radicalization. This chapter builds on that stance by analysing the regime of surveillance: how militant activists (often labelled as 'radicals') respond to the nexus of securitization, radicalization and racialization.

In the context of the securitization of Islam (conceptualized as the reduction of Islam to a topic of security and the reduction of security to Islam), Edmunds makes a distinction between 'hard' and 'soft' modes of regulation and surveillance.[18] The hard surveillance only targets and affects a small number of people (those who are suspected of potentially supporting foreign fighters, for example, or who plan to go to Syria themselves). This type of regime includes practices such as 24/7 monitoring, wiretapping, disturbing all kinds of activities, for example, but also includes the sharper focus that the intelligence services and the Dutch National Coordinator for Security and Counterterrorism (NCTV) now have by identifying 'Salafism' as the main security threat in general and the main Islamic security threat in particular. The soft surveillance involves what Edmunds has called 'the "hyper-legalization" of perceived cultural threats', which can range, for example, from the banning of particular Islamic clothing such as the headscarf or face veil to the outlawing of minarets, because they are all deemed to be a security risk.[19]

Taking the hard and soft surveillance together we are able to see that surveillance is often racialized, that racialization frequently invokes ideas about danger and threats and that this racial surveillance is part of modern society.[20] The racial surveillance of Muslim militant activists that I focus on therefore involves a much wider notion of surveillance than is usually deployed in surveillance studies.[21] I use it more specifically in relation to the answers that Muslim militant activists in my research gave to the question, *'how should I live while being categorized and scrutinized as a security problem?'* Beliefs that people have about how to behave in particular situations go beyond mere imagery, they also relate to concepts determining what a good life or proper conduct is and the particular moral reasoning supporting these convictions. Following Lakoff and Collier, I treat such ideas as specific ethical formations which emerge in uncertain circumstances.[22] These formations or 'regimes of living' are to be seen

> as congeries of moral reasoning and practice that emerge in situations that present ethical problems – that is, situations in which the question of how to live is at stake. Methodologically, the regime of living is abstract: a given regime of living can identify common ethical configurations in diverse situations, and, thus, takes diverse actual forms.[23]

Lakoff and Collier use the concept to bring together different ethical configurations ranging from ethical regulation in Canada, to development and urbanism in Brazil, garrison-entrepôt in the Chad Basin and organ trade in India. The concept of 'regimes of living' is well suited for analysing the responses given by militant activists when asked how they live in a situation of securitization and racialization.[24] The regime of surveillance resembles Pantazis and Pemberton's[25] argument (based on Hillyard's original thesis about the Irish in the UK)[26] that Muslims in Britain have replaced the Irish as the 'suspect community' through the political discourses on counterterrorism that produced and reproduced the idea that Muslims were a problem simply because of their presumed membership to a particular group. Unlike Pantazis and Pemberton, I employ the notion of a 'regime of surveillance' to take into account and emphasize the experiences of the subjects themselves. Using this concept, I explore the different ethical formations constructed by Muslim militant activists in the Netherlands and investigate how they carve out their lives within the context of Dutch society.

Soft surveillance: The experience of being marked as a problem

One of the more well-known militant activists, Abu Muhammad, regarded the debate surrounding Islam as providing him with an important lesson, one that helped him in his efforts to be a good Muslim. Consequently, he no longer mourned the fact that politicians such as the anti-Islam populist Geert Wilders have made the perceived division between Islam and the West the core of their political message:

> In retrospect, I'm glad about it. I have been confronted with the facts since I was a child. We Muslims need someone like Wilders, and the unrest he creates in society. Muslims have to realize that this society doesn't want us. They are waking us up with a good, strong jolt.

Regimes of living are 'configurations of normative, technical, and political elements' providing the means 'for organizing, reasoning about, and "living" ethically'.[27] The excerpt of the conversation I had with Abu Muhammad illustrates the way that he interpreted the Dutch debate on Islam and the role of Freedom Party leader Wilders as a call upon him and the wider Muslim community to wake up. The question of 'how to live' emerges throughout the lives of the militant activists, not only because their behaviour is affected by the hard surveillance (which I will discuss in the next section) but also because the soft surveillance that comes about through the debates and policies regarding Islam, integration and radicalization has an impact as well.

What matters here is that debates, policies and concrete intelligence and monitoring actions are a form of governmentality through regulatory interventions and surveillance: people adjust their attitudes and behaviour towards the state and others based upon the experience of being scrutinized and the idea that there is a world of those being watched (in this case Muslims) and others who watch them. Their experiences of the debates on Islam and integration, with topics ranging from how Muslims take a shower after sports, to national security issues, to the treatment of women, trickle down to the work floor or the school classroom. Muslims feel questioned and interrogated for what other Muslims do in the name of Islam. Following Brubaker, by identifying themselves as Muslims, people are not only responding to being stigmatized and excluded, but also to 'being cast, categorized, queried and held accountable as Muslims in public discourse and private interaction ... for what others say or do as Muslims'.[28] The racialization of danger produces a situation in which policies and debates, as well as concrete intelligence measures, make a distinction between people who are potentially acceptable (safe and not – yet – radical) and potentially unacceptable (a risk or dangerous and – probably – radical). The phenomenon of Salafism is the tie that binds 'the root causes approach' in radicalization together with the ideology (see Fadil and De Koning, Chapter 2 in this volume) and serves as one of the indicators of risk. Note that, the notion of risk implies an uncertainty and, whether acceptable or unacceptable, a system has to be in place to determine whether those considered at risk / a risk are dangerous or not.

The stories recounted by militant activists relating to hard and soft surveillance show how they reason about ethical issues, the good life, how guides for moral action are created, and how moral subjects are formed.[29] Particular events heighten the anticipation of being scrutinized and held accountable. There are also particular events that stand out as so-called 'truth events', in particular 9/11, the murder of Theo van Gogh and the Paris attacks of 2015. In my conversations with militant activists, it was their experiences in schools that stood out in a striking fashion. As AA (twenty-seven, Pakistani-Dutch) told me:

> It was the day after 9/11. We talked about it in class and our teacher showed the video with George W. Bush saying: 'You are either with us or against us'. Then the teacher stood up, pointed at me and asked 'And AA, where do you stand?' I didn't know. But I knew I wasn't with the Americans.

It appears that for many people, such as AA's teacher, events like 9/11 are examples of 'truth events': events that have challenged what is regarded as a consensus on diversity, Islam and multiculturalism and have steered the discourse in a more disciplining and confrontational direction.[30] For AA, this is also a 'truth event'. In his own words, the search for identity began when he increasingly focused on Islam, global political issues (such as the *War on Terror*) and the Dutch debate on Islam. Of course, one might argue that AA does not know what the teacher meant by asking this question. And indeed, a person who feels that he or she is being scrutinized, for example, by a colleague, co-student or teacher, does not always know what the other person is thinking or means when asking a particular question or making a remark. That explains why in discussions among my interlocutors there is not only a recounting of the experience of being scrutinized but also questions such as: '*Are you sure you understood it well? Are you sure it was not just an innocent question?*' These questions are ways to not only divert the negative experience, but they also show a degree of doubt and uncertainty in assessing how outsiders perceive them.[31] AA's reasoning about 9/11 above shows the 'the dynamic process through which a situated form of moral reasoning – a regime of living – is invoked and reworked in a problematic situation to provide a possible guide to action'.[32] He did not know how to answer initially and it made him rethink his own positions as he did not know where he stood but he knew he was not with the Americans. It is in difficult, uncertain situations in which there is a 'perceived gap between the real and the ideal' where regimes of living provide people with possible answers to their questions and struggles.[33] Thus, the event in AA's classroom can be seen as an example of producing a 'truth event' for AA as he felt that he was being put on the spot because of his religion for the first time in his life.

Routinization: 'That's just how it is'

Many people among the militant activist groups refer to stories like the one recounted by AA as examples of intolerance, describing them as unfair and 'yet another example' of the double standards applied to Muslims (compared to others). But the most dominant reaction is one of resignation: 'That's just how it is'. In dealing with these interruptions in their daily routines, the militant activists demonstrate similar coping strategies to those Siebers found in his research on migrant hostility in work settings.[34] Some of Siebers's informants reported that they responded to intolerant remarks as if they referred to others rather than themselves, adding that trying to explain things was pointless. Thus, they attempt to immunize themselves by avoiding these conversations. The phrase: 'That's just how it is', is not necessarily the same as submitting to the racist intolerance or being defeated by it. It is a conscious attempt to protect what matters to them in daily life (having an education or a job) from interactions that distract them from it in multiple ways (from diverting their focus to prompting the feeling that they have to continuously defend themselves). In her article on how Palestinians live under Israeli occupation, Allen focuses on the normalization of violence and how people are 'getting by' as a way to describe and analyse one of the agentic options people have in that particular sociopolitical field.[35] Her analysis of 'getting by' and my analysis of routinization point to a form of agency that is neither open resistance, nor surrender or apathy, but that is available to people within the structures that determine everyday life and shows the different interests and loyalties they have to negotiate.[36] For many men in my research, including the militant activists, their reasoning about how to respond was not only determined by their ambitions to be a pious Muslim but also about how to behave as a husband, father and member of a family.[37] Many feared that publicly resisting the racialization and securitization could endanger their families and would therefore interfere with the roles, responsibilities and loyalties they had towards their families and children.[38]

The activists were keen to protect their private lives, and in particular their families, from undesirable influences that would lead them astray from the right path. Their private domain did not include just the home but extended beyond it too, as they walked together down the street, played sports together and attended lectures. It was also a domain in which, ideally, spirituality and the worshipping of Allah were more important than material gain, wealth and status based on matters that, according to them, had nothing to do with Islam or went against its principles. Some of the activists told me that they preferred not to have a paid job, but to devote their time (together with their wives and families) to reading the Qur'an and studying Islam.

The activists claim that they were distracted from their focus on their faith because of the debate on Islam, by (as they saw it) unnecessary apprehensions by police in the street, identity checks, accusatory questions from colleagues and fellow students about Islam, the arrests of 'innocent brothers', and unbelievers' insults relating to Islam and the Prophet. This was a reference to an important effect of the surveillance of Muslims, namely the idea that someone was always harassing them, holding them accountable, calling them to order and looking over their shoulders. This besieging of their private lives, as they experienced it, led them to withdraw into their own circle of family and friends. Here they found the support, friendship, spirituality and brotherhood that they did not find anywhere else (especially since other Muslims did not want to be associated with them). They claimed that family and friends protected them from intrusive comments, policy measures and debates. This led them to maintain a stronger boundary between their private lives and the influence of outsiders but subsequently this withdrawal presented them with a dilemma. While the withdrawal may well offer protection from a hostile world it also meant, in their own view, that they were adopting a submissive attitude towards the enemy that was not fitting behaviour for a good Muslim. It was necessary to stand up for Allah and his Prophet, and for the Muslim community – many of the activists stated. But this increased the risk of coming under even closer scrutiny, which would threaten their private lives even more.

Mobilization: 'Yes, we are radical'

On the one hand, the routinization of surveillance in daily life and the attempts to avoid confrontation provide a sharp contrast with the public actions the militant activists took, but also fed the activism in multiple ways. The same mechanisms that the state used to control the conduct of individuals, such as the categorization of people as 'radical' (see Chapter 11 by Lechkar in this volume), also created a space for forms of resistance to develop which enable dissidents to behave in a 'deviant' way and claim the 'right to be different'.[39] The phrase 'That's just how it is' in the context of mobilization also serves, I suggest, as a 'truth phrase': when people utter this statement they express the idea that this injustice is part of daily life and, moreover, that this is the 'true face' of Dutch society. This is the message they disseminated in their 2011 demonstration 'The war has begun' against a possible ban on wearing the face veil in the Netherlands. They criticized Dutch politicians for having double standards and claiming to promote freedom while imposing a ban on wearing the face veil. They did not believe that their protests would be effective (in the sense of stopping the ban), but they wanted to make a statement anyway. By being vocal they were also able to criticize those Muslim organizations that did not speak out and expose them as having sold out to the Dutch government. In this way, their protest becomes a means to an end in itself: it is about showing readiness to act on behalf of Muslims and refusing to submit to what they deemed as the unjust regulation of Muslims by the Dutch state. Not acting would be the same as submitting themselves to the Dutch state, or, as they saw it, to a false religion called democracy. Such an attitude would be contrary to their idea as to how a Muslim should behave: steadfast in the face of oppression.

A peculiar mix of politics and anti-politics characterized the militant activists' mode of resistance. It was political because it was part of the 'continuous criticism and politicization' of the policies and debates in the Netherlands concerning the regulation of Muslims and Islam, Islamophobia and the 'War on Terror'.[40] At the same time, it also affected the ways in which governmental power was implemented: their presence at public rallies with the Islamic seal flag (dubbed the 'ISIS flag'), their provocative and sometimes aggressive behaviour and the departure of various activists for Syria all increased the sense of urgency of, and justification for, anti-radicalization policy among politicians, policymakers and opinion leaders.

Their activism was also anti-political. Parvez describes the anti-political (in the case of the face veil) as the 'rejection of state engagement in favor of the valorization of private life, as a substitute for democratic political participation'.[41] The protests against, and disturbance of, debates about Islam and the protest against the proposed ban on the face veil in 2011 were all, partly, framed as acts of resistance and stimulated by the desire 'to be left alone'. At the same time the activists connected their personal impressions with the larger political sphere. During the protest against the film *Innocence of Muslims* in 2012, for example, they responded with the slogan: 'You took our countries, you took our women, but you are not going to take our Prophet'. The activists felt that proposals such as the ban on the face veil were yet another example of how the state was infringing on their private lives. By acting in this manner, the Muslim activists attempted to withdraw from the regulation and politicization of Muslim life but also used the occasion to propagate their idealized version of Islam. The goal was, therefore, not only to resist regulation by the Dutch state but also to strive for a different form of regulation.[42]

The ways the militant activists expressed their grievances were usually considered by many opponents as rude, harsh, aggressive and un-Islamic. A lot of the Muslims we encountered in our research who were outside the militant circles and were often keen to emphasize that they were trying to be pious Muslims, also made clear (often sooner rather than later) that they were not 'radical', 'extreme' and certainly not a 'terrorist'. This reveals how deeply people worry about being categorized as potentially dangerous; something that was expressed when they modified their appearance. One of the women in earlier research stated: 'I do not wear a niqab nor do I wear black. I don't want people to be scared because of the way I look even though I do admire my sisters who are steadfast enough to wear the niqab.' Such a 'performance of safety'[43] is heavily criticized by the militant activists in my research. Although they do adjust their attire in daily life so they do not stand out (for example, when shopping for groceries) they regard such an attitude as evidence of submission to the *kufar* (infidel) and defeat in the war against Islam. In general, this kind of criticism is never levelled against 'ordinary' Muslims, as the activists do not want to appear unreasonable and claim that they understand the reasoning behind it. However, when it comes to other Muslims, who are visible in the public debate, their criticism becomes fierce and harsh. Borrowing from Malcolm X's exposé on the 'house negro' versus the 'field negro', the Muslims who publicly oppose 'radicalism', condemn terrorist attacks in Europe and cooperate with the government, are accused of being 'house Muslims': domesticated Muslims who dilute (or even leave) Islam in order to guarantee a government subsidy, or social standing and acceptance. Furthermore, after the publication of research results by Koopmans[44] on fundamentalism among Muslims triggered a media outcry, the activists responded with a new article on their website called: 'It's true, we are radical'. They explained that, according to them, radicalism meant holding on to the fundamentals of Islam and not giving in to the idea that Muslims have to dilute Islam in order to be accepted as citizens (which according to them would not work anyway as Muslims would still be regarded as second-class citizens at best). In so doing they embraced, redefined and re-appropriated the label 'radical' to present themselves as steadfast Muslims. And here a paradox of militant activism emerges: by making clear that they wanted to be left alone in a harsh and provocative way, they draw more attention to themselves and their daily lives as so-called 'radical Muslims'. They used the debates and the labels in the debates to draw attention to their messages, but through their provocative and sometimes aggressive stands, the security gaze only became stronger. In the end their performance of steadfastness resulted in an intensification of counter-radicalization policy.

Hard surveillance: 'We are being watched'

The militant activists I worked with were troubled not only by the debates and policies regarding Islam influencing their private lives, but also by being watched and monitored by the security services. Here routinization, much more than mobilization, was the most common reaction. Here, for example, is an excerpt of a phone conversation:

> OA: Martijn, before we continue, you do realize this phone is being tapped, right?
> MdK: Most likely, yes.
> OA: OK, I just thought I should mention it; we have to be careful, although I have nothing to hide.
> MdK: No problem, I understand.

This conversation took place at the beginning of a phone call I had with a friend of a militant activist who had been convicted for incitement and for being a member of a criminal organization with a terrorist intent. This shows a clear awareness, or anticipation, that police or security services were monitoring the call, and is followed by an explicit statement that the person had nothing to hide anyway. As Ali explains, hard surveillance is not only about the practice itself but also about the expectation that it is being done at that specific moment.[45] My interlocutor's behaviour is attuned to that expectation even though, or perhaps especially because, he cannot know what the person who is listening in (if at all) is looking for. He does so, not to stop the conversation, but to be able to continue it. My interlocutors often made statements like this, which, in the same way as it does with soft surveillance, points to the routinization of being monitored by the police and security services. Most of the people I talked to have reasons for thinking they are being monitored. Many activists were monitored almost continuously by police officers and the intelligence services, and police officers were present during demonstrations as well as leisure activities. Some officers of the security services and police were also known by the activists as the individuals who were monitoring them. Although this form of surveillance led to some hilarity among the activists, it also appeared to give them a certain status ('It proves we matter', one of them told me).

While this chapter focuses on the hard surveillance of militant activists, it is important to note that this surveillance tactic is not restricted to this group only. Other Muslims (or people who may 'look Muslim') can also be targeted if they are in the 'wrong' places – places that are deemed a risk. Many activist networks (mostly Salafi but not all) have shared their stories about sudden visits by the police or other institutions (this is not always clear to them). This would often occur right after they established an organization with a political orientation that was unclear to outsiders. As Ali shows in his research with Muslim students in the United States, the surveillance of Muslims 'is enacted upon individuals and communities deemed suspicious by the state rather than simply as a response to a specific act'.[46] In the autumn of 2016, the police at Schiphol airport approached a young man. According to his own account, on Facebook, he was interrogated and then released. After his lawyer asked the Royal Netherlands Marechaussee (who are responsible for airport security) for information; he got an official letter stating that the man had been arrested and investigated because 'he fitted a profile that matches jihadism'.[47] For obvious reasons the Marechaussee refused to disclose the content of such a profile although behaviour and outward appearances were probably part of it.[48] The letter also stated that no further investigations against the man were being conducted and that he was not a suspect. As the person in question was not working as an activist in any way, and opposed ISIS and Jabhat al-Nusra on his Facebook pages, the declaration that he had 'a profile that matches jihadism' opened the door to the widest speculation. In this way the system does not only try to expose those racialized as Muslims who may indeed be a potential threat, it also stigmatizes those who are at risk (but not considered a risk anymore). The example also shows how hard surveillance, which is meant to increase safety, can transform a space into one which is potentially unsafe for particular individuals; something which many Muslims in my research (militant activists and others) were keenly aware of.

The main reaction among the militant activists to hard surveillance is similar to their responses to soft surveillance: 'That's just how it is'. This response to hard surveillance can be seen as a mode of attuning oneself to living in a situation in which one knows one is being monitored or one expects to be. It is a form of 'inattention' as Larkin explains in relation to how people in Nigeria engage with the disruptions in daily life that are caused by all kinds of attention-seeking technologies (such as the public call to prayer).[49] In particular, because of the reoccurring politico-religious conflicts, one has to cultivate 'inattention' to be able to live and work in the urban areas. People do pay attention to the violent messages but develop the skill to not openly display attention: 'it is a conscious, wilful act and not simply an inability to attend'.[50] With a little twist we can argue the same for the militant activists. Through their construction and protection of a space where everything conforms to their own rules (instead of the government's), they try not to be affected by the surveillance and to create a condition that enables them to continue with their activism and to develop the necessary skills to do so.

Sometimes, however, this deliberate inattention does not work. Take, for example, my conversations with AZ, one of the militant activists who was under surveillance by the police and security services. During a conversation we were having in a restaurant in The Hague, after a few minutes, he suggested moving seats because: '*I have to have a clear view of what is going on here and I want to be able to leave as quickly as possible if necessary*'. A few days later when we met in the

Public Library of The Hague, he grew visibly nervous during our conversation, looking around, staring at people passing by and losing focus on the topic of the conversation. '*Those three guys, with similar rucksacks and those shoes, they're walking around but always stay close to us. They are watching us.*' Changing places and monitoring one's environment for people who seem out of place become ways of maintaining a certain degree of control but it also converts the space into one full of danger and suspicion, often expressed through statements like: 'But maybe we are just getting paranoid'.

This explicit, and frequently made, reference to paranoia is an expression of a desire to be unaffected by the hard surveillance without challenging it publicly. In this particular case the routinization failed and gave way to surveillance paranoia: changing places or changing the venue is then a way to restore the routinization. Another method of routinization is to make jokes about the surveillance. Sometimes this happens right in front of known officers of the police and security services but also often among themselves. For example, at the start of a meeting I attended, one of the speakers not only welcomed the visitors, the press and the researcher, but also 'the security services, those poor guys who are now going to listen to one of the most inciting, sorry, boring lectures ever'.

Humour such as this functioned as a way of bonding and instilled in those present that they were among like-minded people who had to deal with similar circumstances, challenges and questions. At the same time, being among each other also appeared to be a way to continue the routinization of the regime of surveillance: being less vulnerable and more shielded against any disturbance of their daily lives by the hard surveillance. Furthermore, even tougher measures such as the arrests of a few militants some years prior to the Syria conflict was explained as part and parcel of being a 'true' Muslim. Abu Muhammad, for example, then explained:[51]

> This is all a political game, but the more Islam is attacked the stronger your *imaan* (inner faith) becomes since the Prophet Muhammad, peace be upon him, predicted this, that Islam will start as something strange and will end as something strange. And then yes, we are the strangers or *ghuraba*.

The narrative of the *ghuraba* is based upon two Hadiths, which are believed to represent the true Muslim as a travelling stranger in this world who acquiesces to his fate. Abu Muhammad like several of his friends believe that persecution and living in isolation is a consequence of being steadfast believers just as it was for Prophet Muhammad. As a consequence, they live on the margins of a godless society; reliving the idea that Islam began as something strange, or at odds with the status quo of that time, and will end as such.[52] This example also shows that being under surveillance helps to form the self-understanding of these militant activists and supports their internal construction of a 'true' Muslim, a committed, steadfast activist. Furthermore, both the hard and soft surveillance contributed to them seeing the state as their enemy. They presented themselves as hardliners who were going against the oppressive tactics of the state. For instance, they once released a video in which they allegedly disclosed how the police monitored and traced them while they were driving through The Hague in a car. Yet, they were often accommodating and very friendly to the police during demonstrations. Furthermore, several of the activists also depended on the state for welfare benefits. As such, being the subject of soft and hard surveillance resulted in the individual having a very complicated and ambivalent relationship with the state.

The Hondius case: How mobilization and routinization interfere

In the former sections, I showed how strategies of routinization and mobilization are often deployed by activists in dealing with the dominant context. Yet the use of these tactics also created its own problems and challenges. To illustrate this, I want to focus on what has come to be known as 'the Hondius case'. This affair describes a confrontation that took place in September 2013 between the police and the activists during a friendly football match after an incident occurred during another friendly match a week earlier; an incident which had attracted a lot of media attention.

The weekend football games first started in 2011 as an opportunity to be with like-minded people, brothers and friends who combined their love for football with their love for Islam (there are always lectures as well). These gatherings can be seen as attempts to create a space of their own, one in which they can conduct themselves in the way they want to. It is a space for them in which they are not, or rather were not, bothered by the authorities and the media.

In September 2013, during a football game, they posted a photo of one of the men walking with the flag of the seal of the Prophet Muhammad, which had come to be known as the 'ISIS flag' since this movement rose to power. The following day the photo appeared on the twitter account of ISIS stating that Dutch Muslims supported the Islamic state of Iraq and Syria. The photo was quickly discovered by Dutch journalists and Belgian 'jihad watchers' and caused a controversy; people were incensed by this statement of support and the blatant flag flying. The event also became politicized because of the meanings that were imposed upon the flag (and subsequently also upon the young men) such as the 'al-Qaeda flag' and 'terrorist flag'. The Freedom Party asked questions about it in the Dutch Parliament and called the mayor of The Hague 'a coward' after he stated he disliked the flag but could not do anything about it because it was a matter of the freedom of speech.

Although this controversy was exactly what some activists feared, i.e. their space being threatened by public attention expressed in terms of terrorism and al-Qaeda, others sought to respond to this commotion by organizing a new, larger football gathering with a barbecue the following weekend at the Hondius playground in The Hague. The controversy had prompted the activists to make a political statement, on the one hand, by organizing a larger event and, on the other hand, to ridicule the responses by saying it was 'only football and a barbecue'. According to AM the gathering was just friends playing football and 'there is nothing wrong with that. Obviously, we're not going to do anything crazy, we know the AIVD is monitoring us. It is just a family and friends get together'. This quote is interesting because AM clearly shows that he knows he and his friends are under surveillance and that they take that into account. We see, furthermore, that he expects the public debate about them (the soft surveillance) will lead to police presence (hard surveillance).

The activists expected the police to arrive, and they were right, but in a way they did not anticipate: the police cracked down on the meeting. After holding the activists for several hours at the playground, the police arrested five people for incitement and refusing to show their ID cards.[53] Later that night several activists took a photo of the Islamic seal flag flying over another playing field and sent it to *De Volkskrant* newspaper which published it the very next day. This was a clear demonstration of how the crackdown enabled the activists to construct a counter-subjectivity. In the article and the photo, they presented themselves not as moderate or liberal Muslims who complied with the wishes of the Dutch authorities, but as Muslims who defied and challenged these authorities by going on a field at night with the flag, posting a photo online and announcing more 'football actions.' The Hondius event did not only have a political value for the militant activists, it also had an ethical one since it provided them with a sense of being prosecuted as Muslims and of having proudly and steadfastly stood up against it: exactly the way 'true' Muslims should conduct themselves. This made their resistance, in their eyes, an action, a choice, not just a reaction against the state's policies and media attention. Their subjectivity was enabled by the publicity and police actions but it also escaped it because it did not submit (in the fullest sense) to the governmentalities of the state. Furthermore, the event and their reaction to it established a particular kind of reputation for them among other Muslims who saw them as intimidating or even threatening. Many of the Salafi Muslims from mainstream Salafi networks who were present at 'Hondius' did not agree with the way the BehindBars network handled the confrontation and did not want their studies or professional careers jeopardized by confronting the police (something they stated afterwards, not during the event itself). The event therefore created a greater division between the BehindBars network and other (Salafi) Muslims.

The debate about the flag could not have emerged without the ongoing racialization of danger (itself exacerbated because of the rise of ISIS and its relentless actions). This subsequently produced a situation in which the soft surveillance and hard surveillance endured by these militant activists came together in the crackdown on this event. In turn, the event (which they called the 'Battle of Hondius') enabled a 'performance of radicalism' (instead of a performance of safety) by the militant activists. At the same time, however, the authorities and the media labelled them as 'radical Muslims', their football gathering as a political manifestation and, in the later indictments, as 'a meeting of jihadists who were recruiting'. In 2015, during the trial of ten activists and foreign fighters (most of whom were present at Hondius), it became clear that the 'Hondius meeting' triggered the start of the inquiry into the militants' activities initiated by the public prosecutor and represented the beginning of the collapse of both the routinization and mobilization.[54]

Conclusion

The securitization of Islam and the racialization of danger create an exclusive security gaze on Muslims within a specific arrangement of the Dutch nation-state, race and religion. Drawing on different ways of constructing Muslims as a danger through policies and debates concerning Islam, integration and counter-radicalization, Muslims, or people who 'look like' Muslims and, in particular, look like 'radical Muslims', have become more visible and potentially dangerous and suspect. In this chapter I have analysed how a network of friends and acquaintances operating under names such as BehindBars, who were labelled as a potential threat to security, responded to modes of hard and soft surveillance. These forms of surveillance had direct and indirect consequences for these individuals' lives and work. The practices of routinization and mobilization are part of the regime of surveillance, a regime of living that offers a possible answer to the question, 'How should I live when I am a security problem?' In analysing this regime of surveillance this study adds to the existing critical studies on the apparatus of security – by highlighting and interpreting the perspectives and experiences of those who are directly targeted by the security state.

For the militant activists, the soft and hard surveillance produced a situation in which they were continually checking themselves and asking themselves how they should live. As Lakoff and Collier point out, regimes of living may provide answers to an uncertain situation but they can also raise new ethical problems.[55] The tension that arose between the desire to live one's life without interference, and the desire not to submit, was an important feature of how a very small and specific group of militant activists behaved in a context of the monitoring and surveillance carried out by the security services and police.

Although the militant activists state that they get used to these tactics and that dealing with them becomes a routine, in some cases, when their personal sphere (not necessarily private sphere) is invaded and the routinization hindered, they have to devise new responses to the question, 'how do we live (or act) now?' This question also emerges from their deliberations about what kind of protest they want to stage. At the same time, they also want to be 'left alone' and have their own free space, a space in which they can live according to an alternative type of self-regulation than what is proposed by the state: an Islamic one. The phrase 'That's just how it is' is an attempt to avoid confronting the situation, but the same statement also reveals an alienation from a society that treats Muslims with double standards and is, at the same time, a critique of Dutch society.

Analysing the regime of surveillance of the militants provides us with insight into the ways that people understand themselves in relation to other members of Dutch society (including other Muslims) and in relation to the counter-radicalization practices of the state. For militant activists it was important to be able to continue their lives as they saw fit: on the one hand being inconspicuous and on the other not submitting to the practices of the state. As Yuval-Davis reminds us, challenging what the state regards as public and private is a political act.[56] Liberal states intervene differently in matters that are regarded as private than they do in public matters. The racialization of danger and the threat that may come from the militant activists, in particular, has legitimized and enabled the state to monitor the private lives of these people, especially after they were categorized as a potential terrorist threat. The fact that the investigation and intelligence agencies focused on the activists' private lives means that this sphere also became politicized – a public domain – whether the activists wanted this or not. As long as they did not break the law, the authorities had only limited control over them, but the militant activists couldn't manage to elude their grasp entirely. For the activists, the boundaries between politics and religion and between public and private thus become completely blurred.

The regime of surveillance for militant activists links and mediates their formation of ethics with the debates and policies regarding ('radical' and 'radicalizing') Muslims. It reinforces their views on what it means to be steadfast Muslims and activists, underlines their daily responsibilities as husbands, fathers and family members and clarifies their tactical and strategic thinking as activists. Routinization and mobilization do, therefore, point to a series of related questions, uncertainties and ambiguities pertaining to the ethical and practical problem of how to live and how to be an activist, a Muslim, a father and a husband. These ambiguities are partly linked to the issue of uncertainty: one does not always know how to interpret a particular question from a colleague or if one is monitored or not. In this sense, counter-radicalization can be seen as a way to manage the uncertainty of knowing who is a risk and who is at risk through racializing danger. Yet, those at risk may also be targeted as a risk when they meet the criteria of 'a profile that matches with jihadism'. In the case of the militant activists in my research, they construct regimes of living to deal with the uncertainties and ambiguities that come with being the object of the racialized security gaze but they also use the racialized security to construct themselves as steadfast Muslims and activists.

At the same time, as the Hondius case in 2013 shows, the process of combining routinization and mobilization is, at least for the activists, self-defeating. They struggled to keep up the routinization and became more careless when it came to mobilization, which led to several of them being arrested almost a year later. The idea that one should be steadfast, and the desire to be regulated in an alternative manner, may give the activists' regime of living a certain coherent and stable appearance but did not achieve any level of institutional stability while it faces growing pressures from outside.

Notes

1   De Koning, Roex, Becker and Aarns, *Eilanden in een zee van ongeloof*. The project also included networks in Belgium and Germany. This chapter will focus on the Dutch network. The project was funded by the University of Amsterdam, Radboud University, Nijmegen, the Ministry of Security and Justice and by the Netherlands Organization for Scientific Research (NWO) for the project 'Forces That Bind and/or Divide' of the Department of Anthropology of the University of Amsterdam.

2   This section summarizes and builds on Martijn de Koning, ' "You Need to Present a Counter-Message" – The Racialisation of Dutch Muslims and Anti-Islamophobia Initiatives', *Journal of Muslims in Europe* 5, no. 2 (2016): 170–89.

3   Scholten, *Framing Immigrant Integration.*

4   Ibid.

5   Fermin, *Nederlandse politieke partijen.*

6   *Verslag van de vaste Commissie voor de inlichtingen en veiligheidsdiensten over haar werksaamheden (juli 1990–juli 1991)*, Tweede Kamer, vergaderjaar 1991–2, 22463, nr. 3.

7   Paul Mepschen, Jan-Willem Duyvendak and Evelien Tonkens, 'Sexual Politics, Orientalism and Multicultural Citizenship in the Netherlands', *Sociology* 44, no. 5 (2010): 962–79.

8   Ellie Vasta, 'From Ethnic Minorities to Ethnic Majority Policy: Multiculturalism and the Shift to Assimilationism in the Netherlands', *Ethnic and Racial Studies* 30, no. 5 (2007): 713–40.

9   Dvora Yanow and Marleen van der Haar, 'People Out of Place: Allochthony and Autochthony in the Netherlands' Identity Discourse—Metaphors and Categories in Action', *Journal of International Relations and Development* 16, no. 2 (2015): 227–61.

10 Peter Geschiere, *The Perils of Belonging: Autochthony, Citizenship, and Exclusion in Africa and Europe* (Chicago, IL: University of Chicago Press, 2009).

11 Dieke Hondius, 'Black Dutch Voices: Reports from a Country that Leaves Racism Unchallenged', in *Dutch Racism*, eds. Philomena Essed and Isabel Hoving (Amsterdam: Rodopi, 2014).

12 Adam James Tebble, 'Exclusion for Democracy', *Political Theory* 34, no. 4 (2006): 463–87.

13 De Koning, 'You Need to Present a Counter-Message'.

14 Rens Vliegenthart, *Framing Immigration and Integration: Facts, Parliament, Media and Anti-Immigrant Party Support in the Netherlands* (Amsterdam: Vrije Universiteit, 2007); and De Graaf, 'Religion Bites'.

15 Stuart Croft, *Securitizing Islam: Identity and the Search for Security* (Cambridge: Cambridge University Press, 2012).

16 Ibid., 91.

17 Clara Eroukhmanoff, 'The Remote Securitisation of Islam in the US Post-9/11: Euphemisation, Metaphors and the "Logic of Expected Consequences" in Counter-Radicalization Discourse', *Critical Studies on Terrorism* 8, no. 2 (2015): 246–65.

18 Edmunds, 'The "New" Barbarians'.

19 Ibid., p. 73.

20 Seda Gürses, Arun Kundnani and Joris van Hoboken, 'Crypto and Empire: The Contradictions of Counter-Surveillance Advocacy', *Media Culture & Society* 38, no. 4 (2016): 579. See also David Theo Goldberg, 'Militarizing Race', *Social Text* 34, no. 4 (2016): 19–40; Sanjay Sharma and Nijjar Jasbinder, 'The Racialized Surveillant Assemblage: Islam and the Fear of Terrorism', *Popular Communication* 16, no. 1 (2018): 72–85; David Moffette and Vadasaria Shaira, 'Uninhibited Violence: Race and the Securitization of Immigration', *Critical Studies on Security* 4, no. 3 (2016): 291–305; Junaid Rana, 'The Racial Infrastructure of the Terror-Industrial Complex', *Social Text* 34, no. 4 (2016): 111–38.

21 These studies often draw upon Foucault's ideas of the panopticon and focus on the techno-social realities of surveillance and the institutions which perform it. For example, see Nicola Green and Nils Zurawski, 'Surveillance and Ethnography:

Researching Surveillance as Everyday Life', *Surveillance & Society* 13, no. 1 (2015): 27–43.

22 Andrew Lakoff and Stephen J. Collier, 'Ethics and the Anthropology of Modern Reason', *Anthropological Theory* 4, no. 4 (2004): 419–34.

23 Ibid., p. 420.

24 I have explained the idea of regimes of living in more in detail in Martijn de Koning, 'How Should I Live as a "True" Muslim? Regimes of Living among Dutch Muslims in the Salafi Movement', *Etnofoor* 25, no. 2 (2013): 53–72.

25 Pantazis and Pemberton, 'From the "Old" to the "New" Suspect Community'.

26 Paddy Hillyard, *Suspect Community* (London: Pluto Press, 1993).

27 Stephen J. Collier and Andrew Lakoff, 'On Regimes of Living', in *Global Assemblages*, eds. Aihwa Ong and Stephen J. Collier (Oxford: Blackwell, 2008).

28 Rogers Brubaker, 'Categories of Analysis and Categories of Practice: A Note on the Study of Muslims in European Countries of Immigration', *Ethnic and Racial Studies* 36, no. 1 (2013): 3. The quote is from Werner Schiffauer, 'Vom Exil-zum Diaspora-Islam: Muslimische Identitäten in Europa', *Soziale Welt* 55, no. 4 (2004): 348.

29 Collier and Lakoff, 'On Regimes of Living', p. 29.

30 Alana Lentin and Gavan Titley, *The Crisis of Multiculturalism: Racism in a Neoliberal Age* (London: Zed Books, 2011), p. 134.

31 In discussing the Danish asylum procedure, Whyte explores how uncertainty is an important part of the security gaze and how the objects of this gaze respond to it. See Zachary Whyte, 'Enter the Myopticon: Uncertain Surveillance in the Danish Asylum System', *Anthropology Today* 27, no. 3 (2013): 18–21.

32 Lakoff and Collier, 'Ethics and the Anthropology of Modern Reason', pp. 422–23.

33 Collier and Lakoff, 'On Regimes of Living', p. 32.

34 Hans Siebers, 'The Impact of Migrant-Hostile Discourse in the Media and Politics on Racioethnic Closure in Career Development in the Netherlands', *International Sociology* 25, no. 4 (2010): 475–500.

35 Lori Allen, 'Getting by the Occupation: How Violence Became Normal during the Second Palestinian Intifada', *Cultural Anthropology* 23, no. 3 (2008): 453–87.

36 Allen, 'Getting by the Occupation', p. 457.

37 Of course an attempt to be a good father can also be part of the effort to be a pious Muslim, and vice versa.

38 De Koning, Roex, Becker and Aarns, *Eilanden in een zee van ongeloof*.

39 Foucault, *Security, Territory, Population*, pp. 194–95; Michel Foucault, 'The Subject and Power', *Critical Inquiry* 8, no. 4 (1982): 781.

40 Carl Death, 'Counter-Conducts: A Foucauldian Analytics of Protest', *Social Movement Studies* 9, no. 3 (2010): 248.

41 Fareen Z. Parvez, 'Debating the Burqa in France: The Antipolitics of Islamic Revival.' *Qualitative Sociology* 34, no. 2 (2011): 289.

42 De Koning, Becker, Roex and Aarns, *Eilanden in een zee van ongeloof*.

43 Gabe Mythen, Sandra Walklate and Fatima Khan, ' "I'm a Muslim, but I'm Not a Terrorist": Victimization, Risky Identities and the Performance of Safety', *British Journal of Criminology* 49, no. 6 (2009): 736–54.

44 Ruud Koopmans, 'Religious Fundamentalism and Hostility against Out-Groups: A Comparison of Muslims and Christians in Western Europe', *Journal of Ethnic and Migration Studies* 41, no. 1 (2015): 33–57.

45 Arshad Imitaz Ali, 'Citizens under Suspicion: Responsive Research with Community under Surveillance', *Anthropology & Education Quarterly* 47, no. 1 (2016): 86.

46 Ibid., p. 80.

47 My translation. Original: '. . . daar hij voldeed aan het profiel dat past bij jihadisme'.

48 Based upon an informal conversation with an employee of the Royal Netherlands
    Marechaussee (RNM). In a formal reply by the press agents
    of the RNM, it was stated that a profile consists of several aspects based upon
    information from different police and intelligence services and is checked for validity.
    Someone who fits the profile is not immediately a suspect, but will be investigated.
    According to the RNM 'profiles assist the Marechaussee agents in executing their task'
    (Email, 16 September 2016).

49 Brian Larkin, 'Techniques of Inattention: The Mediality of Loudspeakers in Nigeria',
    Anthropological Quarterly 87, no. 4 (2014): 989–1015.

50 Ibid., p. 1006.

51 Also published in De Koning, 'How Should I Live as a "True" Muslim?', p. 65.

52 Carmen Becker, *Learning to Be Authentic: Religious Practices of German and Dutch
    Muslims following the Salafiyya in Forums and Chat Rooms* (Nijmegen: Radboud
    University, 2013).

53 I stayed with the activists and like most of them was free to go after showing my ID
    and allowing it to be copied.

54 On this court case, see De Graaf (Chapter 4 in this volume).

55 Lakoff and Collier, 'Ethics and the Anthropology of Modern Reason', p. 430.

56 Nira Yuval-Davis, *Gender and Nation* (London: Sage, 1997), p. 83.

Chapter 9

CAN THE 'MUHAJIR' SPEAK? EUROPEAN SYRIA FIGHTERS AND THE DIGITAL UN/MAKING OF HOME

Jaafar Alloul

In May 2014, a man calling himself Abu Fulaan from Antwerp[1] posted a video on YouTube explicitly addressing his audience as *drari*, Maghrebi Arabic vernacular (*Darija*) for 'brothers'. In his talk, Abu Fulaan is clearly concerned with presenting life after emigration as good, if not *better* than (staying put at home) in Europe. Driving his car somewhere in northern Syria, and filming himself with his dash camera, he claims repeatedly in Dutch that 'life is *very* normal here', adding that 'in some cases we're even better off than you guys in Belgium'.[2] Fulaan's aversion for the institutional order of things in Europe comes to the fore when he refers to Belgian political parties, which are usually deemed sympathetic to minority concerns, but by whom he seems to feel betrayed, as follows:

> *Sp.A* [socialist party] and *Groen* [green party], it's all bullshit! It's all the same. *Vlaams Blok*! [far-right party] They are the least troublesome of all those democrats over there [Belgium]. Why? Because they say it out loud: All *makkakken*[3] out. Muslims shouldn't be here.[4]

Fulaan then even urges *his* social group, that is, Belgian-Moroccans, to reconsider their supposedly docile voting habits: 'There are many people who say that if we don't vote the extreme right will win the elections and we will be the victims of that, and therefore we should all vote left-wing parties. ... Those politicians for whom most Moroccans ... most Muslims, vote – they do vote indeed – have never solved anything for us Muslims'.[5] To outside observers, it is striking that although Abu Fulaan is based in war-torn Syria, he focuses primarily on Belgium, fulminating, 'I have followed the [Flemish] news', and 'in a few days there will be elections, so people are urging each other to go vote'.[6] These utterings clearly indicate an ongoing emotional investment in the home country, as well as a desire to politicize life there. For instance, in another of several YouTube episodes, he and his Dutch co-driver, referring to Sharia law, urge youngsters *not* to go vote and to stage protests simultaneously: 'Go and hold up pamphlets and distribute flyers in order to raise political awareness'.[7]

The presence of Belgian nationals in Syria first came to the general public's attention in Flanders during the summer of 2012. Belgium now holds the highest per capita contingent of EU 'foreign fighters' in Syria. As of February 2018, the total number of Belgian legal subjects having engaged in migration efforts to Syria ever since 2012 was estimated at 550–600, including both failed attempts and 'returnees'.[8] This entire group has been described as comprising a variety of 'teenagers and tweens, girls as well as boys, sometimes entire families, or mothers with small children'.[9] Also, 75 per cent of the estimated total of 137 Belgian children in Syria was born on site. Of the 413 *adult* Belgian 'Syria fighters' or 'foreign terrorist fighters' (FTF) – as they are now dubbed by most agencies of the Belgian government – who managed to reach Syria and Iraq, 80 per cent 'are young men with a typical age range between twenty and thirty', and three-quarters reportedly 'joined the Islamic State (ISIS)'.[10] By February 2018, the Dutch FTF group believed to have travelled to Syria and Iraq was estimated at 280 nationals, with at least 42 killed on site, 50 returnees, and 140 remaining in the region.[11] For the joint Belgian and Dutch cases for which information is available, unemployment was estimated at 32 per cent for the Belgian cohort and 41 per cent for the Dutch group, with those employed mainly categorized as unskilled workers.[12] Moreover, some estimates suggest that around 80 per cent of the Belgian Syria fighters held a Maghrebi *minority* background, while at least a disaggregated 41 per cent of the Dutch fighters is reported to have a Moroccan background.[13]

In September 2014, the largest ever terrorism prosecution in Belgian history began. Members of an association named 'Sharia4Belgium' and a set of Syria fighters were put on trial, some in absentia. Speculation about the role of Belgian nationals in crimes against humanity committed in Syria has been ongoing, ever since videos surfaced online in mid-2013 in which Belgian 'fighters' allegedly filmed their own acts of beheading their Syrian adversaries.[14] Many other European emigrants – *muhajirun* in their own parlour[15] – also used a variety of social media platforms to record and share their activities in Syria.[16] A French media commentator even remarked on the jubilant editing and publishing process of one such video – in which Belgian national Abdelhamid Abaaoud can be seen driving a pick-up truck in Syria and dragging along the bodies of what he proudly calls the *murtad* (apostates) – '[They] film their jihad, as if it were all a game'.[17] This chapter seeks to unravel some of the meanings behind the fabrication and distribution of such digital-style performances of European Islamist fighters in the disintegrating state(s) of Syria (and Iraq), aimed at local publics at home in Europe.

These inexpensively assembled (YouTube) videos and staged pictures focus primarily on their own mythical engagement in what they call *sham*,[18] and later the *khilafa* (Caliphate), instead of on the Syrian people's struggles. Indeed, social media posts of profane celebrations of 'newfound' material gains in Syria (weapons, cars, villas) appear legion,[19] along with 'jihadi' enactments of what has been coined 'fierce masculinity' in other case studies on the migration of close-knitted male groups.[20] This somewhat narcissistic and consumerist behaviour of some European *muhajirun* in Syria is reminiscent of the 'post-political' characterization of contemporary society.[21] However, a closer look at some of these online performances suggests that concrete *politics* might nevertheless be present. Interestingly though, these politics often relate directly to Europe rather than (only) the Middle East. This chapter therefore also gauges how such digital jihadi enactments can be understood and read as practices of romantic-nationalist 'homemaking', whereby established notions of belonging, (feeling at) home and citizenship are purportedly destabilized in favour of the mythical trope of an idealized 'Islamic home'.

Over time, a series of media polemics and public spectacles have arisen in the Flemish and Dutch media on whether or not these are *really* 'Our boys in Syria?'[22] Moreover, lawmakers across Europe have sought to strip 'them' of their citizenship through new terrorism legislation, thus seeking to redefine the boundaries of the constitutional order and reinforce the cultural form of the 'punitive turn'.[23] In sight of this *muhajir* (migrant) phenomenon to conflict zones and rising security concerns across the EU, some politicians in the Low Countries have started applying the catch phrase 'act normal or leave',[24] insinuating that all sorts of agitation and deviance from the part of 'the people' – in this case exceptional minorities – should be de-territorialized, and preferably so to an (ancestral) elsewhere ('homeland'). Yet, one can also detect a degree of unease among policymakers and academics in Europe on how to best 'define' EU nationals that have left for Syria: 'Syria fighters', 'Syria travellers', 'foreign fighters', 'FTF', or 'jihadi brides' (for women)? It is telling that none of these common institutional signifiers imply any reference to Europe, while at least *some* Europeans in Syria, like Hicham Chaib, have appropriated a *nom de guerre* that denotes precisely such a *spatial* connection: 'Abu Hanifa al-Baljiki [the Belgian]'.

This chapter has three main purposes: (1) to unpack the complex web of coded (Islamic) ideas (*hijra, jihad, sham, umma, ikhwaniyya*) on which some *muhajirun* draw and outline how this infers a set of *relational* societal sensibilities that refer back to Europe; (2) to denaturalize what we pretend to know about 'jihadi radicalization' in Western Europe by foregrounding anthropologically some of the narratives of the actors themselves; and (3) to elucidate some of the ways in which the state in Europe has tried to (re)gain control over these 'anti-citizens' (e.g. by enacting new terrorism legislation, declaring a state of emergency, stripping of citizenship and discursive framing). In the following section, I first review the dominant ways in which social scientific knowledge has thus far been produced about this deviant public. It will be shown how the analytical concepts of 'social space' and 'home', as well as the lens of a political anthropology of migration, offer fruitful venues for inquiry. I then offer a brief note on the applied methodology, before presenting my data and research results.

Knowledge production on radicalization

The considerable focus on the *mahjar* (place of departure in Europe), apparent in the language used by some of the Belgian and Dutch fighters in Syria, earnestly questions key arguments found in the bulk of rapidly emerging radicalization studies, which mostly emphasize (ideological) 'pull factors'.[25] The latter focus often leads to methodological individualism (and *petite histoire* as pathology),[26] and the mystification of explicit and implicit *structures* that may precede such outward mobility, such as the interplay between 'social space' and 'race'.[27] While much of the literature focalizes on the transgressive ideology of such agents, it neglects the context of departure and specific inter-group dynamics at play therein. Some scholars have attempted to address this lacuna, but mostly from *within* the framework of 'radicalization' or 'terrorism'.[28] Although these two strands of inquiry have been put to question in recent years,[29] a genealogical tendency to downplay the local context and prioritize 'international jihadism' remains salient.[30] For instance, in his recent edition on Syria fighters, Patrick Loobuyck puts forth a disquieting scientific reductionism, which the saturated radicalization paradigm now legitimatizes:

> We don't focus on the societal context of poverty, unemployment, disadvantage, discrimination, Islamophobia, equal opportunities, far right [politics], racism and (failed) integration. This does not imply that a debate on these subjects is unimportant; the contrary is true and it is a pity that we need Syria fighters to do so as a matter of speech. But we nevertheless do not treat these topics here in this study, because they do not have particular relevance to better understand Syria fighters, radicalization and the attraction of IS.[31]

While some scholars frame the *muhajirun's* behaviour as 'nihilist',[32] others mention the attraction to 'conspiracy theories'.[33] Both appreciations risk briskly depoliticizing these EU citizens' migratory agency and the very spaces, or 'power-geometries',[34] through which they move, irrespective of their mode of alienation or sense of paranoiac phantasm. Media scholarship either harbours similar ideological premises or gets bogged down in the substantial work that comes with more quantitative analyses.[35] Still others have mostly attended to synthesizing governmental data,[36] while staying largely within the analytical confines of 'integration'.[37] Few have drawn qualitatively on the direct empirical study of such online data as the discursive registers – or ethnographic artefacts – of a mobile but *local* contestation of societal power in Europe.[38] Anthropologists have only recently started exploring European female migrants in Syria (*muhajirat sham*) from such an everyday analytic while applying online methods.[39]

Although the Islamic notion of *jihad* and numerous *mujahidin* have enjoyed considerable attention in social science,[40] the Islamic concept of *hijra* (piety migration) remains much less investigated. Yet, one of the claims put forward here is that it is precisely this critical 'Islamic' notion that commands attention for the conducive context of departure in Europe. Once unpacked, this mobilizing *topos* serves as a cognitive bridge in linking strands of contemporary Islamic vernacular to broader phenomena such as alienation and specific modes of spatial-urban aversion and indignation, which are social, if not existential as well.[41] In fact, *hijra* speaks of the unimaginable: *leaving* wealthy Europe for war-torn Syria because of a negative place attachment in the West. In their own right, scholars of Islamic studies have already connected such underlying semantic registers as *hijra*, and *dar al-harb* ('the house of war', meaning territory outside Muslim rule), to a variety of historical and jurisprudential debates within the Islamic tradition on the prescription of jihad as either an individual (*fard 'ayn*) or communal responsibility (*fard kifaya*), while noting simultaneously dynamic shifts in the ideational spheres of global(izing) Islam(s).[42] Indeed, the verbal Arabic root of *hijra* often features in the Qur'an in concurrence with that of *jihad*.[43] However, *hijra* also inherently references social space. After all, its Arabic meaning literally oscillates between 'forced migration', 'to break away from' and 'render(ed) homeless', encompassing the coatings of structure, instances of agency and a temporal and uprooted state of liminal being. The contemporary mobilization of *hijra* as a politicized category may therefore signal how a set of lived experiences of socio-spatial friction have in turn enabled romantic imaginaries of land (*sham*) and community to take shape. Adopting this angle, 'Islamist' notions such as *hijra, jihad* or *sham* suddenly appear to us as very modernist epistemic classifications.

In this sense, the *muhajir*, as an un-theorized 'mobile figure',[44] thus also embodies the increasingly politicized *emotion* of 'home' in Europe, or what Jan Willem Duyvendak calls the 'crisis of home': heightened social and political concerns for ethno-national belonging and organization. Interestingly, and contrary to what has thus far appeared in social science literature, Duyvendak approaches 'home' as an emotional experience and interactional disposition rather than as a mere physical structure or purely individual sentiment.[45] This then invites us to reflect more profoundly on the uneven experience of what Henri Lefebvre theorized earlier as 'social space' and the 'triple dialectic', that is, the meeting point of situational political economy (materiality) and cultural forms (layered, ideological normativities), reified as actual social environments by the occurrence of everyday interactions. Indeed, 'space' is not a mere passive background to social relations; rather, space is fundamentally social because material context, ideological regimes and everyday social interactions are all mutually constitutive, functioning as a triad or 'socio-spatial dialectic'.[46] My reading of the notion of *hijra* also resonates with debates on the validity of the critique of 'racial capitalism' and its implications for a 'politics of recognition'.[47] Although racialized majority–minority dynamics in Europe have been studied in relation to Muslim publics,[48] few have approached it from the dynamic case-perspective of emigration. Indeed, while studies exist about the impact of 'multicultural' *immigration* on formations of 'race' in the West,[49] rare are those that focus on the impact that 'race' has on *emigration*, that is, as a powerful structure in itself, informing social experience and capable of spurring all sorts of new (individualized) 'migratory dispositions'.[50]

Mainstream social science research in Western Europe still considers 'race' to be a predominantly American issue and therefore an analytic relevant chiefly to US scholarship. Ignored thereby are the basic premises of racial formation theory,[51] such as racial categorizations being dynamic throughout time (and space), in what remains a societal power play between (established) groups (and newcomers) over capital resources and political domination. This ontic and epistemic inertia has become manifest recently in that it is first and foremost US scholars who initiated the significant question, 'Is Islam in Western Europe like race in the United States?'[52]

A small and pioneering number of European scholars have recently sought to address this racial optic trans-historically by positing Islamophobia as 'the new Western racism', flowing out of an older Euro-colonial racism and continental anti-Semitism.[53] Yet, this overall reluctance of taking race seriously as a meaningful category of analysis might stem from the ongoing rescaling of 'methodological nationalism',[54] fixated on all sorts of *immigration* to 'Fortress Europe'.

The following question arises from this critical framework: does *hijra* as a coded form of emigration constitute a spatially contextual and highly symbolic form of minoritarian 'exit' in Europe,[55] one which paradoxically reflects a sense of migratory 'hope',[56] as a modern 'imaginary of mobility'?[57]

Methodology: Complementary practices of looking

Scholars have come to note a general 'lack of primary data' in most studies on Islamist radicalization in Europe.[58] Indeed, while governments limit sharing their sensitive information, social media platforms and companies like YouTube and Facebook are known to erase 'hate speech', nullifying considerable empirical evidence and leaving the public only with impressions. Others have nevertheless noted that, unlike the crises in Bahrain or Yemen, 'Syria is probably the most "socially mediated" conflict in modern history',[59] foregrounding the growing importance of 'online fields' when physical access is restricted.[60] In an attempt to redress this dearth of primary data, this chapter draws on a preliminary sample of videos and pictures that surfaced online, or were sometimes reported on (and stored temporarily) by media outlets, in the early war context of 2012–14, when European Islamist activists and fighters in Syria were still disseminating their self-portrayals. In total, twelve open-source video samples (of anything between one and thirteen minutes) from mainly Dutch-speaking Belgian and Dutch (Maghrebi) nationals, and approximately twenty images were located online, featuring predominantly young men, of which only a portion could be discussed here.

While quantitative research has been conducted on some of the formal propaganda channels of organizations like ISIS, such as the English-language *Dabiq* magazine,[61] or the Twitter and Facebook accounts of vocal figures (in the West) calling for jihad in Syria,[62] this study draws on self-fabricated materials by Europeans in Syria, as well as on secondary ISIS propaganda segments that specifically feature EU nationals. In doing so, it seeks to move the analytical perspective primarily to the protagonists and their own discourses about leaving Europe, seeking to address the question, 'For what and for whom is all this going on, and – indeed – against whom?'[63]

This digital anthropology applied an open-source methodology,[64] employing both direct and indirect data collections. First, open access e-platforms like YouTube were skimmed manually by applying focused search variables, and then other materials (e.g. videos, pictures) were gathered from residual websites, public social media platforms and online media channels that have all reported on and stored such primary data. The overall aim was to isolate these primary materials from any secondary framing so as to explore more directly the perspectives of those engaging in *hijra* to Syria. I do not claim this sample is representative for any (national) group of European *muhajirun*, nor does this chapter provide an exhaustive causal explanation of this complex phenomenon – leaving this to scholars better positioned. Rather, I approach the theme through a body of literature that is seldom integrated during academic discussions of Islamist radicalization in Europe. Given the relative absence of similar studies that foreground e-data *outside* of the framework of radicalization, complementary insights on this *muhajir* public can be attained here, not least by first provoking the Spivakian question, 'Can the *muhajir* speak?'[65] and then carefully listening 'to what people say regarding where and when they feel at home, and what feeling at home means to them'.[66]

Discussion: Jihadi ego in new media

Speaking back to 'home' in Europe

A video featured online on the webpage of a Belgian daily newspaper in October 2013 and saw a Flemish-Maghrebi youth (see Figure 9.1) slander the Belgian population from abroad as 'the descendants of apes and swines', claiming that Belgium was 'fighting Islam with laws' by means of 'a ban on veils in schools'.[67] Despite the ISIS flag in the background, he was referencing *local* municipal politics in Belgium, dating from the late 2000s, namely when the city of Antwerp (led by the socialist mayor Janssens) decided to outlaw headscarves among civil servants in 2007. In 2009, a regional measure was also adopted in the Flemish public-school system, allowing for the prohibition of all displays of religious signs in schools, as an extension of the bureaucratic sartorial legislation.[68] References to such public discussions on the veil ban back in the Low Countries were also made in Abu Fulaan's first episode on YouTube:

> a woman who dresses up gets a fine, while a woman who undresses gets money for it. Yes! . . . The freedom of expression! For us there is no freedom. For us there is dictatorship; using a steel fist against Muslims, that is what we have experienced in Europe, guys.[69]

Here, Fulaan frames such legislative initiatives in the Low Countries as efforts that sought to limit the freedom of religion. Contrary to what one would expect from someone engaged in the Syrian civil war, he chooses to emphasize the claim that his social group has experienced a lack of 'freedom' *in Europe*. We can read in Fulaan's outcry a sense of racialized exclusion and suppression ('steel fist against Muslims'). His narrative appears to stand in opposition to what he perceives as a top-down 'technology' of state (bio)power. Here, the *muhajir*'s rhetoric could be seen to function as an oppositional 'technique' that seeks to undermine the moral authority of the state in Europe.

Figure 9.1 Anonymous Belgian in Syria. Screenshot caption: 'We left everything behind: our family and friends.'

Source: Anonymous 1, in 'Strijder roept in plat antwerps op om aanslagen te plegen en naar Syrië te komen', *Het Nieuwsblad* [online], 23 October 2013. Available at https://www.nieuwsblad.be/article/detail.aspx?articleid=DMF20131022_00804525 (accessed 18 November 2013).

Besides such political controversies, some fighters also share rather banal details of their daily practices in Syria. Abu Fulaan, for instance, occasionally mentions some leisurely routines that seemingly fall outside of any concrete politics: 'I'll be driving to the shop later on to buy some crisps, some drinks, Pepsi and stuff; that's all available here'. However, these mundane references nevertheless allude to a *concrete* urban space and minority milieu in Europe. What Fulaan does here is to tap into a Dutch-*Darija* vernacular language and introduce subtly a sense of *familiarity* or 'home' that appeals directly to an urban youth culture in Europe. Hence, his popular 'urban language' functions as an emotive layer *within* the assemblage of his propaganda effort, rather than outside or alongside it. By infusing his message with familiar social codes, such as consuming snacks with close friends, he first portrays himself as an in-group member, establishing credibility and trust, and only then continues to project his ideology. By inserting *recognizable* elements of daily life in Europe into a larger account of (the war in) Syria, he reshapes the idea of travelling to Syria into something more conceivable; as a groomer, he leads the imagination by example. Such an emigration might otherwise appear alien or distant to European minority youths, as the intricacies of Middle Eastern politics are not familiar *per se* to second- and third-generation Maghrebis, born and raised in Europe. By blending the wider political concerns of minority publics in Europe, like the veil ban, with more banal rites located in the urban everyday of minority youths, Fulaan crafts meanings into the Syria conflict, offering a palatable 'translation'. Such highly emotional amalgamations help to make recruitment efforts echo more widely among alienated publics in Europe.

In his recent work, *Migration and the Search for Home*, Boccagni argues that a combined sense of *security, familiarity* and *control* constitute the three key elements in the social experience (of feeling at) 'home'.[70] Fulaan's negative perception of 'anti-Muslim' legislation takes the form of a dialogical resentment that testifies to a perceived loss of *security* for his specific (piety) group(s). It also conveys an inability, namely the perceived lack of a political means to exert a degree of *control* over contemporary forms of exclusion. Listening to these men's voices when they speak online, one notices a strong ventilation of anger for having gone through some kind of deep-seated, denigrating treatment in Europe – a sort of casting out. In *Purity and Danger*, Mary Douglas describes such negative boundary making, or 'abjection', as the processes by which certain bodies in society are marked by the ruling classes as undesirable for the purpose of enabling a national 'Us' to take shape, precisely by imaginatively emphasizing that which 'We' are *not*.[71]

Moreover, scholars of race studies have suggested that 'social power plays an important role in how people move in the world and how they connect to place',[72] reclaiming the Lefebvrian idea that the ability to exert power over space is ultimately power over life.[73] Hence, 'exiting' social space, in this case by means of an outward migration to Syria, thus becomes analytically meaningful in attaining a symbolic European 'voice' of its own.[74] By 'leaving Europe', and advocating for a new community and polity abroad, this 'migratory voice' is indeed reified. In this sense, migration-as-process becomes an almost existential means for regaining some degree of (political) *control* over life. It is therefore argued here that this emigration dynamic to Syria might relate to a deep-running frustration among Muslim minority publics in Western Europe over their abjected social status as second-class citizens, and consequently, to the remaking or revalorization of this degraded social standing through geographical relocation.

In his second YouTube episode, Fulaan introduces a Dutch companion seated next to him in the car, who is brought in to testify on what they claim is by now a collective and transnational political climate across Western Europe:

> I can tell you that left-wing parties like *Sp.A* and *Groen* have voted for the ban on headscarves and effectuated it. [The same for] ritual slaughter, a ban; Islamic school, a ban! Those weren't the right-wing parties; it was all left-wing parties.[75]

In other words, what they claim is that the targeting of Muslim publics in Europe is no longer the sole currency of the (far) right but that it has become part of the broader political landscape. Some Belgian scholars have suggested that it is precisely such a general, post-9/11 societal backdrop – consumed by 'Islam' and 'migration' – to which contemporary forms of radicalization in Europe can be read: the 'radical-right anti-Islam stance was now joined by the rigorous anticlerical stance of the left in some kind of joint anti-Islamic Kulturkampf', thereby cementing a 'polarizing debate on the compatibility of Islam with Western values'.[76]

In their episode, Fulaan and his Dutch companion first touch upon the situation in Syria. But this evocation of their new 'home' remains relatively brief (one minute), marking a 'discursive silence'; the remaining time (nine minutes) is dedicated to current media affairs in the Low Countries rather than in Syria. The shift in focus occurs abruptly, hastily transitioning: 'actually we want to discuss this'.[77] They then relate how two 'sisters' were arrested at the Belgian international airport on the suspicion of wanting to leave for Syria. They try to legitimize these *muhajirat*'s attempts by referencing the local societal context in Europe, not least the decades-old racist credo that 'they' should leave:

> If you're always shouting, like Filip does [Filip Dewinter, former head of the far-right Flemish Cause party], 'Adapt or get lost'. Well, those two sisters wanted to leave [Belgium]. They were probably sick and tired of it. But why did they want to leave? They left but they were stopped. Why, I don't know . . . . people that want to leave *voluntarily* via official routes are stopped! That's a world upside down . . . . Those guys [far right], I don't know what they want. They want us here; they want us there. What are we supposed to do?[78]

This statement can either be read as incorporating right-wing arguments in order to mock a level of political contradiction at home, or as an illustration of their having fully internalized the racist trope of 'not belonging' to Europe. Either way, their mode of speaking occurs in direct *spatial relation* to the political discourse of the Flemish right wing. Abu Fulaan then asks his anonymous Dutch passenger, 'I don't know whether it's the same at your end?' To which the latter replies, 'At our end, they always say that we *have* to leave. Yes, for the Netherlands it's exactly the same. Adapt to Dutch society or else you don't belong here.'[79] The Dutch phrase that is used to refer to 'not belonging' applies the exact wording of 'or else you are not at home here [*anders hoor je hier niet thuis*]', in which the key sign of 'home' does not merely denote a physical home or even legal citizenship, but clearly connotes belonging to a 'national' community based on ethno-racial or assimilationist ideas of collective identity, in their modernist romantic conception. The speakers in Syria thus present their former 'home' as an experience of friction, grounded in concrete social geographies in Europe (Flanders, the Netherlands). Their referenced subject position as 'Muslims' in Europe imbues the characteristics of 'racial formation' processes in which 'Muslimness' has gradually started operating as a form of religion-coded race,[80] much in the same way that 'Catholic' Irish (and Italian) immigrants to the US were first cast out as 'non-white' by the 'White Anglo-Saxon Protestant' (WASP) majority in power – a racial disciplining process aimed at limiting their access to meaningful positions of power, thus curbing their quest for permanent settlement and discouraging them from feeling at home.[81] The similarly transformative but contrary dynamic goes for former 'ghetto Jews' in Europe, who, over the course of two centuries (1750–1950) became part and parcel of Europe's cultural avant-garde and integrated into its political and financial elites, only for this 'Jewish modernity' to be violently annihilated when 'they' were recast as distinct 'Jews' during the continental crises of 1930–45.[82]

By alluding to their past experiences with racism, these *muhajirun* evoke the idea of 'home' in Europe as a well-policed notion to which their community was *not allowed* to lay claim. Given that most of the cited online media fabrications occur in Dutch, both the symbolism and message do appear located largely within a *European* social field. Such instances display a political indignation from below, however inconvenient this may sound. Their social media activity signals a need to 'speak' (back to 'home') – a social privilege often denied to subaltern publics. However, as Robert Young has pointed out, it is not that 'they' do not know *how* to speak (politics), as the above videos partly indicate, 'but rather that the dominant would not listen'.[83] This tension with which the urge to speak back to Europe from a position (of power) in Syria reflects a dual process of un/making 'home': in Dutch, rather than formal Arabic, European speakers in Syria address *European* publics, and discursively intervene on *local* matters of social and political concern in Europe ('making'), while at the same time discarding ('unmaking') their respective societies as viable social spaces for 'Muslim' life, propagating oppositional horizons of being and community. In doing so, they seem to have internalized the very binary of outsider/*Fremdbild* of the far-right logic.[84]

Indeed, it is striking how the political life-worlds of these *muhajirun* continues to be informed by *European* sensibilities despite their relocation. As migration scholar Pine makes clear, however, 'migration is both a future-oriented and a backward-looking process'.[85] In our case, it calls attention to the importance of lived experiences in the space of departure as being *indicative* of the movement itself: from the alienating urban ghetto in Europe to the Syrian front. Moreover, migration scholars like Ghassan Hage have already demonstrated at length that a sense of 'stuckedness' – that is, the subjective feeling of 'going too slowly' or 'going nowhere'– can play a role in prompting emigration.[86] In such instances, migration operates as a hands-on coping strategy for 'waithood',[87] and as a gateway for a set of future aspirations located or imagined in an elsewhere.

In this light, it comes as no surprise that Belgian scholars have started making the claim that 'all radicalisation is local'.[88] In fact, more alarming analyses also implicate the relevance of the suggested notion of 'home', in very concrete ways: 'Judging by the number of plots and attacks hatched by Syrian returnees, the Islamic State's francophone [French and Belgian] cadre appears to be the most active of the organization's Western contingent. Often operating together in Syria, a number of these recruits showed an early proclivity towards striking their home country'.[89] Indeed, 'immigrant' minorities-turned-*muhajirun* might now symbolize how 'from its place of banishment, the abject does not cease challenging its master'.[90] This ongoing interplay between ego and superego, both online and in the political sphere, raises the question then whether the ensuing aggression by these *muhajirun* inside Europe symbolizes, to a certain degree, a very reactionary revolt of the 'colony within',[91] bearing in mind here the involvement of European citizens in appalling local attacks on European soil who have never themselves ventured out to Syria, like Salah Abdeslam.

Un/making home: Burning the EU passport

A particular *muhajir* rite in Syria is the recording of EU passport burnings, accompanied by slogans like, 'We are honored that we have nothing more to do with [yo]u'[92] in the case of a set of Dutch nationals (see Figure 9.2). Here, the signifier 'you' refers to Dutch society. In part, this type of recorded hyper-media seems manufactured to arouse a non-Syrian, Dutch public. The speaker's claim of not being part of the '*u*' evokes an almost bodily understanding of 'the nation'. During such critical junctures, aversion to the context of departure seems stronger than attraction to Syria or the Middle East. This rite of passage further amplifies the *unmaking* of 'home': subsequent to the burning stage, one passes on to the liminal phase of being stateless and homeless (disaffiliation),[93] after which a combative oath is taken (re-grounding) that clears the way for a reconstitution (re-affiliation) of community (brotherhood/*ikhwaniyya, umma*) in a new 'home' (*sham, khilafa*). Such emblematic rituals in Syria foster newly found social bondage and self-identification.

A similar act was staged by French nationals in Syria, who in a video post (see Figure 9.3) that was published by the *Guardian* in 2014 shout out in an enraged tone of recording, 'You have oppressed us, you have fought our religion, you have insulted our Prophet'. The main speaker adds: 'If you come here, we will fight you.'[94] Here, the signifier of 'you' denotes France and the symbolic institution of the French army. Citizenship thus also represents the (un)willingness to associate with a state and its society. This French discourse of dissent evokes a desire to engage with France in a geographical space that is framed in highly mythological

Figure 9.2 Primary image produced by Dutch nationals in Syria and reported on by UK scholar Shiraz Maher on Twitter (September 2014), showing the ritual burning of passports. Screenshot caption: 'Dutch foreign fighter in Syria burns his passport. His message: "we are honored that we have nothing more to do with u."'

Source: Anonymous 3, retweeted by Dr Shiraz Maher (ICSR, King's College London) (9 April 2014), [Twitter, account '@ShirazMaher']. Available at https://twitter.com/ShirazMaher (accessed 20 April 2014).

Figure 9.3 Screenshot of video by French nationals in Syria.

Source: Anonymous 4, in 'Video: French ISIS Fighters Burn Their Passports', the *Guardian* [online], 20 November 2014. Available at https://www.theguardian.com/world/video/2014/nov/20/french-isis-fighters-burn-passports-video (accessed 6 June 2016).

parole (*sham*, *khilafa*). Syria then becomes a highly symbolic counter-space, or 'consequential geography',[95] for staging actual politics against (a former home in) Europe. *Sham*, founded on the debris of disintegrated states in the Middle East, provides these Europeans with a highly mediated platform from which to voice their power contestation as modern 'anti-citizens' on the move.

By introducing ethnographically the social figure of the *muhajir*, and probing his rituals in Syria, I conceptualize here the analytical figure of the 'anti-citizen', which enables for the expansion of Robin Cohen's triangulation of citizenship categories. Based on his view that 'the modern state has sought to differentiate the various people under its sway by including some in the body politic and according them full civic and social rights, while seeking to exclude others from entering this charmed circle', he conceptualized 'citizens' (e.g. nationals by birth), 'denizens' (e.g. cosmopolitan 'expats', recognized asylum seekers), and 'helots' (e.g. irregular entrants and overstayers, asylum seekers, irregular workers).[96] However, his implicit legalistic focus does not include abjection processes of racialized segments of the citizenry (by birth) that are, subsequent to emigration, downgraded in both their symbolic and legal status, over their political behaviour abroad – either by their own doing (i.e. burning rites) or by authorities in Europe that push for stripping their citizenship status.

There is a well-established discourse in France, and Western Europe for that matter, that propounds that citizens with a non-EU, Muslim background from Maghreb countries are only 'French in passport' or '*français de passeport*', and can therefore be categorized as 'second-', 'third-', or 'fourth-generation immigrants' or '*issue de l'immigration*', irrespective of their place of birth. This amounts to what scholars have dubbed 'differentialist racism' or 'neo-racism'.[97] Rik Coolsaet has recently highlighted that 'social exclusion – the feeling of being considered second-class citizens' constitutes a key element of the conducive context of minority youth's radicalization in Europe, precisely because it operates as a form of relative deprivation.[98] In her study on the experiences of youths of North African origin in France, Nadia Kiwan writes that 'racial and cultural discrimination, in all its forms', is intensely 'present in terms of a conscience' among young men in the *banlieues* of Paris.[99] In the Low Countries, scholars have over the years also noted an increasing 'culturalization of citizenship',[100] operating under the auspices of the disciplinary discourses of 'integration' and 'tolerance'.[101] The salience of such exclusivist ideologies in Western Europe reinforces the primacy of ethno-national ideas (*confer jus sanguinis*) and challenges universalist philosophies on state–subject relations that remain as yet enforced by law in most EU Member States (*jus soli*).

In the French video (Figure 9.3), one of the speakers heatedly utters, 'we disown these passports that you have imposed on us'.[102] Such a claim makes it seem as if a passport is the only thing they share with other segments of French society, despite having been socialized primarily in Europe, suggesting that they have internalized and are now themselves reproducing the racist logic of the European far right. In her work, Barbara Franz has discerned an ongoing 'coloured' (segmented) form of class indignation in Europe, arguing that an underlying negation of social mobility for many West-Europeans with an immigrant-Muslim background has in turn led to a reinforced self-identification as 'Muslims'. In this dialectic process of segregation, dominant notions of otherness (stigma) also feed back into the cultivation of selfhood among besieged minorities.[103]

The *muhajirun*'s narratives, rituals and style performances convey strong negative place attachments to Europe that seem located on a visceral level, based on a series of (traumatic) lived experiences, or '*espace vécu*'.[104] Indeed, the fact that they take the time and effort to speak of their prior condition back in Europe in a heated Syrian war context suggests that Europe continues to occupy a central emotional referent in their life-worlds. Their willingness to engage militarily with the European 'nation-state' indicates that their anger and discourse seem fixated against this previously experienced racialized structure, or 'racial space', in Europe.[105] This renders their Islamist discourse on 'home' very political indeed. It appears that forms of local alienation in urban Europe have translated into a spatially aversive affect, to which emigration (*hijra*) is the answer.

This emerging importance of the European context of departure, unearthed in the online repertoires of European *muhajirun* in Syria, puts to question the overemphasis on foreign ideologies and political movements abroad, as found in the rapidly emerging bulk of radicalization scholarship. Recent studies seem primarily concerned with diagnosing *individual* signs of pre-departure 'radicalization',[106] while often outsourcing the main political references to a social space *abroad*, outside of Europe, namely as 'the attraction of IS'.[107] Yet others displace politics entirely to a sensational cyberspace ('virtual Caliphate'), which allegedly stands disconnected from broader socialization processes. Conveniently so, 'they' then radicalize anywhere but in our midst.[108]

Responding to such a trend, scholars like Franz have long argued for the rehabilitation of social class into the analysis of 'Islamic alienation' in Europe.[109] In a similar vein, more critical explorations into the intricate structure of 'race' have posited racism to be an inherent instrument for class division, catering to the ability of capital to flexibly call upon, or temporarily expel labour segments according to the dictate of market demands (social dumping),[110] precisely through their very inferiorization or selective 'racing',[111] always recreating new 'regimes of human worth'.[112] In this view, racism is not a negligible by-product of modern capitalism but rather an integral function ('social reproduction') to sustaining its very survival. Therefore, if capital organizes itself on a racial basis too, as an underlying *social* relation of production, then 'race' forms an integral device in the hegemonic ideological apparatus of the ruling class and its majoritarian following among the population.

For instance, when yet other Belgian and Dutch *muhajirun* in Syria proclaim, 'Our Prophet is being mocked, use *hikma* [righteous wisdom], and stand up',[113] in direct conjunction with mentioning (Geert) 'Wilders' – the Dutch chairman of a far-right party (*Partij voor de Vrijheid*) – it signifies not only the visceral ways in which 'Muslims' experience the persona of the Prophet, but, also that European minority youths have started mobilizing religion (*hikma*) politically, as a modern vernacular for staging a militant counter-discourse. Most scholars have overlooked the fact that these European *muhajirun* in Syria repeatedly make such telling references to concrete political figures of the far right in Europe. Consequently, one can argue that new and locally emerging ways of collective self-identification (categories of practice) among highly racialized subjects of the working class need to be tied into the global material intricacies at play *within* grotesque spectacles of identity politics. As Cohen has amplified, 'too much attention has been paid to identity formation among ethnic minorities without looking at the shifts in popular consciousness and cultural practices among majority populations'.[114] Hence, shifting the analytical focus from the 'individual' ('Syria fighter') or 'residual' ('Muslims') to the hegemonic and dominant *dispositif* within the socio-spatial (i.e. re-emerging forms of ethnic nationalism) seems expedient.

Today, the notion of *hijra* is actively discussed (online), especially in puritan strands of Salafi-Wahhabism in the West. 'Spokesmen' have been reinforcing its obligatory and literal-physical interpretation – stressing the binary '*dar al-harb*' versus '*dar al-Islam*' as opposed to *hijra* as intention (*niya*) and a domain for self-struggle and repentance (*tawba*).[115] However, it is key to ask ourselves on what societal grounds in Europe this ideational Wahhabi literalism (of 'reborn' Muslims rediscovering their faith) is fostered. One could reference the Qur'an and state that 'they' act merely upon their religious commands; one particular Qur'anic verse seems to have been popularized in Wahhabi circles, namely when the angels are quoted asking the deceased, 'In what condition were you?' They will say, 'We were oppressed in the land.' To which the angels will say, 'Was not the earth of Allah spacious [enough] for you to emigrate therein?'[116] However, the very popularization of this *specific* verse (from the entire Qur'an and body of *Hadiths*) also suggests that 'they' link such historical registers of the Islamic tradition (e.g. the oppression of Prophet Mohammad and his '*hijra al-nabawiyya*' in AD 622) to a *contemporary* climate of societal polarization in Europe and their own negative place attachments.

Un/making race through hijra to sham

In older video segments that were incorporated in a 2017 Belgian-Flemish documentary series on IS, we can hear French-speaking Belgians in Syria propagate the Caliphate, saying 'there is no difference between an Arab and a non-Arab, between a white man and a black man, provided that they are pious'.[117] This claim is bolstered in their video sketch by an image of men of different colour, all dressed up in identical ('egalitarian') army uniforms, all smiling and posing in a *brotherly* fashion (see Figure 9.4). Another image follows showing young men intensely hugging each other in the mosque after prayer. Racial equality and pious brotherhood (*ikhwaniyya*) are two ideas that are drawn upon simultaneously to morally legitimate the Caliphate as a *political* space in opposition to Belgium and Europe. The documentary also featured an anonymous Dutch-speaking Belgian male (see Figure 9.5). Looking into the camera, he proclaims: 'Thank God for giving us the strength to comply with our duty [*hijra, jihad*], and as you can see, we are here with all sorts of people: Africans, Europeans, Americans, Asians. And that kind of racism that you know there is simply not around over here'.[118] He makes this claim while rowing a boat (on the Euphrates, with a child) against the backdrop of a crystal-clear sky. He is then seen lighting a campfire over which fresh food is cooked, enticing the audience with a sense of outdoor adventure. Similar to most of the abovementioned speakers, he narrates in vernacular Dutch to European (in-group) audiences, and in the background one can hear pre-recorded Arabic-language hymns (*anasheeds*) that have been put in place to further evoke a sense of Arab-Muslim authenticity. By unfolding a discursive opposition between 'here' (the Caliphate's self-proclaimed territories) and 'there' (Belgium), he too addresses – as fuel for Wahhabi ISIS propaganda – the contemporary racialization of (coloured) Muslim citizens in Europe.

The documentary then features a video clip dating from August 2014, featuring Hicham Chaib (see Figure 9.6), a former resident of the Belgian city of Antwerp.

Figure 9.4 European IS fabrications. Image of fighters of 'all colours' presented as ideal. Screenshot caption: 'Between an Arab and non-Arab, a white [man] and a black [man]'.

Source: Anonymous 6, in 'Vranckx: IS in het vizier – voor God en Kalifaat' (21 March 2017), [*Canvas* online, episode 1], 26:35–27:06. Available at https://www.vrt.be/vrtnu/a-z/is-in-het-vizier/1/is-in-het-vizier-s1a1-voor-god-en-kalifaat/ (accessed 1 April 2017).

Figure 9.5 Anonymous Belgian-Maghrebi testifying about the absence of racism in the Caliphate. Screenshot caption: 'And the sort of racism that you know there is simply not around over here'.

Source: Anonymous 7, in 'Vranckx: IS in het vizier – voor God en Kalifaat' (21 March 2017), [*Canvas* online, episode 1], 27:25–27:45. Available at https://www.vrt.be/vrtnu/a-z/is-in-het-vizier/1/is-in-het-vizier-s1a1-voor-god-en-kalifaat/ (accessed 1 April 2017).

Figure 9.6 Belgian-Moroccan national Hicham Chaib (August 2014), staging IS propaganda from Raqqa, Syria. Screenshot caption: '[I have never in my life felt like a Muslim as I do] in these moments, over here, amidst all the Muslims'.

Source: Hicham Chaib, in 'Vranckx: IS in het vizier – voor God en Kalifaat' (21 March 2017), [*Canvas* online, episode 1], 27:55–28:15. Available at https://www.vrt.be/vrtnu/a-z/is-in-het-vizier/1/is-in-het-vizier-s1a1-voor-god-en-kalifaat/ (accessed 1 April 2017).

Wearing a turban and 'traditional' garb, he emotionally proclaims in Dutch, 'I have never in my life felt like a Muslim as I do in these moments, over here, amidst all the Muslims, and under the shadow of the *khilafa*. Thank God, we live here very safely and very happily.'[119] At the time of recording in Raqqa, the day is bright and there are few signs of war. Chaib claims that his 'happiness' is derived from concluding *hijra*, evoking the idea of a 'homecoming' and immersion into a reachable Muslim 'body', as some form of kinship, drawing on the pre-national notion of the global *umma*, the ecumenical Islamic community. His reductionist *parole* of equating diversely inhabited territories in Syria to 'Muslims',[120] only makes sense when attending to its reflexive referent: the feeling of not belonging to/in Europe, propagated, or indeed previously experienced, as being equally 'homogenous'. Chaib crafts a migratory horizon where *sham* operates as a 'promised land', portrayed as a gateway towards a more *dignified* life among alleged brethren. Although the signifier of 'Muslim' remains applied in terms of 'situational self-identification' across space – he self-portrays primarily as 'Muslim', first in Europe, then in Syria – its connoted meaning nevertheless holds a wholly different weight subsequent to emigration: majoritarian dominance.[121] Spatial relocation across social formations can thus be imagined or experienced as a beneficial form of (racial) status exchange, and is hereby conceptualized as the process of 'status migration', as a contribution to migration scholarship. In Chaib's case, his own status exchange seems to have come with a concrete pathway to power in Syria, as he reportedly occupied a position in the ranks of the 'religious police' in Raqqa. In fact, other *muhajirun* in Syria, like Abu Fulaan, also celebrated this peculiar inversion of power: 'In Syria, *we* are the police!'[122]

Drawing on colonial history, Cohen was quick to point out that it used to be 'perfectly possible for English and Irish convicts to become landowners and gentlemen farmers in Australia',[123] demonstrating that a drive for upward mobility in the social order has long functioned as an emigration motive, especially for symbolically stained publics that would otherwise remain 'stuck' in their abjected social position.[124] This chapter proposes, however, that such instances of 'status migration' need not be narrowed down economically to labour or mere gains in monetary income, but can simultaneously involve matters of 'race' too. The idea of 'hope' for an alternative social ordering through migration comes to the fore here.[125] One should note also that Chaib does not evoke 'Arabness' in his discourse on community, amplifying the demise of regional Arab nationalism as a mobilizing political force.[126] The militant Wahhabism of European IS-supporters like Chaib and their obsession with the ancient world seems to have blended with the ideational categories of nineteenth-century European racism, approaching therein the discursive structure of the contemporary far right in Europe. This 'glocal' style-embodiment exhibits how certain ideational frameworks can travel, blend with others and re-emerge as hybrid assemblages outside of their foundational sphere(s) of origin.

By coding Syria as *sham* and 'among Muslims', and infusing mythological monotheist sentiments like 'salvation', a 'new beginning', or a 'resurrection' (*nahda* in Arabic) into imagined notions of communitarian space abroad, we see Chaib romantically framing his migration as a transition from membership of an urban outcast minority to a majority *Herrenvolk*. While showcasing subtly his new position in the social hierarchy, the sign of 'Muslim' in Chaib's narrative implies, however, an equally racialized conceptualization. His take on *sham* and the *khilafa* has taken on the form of a Lacanian 'fantasy-space',[127] in which he and his IS affiliates are positioned centre stage as a 'chosen people', surrounded by object-like

others – framed as 'pagan intruders', 'non-people', or 'rejectionist apostates' (*kuffar,
tawaghit, murtad, rafidin*) – whose very existence defies the propagated myth.
These ideational exponents of his language use – romantic *terra*, default 'nation' in
Europe's mirror image – partly highlight the reproduction of *European* social
space in Syria. As Neely and Samura have aptly pointed out, 'the making and
remaking of space is also about the making and remaking of race'.[128] This also
resonates with Spivak's critique of 'colonized minds': subalterns ending up
reproducing the very 'Western fantasies' of their (former) 'masters'.[129] These young
men seem to produce the stereotypical image of the antithetical Orient that has so
long been propagated by the centres of Empire, prompting the question of whether
their styling efforts, in all their disconnect from the many concrete struggles of the
Syrian peoples, present us paradoxically with yet another Fanonian permutation
of 'brown skin, white masks'.[130] Indeed, Chaib's narrative strikes us as an extremely
dualist, centre-periphery discourse and demonstrates the modernist racialism at
the heart of IS's ideology. His language points yet again to the importance of
Boccagni's aforementioned element of (re/gaining a sense of) *control* over life; in
this case, by violently remaking Syria as a cleansed 'Muslim home'.

Performing *hijra* to Syria-as-*sham* appears to constitute a highly relational
quest for community and belonging, masking modes of individual alienation
and racialized abjection in Europe. This indignant procession of self-exile
then becomes a late-modern phenomenon, occurring to a certain degree in a
dialectic relationship to forms of exacerbated nationalism and racist exclusion
by majoritarian publics in the West. This suggests that fringe elements of an
oppositional minority politics have morphed into a far-right *modus operandi*,
transposed abroad (on)to the Syrian conflict;[131] as radical elements that might
otherwise have served as fuel for a progressive social movement at home in the
face of wide-ranging, dislocating social transformations in Europe.

Conclusion

Migration scholars Narotzky and Besnier rightly remind us that 'past experiences
provide a horizon of expectations configuring present aspirations and hopes for
the future'.[132] Indeed, space and spatially situational behaviour are, at least in part,
social products. However, when it comes to the study of the phenomenon of 'Syria
fighters', the societal context of departure has generally been ignored in favour of
the ideology of 'international jihadism', obfuscating some of the more structural
psychosocial modalities that may partly inform such a peculiar emigration in the
first place. By means of carefully studying the online narratives of some of the
more vocal *muhajirun* in Syria and Iraq, this study has unearthed a strong focus on
Europe (despite their emigration), as well as a relational language that articulates
highly racialized experiences as 'Muslims' in their respective societies of departure.
This discursive focus on 'home' in Europe is clearly political, for it speaks of a
viscerally experienced abjection as second-class citizens. In fact, some of the
recorded jihadi (body) language used in Syria seems to occur in Dutch rather than

formal Arabic, and it often stands in a dialogical relationship to European rather than Middle Eastern societal affairs. In particular, these *muhajirun* can be seen interpellating the racist discourse of the European far right, applying such 'antithetical' political referents to make resonate further their (IS) propaganda among other minority youths in their home countries back in Europe. These elements run against the mainstream assertion that these 'Syria fighters' are somehow *foreign* to our societies in Europe.

Focusing on what is said about the home context of departure in the online narratives of some West European 'Syria fighters' suggests that the pervasiveness of 'racial space' in Europe might have partly provided a basis for spurring such migratory dispositions. This 'voice of exit' comes about through discursive references to a *lived* status degradation in Europe, and through visceral rites of un/making 'home' in Syria, like ritual passport burnings that first abort and then renew community abroad. To a certain extent, migration to *sham* could be seen as a globalized form of rebellious hyper-locality: a numerically small minority technique that seems aimed at subverting a European nationalist governmentality that is claimed to premeditate the inferior status of specifically 'Muslim' life forms in the social order. In their case, outward migration then appears to function as both a means to navigate hampering racial stigmas in Europe, and as a pathway to attaining increased material privilege, social standing and even dominance abroad; a spatial process of radical status exchange that I have coined here as 'status migration'.

Moreover, in undertaking *hijra* to Syria (and affiliating often with such groups as IS), *muhajirun* from the Low Countries seem to *reproduce* the ideational tenets of a *lived* European racism, on the rise since 9/11. This is clear from their highly selective, particularly narrow, and ultimately modernist appropriation of a series of Islamic notions (*hijra, jihad, sham, khilafa, umma*, etc.) that are preoccupied with demographic homogeneity, ancient myths of land and political demagoguery. Consequently, it could be argued that such European (minority) youths on the move have cultivated a far-right-wing political extremism of their own, coded in 'Islamic' vernacular yet occurring in dialogic relation to the racist nationalism of majoritarian far-right groups in Europe. These 'Islamists', born and socialized in Europe, thus partly transpose and reproduce a highly racialized *European* 'social space' in Syria, possibly reinstating and multiplying modes of injustice on site. Instead of struggling politically in Europe to ameliorate their outcast condition, minority trajectories of lived exclusion seem to have been displaced abroad, in a propagated fantasy-space like the Caliphate, which legitimizes inverted cycles of quick-fix dominance and new modes of dislocating violence, and even ethnic cleansing.

Today this *muhajir* public is disowned by the state in Europe through both ideological naming efforts that cast them out as allegedly *foreign* to the national body (e.g. 'Syria fighter', 'foreign terrorist fighter'/FTF, 'jihadi bride'), as well as the stripping of their citizenship without much judicial supervision (in the early phase of this phenomenon). In turn, their (online) threats and highly mediated societal role seem to expedite a gradual redefinition of state–citizen relations that altogether reimagine constitutional boundaries. Surely, some *muhajirun* returning from Syria with military know-how will continue to pose a threat to society in Europe, as shown by the abhorrent attacks in Paris (2015) and Brussels (2016), raising a whole series of further questions on prevention and monitoring mechanisms. But what is less mentioned is that they, as Belgian and Dutch IS affiliates, also provide the fuel for the public legitimation of costly and long-term 'perpetual' warfare of various EU Member States in Middle Eastern countries like Syria and Iraq. As such, this specific *muhajir* public has moved from the functional character of being a principle Other *within* Europe to what I see as 'anti-citizens' *on the move*, serving as a welcome nemesis in the teleological crafting of a more militarized European national self-image. The social figure of the *muhajir*, willingly performing the role of the jihadi anti-citizen and potentially fulfilling its reactionary credentials abroad, thus helps facilitate gradually this *normative shift* in societal governance in Europe, away from preventive redistribution and curative recognition in favour of a more punitive security turn.

Notes

1 Mimicking the critical sketches of Belgian-Moroccan comedian and Facebook-hit Rachid Abourig.
2 Abu Fulaan, 'Bear Grills in Syrië' (11 May 2014), [YouTube, account 'De Basis', episode 1]. Available at https://www.youtube.com/watch?v=QmERKBlnqcc (accessed 16 June 2016).
3 Flemish-Dutch slang and racist sign, translatable as 'shitty monkeys', referring to both a type of ape (*makaak*) while denoting simultaneously the Dutch signifier of '*kak*' or 'shit'.
4 Fulaan, 'Bear Grills', ep. 1.
5 Ibid.
6 Ibid.
7 Abu Fulaan, 'Bear Grills in Syrië' (23 May 2014), [YouTube, account 'De Basis', episode 3]. Available at https://www.youtube.com/watch?v=FDkfjoNC-ZU (accessed 16 June 2016).
8 Thomas Renard and Rik Coolsaet, 'From the Kingdom to the Caliphate and Back: Returnees in Belgium', in 'Returnees: Who Are They, Why Are They (Not) Coming Back and How Should We Deal with Them? Assessing Policies on Returning Foreign Terrorist Fighters in Belgium, Germany and the Netherlands', *Egmont Papers* 101 (2018): 19.
9 Rik Coolsaet, 'Facing the Fourth Foreign Fighters Wave: What Drives Europeans to Syria and to Islamic State?', Egmont Papers 81 (2016): 42.
10 Renard and Coolsaet, 'From the Kingdom to the Caliphate and Back', p. 19.
11 Bibi van Ginkel and Simon Minks, 'Addressing the Challenge of Returnees: Threat Perceptions, Policies, and Practices in the Netherlands', in 'Returnees: Who Are They', *Egmont Papers* 101 (2018): 55.
12 Edwin Bakker and Roel de Bont, 'Belgian and Dutch Jihadist Foreign Fighters (2012–2015): Characteristics, Motivations, and Roles in the War in Syria and Iraq', *Small Wars & Insurgencies* 27, no. 5 (2016): 843.
13 Coolsaet, 'Facing the Fourth Foreign Fighters Wave', p. 9; Bakker and De Bont, 'Belgian and Dutch Jihadist Foreign Fighters', pp. 840–1.

14 Ayfer Erkul, Maud Oeyen and Koen Vidal, 'Syriëstrijders begaan oorlogsmisdaden', *De Morgen*, 8 June 2013.

15 See 'Abu Maariya Al Muhajir', in 'Martelaar aan de frontlinie' (27 May 2014), [YouTube, account 'De Basis'], 7:10-07:33. Available at https://www.youtube.com/watch?v=tyIsIcIHkGw (accessed 6 June 2016).

16 Janny Groen, 'Nederlandse syriëganger op de foto met vijf afgehakte hoofden', *De Volkskrant*, 17 March 2014.

17 France24, 'Gruesome video of European jihadists in Syria shocks France', *France24*, 27 March 2014. Available at http://www.france24.com/en/20140327-syria-french-jihadist-video-shocks-france/ (accessed 20 April 2016).

18 A historical endonym denoting the most populous and fertile areas of the north-western rim of the Middle East, known as the Levant or *Bilad al-Sham* (Syria, Lebanon, Palestine, Jordan, Southern Turkey), featuring as a mythological region in Islamic eschatology (e.g. 'Great battle of the final hour'/*Al-Malhama al-Kubra*).

19 *De Morgen*, 'Video: Vlaamse strijders baden in luxe in Syrië', 19 April 2014.

20 Dunbar Moodie and Vivienne Ndatshe, *Going for Gold: Men, Mines and Migration* (Berkeley, CA: University of California Press, 1994), p. 18.

21 Alana Lentin, 'Post-Race, Post Politics: The Paradoxical Rise of Culture after Multiculturalism', *Ethnic and Racial Studies* 37, no. 8 (2012): 1271.

22 Yves Desmet, 'Onze jongens in Syrië', *De Morgen*, 8 June 2013; Marc van Dijck, 'Zijn dat "onze jongens" in Syrië?', *Trouw*, 14 March 2013.

23 David Garland, *The Culture of Control* (Chicago: University of Chicago Press, 2001).

24 *De Morgen*, 'Burgemeester Rotterdam: "Als het je hier niet bevalt, rot dan op"', 8 May 2015. Also, in January 2015, Dutch Prime Minister Mark Rutte used the catch phrase '*pleur op*' or 'piss off', mimicked in Belgium by Gwendolyn Rutten.

25 Lorne Dawson and Amarnath Amarasingam, 'Talking to Foreign Fighters: Insights into Motivations for Hijrah to Syria and Iraq', *Studies in Conflict & Terrorism* 40, no. 30 (2017): 193.

26 See Wright Mills, *The Sociological Imagination* (Oxford: Oxford University Press, 2000 [1959]).

27 Brooke Neely and Michelle Samura, 'Social Geographies of Race: Connecting Race and Space', *Ethnic and Racial Studies* 34, no. 11 (2011): 1933–52, especially 1940 and 1947.

28 Mohammed Hafez and Creighton Mullins, 'The Radicalization Puzzle: A Theoretical Synthesis of Empirical Approaches to Homegrown Extremism', Studies in Conflict & Terrorism 38, no. 11 (2015): 958–75. Daan Weggemans, Edwin Bakker and Peter Grol, 'Who Are They and Why Do They Go? The Radicalization and Preparatory Processes of Dutch Jihadist Foreign Fighters', *Perspectives on Terrorism* 8, no. 4 (2014): 100–10; Jytte Klausen, 'Tweeting the Jihad: Social Media Networks of Western Foreign Fighters in Syria and Iraq', *Studies in Conflict & Terrorism* 38, no. 1 (2015): 1–22.

29 Arun Kundnani, 'Radicalisation: The Journey of a Concept', Race & Class 54, no. 2 (2012): 3–25; Lisa Stampnitzky, *Disciplining Terror: How Experts Invented Terrorism* (New York: Cambridge University Press, 2013).

30 Sageman, *Understanding Terror Networks* (Philadelphia: University of Pennsylvania Press, 2004).

31 Patrick Loobuyck, 'Introduction', in *De Lokroep van IS: Syriëstrijders en (De) radicalisering*, ed. Patrick Loobuyck (Kalmthout: Pelckmans, 2015), p. 16.

32 Olivier Roy, 'Interview: Lure of the Death Cult – Olivier Roy on Europe's Failure to Understand the Roots of Radicalization', *The World Today*, February and March edition (2017).

33 Johan Leman, 'Van radicalisering tot jihadisering: Een antropologische kijk', in *De Lokroep van IS: Syriëstrijders en (De)radicalisering*, ed. Patrick Loobuyck (Kalmthout: Pelckmans, 2015), p. 55.

34 Doreen Massey, 'Politics and Space/Time', in *Place, Space and the Politics of Identity*, eds. Michael Keith and Steve Pile (London and New York: Routledge, 1993), pp. 141–61.

35 Joseph Carter, Shiraz Maher and Peter Neumann, '#Greenbirds: Measuring Importance and Influence in Syrian Foreign Fighter Networks', *ICSR Paper* (2014): 1–32; Anna Berbers, Willem Joris, Jan Boesman, Leen D'Haenens, Joyce Koeman and Baldwin van Gorp, 'The News Framing of the "Syria Fighters" in Flanders and the Netherlands', *Ethnicities* 16, no. 6 (2016): 798–818.

36 Bakker and De Bont, 'Belgian and Dutch Jihadist Foreign Fighters'.

37 Sean Reynolds and Mohammed Hafez, 'Social Network Analysis of German Foreign Fighters in Syria', *Terrorism and Political Violence* (2017): 1–26. Published online at https://doi.org/10.1080/09546553.2016.1272456.

38 Mobilizing discourses (pull factors) from religious figures in the Middle East remain relevant given that they are read as *political* rhetoric. For instance, on 13 June 2013, a joint statement was issued in Cairo by a number of Sunni clerics declaring 'jihad' in Syria as '*wajib*' (obligatory), in order 'to help our brothers in Syria by sending them money and weapons' (*Al Arabiya*, 2013). It featured prominent, *state-affiliated* clerics like Saudi preacher Abdulaziz al-Shaikh, Youssef al-Qaradawi, the prolific Egyptian preacher based in Qatar, and Hassan al-Shafai, a senior cleric of the Al-Azhar academy. This event coincided with the first military victory of the Iranian-backed Lebanese Hezbollah movement in Syria, namely the strategic capture of the city of Al-Qusayr in early June 2013. These regional political dimensions shed further light on the precise timing (summer 2013) by which militant 'Islamist foreigners' influenced by Wahhabi ideology, both in Europe and elsewhere, decided to leave their home countries and travel to Syria in particular (and not to Bahrain, for example).

39 Aysha Navest, Martijn de Koning and Annelies Moors, 'Chatting about Marriage with Female Migrants to Syria', *Anthropology Today* 32, no. 2 (2016): 22–5.

40 David Cook, *Understanding Jihad* (Berkeley, CA: University of California Press, 2005).

41 Bertell Ollman, *Alienation: Marx's Conception of Man in a Capitalist Society* (Cambridge: Cambridge University Press, 1977); Henri Lefebvre, *La révolution urbaine* (Paris: Gallimard, 1970).

42 Stijn Aerts and John Nawas, 'Hoe Islamitisch is Islamitisch radicalisme', in *De Lokroep van IS: Syriëstrijders en (De)radicalisering*, ed. Patrick Loobuyck (Kalmthout: Pelckmans, 2015), pp. 107, 109, 114.

43 See, for instance, Qur'an 8: 72.

44 Noel Salazar, 'Key Figures of Mobility: An Introduction', *Social Anthropology* 25, no. 1 (2017): 5–12.

45 Jan Willem Duyvendak, *The Politics of Home: Belonging and Nostalgia in Europe and the United States* (Basingstoke: Palgrave Macmillan, 2011).

46 Henri Lefebvre, *The Production of Space* (Oxford: Wiley-Blackwell, 1992 [1974]).

47 Cedric Robinson, *Black Marxism: The Making of the Black Radical Tradition* (Chapel Hill, NC: University of North Carolina Press, 2000 [1983]); Nancy Fraser, 'From Redistribution to Recognition', *New Left Review* I, no. 212 (1995): 68–93.

48 Nadia Fadil, ' "Are We All Secular/ized Yet?" Reflections on David Goldberg's "Are We All Post-Racial Yet?" ', *Ethnic and Racial Studies* 39, no. 13 (2016): 2261–8; Tariq Modood, *Multiculturalism* (Cambridge: Polity Press, 2007).

49 Ghassan Hage, *White Nation: Fantasies of White Supremacy in a Multicultural Society* (New York: Routledge, 2000); Etienne Balibar and Immanuel Wallerstein, *Race, Nation, Class: Ambiguous Identities* (London and New York: Verso, 1991).

50 Barak Kalir, 'The Development of a Migratory Disposition: Explaining a "New Emigration", *International Migration* 43, no. 4 (2005): 167–96.

51 Michael Omi and Howard Winant, *Racial Formation in the United States: From the 1960s to the 1980s* (Abingdon: Routledge, 1986).

52 Nancy Foner, 'Is Islam in Western Europe like Race in the United States', *Sociological Forum* 30, no. 4 (2015): 885–99.

53 Enzo Traverso, *The End of Jewish Modernity* (London: Pluto Press, 2016): 94–96.

54 Andreas Wimmer and Nina Glick-Schiller, 'Methodological Nationalism, the Social Sciences, and the Study of Migration: An Essay in Historical Epistemology', *The International Migration Review* 37, no. 3 (2003): 576–610.

55 Nicholas Van Hear, 'Reconsidering Migration and Class', *International Migration Review* 48, S1 (2014): S116.

56 Frances Pine, 'Migration as Hope: Space, Time, and Imagining the Future', *Current Anthropology* 55, S9 (2014): S95–S104.

57 Noel Salazar, 'Imagining Mobility at the "End of the World"', *History and Anthropology* 24, no. 2 (2013): 233–52.

58 Daniela Pisoiu, 'Coming to Believe "Truths" about Islamist Radicalization in Europe', *Terrorism and Political Violence* 25, no. 2 (2013): 247.

59 Thomas Hegghammer, 'Syria's Foreign Fighters', *Foreign Policy*, 9 December 2013.

60 Nic Craight and Emma Hill, 'Re-Locating the Ethnographic Field: From "Being There" to "Being There"', *Anthropological Journal for European Cultures* 24, no. 1 (2015): 42–62.

61 Thomas Frissen and Leen d'Haenens, 'Legitimizing the Caliphate and Its Politics: Moral Disengagement Rhetoric in ISIL's *Dabiq*', in *Authoritarian and Populist Influences in the New Media*, ed. Sai Felicia Krishna-Hensel (Abingdon: Routledge, 2017), pp. 138–64.

62 Carter, Maher and Neumann, '#Greenbirds', pp. 1–32.

63 Eric Wolf, *Pathways of Power: Building an Anthropology of the Modern World* (Berkeley, CA: University of California Press, 2001), p. 392.

64 Miriyam Aouragh, 'Digital Anthropology', in *The International Encyclopedia of Anthropology*, ed. H. Callan (Chichester: Wiley-Blackwell, 2018).

65 Gayatri Spivak, 'Can the Subaltern Speak?', in *Marxism and the Interpretation of Culture*, eds. C. Nelson and L. Grossberg (Urbana, IL: University of Illinois Press, 1988), pp. 271–313.

66 Duyvendak, *The Politics of Home*, pp. 37–8.

67 Anonymous 1, in 'Strijder roept in plat antwerps op om aanslagen te plegen en naar Syrië te komen', *Het Nieuwsblad* [online], 23 October 2013. Available at https://www.nieuwsblad.be/article/detail.aspx?articleid=DMF20131022_00804525 (accessed 18 November 2013).

68 Eva Brems, Jogchum Vrielink and Saïla Ouald Chaib, 'Uncovering French and Belgian Face Covering Bans', *Journal of Law, Religion & State* 2, no. 1 (2013): 69–99.

69 Fulaan, 'Bear Grills', ep. 1.

70 Paolo Boccagni, *Migration and the Search for Home: Mapping Domestic Space in Migrants' Everyday Lives* (New York: Palgrave Macmillan, 2017), p. 7.

71 Mary Douglas, *Purity and Danger: An Analysis of Concepts of Pollution and Taboo* (New York: Routledge, 2002 [1966]).

72 Neely and Samura, 'Social Geographies of Race', p. 1937.

73   Henri Lefebvre, 'The Production of Space', in *Space and Social Theory*, ed. Andrzej Zieleniec (London: Sage, 2008), p. 85.

74   Van Hear, 'Reconsidering Migration', p. S116.

75   Anonymous 2, in 'Bear Grills in Syrië' (23 May 2014), [YouTube, account 'De Basis', episode 3]. Available at https://www.youtube.com/watch?v=FDkfjoNC-ZU (accessed 16 June 2016).

76   Rik Coolsaet, 'Anticipating the Post-Daesh Landscape', *Egmont Papers* 97 (2017): 30.

77   Fulaan, 'Bear Grills', ep. 3.

78   Ibid.

79   Anonymous 2, in 'Bear Grills', ep. 3.

80   Omi and Winant, *Racial Formation in the United States*.

81   Noel Ignatiev, *How the Irish Became White* (New York: Routledge, 2008).

82   Traverso, *The End of Jewish Modernity*, pp. 7–19.

83   Robert Young, *White Mythologies* (New York: Routledge, 2004 [1991]), p. 5.

84   Georg Simmel, 'The Stranger', in *Georg Simmel on Individuality and Social Forms*, ed. M. Janowitz (Chicago, IL: University of Chicago Press, 1972 [1908]), pp. 143–9.

85   Pine, 'Migration as Hope', p. S95.

86   Ghassan Hage, 'A Not So Multi-Sited Ethnography of a Not So Imagined Community', *Anthropological Theory* 5, no. 4 (2005): 471; Ghassan Hage, 'Waiting Out the Crisis: On Stuckedness and Governmentality', in *Waiting*, ed. G. Hage (Carlton: Melbourne University Press, 2009), pp. 97–106.

87   Alcinda Honwana, *The Time of Youth: Work, Social Change, and Politics in Africa* (Sterling, VA: Kumarian Press, 2012).

88   Rik Coolsaet, 'All Radicalisation is Local: The Genesis and Drawbacks of an Elusive Concept', Egmont Papers 84 (2016).

89   Jean-Charles Brisard and Kevin Jackson, 'The Islamic State's External Operations and the French-Belgian Nexus', *CTC Sentinel* 9, no. 11 (2016): 8.

90   Julia Kristeva, quoted in Yael Navaro-Yashin, *The Make-Believe Space: Affective Geography in a Postwar Polity* (Durham, NC, and London: Duke University Press, 2012), p. 147.

91   Frantz Fanon, *Black Skin, White Masks* (New York: Grove Press, 1967 [1952]); Chris Hayes, *A Colony in a Nation* (New York: W. W. Norton & Company, 2017).

92   Anonymous 3, retweeted by Dr Shiraz Maher (ICSR, King's College London) (9 April 2014), [Twitter, account '@ShirazMaher']. Available at https://twitter.com/ ShirazMaher (accessed 20 April 2014).

93   Anthropologists have noted that Belgian *muhajirun* in Syria tend to stage a fundamental break with their mothers back in Europe – even denouncing them as apostates in a *takfiri* fashion that characterizes the Wahhabi strand of modern Islam – signalling other mental thresholds in the ritualistic redefinition of belonging in Syria (see Leman, 'Van radicalisering tot jihadisering', pp. 53–4).

94   Anonymous 4, in 'Video: French ISIS Fighters Burn Their Passports', the *Guardian* [online], 20 November 2014. Available at https://www.theguardian.com/world/ video/2014/nov/20/french-isis-fighters-burn-passports-video (accessed 6 June 2016).

95   Edward Soja, *Seeking Spatial Justice* (Minneapolis, MN, and London: University of Minnesota Press, 2010).

96   Robin Cohen, *Migration and Its Enemies: Global Capital, Migrant Labour and the Nation-State* (Burlington, VT: Ashgate, 2006), p. 149.

97   Pierre-André Taguieff, 'The New Cultural Racism in France', *Telos* 83 (1990): 109–22; Etienne Balibar, 'Is There a "Neo-Racism"?', in *Race, Nation, Class: Ambiguous Identities*, eds. E. Balibar and I. Wallerstein (London and New York: Verso, 1991), pp. 17–28.

98   Coolsaet, 'Anticipating the Post-Daesh Landscape', p. 46.
99   Nadia Kiwan, *Identities, Discourses and Experiences: Young People of North African Origin in France* (Manchester: Manchester University Press, 2009), p. 153.
100 Amelies Moors, 'The Dutch and the Face-Veil: The Politics of Discomfort', Social Anthropology 17, no. 4 (2009), p. 394.
101 Bowen Paulle and Barak Kalir, 'The Integration Matrix Reloaded: From Ethnic Fixations to Established versus Outsiders Dynamics in the Netherlands', *Journal of Ethnic and Migration Studies* 40, no. 9 (2014): 1354–74; Slavoj Zizek, 'Tolerance as an Ideological Category', *Critical Inquiry* 34, no. 4 (2008): 660–82.
102 Anonymous 4, in 'Video: French ISIS Fighters'.
103 Barbara Franz, 'Europe's Muslim Youth: An Inquiry into the Politics of Discrimination, Relative Deprivation, and Identity Formation', *Mediterranean Quarterly* 28, no. 1 (2007): 89–112.
104 Lefebvre, *The Production of Space.*
105 Neely and Samura, 'Social Geographies of Race', pp. 1933–52.
106 See, for instance, Marion van San, 'Onze kinderen zijn geen terroristen': families van Belgische en Nederlandse Syriëgangers over het vertrek van hun geliefden', *Tijdschrijft voor Criminologie* 57, no. 3 (2015): 308.
107 See, for instance, Loobuyck, 'Introduction', p. 16.
108 Cristina Archetti, 'Terrorism, Communication and New Media: Explaining Radicalization in the Digital Age', *Perspectives on Terrorism* 9, no. 1 (2015): 49–59.
109 Franz, 'Europe's Muslim Youth', pp. 89–90.
110 Robinson, *Black Marxism*; David Roediger, *The Wages of Whiteness: Race and the Making of the American Working Class* (New York: Verso, 2007).
111 David Roberts and Minelle Mahtani, 'Neoliberalizing Race, Racing Neoliberalism: Placing "Race" in Neoliberal Discourses', *Antipode* 42, no. 2 (2010): 248–57.
112 Aihwa Ong, *Neoliberalism as Exception: Mutations in Citizenship and Sovereignty* (Durham, NC, and London: Duke University Press, 2006), p. 181.
113 Anonymous 5 [vocals ascribed to De Mulder but likely an anonymous Maghrebi youth (i.c. of Fig. 9.1)], in 'Video: Brian De Mulder dreigt met bloedige aanslag op België', *De Standaard* [online], 10 December 2013. Available at https://www. standaard.be/cnt/dmf20131210_052 (accessed 10 December 2013).
114 Cohen, *Migration and Its Enemies*, p. 108.
115 Alan Verskin, *Islamic Law and the Crisis of the Reconquista: The Debate on the Status of Muslim Communities in Christendom* (Leiden and Boston, MA: Brill, 2015), p. 33; Daoud Casewit, 'Hijra as History and Metaphor: A Survey of Qur'anic and Hadith Sources', *The Muslim World – Hartford* 88, no. 2 (1998): 105–28.
116 See Qur'an 4: 97.
117 Anonymous 6, in 'Vranckx: IS in het vizier – voor God en Kalifaat' (21 March 2017), [*Canvas* online, episode 1], 26:35–27:06. Available at https://www.vrt.be/vrtnu/a-z/ is-in-het-vizier/1/is-in-het-vizier-s1a1-voor-god-en-kalifaat/ (accessed 1 April 2017).
118 Anonymous 7, in 'Vranckx: IS in het vizier – voor God en Kalifaat' (21 March 2017), [*Canvas* online, episode 1], 27:25–27:45. Available at https://www.vrt.be/vrtnu/a-z/ is-in-het-vizier/1/is-in-het-vizier-s1a1-voor-god-en-kalifaat/ (accessed 1 April 2017).
119 Hicham Chaib in 'Vranckx: IS in het vizier – voor God en Kalifaat' (21 March 2017), [*Canvas* online, episode 1], 27:55–28:15. Available at https://www.vrt.be/vrtnu/a-z/ is-in-het-vizier/1/is-in-het-vizier-s1a1-voor-god-en-kalifaat/ (accessed 1 April 2017).
120 Media reports about ethnic cleansing of (e.g. Yazidi and Kurdish) villages in the vicinity of Kobani by IS militants in September 2014 come to mind here.

121 Cohen, *Migration and Its Enemies*, p. 102.
122 Fulaan, 'Bear Grills', ep. 1.
123 Cohen, *Migration and Its Enemies*, p. 153.
124 Hage, 'Waiting Out the Crisis'.
125 Pine, 'Migration as Hope', pp. S95–S104.
126 Neither is a form of 'Maghrebi diaspora' consciousness evoked (e.g. 'Moroccanness' or even the *Amazigh* identification, each harbouring its own distinctive politics).
127 Zizek, quoted in Hage, *White Nation*, p. 98.
128 Neely and Samura, 'Social Geographies of Race', p. 1934.
129 Spivak, quoted in Young, *White Mythologies*, p. 211 and p. 218.
130 Hamid Dabashi, *Brown Skin, White Masks* (New York: Pluto Press, 2011).
131 Abu Fulaan literally urges youngsters to stay away from crime ('breaking stuff down'), providing them with a *political* alternative: 'If you do have the excess energy, then come here'. See Abu Fulaan, 'Bear Grills in Syrië' (16 June 2014), [YouTube, account 'De Basis', episode 5]. Available at https://www.youtube.com/watch?v=U2LweJEB3AQ&t=5s (accessed 16 June 2016).
132 Susana Narotzky and Niko Besnier, 'Crisis, Value, and Hope: Rethinking the Economy', *Current Anthropology* 55, no. 9 (2014), p. S5.

Chapter 10

NO ESCAPE: THE FORCE OF THE SECURITY FRAME IN ACADEMIA AND BEYOND[1]

Annelies Moors

In April 2016 Aysha Navest, Martijn de Koning and Annelies Moors published a three-page article, 'Chatting about Marriage with Female Migrants to Syria', in the peer-reviewed, popular-scientific journal *Anthropology Today*.[2] Nine months later, a journalist of an upscale Dutch daily, *NRC Handelsblad* (hereafter the *NRC*), wrote a three-page article about our publication.[3] He accused the first author, a junior researcher, of sympathizing with the violent jihad, and the research team of a lack of transparency, as we had not acknowledged this in the article. Moreover, according to the *NRC*, our methodology was flawed, as we had allowed our interlocutors to remain anonymous, while our conclusion could be used to undermine the attempts of the security services to prosecute women returning from IS-held territory. The *NRC* article circulated widely online, became a hit in the alt-right blogosphere (such as Breitbart), and in the aftermath three political parties posted a total of twenty-two parliamentary questions.[4]

This brief auto-ethnographic contribution reflects on these events to gain insight into the force of the security discourse in academia, the unequal division of trust and distrust, and its performative effects.[5] Our aim is to understand how a text that focused on marriage and was written to remain outside of the security and radicalization frame, was nonetheless unable to escape such framing. Starting with an analysis of the reception of our publication in the *NRC*, we soon discovered that we needed to take two aspects far more seriously than we had expected, namely, public views on authorship and academic discipline. In the following, we first summarize how we started our research project, the kinds of methods we used, and the conclusions we have drawn. We then analyse how the *NRC* framed our text in such a way as to turn it into something akin to 'a security problem'. In order to understand how this shift from marriage to security occurred, we investigate how distrust about the positionality of the junior researcher and of anthropology as a discipline was produced. As it turned out, invading the private life of the junior researcher and a disregard for the ethical requirements and epistemological grounding of anthropological research were justified by the need for increased surveillance due to the growing threat of terrorism.

Our point of departure: Academic and public debates

Our work concerning the marriages of *muhajirat sham*[6] is firmly located in academia. In line with critical studies on kinship, we consider marriage not simply as a private affair, but as a key institution for the regulation of sexuality and procreation, for the production of kinship, the organization of care and the transfer of property (as dower). Marriage is central to the production and reproduction of families, ethnicities, religious groups, nations and other social formations.[7] It is no surprise then that a variety of parties such as family members, religious authorities and state actors have an interest in how marriages come to pass.

Chatting about marriage is part of a larger anthropological research programme, started in 2013, that explores what kinds of Muslim marriages have become problematized, and how this problematization relates to the perspectives and desires of those carrying out these marriages.[8] In other words, actively engaging with societal concerns, this research programme focuses on marriage forms that have become the object of controversy in various parts of the world, such as mixed marriages, transnational marriages and unregistered marriages. A superficial glance at media discourse indicates that the marriages of the *muhajirat* easily fit into this category. The frequent use of terms such as jihadi brides, sexual jihad, and temporary marriages evokes an imaginary of 'sex, violence and women's oppression' that works as a magnet to draw the attention of readers.[9] This then raises the question, how do the women concerned perceive of how they enter into marriage?

Turning to the literature, we did not only quickly discover that there was no reliable information available about how such marriages were carried out, but we were also more generally struck by a strong bias in publications about the *muhajirat*. A rather narrow range of questions dominated the literature: the motivations of women to travel to Syria, the extent to which they are or will become a security risk, and how to develop successful trajectories for deradicalization.[10] In other words, a radicalization and security frame is central to these publications.

Taking a closer look at the perspectives used in these writings, women's agency tends to be either underrated ('women as victims of devious men') or overrated ('women as trying to outdo their male counterparts'). Tropes like 'sexual jihad' and 'jihadi brides' often present the *muhajirat* as victims of unscrupulous men who lure them to Syria.[11] This is rather similar to how politicians, the security services, and the media had discussed 'informal Islamic marriages' as a security risk a decade earlier.[12]

Over the course of time, the trope of the 'jihadi bride' has become increasingly criticized in the academic literature. The *muhajirat*'s growing public online presence has contributed to a shift in the dominant discourse towards recognizing these women as actors and even as militant activists who function as propagandists and recruiters for IS. Some authors use the term 'female foreign fighters' to refer to the *muharijat*,[13] or point to their potential engagement in violent extremism, comparing them with the earlier presence of female fighters in left-wing groups and the more recent female suicide bombers recruited by Islamist groups.[14] In so far as these authors include the perspectives of the *muhajirat* themselves, they largely rely on the *muhajirat's* publicly accessible posts on social media. Such an approach in itself privileges the more ideologically engaged women and, in turn, amplifies their voices.

Methods used and insights gained

In order to gain insight into how the *muhajirat* conclude their marriages, we needed other sources and methods. Because of restrictions on doing fieldwork in Syria, the best alternative was private chatting. We recognize that this is far removed from the longer-term immersion that is the hallmark of anthropology. It is in some ways more similar to interviews, as it remains at the level of discourse (what people say) rather than allowing for the observation of people's practices (what people do). In addition, the absence of face-to-face contact makes it more difficult to assess the presence of our interlocutors, their body language and intonation. Also, answers are often briefer, it is more difficult to talk in depth, and chats are easily interrupted.

Similar to anthropological fieldwork, private chatting also requires the development of some level of trust between the researcher and her interlocutors, so we needed to work with someone who would be able to build such a relationship. We were fortunate to find a suitable junior researcher who had known a few of the *muhajirat* prior to their departure and was familiar with the kind of language they use (that is Dutch, but with very frequent use of Arabic-Islamic greetings, terms and interjections). Because of internet connectivity issues, we could not use Skype, so we turned to Facebook and WhatsApp. We worked with a topic list and open conversations, that is, we employed an interactive and cyclical approach, using insights gained from one conversation in the course of later conversations.[15] We were able to contact twenty-two *muhajirat*, and consider ten of them as our key interlocutors as they were both willing and able to provide insights into how the enactment of marriages came about.[16] The number of chats per person varied from less than five to over thirty, and after the initial contact from our side they were initiated by both parties.

Although we cannot claim that the women we talked with are a representative sample, some interesting patterns emerged nonetheless. The large majority of our interlocutors (here we refer to the twenty-two women we contacted) were young adults in their early to mid-twenties. Many were Moroccan-Dutch (a few were Moroccan-Flemish), while a little over a quarter were converts (of various ethnic backgrounds). Over two-thirds of the *muhajirat* only married after arriving in Syria, while the remainder either travelled together with their husbands to Syria or followed them later. Most of the women – also those marrying in Syria – married partners from the same ethnic background, or if not, then with a convert, or a migrant who had grown up in another Western country. None of our interlocutors had married a Syrian. By the end of our research period, in the early summer of 2015, already half of the women had been widowed.

Looking more closely at *how* the *muhajirat* married (that is, turning to our ten key interlocutors), it became evident that they held strong opinions about the trajectory towards marriage. Critical of premarital contact with men, they only agreed to meet their partner a limited number of times before marriage and preferably in the presence of others. Instead of focusing on material matters – a high dower or a lavish wedding – their main concern was to find 'a practising brother', even if their own religious knowledge was sometimes limited. By doing so, they not only rejected mainstream notions of free dating, but also those arranged marriages that have material and familial interests as their main concern.

Both those marrying in the Netherlands and the early arrivals among our interlocutors who came to Syria from early 2013 onwards, reported that their marriages were effected informally. The marriage contract was often carried out at home, sometimes at first only orally, the dower often had little or no material value, and some women reported that they had chosen their own *wali* (marriage guardian). However, after the Caliphate was proclaimed, IS officials increasingly attempted to control and regulate the enactment of marriages, restricting the freedom of action of both the bride and the groom.

This was similar to what had happened during processes of state formation elsewhere. In line with the Syrian Law of Personal Status, IS also started to require that marriages either took place at the Sharia court or at home in the presence of an official who would then register the marriage at the court. Standard Islamic rules about who should function as a woman's *wali* were implemented, starting with the father and proceeding in a fixed order; while for converts the *qadi* (judge) at the Sharia court was to function as *wali*.

Other attempts made by IS officials to regulate marriages were less conventional. They imposed heavy restrictions on private premarital contact between men and women. Men did not only need the approval of the *wali* of their prospective wife, but also the leader of their group (the *amir*) needed to give his permission. Moreover, IS made attempts to impose a *minimum* amount of dower (our interlocutors mentioned $500) in order to make marriage a more serious commitment and to protect the *muhajirat* from men who would only marry them because they would ask for so little compared to Syrian women.[17]

Textual politics: From marriage to a 'security issue'

In the section above we have presented our work on the marriages of the *muhajirat* quite extensively because that was the central focus of our publication in *Anthropology Today*. We ended our article with a brief, more general observation. In the light of the commotion it caused, it is worthwhile to cite this last paragraph in full:

> We do not claim that the insights we gained through our chats are representative of the whole population of female migrants from the Netherlands (and even less so for those from Belgium) to Syria. We can, however, state with confidence that

a substantial number of *muhajirat* are adult women in their twenties who went to Syria because they desired to live under IS rule. Considering them either as victims or as militant activists does not tally with how they talk about their lives. Rather than expressing an interest in joining the violent jihad, they see themselves as first and foremost responsible for domestic life. This does not imply that giving birth, raising children and caring for husbands are not central to the reproduction of social formations, in this case IS. Yet, in contrast to other cases, where women themselves highlight the political nature of motherhood, our interlocutors were rather reluctant to consider their domestic activities as part and parcel of the world of politics.[18] Their main investment seems to be in attempting to normalize life under IS rule. This normalization remains, however, fragile, as many of the women – a staggering half of our interlocutors – have experienced widowhood in the past couple of years.[19]

We had included this last paragraph because it contradicted one of our own assumptions. We had expected women who had taken the huge step to leave their homeland and to travel to Syria, engaging in an act that many orthodox Muslims would denounce (travelling without a male relative or husband), to become more involved with their environment and with the broader process of state-building. As this hardly seemed the case, we considered it worthwhile to share this observation with our readers. Little did we expect this carefully worded paragraph would engender major media hype and parliamentary debate.

After our article was published in *Anthropology Today* in April 2016, we sent it to a few journalists to see whether they would be interested in writing about it for the Dutch-language media. In July 2016, an *NRC* journalist sent us the draft of an article he intended to publish. At the time he considered our work to be 'cool research'.[20] Using the case of Laura H. – who had just returned from IS-held territory – as an anchor, he summarized some of our findings quite adequately, including those on marriage. However, this article never saw the light of day, as the *NRC* deemed it insufficiently newsworthy.

Half a year later the *NRC* published, instead, a very different article by the same journalist about the same *Anthropology Today* article. Entitled *Jihad Researcher from University of Amsterdam Expressed Support for IS fighters* it appeared as the third and last episode in a high-profile series on Cyberjihadism. This series coincided, as the editorial op-ed stated, with the public announcement of the formation of a special police unit to fight Cyberjihadism. More than half of the front page was dedicated to the over 1500-word article as well as two pages in the middle, with much space devoted to a large colourful drawing of a covered woman working on a tablet. Headings included 'sympathy for the jihad', 'a contribution to terror', 'jihadist posts', and 'no openness'; in fact, the term jihad was mentioned over eighteen times in the article.

How did the *NRC* frame our article? It started with the statement that the junior researcher had already, prior to research, expressed the opinion that these women were not recruited and used for the sexual jihad, but that they had opted themselves to leave for Syria and were just married. The journalist claimed to have learned this, after allegedly discovering the pseudonym she had used for postings on a web forum, which also included some posts that could be read as 'pro-jihadist'. He reproached us for not being transparent about her 'jihadist sympathies'. In his eyes, this was particularly problematic as our argument that many women expressed no interest in militant activism could be used by the lawyers of women returning from IS-held areas. His mistrust was further evoked by the fact that, according to him, our results did not tally with those of other researchers, our study lacked openness about the questions asked, and our refusal to register the women's real names was highly unusual. To underscore this point, he quoted other academics who allegedly criticized our study for a lack of transparency.

In its reporting, the *NRC* publication completely ignored both the research question and the main conclusions of our article. It is hard to overstate this. Not a word was written about the marriages of the *muhajirat*. No mention was made about dating practices, partner choice in relation to ethnic-national boundary making, the informal nature of carrying out these marriages, and the conventional and less conventional ways in which IS attempted to regulate marriages. Instead, our conclusions were reduced, in one sentence, to 'a large number of the women with IS willingly embrace the strict rules of the terrorist organization'.[21] Others then translated this into statements such as 'those ladies who had been with IS and had liked it very much',[22] or 'the main conclusion was that the women were very content with their domestic life with IS'.[23] We had, of course, no evidence whether the *muhajirat* 'liked it' there or 'were very content' and we seriously doubt whether we would have been able to provide a well-grounded answer to such a question on the basis of chatting. We had only stated that *in the field of marriage*, 'the women willingly submitted to IS regulations'. But the *NRC* and, in its slipstream, other media, were not interested in marriages.

Countering the security frame: An appeal to reason

The main substantial issue the *NRC* raised was that presenting these women as only involved in domestic tasks, would be helpful for lawyers defending the *muhajirat* after their possible return to the Netherlands. In other words, we, as authors of the text, obstructed the work of the security services. We found this line of argumentation puzzling, as, on the basis of our text, one may argue as well that the public prosecution could use our article to undermine the argument that the *muhajirat* were victims of unscrupulous men trying to recruit them. In fact, either one of these deductions is problematic, as we explicitly stated that our results could not be generalized for the whole population of *muhajirat* in Syria. When we reported that a substantial number of the *muhajirat* presented themselves neither as victims nor as militant activists, we were referring to our interlocutors *only*, about one-third of the estimated number present in Syria at the time. We explicitly stated that we cannot claim that these women are representative for the whole category of *muhajirat*. It would simply be incorrect to conclude on the basis of our publication that there are *no* women who are either victims or militant activists; in fact, we mention one woman among our interlocutors who could be considered as belonging to the latter category. We only stated that there is *also* a category that does not seem to fit either of these two descriptions. Moreover, we then qualified our statement further with the observation that even if the *muhajirat* only engage in caring tasks, they may still be considered as involved in the reproduction of IS as a social formation. How careful can one be?

In hindsight, it may well have been the very fact that we were so cautious in our statements about the *muhajirat* that caused discomfort. We highlighted that our article in *Anthropology Today* was part of the 'narrative' section, and explicitly presented it as explorative. Rather than drawing firm and unequivocal conclusions about their activities, we focused on how they presented themselves to us. We pointed out that our results could not be generalized, and argued that their engagement in domestic tasks could be interpreted in different ways. In other words, as is often the case in anthropological research, we showed the complexity and multi-layeredness of apparently simple questions (such as whether the *muhajirat* are victims or activists) instead of providing clear and unambiguous answers.

What makes it even more difficult to understand why the NRC considered our last paragraph so scandalous, is that, in contrast to the claims of the NRC, it is rather similar to what others have argued. Take, for instance, how the very same NRC had presented *Destination Syria,* a report about the everyday life of Dutch emigrants to Syria, in relation to the court case against Laura H. First, the NRC criticized how the public prosecutor used the *Destination Syria* report: 'According to the public prosecutor the report indicates that all female emigrants to Syria are involved in the armed struggle. The authors deny this.'[24] Next, the NRC quotes two of the authors. One of them, an emeritus professor of Arabic and Islamic Studies states, 'There are plenty of women there who are sitting at home, are married and take care of the children', while, according to the other, a professor of terrorism studies, 'Many girls naively assume that they can live best as a Muslim in the Caliphate'. In other words, these conclusions resonate strongly with what we had stated in our publication.[25] However, in January 2017, the NRC argued that our conclusion 'is at odds with those of other studies', adding to this that our argument that these women are only involved in domestic tasks may obstruct the work of the security services.

Authorship matters

How had our article turned from 'cool research' in July 2016 into a case of 'jihadism at the University of Amsterdam' in January 2017? As the journalist told us, he had first discovered that the junior researcher had a close relationship with someone ('a jihadist'), with whom he had a long-standing conflictual relationship. He had then allegedly found out that the junior researcher had in the past posted some pro-jihadist messages on a web forum under a nickname. These 'bits of information' had apparently prompted him to re-read our article as a pro-IS text.

In the course of two long conversations with the journalist, we first explained that we did not intend to make a public statement about what someone may or may not have posted under a nickname prior to our working relationship.[26] Also, we made it clear that we would not investigate (and publicly disclose) other aspects of our co-author's personal life, as we considered that an infringement of her right to privacy. The risk of taking such a principled stance was, of course, that it would raise more suspicion among the wider public, especially in the present-day political climate in which Muslims are already singled out for surveillance. Still, we felt that it was important to draw a line, as we were very concerned about providing a precedent to further infringements to the right to privacy that is already in itself often seen as standing in a tense relation with security concerns and hence increasingly under attack.

We found it hard to understand how our last paragraph (mentioned above) had given rise to so much suspicion. We explained in detail how we had worked and discussed the ethical requirements of anthropological research, such as the need to protect the identity of our interlocutors. In hindsight, our expectation that a rational discussion about *the content* of our article would take away the concerns of the *NRC* was far too optimistic. Whereas we cannot be certain about the motivations of the journalist and the *NRC* to publish the article in the format chosen, be it a personal grudge of the journalist, click-bait for a newspaper concerned about its financial position, or a blinding concern for state security, it was evident that we had underestimated the force of emotion in this case. It was our rational line of argumentation, and the relatively neutral language we used, that caused considerable discomfort. In the case of IS, apparently the only acceptable discursive format and style was one of affective rejection.[27] We were, however, not the only ones using a relatively neutral language – the authors of *Destination Syria*, for instance, also did so.[28] To understand what made our publication particularly suspect, we need to further investigate authorship.

Positionality and the unequal division of distrust

As the above indicates, claiming a researcher's rights to privacy and refusing to be drawn into a security frame, was unacceptable to the *NRC*, members of parliament and the public at large. In an attempt to counter misinterpretations of our position, we decided to make a public statement about our personal views about the violent jihad. In our response to the *NRC* article we explicitly stated, that 'none of the authors is a supporter of the violent jihad'. This we also did, because the *NRC* had accused us of a lack of transparency, as we had not acknowledged such support in our publication. At the time we simply had not done so because none of us held such sympathies.[29] But this push for disclosure also raises the more fundamental question of whether researchers actually need to state their personal preferences.

Taking a step back and reflecting on the *NRC*'s line of argumentation about authorship, two different sets of objections emerged. First, the junior author should not have taken part in the research project at all, because she was allegedly biased.

Such a position cannot be defended. The ideal researcher would then be the imaginary tabula rasa, hardly a real-life figure. What matters is that we as researchers reflect on our own positionality and develop an awareness of the assumptions we all work with. Being a 'relative outsider' does not make one necessarily less biased than when one is a 'relative insider'. In fact, those who are generally considered as the closest to the ideal of neutrality (the paradigmatic secular white men) run the greatest risk of lacking an awareness of how their own assumptions and backgrounds may impact their research.

Secondly, researchers may hold particular opinions about their subject matter, but, for the sake of transparency, they need to make the opinions they hold available to the public. Although we agree that transparency is important in our interactions *with our interlocutors* in so far as it is appropriate, publicly reporting on one's opinions is a different kind of demand. In many cases it may be irresponsible or culturally insensitive to do so. Authors disclosing their political preferences may endanger both their interlocutors and themselves, and could result in their being barred from research sites. Demanding that researchers disclose their opinions about, for instance, sexual preferences, abortion or religious convictions, may jeopardize their ability to work in particular settings and may also impact their personal lives. After all, in contrast to their interlocutors, authors cannot remain anonymous, and may well need to exert some kinds of self-censorship, as we all do in social life.

Such demands of disclosure are also problematic because they often involve double standards. If one is obliged to report support for the violent jihad for the sake of transparency, wouldn't one, then, in a similar vein, be equally obliged to report an aversion to the violent jihad? There is, of course, the very real risk that such transparency is only required of those holding non-mainstream, transgressive opinions. And it does not stop there. Once it is accepted that one needs to report on personal opinions, the next demand would be to provide evidence that one does so truthfully. It is evident that in the eyes of the *NRC*, the junior researcher had expressed her real opinions in internet posts (without evidence that she had actually written and posted these); it considered her public statement that she does not support the violent jihad as inconsequential. Once the seeds of doubt and suspicion have been sown, it becomes impossible to correct this, especially when an appeal to Cyberjihadism fits so well with the hegemonic security frame.

The main point is, however, that the ability to do so is unequally distributed. It is far easier to create doubt about a research project if the researcher concerned belongs to a category ('a committed or orthodox Muslim') that is already under surveillance and hence an object of suspicion. What matters is not simply *what* is said and *how* it is said, but above all *who* says it. It is precisely because the researcher targeted is a Muslim woman, that it becomes so easy to render our reasoned arguments suspect. This is not only an ethical issue, but it also has serious epistemological consequences. It de facto disqualifies certain categories of researchers (those with a recognizable Muslim presence) as producers of knowledge. The net effect is then that particular forms of experiential knowledge are excluded from the process of knowledge production.

The research process: The vulnerability of anthropology

In addition to a 'jihad-friendly' text and a biased junior researcher, the NRC had yet another axe to grind with our methodology – private chatting with interlocutors whose official names were unknown. While in our publication we had elaborated on the drawbacks of this method, we also explained why we nonetheless had opted to try this out. As existing studies heavily lean on publicly available internet postings, amplifying the voices of those opting for a public presence, we were interested to discover whether private chatting would yield different kinds of knowledge. The NRC's claim that we did not know the questions our interlocutors had been asked was simply incorrect. Perhaps because the NRC had overlooked the fact that the focus of our research project was on how the *muhajirat* enter into marriages, our questions about marriage had also dropped off the radar.

The NRC's main objection, however, centred on the anonymity of our interlocutors, that is, the fact that we did not record the full official names of our interlocutors. On the record we were asked the following question: 'You did not establish through ID cards or passports that the research subjects were present in Syria. In hindsight, shouldn't you have done so?'[30] Besides the fact that it is not clear how a picture of an ID card would work as evidence of someone's presence in a particular location, this question also indicates the different ways in which journalists and anthropologists work with anonymity. Whereas journalists prefer to include official names and other identifiers in their publications, for anthropologists it is standard practice *not* to mention people's real names and to be careful with other identifiers. This is because one important ethical consideration in the field of anthropology is the principle of 'doing no harm'.

In order to protect the safety of our interlocutors we refrained from asking individual's official names, and from disclosing other information that would make them easily identifiable. We were already aware of the need to do so when we started our research. When we had submitted our larger research project to the relevant ethical committees, we had committed ourselves contractually to refrain from recording, and even asking about, official names. This issue became even more pressing when the AIVD changed its policy in January 2016, considering anyone present in an IS-held area as involved in a terrorist organization.[31] This was further compounded when, in early 2017, public prosecutors started to prepare cases against those present in IS-held territory, including women and children.[32] The substantive value of the requirement of anonymity became evident in the course of the contestations about our research project. One of the parliamentary questions addressed to the Minister of Security and Justice centred on the identity of the woman that we had considered as the only one actively involved and committed to IS state-building: Was her name known to the public prosecutor and would a criminal investigation be started against her?

As social scientists we also face the problem that we do not have the legal right to protect our sources. This places us in a double bind. It is thanks to our contextual knowledge about the *muhajirat* that we felt a strong measure of confidence about the quality of the insights and the information our interlocutors had provided us with. Yet, we needed to be careful about the extent to which we publicly report this, precisely because we cannot claim the right to protect our sources. There is then a strong contrast between journalists who are not bound by the 'doing no harm' principle (they may, in contrast, consider it their task to expose individuals), yet enjoy a measure of legal protection of sources, and anthropologists who are bound to an ethics of care and do not have such legal protection.[33]

There is yet another reason why anonymity is the default option in anthropology. Much anthropological research is based on the fact that we develop relations of trust with our interlocutors. Based on such relations of trust, people share all kinds of details of their lives with us – which are sometimes very private – expecting that we will act responsibly and use this information prudently. A precondition for the development of such relations of trust is the promise of confidentiality. If we were to identify our interlocutors by name this would no doubt affect the quality of our work negatively. For most anthropological research, there is no methodological need to link a particular practice to a named individual, as we tend to focus on patterns emerging from individual practices, rather than on specific individuals. If we were to ask our interlocutors for their official names, there is a good chance that they would simply refuse to talk to us, and if they would still be willing to do so, they would then be well aware of the fact that they are 'on stage', that they are addressing a broader public while talking to us. This would have a considerable impact on the kinds of insight and information they would be willing to share with us.

A brief reflection: Overdetermined by the security discourse

When we were confronted with the controversy about our article and especially with the personal attacks on the junior researcher, we asked ourselves the following question: should we, in hindsight, not have published this article? After going through our material once more, revisiting our analysis and asking colleagues to critically read our text, we concluded that we stand behind our publication, both in terms of the choice of genre (a brief, explorative article in the 'narrative' section of *Anthropology Today*) and in terms of its content.[34] We could only have avoided the commotion if we would not have mentioned the junior researcher by name. Doing so would, however, have entailed another ethical and integrity issue, the denial of authorship.

The *NRC*'s framing of our article was accepted uncritically, also among those who would generally be critical of more sensationalist styles of reporting. Part of the reason is that the *NRC* is considered an upscale, quality paper, widely read among the administrative and professional elite of the country. But we had also failed to recognize that we were in a highly vulnerable position. We had overlooked the affective force of the security discourse, which appeals so strongly to emotions and is so forcibly and dominantly present in public debate that it is hard not to be affected by it.

We had, in particular, miscalculated how easily such a discourse could be triggered when the targets are 'already under suspicion', that is a Muslim researcher and anthropology as a discipline. In a political climate in which especially more orthodox Muslims are *a priori* considered as 'suspicious', Muslim researchers are particularly vulnerable to allegations about bias, and hence subject to unequal treatment. In an academic climate in which interpretative social sciences and the humanities are increasingly under attack, anthropology as a discipline that is intersubjective rather than positivistic, highlights ambiguity and fluidity rather than certainty, values heterogeneity over homogeneity, and foregrounds responsibility towards one's interlocutors over institutional interests, is an easy target.

There was no escape. Our attempts to counter accusations by reasoned argumentation were, at times, counterproductive. The combination of the affective hegemony of the security frame and a style of reporting of a quality paper that is increasingly bent on enticing its audiences through click-bait, enabled the *NRC* to turn our article on marriage into something akin to a security threat. If we had followed the journalist's lead, and had investigated the private life of our colleague and disclosed the names of our interlocutors, we would have functioned as some kind of security agents ourselves. Moreover, the security discourse also tried to pressure us to transgress both anthropological ethics and the law, be it by violating the right to privacy of a colleague or by non-compliance with contractual obligations about anonymity. But not only ethics and the law are at stake, there are also serious epistemological consequences. Disqualifying particular categories of researchers implies a disregard for their experiential knowledge, while refusing to provide confidentiality to our interlocutors will make them very hesitant to openly share their insights with us. This would seriously affect the quality of our work, and, more generally, that of our academic field.

Notes

1 Research for this project is funded by the European Research Council advanced grant 'Problematizing "Muslim Marriages": Ambiguities and Contestations' (project 2013-AdG-324180). The author wishes to thank Nadia Fadil for her comments that helped sharpen the line of argumentation.
2 http://onlinelibrary.wiley.com/doi/10.1111/1467-8322.12241/epdf. Although this contribution is written by Annelies Moors, both Martijn de Koning and Aysha Navest, co-authors of the *Anthropology Today* article agree with the line of argumentation. Depending on the context, the 'we' in this text refers either to the three authors of the article, or to the two senior authors. All translations from Dutch are by the author. The first section of this contribution draws heavily on the *Anthropology Today* article.
3 Andreas Kouwenhoven, 'Zuster Aicha: Cyberjihadist en UvA-wetenschapper', *NRC Handelsblad*, 16 January 2017. Available at https://www.nrc.nl/nieuws/2017/01/16/aicha-cyberjihadist-en-wetenschapper-6242123-a1541543. For our first response (on the university website), see http://www.uva.nl/content/nieuws/nieuwsberichten/2017/01/reactie-uva-op-artikel-nrc-handelsblad.html.

4 Parliamentary questions were submitted on 18 January 2017 and answered on 23
   February 2017: https://zoek.officielebekendmakingen.nl/ah-tk-20162017-1264.html;
   https://zoek.officielebekendmakingen.nl/ah-tk-20162017-1263.html; https://zoek.
   officielebekendmakingen.nl/ah-tk-20162017-1262.html; No doubt timing matters.
   These questions were posed during the pre-election campaign, and they functioned as
   a quick and convenient means for political parties to draw the attention of their
   constituencies.
5 With 'auto-ethnography', we refer to an analysis of experiences that did not first occur
   as part of a fieldwork project and pertain to a 'field' the researcher cannot simply
   choose to leave (see Sara Crawley, 'Autoethnography as Feminist Self-Interview', in *The
   Sage Handbook of Interview Research*, 2nd edn, eds. Jaber F. Gubrium, James A.
   Holstein, Amir B. Marvasti and Karyn D. McKinney (Thousand Oaks, CA: Sage, 2012).
6 In this article we use the term *muhajirat sham* (emigrants to Greater Syria) as this is
   the term the women use to refer to themselves. We also use terms such as Islamic State,
   hijra, and jihad as emic terms. Many Muslims strongly disagree with the political
   theology ISIS has developed about the Caliphate, *hijra* and jihad and object to its claim
   to Islamic statehood.
7 See Kate Young, Carol Wolkowitz and Roslyn McCullagh, *Of Marriage and the Market:
   Women's Subordination in International Perspective* (London: CSE Books, 1981);
   Frances Hasso, *Consuming Desires: Family Crisis and the State in the Middle East*
   (Stanford, CA: Stanford University Press, 2011); and Sarah Franklin and Susan
   McKinnon, 'New Directions in Kinship Study: A Core Concept Revisited', *Current
   Anthropology* 41, no. 2 (2000): 278.
8 Carol Bacchi, 'The Turn to Problematization: Political Implications of Contrasting
   Interpretive and Poststructural Adaptations', *Open Journal of Political Science* 5, no. 1
   (2015): 1–12.
9 Our discussions about the tropes of 'sexual jihad' and 'jihadi brides' are limited to
   Muslim women who actively desire to live under IS rule. It does not include the
   experiences of the Yazidi women and others who are forced to live under IS rule.
10 Examples of such studies are Edwin Bakker and Seran de Leede, 'European Female
   Jihadists in Syria: Exploring an under-researched Topic', *ICCT Background Note* (The
   Hague: ICCT, 2015). Available at http://www.icct.nl/download/file/ICCT-Bakker-de-
   Leede-European-Female-Jihadists-In-Syria-Exploring-An-Under-Researched-Topic-
   April2015%281%29.pdf (accessed 8 December 2015); Claudia Carvalho, ' "Okhti"
   Online – Spanish Muslim Women Engaging Online Jihad – A Facebook Case Study',
   Online: Heidelberg Journal of Religions on the Internet 6 (2014): 24–42. Available at
   https://heiup.uni-heidelberg.de/journals/index.php/religions/article/view/17358
   (accessed 8 December 2015); Carolyn Hoyle, Alexandra Bradford and Ross Frenett,
   Becoming Mulan? Female Western migrants to ISIS (London: Institute for Strategic
   Dialogue, 2015). Available at http://www.strategicdialogue.org/ISDJ2969_Becoming_
   Mulan_01.15_WEB.PDF (accessed 8 December 2015); Brigitte L. Nacos, 'The
   Portrayal of Female Terrorists in the Media: Similar Framing Patterns in the News
   Coverage of Women in Politics and in Terrorism', *Studies in Conflict & Terrorism* 28,
   no. 5 (2005): 435–51; Anita Perešin, 'Fatal Attraction: Western Muslimas and ISIS',
   Perspectives on Terrorism 9, no. 3 (2015): 21–38. Available at http://www.
   terrorismanalysts.com/pt/index.php/pot/article/view/427 (accessed 8 December 2015);
   Anita Perešin and Alberto Cervone, 'The Western *Muhajirat* of ISIS', *Studies in Conflict
   and Terrorism* 38, no. 7 (2015): 1–15; Erin Marie Saltman and Melanie Smith, *Till
   Martyrdom Do Us Part: Gender and the ISIS Phenomenon* (London: : Institute for

Strategic Dialogue, 2015). Available at http://www.strategicdialogue.org/Till_
Martyrdom_Do_Us_Part_Gender_and_the_ISIS_Phenomenon.pdf (accessed
8 December 2015); Marion van San, 'Striving in the Way of God: Justifying Jihad by
Young Belgian and Dutch Muslims', *Studies in Conflict & Terrorism* 38, no. 5 (2015):
328–42; and Rafia Zakaria, 'Women and Islamic Militancy', *Dissent* 62, no. 1 (2015):
118–25. Available at https://www.dissentmagazine.org/article/why-women-choose-isis-
islamic-militancy (accessed 8 December 2015).

11 Perešin and Cervone, 'The Western *Muhajirat* of ISIS', p. 6; Zakaria, 'Women and
Islamic Militancy', p. 119.

12 See, in this context, Annelies Moors, 'Unregistered Islamic marriages'; and NCTb,
Informele islamitische huwelijken: Het verschijnsel en de (veiligheids)risico's (Den Haag:
NCTb, 2006), p. 22. Available at https://217.26.122.24/uploads/84/e4/84e4319aa2c1f72
1c2c050cb05ed27a7/Rapport-informele-islamitische-huwelijken_tcm50-138594-1.pdf
(accessed 8 December 2015).

13 Bakker and De Leede, 'European Female Jihadists in Syria'.

14 Zakaria, 'Women and Islamic Militancy'; Bakker and De Leede, 'European Female
Jihadists in Syria'; and Nacos, 'The Portrayal of Female Terrorists in the Media'.

15 Daniel Bertaux, 'From the Life-History Approach to the Transformation of Sociological
Practice', in *Biography and Society: The Life-History Approach in the Social Sciences*,
ed. Daniel Bertaux (London: Sage, 1981).

16 Some women did not want to participate in the research because they considered it too
risky (and were concerned about their families living in the Netherlands or Belgium),
had a previously negative experience of journalists, researchers, or the security services,
or did not expect much good to come from engaging with those who did not share
their worldview. Others were willing and sometimes eager to participate in the
research, but circumstances – be they personal, infrastructural or war related – did not
always allow for substantial chat sessions.

17 This stands in contrast to developments elsewhere in the Arab world, where attempts
to regulate the dower or the costs of marriage entail setting a *maximum* amount in
order to facilitate marriage – that is, to counter the trend towards delayed marriage. See
Welchman, *Women and Muslim Family Laws in Arab States* (Amsterdam: Amsterdam
University Press, 2007), pp. 91–2; Hasso, *Consuming Desires*, 62–63ff., 80–81ff.

18 Julie Peteet, 'Icons and Militants: Mothering in the Danger Zone', *Signs* 23, no. 1 (1997):
103 and 114, for instance, writes about 'activist mothering' (birthing and nurturing
children) under warlike conditions in the case of Palestinians in the camps in Lebanon;
and Jeanette S. Jouili and Schirin Amir-Moazami, 'Knowledge, Empowerment and
Religious Authority among Pious Muslim Women in France and Germany'. *The Muslim
World*, 96, no. 4 (2006): 622–3, refer to the term 'political motherhood' when analysing
the involvement of mothers in the transfer of Islamic knowledge to the next generation
of Muslims in Europe.

19 Aysha Navest, Martijn de Koning and Annelies Moors, 'Chatting about Marriage with
Female Migrants to Syria', p. 24.

20 Email, 14 July 2016.

21 Andreas Kouwenhoven, 'Jihadonderzoeker UvA uitte zelf steun voor strijders van IS',
NRC Handelsblad, 17 January 2017.

22 Pieter Duisenberg, member of parliament for the VVD, a right-wing party with the
largest number of seats in parliament, 'VVD wil onderzoek politieke voorkeur
wetenschappers', *Science Guide* [website], 26 January 2017. Available at http://www.
scienceguide.nl/201701/vvd-wil-onderzoek-politieke-voorkeur-wetenschappers.aspx.

23 Nikki Sterkenburg, 'Onder antropologen', *Elsevier* 73, no. 4 (2017): 30.

24 Andreas Kouwenhoven and Kees Versteegh, 'In crucial Syrië-rapport werd geschrapt', *NRC Handelsblad*, 16 August 2016.

25 It is rather ironic that one of the (anonymous) sources of *Destination Syria* is Martijn de Koning, co-author of our *Anthropology Today* article. As *Destination Syria* does not identify its sources by name, but only by function (such as 'researcher' or 'journalist'), the *NRC* journalist did not know this.

26 Conversations with journalist, 18 October 2016 and 17 November 2016.

27 This was clearly expressed in a contribution by Gert Jan Geling. He argues that as our research may influence the judicial powers (in dealing with those returning from IS-held areas), the greatest possible objectivity and neutrality is required. In his view, this is not the case in our research, as we are taking up a strongly relativistic position. This is evidenced by the use of terms such as 'female migrants' (rather than an explicit reference to a terrorist organization). See Gert Jan Geling, 'Frame mij niet als islamcriticus uit Leidse stal', *deKanttekening*, 8 February 2017. Available at https://dekanttekening.nl/opinie/frame-mij-niet-als-islamcriticus-uit-de-leidse-stal/.

28 Daan Weggemans, Ruud Peters, Edwin Bakker and Roel de Bont, *Destination Syria: An Exploratory Study into the Daily Lives of Dutch 'Syria Travellers'* (Leiden: Leiden University, Institute of Security and Global Affairs, 2016), p. 10.

29 We recognize that the very act of making such a statement of non-support for the violent jihad to counter misinterpretations, runs the risk of normalizing the need to respond to such accusations.

30 Email, 13 December 2016.

31 AIVD, 'Leven bij ISIS, de mythe ontrafeld' (Den Haag: AIVD, 2016), p. 15.

32 Janny Groen, 'OM wil Nederlandse jihadisten veroordelen voor terugkomst uit klalifaat', *De Volkskrant*, 16 February 2017.

33 The journalist himself stated to us that he was well aware of the fact that publishing and linking particular internet posts to her by name could harm the junior researcher 'in a possibly fatal way', interview with journalist, 17 November 2016.

34 The two anthropologists mentioned in the *NRC* article both stated that they do *not* share the journalist's criticism. One of them, professor Thijl Sunier, had not even been told by the journalist that the questions about transparency he had posed concerned our article. The *NRC* also refused to publish his letter to the editor.

CONCLUSIONS

Chapter 11

FROM CONVERT TO RADICAL: MAKING CRITIQUE ILLEGIBLE

Iman Lechkar[1]

'Radical change' of worldview and identity is an important supposition in both the categories of 'religious conversion' and of 'radicalization'. Since 1902, research on religious conversion makes an irrevocable correlation between conversion and radical change, linking conversion to a transformation from 'a previous infernal life to a utopian existence'.[2] This idea, that conversion entails a psycho-pathological condition and radical change, can even be found in some more recent research on conversion to Islam. Stefano Allievi, for instance, frames the conversion as follows: 'Conversion, as entry into another culture and another religion, presupposes strong moments that symbolically sanction the conversion itself and reinforce its significance as a radical change and clean break with the past'.[3] This view on conversion also extends to the bodily practices such as wearing a veil or circumcising, for, he continues, 'From this point of view, the main functions of the hijab seem to be the following. First, it helps women to convert (obliges them, from a certain point of view), to keep to the new choice, to "enter" it in a radical way, like circumcision for men (which is far more "definitive"). Second, it helps them to be accepted by their new "significant others"'.[4]

As noted by Fadil and De Koning (see Chapter 2 in this volume), the term radicalization was introduced by the AIVD as a concept to capture a process of radical change that could potentially result in a security threat. Although the AIVD used radicalization mainly to refer to 'Islamic forms of militancy', some scholars have tried to bring the term back to its broader meaning, indicating a generic process of alienation. Because of the quintessential presence of 'radical change' in the notion of radicalization, it was inevitable that radicalization would also be understood as and linked with conversion.[5] We find it, for instance, in the popular depiction of Belgian converts Jejoen Bontick, Younes Delefortrie or Brian de Mulder, who have often been framed as individuals who have fallen prey to the extremist ideologies of Sharia4Belgium or Syria foreign fighters. We find it also in the various models on radicalization where a 'radical shift' towards Islam is often seen as a disturbing sign (see Fadil and De Koning, Chapter 2 in this volume; and Jaminé and Fadil, Chapter 7 in this volume).[6]

In what follows, I would like to offer a reflection on this notion of 'radicalization' by putting it in relation with the literature on conversion that has traditionally considered this idea of 'radical shift' as a problem. I want to suggest that, just like in the literature on conversion, this focus on 'radical shift' tends to not only problematically reify and naturalize particular modes of being, but it becomes also a strategy of dismissal and silencing of particular forms of political critique.

Conversion is radical

In his foundational work *The Varieties of Religious Experience* (1902), the psychologist and philosopher William James (1842–1910) describes a wide variety of different religious experiences. He makes a distinction between 'the healthy-minded, who need to be born only once, and the sick souls, who must be twice-born in order to be happy'.[7] These sick souls are characterized by a crisis, while 'once-born souls only know a gradual growth in holiness without a cataclysm'.[8] James understands conversion as the unification of a divided self. The author explains that the features of the pre-convert include being divided, feeling inferior and unhappy and that through conversion, the convert 'receives grace, experiences religion, gains assurance by which a self-hitherto divided and consciously wrong, inferior and unhappy becomes unified and consciously right, superior and happy'.[9] At the heart of James's account lies a binary that consists of the transformation from a previous infernal life to a utopian existence and is embedded in a dramatic and sudden change. James goes on to write that 'the alterations can only be radical or the completest of the ways a self may be divided'[10] and it is 'through a crisis that a change of place in the system occurs and that peripheral ideas become more central'.[11]

Ever since James suggested that conversion is symptomatic of a divided self, there have been a number of studies that have critically challenged this interrelationship between radicalism and conversion.[12] The volume *The Anthropology of Religious Conversion*, edited by Andrew Buckser and Stephen D. Glazier, questions, for instance, many aspects in the psychological and sociological models and offers a major insight into understanding conversion as a 'continuing practice' rather than something radical that would be based on 'a singular experience, paranormal or otherwise, or on an absolute breach with a former life'; an understanding in which 'conversion is a passage: constituted and reconstituted through social practice and the articulation of new forms of relatedness'.[13]

Because of the shifting meanings of 'radical' and the ideological underpinning in the usage of the concept, the anthropologist Talal Asad has challenged the explanatory value of the concept of 'conversion', arguing that the latter is imbued with value judgements entailing an assumption on a 'natural' body, thus neglecting the way in which bodies are continuously made and remade.[14] Asad rightly remarks that the 'secular body is naturalized as the space of human action – pure and simple – and the religious becomes subsumed by it as a social phenomenon to be characterized in terms of that ontological space'.[15] The idea of 'conversion' presupposes – on the other hand – a state of normalcy, which normalizes and naturalizes *certain* bodily iterations and practices framed as 'secular'.[16] Undoing religious bodies from their Islamic practices and symbols (such as not fasting, premarital sex, unveiling) can, however, also be viewed as an instance of 'conversion' or 'radical change', yet they are rarely read as such.[17] Islamic practices such as veiling among white female converts or circumcision among white male converts are, on the other hand, predominantly understood as radical changes.[18] By denoting conversion or particular practices executed by converts as radical, our understanding becomes blurry with regards to conversion as a distinctive form of bodily cultivation.

Dismissing liberal-secular critique

Yet, another notion of 'radical change' is present as well, one that points to conversion and radicalization as a critique on society. The notion of radicalization also points to the desire people acquire to bring about 'radical change' or 'deep change' in society (see Fadil and De Koning, Chapter 2 in this volume). One of the important consequences of this language of conversion is the relative neglect and disregard for the political and critical positioning one can adopt vis-à-vis dominant society throughout one's life trajectory. One of the main insights gained through my ethnographic fieldwork with converts between 2007 and 2011 was that their conversion to Islam often coincided with and articulated a sharp critique of neoliberal forms of consumerism and sociability. Several of my informants critically challenged liberal-secular values such as the disappearance of religious structures, individualism, the consumption culture, materialism and status anxiety, which they linked with the omnipresence of liberal-secular traditions. Through conversion, they hoped to become part of a community in which values such as solidarity, generosity and sense of community were thought to have a more prominent place.[19] They criticized the liberal rat race and were attracted to values of solidarity, hospitality, family and community ties.[20]

Yet these critiques often get lost in the general framing of 'converts' who are often treated as unstable people or even as a potential threat in the national imaginary. In her book *Outside the Fold*, Gauri Viswanathan states that the adoption of a different religious tradition 'undoes the settled practices of a community's composition and the certainty with which its practices are followed and regularized'.[21] Conversion *away* from the dominant religious tradition is indeed often experienced as unsettling, which can even result in public accusations. Esra Özyürek depicts, for instance, how German converts are often seen as national threats. She shows how an incident with two converts who were caught collecting chemicals in order to make explosives resulted in a call by Christian Democrat Wolfgang Bosbach to establish a convert registry because, so he claimed, 'we know some of them may be radicalized after converting'.[22] Özyürek explains that converts in Germany are often understood in terms of 'dangerous hybrids, polluting and challenging the cultural superiority and purity of the dominant group'.[23] Converts are viewed as threats and traitors because they remind national and supra national powers of the 'unfinished job of national, religious, and cultural homogenization'.[24] Unlike ethnic minorities or born religious minorities, German converts give up their homogenous racial, cultural and religious privileged position to become part of the greater group of minorities, a synonym for 'metaphors and reminders of the betrayal of the classical national project'.[25]

Conclusion

Whereas the discourse on radicalization might be viewed as a new development, the understanding that 'radical change' might potentially pose a threat is not necessarily new. As shown in the early works on conversion, the idea of 'radical change' (in particular into a different religious tradition than the national one) has always been met with suspicion and viewed as deviant. Yet one of the important consequences of these categories, whether it is that of 'conversion' or that of 'radicalization', is the incapacity to acknowledge and understand the societal critique that is often entailed in these life-journeys. Categories such as 'radical' and/or 'radicalization' blur not only motivations of people who convert to Islam but also the political claims towards society at large through their 'conversion'. If societal and political critique is systematically delegitimized through a conversion, radicalism and/or a radicalization discourse, how can we really understand what the religious, economic, social and political struggle of Muslim converts in particular and Muslims in general consists of?

Notes

1 I would like to thank Nadia Fadil and Martijn de Koning for their valuable feedback.
2 William James, *The Varieties of Religious Experience: A Study in Human Nature* (New York: New American Library, 1958 [1902]); Richard Travisano, 'Alternation and Conversion as Qualitatively Different Transformations', in *Social Psychology through Symbolic Interaction*, eds. Gregory Stone and Harvey Faberman (Waltham: Ginn-Blaisdell, 1970).
3 Stefano Allievi, 'Shifting Significance of the Halal/Haral Frontier: Narratives on the Hijab and Other Issues', in *Women Embracing Islam: Gender and Conversions in the West*, ed. Karin van Nieuwkerk (Texas: University of Texas Press, 2006), p. 124.
4 Ibid., p. 145.
5 Wim Meeus, 'Why Do Young People Become Jihadists? A Theoretical Account on Radical Identity Development', *European Journal of Developmental Psychology* 12, no. 3 (2015): 275–81; Neil Ferguson and Eve Binks, 'Understanding Radicalization and Engagement in Terrorism through Religious Conversion Motifs', *Journal of Strategic Security* 8, no. 1 (2015): 16–26.
6 For how conversion and radicalization can be conflated, see also Olivier Roy, 'The Long Read: Who Are the New Jihadis?', the *Guardian*, 13 April 2017. Available at https://www.theguardian.com/news/2017/apr/13/who-are-the-new-jihadis.
7 James, *The Varieties of Religious Experience*, p. 112.

8 Ibid., p. 161.
9 Ibid., p. 189.
10 Ibid., p. 194.
11 Ibid., p. 196.
12 See, in this respect, John Lofland and Rodney Stark, 'Becoming a World-Saver: A Theory of Conversion to a Deviant Perspective', *American Sociological Review* 30, no. 6 (1965): 862–75; Talal Asad, 'Comments on Conversion', in *Conversion to Modernities: The Globalization of Christianity*, ed. Peter van der Veer (New York: Routledge, 1996). See also, Lewis R. Rambo, *Understanding Religious Conversion* (New Haven, CT: Yale University Press, 1993); Henri Gooren, 'Reassessing Conventional Approaches to Conversion: Toward a New Synthesis', *Journal for the Scientific Study of Religion* 46, no. 3 (2007): 337–53; Andrew Buckser and Steven Glazier, eds., *The Anthropology of Religious Conversion* (Lanham, MD: Rowman & Littlefield, 2003).
13 Diane Austin-Broos, 'The Anthropology of Conversion: An Introduction', in *The Anthropology of Religious Conversion*, eds. Andrew Buckser and Steven Glazier (Lanham, MD: Rowman & Littlefield, 2003), p. 9.
14 Asad, *Genealogies of Religion*.
15 Ibid., p. 266.
16 Ibid.; Asad, 'Comments on Conversion'; Talal Asad, *Formation of the Secular: Christianity, Islam and Modernity* (Stanford, CA: Stanford University Press, 2003); Mahmood, *Politics of Piety*; Fadil, 'Submitting to God'; Fadil, 'Not-/Unveiling as an Ethical Practice' (Report), *Feminist Review* 98, no. 1 (2011): 83–109; Iman Lechkar, 'Striving and Stumbling in the Name of Allah: Neo-Sunnis and Neo-Shi'ites in a Belgian Context' (PhD diss., KU Leuven, 2012).
17 See, in this context, Fadil, 'Submitting to God'; and Fadil, 'Not-/Unveiling as an Ethical Practice'.
18 For an interesting account on the racialization of Muslim practices, see Vanessa E. Vroon, *Sisters in Islam: Women's Conversion and the Politics of Belonging: A Dutch Case Study* (PhD diss., University of Amsterdam, 2012).
19 Lechkar, 'Striving and Stumbling in the Name of Allah'.
20 Ibid.
21 Gauri Viswanathan, *Outside the Fold: Conversion, Modernity and Belief* (Princeton, NJ: Princeton University Press, 1998).
22 Esra Özyürek, 'Convert Alert: German Muslims and Turkish Christians as Threats to Security in the New Europe', *Comparative Studies in Society and History* 5, no. 1 (2009): 91.
23 Ibid., p. 95.
24 Ibid.
25 Ibid.

Chapter 12

THE MAZE OF RADICALIZATION: JUSTIFICATION AND PROFESSIONAL INTERESTS

Didier Bigo

The previous chapters have discussed in detail on the one hand the logics of discrimination resulting from the politics of counter-radicalization – be they hard or soft; and on the other, the logics of hyper-specialization, which have transformed the professional field of specialists in internal security and counterterrorism in Europe. Inside this field, we have seen a process which in my previous work I analysed under the notion of 'semi-autonomization', namely a process through which a social field (in this case, counterterrorism professionals) increasingly determines its own priorities and objectives independently from other fields (for example, from politicians, understood as the field of 'professionals of politics'[1]). From 2005, and even more so after 2015, a group of practitioners and academics have gained this semi-autonomy through the terminology of 'radicalization', distinguishing themselves from the traditional professionals of counterterrorism.

This group of *pracademics* – a term coined by Monique Jo Beerli in her doctoral thesis[2] – is in competition with the traditional actors of counterterrorism for a large number of objectives, including increasing their status and importance in the state apparatus, as illustrated, for example, through their share of public budgets and their access to public–private partnerships. In this competition, the idea of 'alternative solutions' carried by the notion of 'radicalization', often in the name of a more 'societal' approach, becomes an instrumental asset in gaining the upper hand. Yet the promotion of this term and the development of media attention have not resolved the controversies surrounding the label of 'radicalization'. On the contrary, it has exacerbated the competition among actors who carry different forms of knowledge, gathered in different disciplines, all aiming to impose their views on how to tackle 'radicalism' and prevent terrorism.

These two phenomena – discrimination and the development of so-called expert knowledge on the societal prevention of terrorism – are not parallel developments; rather, they are deeply intertwined. They call not only for a critique of such preventive policies, in that they generate a climate of suspicion affecting large groups of people (beyond the suspects for whom a reasonable doubt exists), but they also call into question the responsibility of those academics who think through the terminology of radicalization in order to understand what is at stake in Belgium, the Netherlands and more generally in Europe when discussing political violence after 2015.

If reflexivity is a central feature in the social sciences, and in critical security studies in particular, this book clearly illustrates that much work remains to be done when it comes to the literature on radicalization. Scholars and 'experts' who for the most part genuinely want to help governments by providing advice on their policies for terrorism prevention end up willingly or unwillingly reproducing forms of statistical discrimination and folk theories emerging from the discourse of security professionals and their *pracademics*. By doing so, they unfortunately participate in reinforcing the process of discrimination documented in this book. This last point will be the focus of my conclusion.

Radicalization: A regime of justification used for preventive strategies

The belief that the terminology of radicalization – used to explain the supposedly new phenomenon of jihadism and foreign fighters – is a recent development is misguided. A sociogenesis of preventive policies in the matter of counterterrorism reveals that the conceptual origins of the discourse emerged in the mid-seventies. The idea of criminalizing preparatory acts or even preliminary meetings that considered the possible use of violence against civil targets was first discussed around that period.[3]

At the time, the idea of 'revolution' dominated political activity, and clandestine organizations were keen to describe themselves as 'avant-garde' by carrying out violent actions they understood to be a form of 'propaganda by the deed'.[4] Activists sought to encourage people to protest, including through violent means. In this context, 'radicals' were seen by these clandestine organizations as individuals capable of mere 'talk' and no 'action' – that is, as individuals insufficiently mature to carry out a revolution. Violent groups thus considered it necessary to push radicals to extremism and to a revolutionary consciousness. Consequently, 'radical' was the label given by violent organizations to those groups who occupied the middle ground between violent and non-violent methods: capable of forcefully opposing the authorities during demonstrations, but unwilling to go further.[5]

The same terminology, when used by the police, served to designate the groups of people in the middle of the continuum between the far-left parties and clandestine organizations. They were thus a different concern than the clandestine actors, but were not at the core of the discussions.[6] The international institutions of police emerging to tackle terrorism at the time made this distinction as well. The TREVI group[7], for example, was created in 1976 and named ten years after by an acronym that specifically distinguished Terrorism, Radicalism, Extremism, Violence and Internationalism. In this context, radicalism was part of a process of escalation that needed to be tackled, but not the focus of attention itself.

A change occurred when legislation in Italy and the Federal Republic of Germany introduced the idea that justifying combat was already a form of combat that could be punished.[8] Words were considered to be performative: 'saying' (justifying) became almost equated with violence itself. In the intellectual and academic field, intellectuals such as Jean Paul Sartre and Jean Genet contested such measures on the basis that they endangered freedom of speech and the right to self-defence, arguing that it was impossible to predict human behaviour without entering into a totalitarian logic.[9] The 'performative approach' to violence, which considers that the spiral of violence begins with violent words, became increasingly accepted as a credo in antiterrorist, judiciary and academic circles. This led to the delegitimization of acts of violent physical protest and the arguments sustaining them.[10] Philosophical and political principles grounded in Sartre's existentialism, as well as in Hegel's understanding of the penal logic as being aimed towards human rehabilitation gave way to different new views. The new approach emphasized the need to enforce safety measures in the name of defending society, linking penalty with risk and danger, and no longer with the individual as such.[11] This approach relied on new statistical and actuarial approaches which started to be developed in the analysis of 'reoffending'. They claimed that individuals engaged in trajectories of 'radicalism' could similarly not escape their fate.[12] The debate in the mid-eighties and nineties further changed the paradigm of liberty versus security. Social scientific production began questioning the legitimacy of certain kinds of political violence embedded in postcolonial struggles and revolutionary projects. Instead it developed conceptual frameworks focused on 'relative deprivation',[13] anticipations on why, how and when people rebel, and on actuarial justice[14] in an attempt to introduce a 'social science' reasoning based on statistics instead of a political judgement about the justification of violence.[15]

By the mid-nineties, most of these arguments about the notion of 'values' – especially the idea of a value-neutral science applied to political violence – were being called into question. Their pretence to anticipate human behaviour became distrusted. Statistics were revealed not to be a reliable instrument for the scientific prediction of human behaviour, but merely a tool providing uncertain forecasts. Radicals were thus recast as free, unpredictable electrons. The key questions became the following: Why is political violence so rare in democracies despite the possibility to act? What makes democracies unique and stronger than dictatorships despite the low level of their security apparatus? The answers were found in the democracies' capacities for resilience and the strength of trust in real political communities. If the argument was no longer a political judgement in relation to history, it nevertheless still existed as a belief that freedom was not totally paralyzed against violence and was in fact a better 'engine' than the reinforcement of security and surveillance measures to combat violence coming from all sides, be it from the initial clandestine groups and/or the state violence itself in its 'answer'.[16]

The idea of predictability entered into the discussion again, but was mostly restricted to repetitive, opportunistic petty crimes that are not really dependent on police actions. Predictability was not working for highly motivated and conscious terrorists, who foiled the patterns of profiling the police used.[17] As a result, preventive attitudes and anticipation by the police became more tolerated if they were seen as necessary and proportionate. Yet these anticipatory practices were still considered a last resort in the criminal justice system and strongly controlled by judges in order to avoid the violence between clandestine groups and police services escalating and degenerating into riots and further claims for independence or global justice.

The illegality of policing by anticipative and disruptive methods was condemned with almost the same severity as the illegal actions of the clandestine groups. The cases related to the MI6 actions against the IRA and Sinn Fein in Belfast and Manchester, or the GAL (*Grupos Antiterroristas de Liberación*)[18] and *Guardia Civil* (Spanish police force) against ETA and Basque radical political parties showed that suspicion and anticipation of a potential crime were not sufficient to legitimize an illegal 'neutralization' of the enemy.[19]

The war on terror and the normalization of pre-emptive interventions

After the violent actions of September 11 on the other side of the Atlantic, the eruption of the Global War on Terror and the idea that these actions were a 'war' changed these equilibriums. Because of the large number of victims inflicted by a single action and the potential for future violence, the reasoning according to which it was impossible to wait and 'fight back' gained currency. Acting 'first' was presented as necessary in order to protect vulnerable and innocent populations against mass terror. Grounded in the folk theory that any new act of terrorism will be ten times more dangerous than the attacks of September 11,[20] and that there might be biological (e.g. anthrax), chemical or nuclear attacks, the narrative of risk prevention became detached from a justification through statistical recurrence. The security discourse shifted from a logic of risk management to one of risk probability linked to one catastrophic event whose consequences would be purely and simply unacceptable for a government protecting its population.[21] This argument justified a de facto move towards a 'prevention' approach that is more or less independent of a beginning defined by proof and evidence.

Prevention became equivalent to suspicion. Antiterrorism, led by law enforcement and criminal justice experts, had to be replaced by counterterrorism, led by military strategists and intelligence services working both abroad and internally. Their task was to collect all the signs of activity that may indicate an attempt of intrusive actions by a very small group of individuals. Consequently, the meticulous work of infiltrating cells of clandestine groups with human specialists was presented as artisanal and obsolete. Large-scale surveillance implying large technical capabilities had to be deployed at an industrial scale to detect 'weak signals'. 'Connecting the dots' in order to extract information from human beings and/or their computers became the mantra of the Bush administration. Rear Admiral Poindexter can be considered one of the men who framed this narrative of predictive policing by instrumentalizing the fear to have fear: not just 'the fear of the other', but the fear of everybody, including the fear of one's population, which took hold of the neoconservative American government following the 9/11 attacks and the anthrax attacks.[22] He succeeded, in part, in destabilizing the credibility of traditional security measures employed by the criminal justice prosecution and the FBI as well as in pushing the use of data technologies along with automatic identification technologies for fingerprints, digital photographs, iris recognition and/or genetic fingerprinting. These are the technologies the American government and the intelligence services invested most heavily in before 9/11, thereby giving rise to the different representations of the enemy as a suspect who could be tackled via digital surveillance, by intercepting their communications, and by tracking their past movements to predict their future moves.

Some politicians implemented these technologies while others remained wary of them. But these technological 'answers' have constructed a new *doxa* (i.e. a taken-for-granted set of assumptions about how a problem is framed) in the strongest sense of the word.[23] This doxa now serves as the discursive limits beyond which it is not possible to structure controversies around the figure of the enemy and the smokescreens that Western politicians put up collectively. The CIA opted for extraordinary rendition and torture abroad while the NSA and its 'Five Eyes' allies launched a surveillance of suspects of terrorism via the surveillance of their computers and their financing, ultimately rerouting part of their economic intelligence activities abroad and foreign policy analysis into surveillance of pre-terrorists and profiles of 'radicals'.[24]

Initially sceptic about this strategy and weary of the cost in terms of legitimacy for the police and the governments involved, the European allies – especially Tony Blair in the UK – avoided a logic of restructuring their homeland security departments and the practical consequences, such as the creation of 'fusion centres'. This was in part motivated by the fear of the resilience of their judges if a militarization of terrorism was to be undertaken. Nevertheless, European governments asked for derogations to human rights charter and more investigative power for their intelligence services. Prevention was now associated with detection, vulnerability and protection. Reinforcement of surveillance at the borders and intelligence abroad were considered the key elements of the new policy. New laws against terrorism were passed, but the previous ones were the most used at the time. It was central to convince the judiciary to change its views about necessity and proportionality and to 'educate' them on this change in the catastrophic risk approach. Optimism was strong during the first three years, but the bombings of Madrid in 2004 and even more so those of London in July 2005 again moved the cursor.[25] Individuals belonging to clandestine groups were not the only ones who could infiltrate the country despite surveillance measures and despite being outside the Schengen area of freedom of movement. From now on, this logic extended to those who belonged to the UK soil. They were born there. They were citizens choosing to fight against their own government and in support of their adversaries.

The spectre of the enemy from within thus returned. For EU governments, surveillance could not be limited to people on the move, crossing borders. It was necessary to expand the scope geographically to apply inside the borders the kind of surveillance deployed abroad in order to detect who was potentially a traitor, a 'mole' waiting for orders to come from abroad. The insiders were seen to be de facto ideologically infiltrated foreign fighters, despite their UK citizenship. The geographical borders were no longer the main focus. They were important, but insufficient to prevent the new risks.

It became crucial to monitor digital forms of control of anyone having contact, by phone or email, with a foreigner and to treat him as a foreigner himself, not as a UK citizen; this was made possible in part by the digitization of EU borders. It was also necessary to create a temporal border by tracing back the potential suspects' activities in the previous years of their presence in the UK and to develop elaborate profiles in terms of what they may do, using examples of what happened to those who had to take action. Radicals became 'foreigners' and friends of 'foreigners' – namely, anti-citizens. A different semantic connection was created by reducing the meaning of the word 'radicalism' to jihadism.[26] Prevention was no longer an exception or even a necessary but lesser evil; it had to become a routine check, built on risk indicators of all the UK citizens considered to have strong links with foreign ideologies. The process meant detecting pre-terrorist acts in active support of groups fighting abroad against the UK and its allies. It meant identifying anonymous blogs justifying these actions on the internet and in their local communities. Finally, the terminology of radicals and radicalization gave way to the possibility of detecting 'signs' of potential traitors – in sum, signs of citizens becoming de facto foreigners. This temporal border became framed as one from which no return was considered possible. According to this view, individuals engaged in this process would become terrorists. This way of thinking, post 2005, has not only influenced the organization of the struggle against terrorism (to an effort certainly less militarized than that of the US, but still strongly led by the UK intelligence services), but it has also influenced the whole of the European Union's policies regarding antiterrorism.[27]

The polysemy of a policy

As this book has shown in detail, this process was not the result of a straightforward, one-way influence of the UK on other countries. The notion of radicalism had already very different connotations and meanings for the Netherlands, Belgium, Denmark and France. Radicalization became an object of competition in terms of its meaning and definition, its connection with 'foreignness' and 'ideology', and its link with extremist forms of religious feelings justifying violent acts. It also emerged as a term for competition between the actors claiming ownership over counterterrorism. These were divided between those who saw counterterrorism as a vital combat effort for liberal values on one side and the more traditional law enforcement and criminal justice services on the other. The latter envisaged counter-radicalization as a way to tackle and predict behaviour leading to terrorism not by logics of technological surveillance, but through the mobilization of civil society through the co-optation of community leaders considered capable of reporting and controlling those who may have become so apologetic of violence that they could be considered as already violent.

The solutions were coming from a slow process involving larger groups of policy actors, using forms of 'benevolent' mentoring acting 'upstream' of the process. Radicalization was a larger enterprise which needed more people, more human needs, more educational projects and even some forms of rehabilitation. Some chapters of this book are quite illuminating regarding this second position and its capacity to stop – or at least limit for a while – the first approach. Most academics were enthusiastic about a more 'inclusive' approach, a soft way to tackle the problem of radicalization, but they were just reproducing the same magical thought in reverse.[28] It was even looking successful in the way that, in almost every country, including the UK, practitioners insisted that the fight against radicalism was increasingly a way to go 'societal' and innerve communities with a logic of small tools of surveillance instead of continuing with the logic of technologization and interoperability that others were asking for. But they were in fact just defending their own services and an indigenous vision against the US NSA technological and theological vision of finding the pre-terrorist in anticipating its acts, opinions and even thoughts.[29]

But by 2015, the end of al-Qaeda leadership helped push for the first direction and attempted to take care of 'radicals' by de-radicalizing them as if they were suffering from some type of sickness. However, the acceleration of the departures towards Syria of these potential 'traitors', who were following the same de facto road of their national military but to fight in the other camp, again changed the configuration of what radicalization was doing and meaning by re-enacting the argument of a strategic actor.[30] If between 2005 and 2015 'radicalization' designated the process of those considered to deserve surveillance because they were on the path to 'home-grown' terrorism, then from 2015 it designated those on the path to become foreign fighters, who had to be blocked from leaving and – even more importantly – from returning.[31] The militarization of the conflicts in Syria and the situation of the opposition against Syrian President Assad recalibrated the discourse on radicalization. From a narrative of radicalization framed as a problem of 'home-grown' citizens brainwashed by foreign ideologies, the frame shifted to that of 'foreign fighters' leaving the UK, Belgian or French territories. The new narrative of 'foreign fighters' further emphasized the *foreignness* of these individuals, making it even less likely that rehabilitation or disengagement policies could ever be successful.

Considering the number of people who saw themselves joining Daesh as part of an international brigade fighting against a dictator, a remilitarization of the approach to radicalism was a way to justify a potential global civil war by Daesh and the necessity to fight against it at all levels, especially on the ideological terrain. In France and in other countries, denationalization became a way to punish radicals and to consecrate the distinction between good loyal citizens and unfaithful ones.[32] Obviously symbolic, the measure was there to frame the process of radicalization as a military engagement against France's enemies. In doing so, radicals were considered to betray their origins and their values to the point that denationalization was legitimate from the part of the state. The fact that it did not much affect the so-called fighters in practice was not important.

The frame of radicals as 'traitors' whether they leave, stay or return was set up within the broader context of a discourse on French or Belgian *'laïcité'* (secularism).[33] This form of *'laïcité'* as an extreme form of republicanism is now back on the agenda as a revival of the old project of Jean-Pierre Chevènement. The former Minister of Interior under Mitterrand wanted to oblige school teachers to introduce the values of the republic as a 'small catechism' delivered by history professors, with the requirement to sing the Marseillaise and show respect to the teachers.[34]

Academics from the 'new criminology' approach, who maintain strong networks with police forces, freemason networks and the private security sector, were active in promoting the thesis of 'gangstero-criminalism'. This approach refuted both the strategic military-actor thesis and the more psychological approaches.[35] It involved psychologists and childhood psychiatrists, scholars from neurosciences, and specialists in 'crisis management' in the suburbs as well as some actors from the European Union's 'radical awareness network' (RAN) to establish links between jails, criminality, radicalization and terrorism through the implicit connection between crime and poverty.

Radicalization as a folk theory and the responsibility of academics

Without wanting to sound like a broken record of Albert Camus, is there not some truth in the saying that to misname things is to add to the world's unhappiness?[36] When this label is a social mechanism of distributing the 'social bad' via an administrative and political term used to label suspects, what can academics do?[37] Can they validate the term 'radicals' if it means that some human beings are inscribed into a destiny where no change of behaviour is possible?

The notion of radicalization is now associated with the image of citizens supporting a foreign ideology who are impossible to integrate and masked as a re-packaged problem of religion. This pushes us to be doubtful about the validity of the term. One of the worrisome aspects about this development is that the term radicalism today has become associated with the image of an enemy from within, which feeds into a concern with so-called traitors who have not accepted the myth and practices of national identity. Certainly, if radicalization would make sense, it is as a relational process where the origins of violence are displaced from the role of discourse towards physical violence and which moves away from a vision of the pre-destination of human beings that can be traced by their past actions. It is not simply a matter of individual decision and choice, as the caricature of self-radicalization leads us to believe. Individuals are never cut from society and reality, and radicals are not 'mad'; they are angry men with political justifications and never fall into a single category.[38] Each of them is a moment into a trajectory that may create escalation (or not).

The art of asking the right question

In conclusion, to avoid discussing radicalism outside of the frame of peace and conflict studies, it is necessary to start by asking the right questions. Following what Charles Tilly said to Ted Gurr in the 1970s, the question is not 'why do men rebel' but rather 'why do they not rebel more often?' In this way, the question of formal obedience to power is finally opened.[39] In the 1980s, Rémy Leveau raised the same point when people overwhelmingly predicted the revolt that occurred in the French suburbs, the *banlieues*, in the wake of the First Palestinian Intifada. He directed his attention to the prerequisites for the avoidance of mass violence while accepting that there may nevertheless be isolated instances of violence. His article is still considered essential reading in the current climate of fear for its serene alternative.[40] However, his lessons seem to have fallen on deaf ears because they go against the interests of the little cottage industry of think tanks.

The arbitrariness of the practices of naming the situation of others as possessing a 'personality' which can be radicalized depending on the context cannot be rationalized as a specific category underpinning a specific public policy. The terminology of radicalization is a folk theory elaborated as a doctrine by the intelligence services and needs to be studied as such. It is a 'theoretical practice' that is used in the competition between various security actors, which has less to do with the characterization and the analysis of the problem of political violence itself, and more to do with the interests of the various agencies in defining it in such way as to securing funding and ownership of the issue.[41] Using the terminology for research is therefore implicitly validating the position of those who control the circulation of ideas into their sub-field as 'epistemic' authorities into the field of professionals of security – a position that may be best avoided or stated explicitly.

Terminology is never the monopoly of one group, who would have their doctrinal position accepted by others. It is far more often the unexpected result of struggles between different interests and strategies of distinction used in order to 'segment' or fracture the field of academic knowledge. It becomes the way to find a 'niche' where it is possible to develop a small but profitable cottage industry. In the specific case of radicalization, there seems to be an underlying conflict between the various disciplines of the social sciences. Psychologists, psychiatrists and data analysts working on artificial intelligence promote a perspective which disconnects the individual from the social and tries to explain violence not as an agonistic relation between social groups as some other disciplines do, but as a psychological abnormality in a democratic setting. These disciplines are directly responsible for the social acceptance of radicalization as a valid notion.

Radicalization is not a notion or an academic concept, but an accusation – a way to purify the so-called reactive violence by assigning the blame to one side only. As such, objectifying the different tactical moves of the actors who use the term, and the struggles they encounter in so doing, is the only reflexive approach possible. Radicalization is therefore the name by which it is possible to occult the dynamics of mimetic rivalry and escalation among all actors,[42] which is also why – despite the quantity of research on the theme of radicalization – it is very rare to find books like this one, where researchers begin to investigate seriously what is the exact opposite of radicalization – namely, not integration but the decision to not engage in violence, and to reject the propaganda of all sides. This may be the next direction to develop in order to continue the deconstruction of the so-called process of radicalization that this excellent book proposes.

Notes

1 Didier Bigo, 'International Political Sociology: Rethinking the International through Field(S) of Power' in *International Political Sociology: Transversal Lines*, eds. Tugba Basaran, Didier Bigo, Emmanuel-Pierre Guittet and R. B. J. Walker (London: Routledge, 2016), pp. 24–48. Max Weber in *Politik als Beruf* means by the word 'beruf' both a 'profession' and a 'vocation', as Lassman and Speirs indicate in their translation (see *Weber: Political Writings*, eds. Peter Lassman and Ronald Speirs (Cambridge and New York: Cambridge University Press, 1994)); this is why I avoid the notion of politicians and I use 'professionals of politics'.

2 On 'pracademics', see Monique J. Beerli, 'Saving the Saviors: Security Practices and Professional Struggles in the Humanitarian Space' (PhD diss., Sciences-Po, Paris & Geneva, 2017).

3 Gérard Mauger, 'Sur la "radicalisation islamiste"', *Savoir/Agir* 37, no. 3 (2013): 91–9.

4 Walter Badier, *Émile Henry: De la propagande par le fait au terrorisme anarchiste* (Chaucre: Éditions libertaires, 2007).

5 See Robert O. Paxton and Julie Hessler, *L'Europe au XXe siècle*, trans. Evelyn Werth (Paris: Tallandier, 2011), especially chapter 19; see also François Furet, *Terrorisme et démocratie* (Paris: Fayard, 1985).

6 Larry Portis, 'La sociologie consensuelle et le terrorisme: De la propagande par le fait à Unabomber', *L'Homme et la Société* 123–24 (1997): 57–74.

7 The TREVI group was set up in 1976 by Italian, German, French, Dutch and Belgian specialized services on antiterrorism. Its existence was revealed to the public with this acronym only in 1986. See, in this respect, Didier Bigo, *Polices en réseaux: L'expérience européenne* (Paris: Presses de Sciences Politiques, 1996).

8 Tony Bunyan 'Trevi, Europol and the European State', in *Statewatching the New Europe: A Handbook on the European State*, ed. Tony Bunyan (London: Statewatch, 1993).

9 Ulrike Meinhof, *Textes des prisonniers de la 'Fraction armée rouge' et dernières lettres d'Ulrike Meinhof*, Cahiers libres no. 337 (Paris: La Découverte, 1977).

10 Jörg Requate and Philipp Zessin, 'Comment sortir du "terrorisme"? La violence politique et les conditions de sa disparition en France et en République Fédérale d'Allemagne 1970–1990', *European Review of History—Revue européenne d'Histoire* 14, no. 3 (2007): 423–45.

11 David Garland, 'Les contradictions de la "société punitive": Le cas britannique', *Actes de la Recherche en Sciences Sociales* 124, no. 1 (1994): 49–67.

12 Maurice Cusson, *L'art de la sécurité: Ce que l'histoire de la criminologie nous enseigne* (Lausanne: Presses Polytechniques et Universitaires Romandes, 2011).

13 Ted Robert Gurr, *Handbook of Political Conflict: Theory and Research* (New York: Free Press, 1980).

14 Zedner, 'Pre-Crime and Post-Criminology?'

15 Didier Bigo and Daniel Hermant, 'La relation terroriste: Cadre sociologique pour une approche comparatiste', *Études Polémologiques* 47, no. 3 (1988): 13–79.

16 John Mueller, 'Six Rather Unusual Propositions about Terrorism', *Terrorism and Political Violence* 17, no. 4 (2005): 487–505.

17 Bernard E. Harcourt, *Against Prediction: Profiling, Policing, and Punishing in an Actuarial Age* (Chicago IL: University of Chicago Press, 2008).

18 The GAL were a paramilitary group created by the Spanish government to fight illegally against the ETA.

19 Emmanuel-Pierre Guittet, *Antiterrorisme clandestin, antiterrorisme officiel* (Outremont, Athéna Editions, 2010).

20 As Georges Bush said immediately after September 11, 2001, 'we cannot wait for the final proof, the smoking gun that could come in the form of a mushroom cloud' (see Simon Jeffery and agencies, 'We Cannot Wait for the Smoking Gun', the *Guardian*, 8 October 2002. Available at https://www.theguardian.com/world/2002/oct/08/iraq.usa).

21 Ulrich Beck, 'The Terrorist Threat: World Risk Society Revisited', *Theory, Culture & Society* 19, no. 4 (2002): 39–55; Richard Ericson and Aaron Doyle, 'Catastrophe Risk, Insurance and Terrorism', *Economy and Society* 33, no. 2 (2004): 135–73.

22 Shane Harris, *The Watchers: The Rise of America's Surveillance State* (New York: Penguin Books, 2010).

23 On the notion of doxa, as developed by Pierre Bourdieu, see Pierre Bourdieu and Terry Eagleton, 'Doxa and Common Life', *New Left Review* I, no. 191 (1992): 111–21.

24 David Murakami Wood and Steve Wright, 'Before and After Snowden', *Surveillance and Society* 13, no. 2 (2015): 132–38; and Didier Bigo 'Digital Surveillance and Everyday Democracy', in *The Routledge International Handbook of Criminology and Human Rights*, eds. Leanne Weber, Elaine Fishwick and Marinella Marmo (London: Routledge, 2016).

25 Dan Bulley, ' "Foreign" Terror? London Bombings, Resistance and the Failing State', *The British Journal of Politics & International Relations* 10, no. 3 (2008): 379–94.

26 Jacqueline O'Rourke, *Representing Jihad: The Appearing and Disappearing Radical* (London: Zed Books, 2012).

27 Didier Bigo and Anastassia Tsoukala, eds., *Terror, Insecurity and Liberty: Illiberal Practices of Liberal Regimes after 9/11* (Abingdon: Routledge, 2008).

28 Francesco Ragazzi, 'La lutte contre la radicalisation ou deux formes de la pensée magique', *Mouvements* 88, no. 4 (2016): 151–8.

29 Reg Whitaker, 'A Faustian Bargain? America and the Dream of Total Information Awareness'. In *The New Politics of Surveillance and Visibility*, eds. Kevin D. Haggerty and Richard V. Ericson (Toronto: University of Toronto Press, 2006): 141–70.

30 Coppock and McGovern 'Dangerous Minds'.

31 Julie Ræstad Owe, 'Runaway Jihadi Bride: Media Framing of Western Female Foreign Fighters to ISIS' (MA diss., University of Oslo, 2017).

32 Lucia Zedner, 'Citizenship Deprivation, Security and Human Rights', *European Journal of Migration and Law* 18, no. 2 (2016): 222–42.

33 Didier Bigo, Evelien Brouwer, Sergio Carrera, Elspeth Guild, Emmanuel-Pierre Guittet, Julien Jeandesboz, Francesco Ragazzi and Amandine Scherrer, *The EU Counter-Terrorism Policy Responses to the Attacks in Paris: Towards an EU Security and Liberty Agenda* (Brussels: Centre for European Policy Studies, 2015); Nora El Qadim, 'The January 2015 Attacks and the Debate on Deprivation of Citizenship in France', *Reviews and Critical Commentary (CritCom): A Forum for Research and Commentary on Europe*, 10 August 2015 [online article]. Available at http://critcom.

councilforeuropeanstudies.org/the-january-2015-attacks-and-the-debate-on-deprivation-of-citizenship-in-france/ (accessed May 2018).

34 'La Marseillaise au Programme', *Libération*, 21 February 2005 [online article]. Available at http://www.liberation.fr/societe/2005/02/21/la-marseillaise-au-programme_510389 (accessed May 2018).

35 Alain Bauer, 'Le djihad "uberisé"', *Sécurité Globale* 5, no. 1 (2016): 113–18. For an opposing view, see Didier Bigo and Laurent Bonelli, 'Critique de la raison criminologique', *Cultures & Conflits*, 94-95-96 (2014): 7–26.

36 Albert Camus, *Resistance, Rebellion, and Death: Essays* (New York: Alfred A. Knopf, 2012).

37 Richard V. Ericson, 'British Criminology: A New Subject or Old Politics', *Canadian Journal of Criminology and Corrections* 16 (1974): 352–60; Laurent Bonelli, 'The Control of the Enemy Within? Police Intelligence in the French Suburbs (*banlieues*) and Its Relevance for Globalization', *Controlling Frontiers: Free Movement into and within Europe*, eds. Elspeth Guild and Didier Bigo (London: Ashgate, 2005).

38 Laurent Bonelli and Fabien Carrié, *Radicalité engagée, radicalités révoltées: Un enquête sur les mineurs suivis par la protection judicaire de la jeunesse* (Paris: Ministère de la Justice, 2018).

39 Charles Tilly, 'Review of Why Men Rebel by Ted Robert Gurr', *Journal of Social History* 4, no. 4 (1971): 416–20.

40 Rémy Leveau, 'Réflexions sur le non passage au terrorisme dans l'immigration maghrébine', *Études Polémologiques: Terrorisme, Pouvoirs Publics et Sociétés* 49, no. 1 (1989): 141–56.

41 Philippe Bonditti and Christian Olsson, 'War, Violence and Security Knowledge: Between Theoretical Practices and Practical Theories', in *International Political Sociology: Transversal Lines*, eds. Tugba Basaran, Didier Bigo, Emmanuel-Pierre Guittet and R. B. J. Walker (London: Routledge, 2016).

42 On mimetic rivalry, see René Girard, *La violence et le sacré* (Paris: Hachette, 1982).

AFTERWORD

A DE/RADICALIZED FUTURE

Paul A. Silverstein

Deradicalization has become the new *mot d'ordre* (command word) of contemporary Europe. The ongoing banal bureaucracy of harmonizing agricultural, cultural, educational, employment, environmental, industrial, scientific, social and trade policies within the European Union has been increasingly subsumed into a broader organizing logic of securitization and interdiction. 'Hard' counterterrorism measures strengthening border security, militarizing cityscapes, expanding surveillance and increasing detentions and deportations blur into 'soft', 'prevention' practices which deploy teachers, social workers, community organizers and other 'street-level bureaucrats' to police at-risk youth, pre-empt their radicalization and intervene to return them onto the righteous path of democratic citizenship. In the process, Muslim Europeans have had to learn to navigate an anxious public space where their embodied practices have become the object of suspicion, and their religious dress and architecture subject to 'hyper-legalization' (see De Koning, Chapter 8 in this volume), if not outright criminalization. They experience postcolonial Europe as an eerily familiar Manichean universe, structured not around institutionalized dichotomies of colonizer and colonized as such, but still lived through racialized categories of 'autochthon' and 'allochthon', 'moderate' and 'Salafi' Muslim, the surveiller and the surveilled. And, throughout, violence maintains its latent, haunting presence.

Martijn de Koning, Nadia Fadil, Francesco Ragazzi and the other authors of this volume, have done incredibly important work in unpacking the de/radicalization *dispositif* at the core of this tense environment of suspicion and interdiction. As an assemblage of individuals and institutions, policies and processes, de/radicalization, they show, calls forth strategic organizational forms, orchestrates politicized public performances and produces new vulnerable subjects. They trace its genealogy to a set of security policies, reports and coordinating efforts originating in Belgium and the Netherlands in the first years of the twenty-first century. Building on the earlier work of Kundnani and Neumann,[1] they emphasize the de/radicalization assemblage's localization within the Low Countries, both to engage the specificity of its emergence and application, and to counter the facile Anglocentric narrative of the planetary diffusion of the United States' 'global war on terror'. In so doing, they complicate our taken-for-granted notions of the 'state' as a single, homogeneous actor and the correct scale of policy investigation (see Jaminé and Fadil, Chapter 7 in this volume). They trace the transnational trajectories through which local, municipal initiatives (in cities like Antwerp) scale up to EU directives, or the ways in which a national deradicalization 'toolbox' is translated and adapted by regional administrations and community organizations (Ragazzi and De Jongh, Chapter 6 in this volume). They draw our attention to the everyday mechanisms through which security regimes operate and the gravitational pull they exert on local actors through 'collaborations' and 'partnerships' (see Roex and Vermeulen, Chapter 5 in this volume). Drawing on concrete ethnographic cases, they highlight the costs, trade-offs and double binds experienced by European-Muslim subjects/suspects when they participate in the pastoral care and pedagogical work of deradicalization.

As the preceding chapters demonstrate, the paradigm shift represented by the radicalization hypothesis carries with it certain presuppositions and entailments. Past approaches to counterterrorism, if anything, tended to over-rate the agency of militants and the centrality of their ideological positions. In general, Cold War security models have tended to perdure in the projection of a new 'clash of civilizations' where Islamic fundamentalism replaced communism as the central challenge to the global hegemony of Western democracies. The radicalization approach, while similarly equating all challenges to 'the democratic order' as potentially commensurable, is decidedly less concerned with their internal ideological coherence and focuses more on their oppositional stance and the 'undemocratic means' through which they are expressed. In the process, 'democracy' becomes reified as the defining feature of Europe and the measure of legitimate belonging, less in terms of a determined set of liberal political values and institutions than as a set of expected embodied performances of citizenship. European democratic subjects, by this measure, attend public schools, vote in elections, consume local media, navigate state bureaucracies and sincerely participate in national rituals. They exchange political quiescence for physical comfort and economic well-being.

Radical subjects, in contrast, refuse prescribed avenues of civic engagement, criticize enduring forms of racialized exclusion, and disrupt or even sabotage capitalist markets and the state functions which sustain them. Radical subjects embrace the hyper-visible signs of their marked presence, often literally wearing them on their proverbial sleeve. They agentively enact their social and political critique, by whatever means necessary, sometimes spectacularly so. They build communities of belonging at both local and transnational scales which refuse the nation-state's putative monopoly of patriotism. They reject the liberal bargain as ultimately a bad deal for all but the privileged few. They are radical insofar as they take the egalitarian promises of democracy literally and seek to hold a self-proclaimed democratic Europe accountable for its failures to live up to them.

Regardless of the particular ethical tradition in which their social critique is grounded, radicals thus emerge as the abject subjects of European realpolitik, branded as terrorists and cast out as inassimilable enemies. If the 'war on terror' initially drew on the precedent of a past war on piracy, with terrorists projected as unredeemable, killable *hostis humani generis* who had implicitly declared war on mankind as a whole,[2] the new de/radicalization paradigm arguably recalls the so-called 'war on drugs' (a staple of US foreign policy since the early 1970s) to be fought on both the supply and demand sides, against both the traffickers and consumers of radicalism. Initially some security experts and policymakers pushed for a reflexive examination into the 'root causes' of domestic terrorism, as connected to European states' participation in wars in the Middle East and Muslim Europeans' particular experiences of racialized discrimination (see Coolsaet, Chapter 1 in this volume). They further linked post-9/11 attacks to an earlier history of Basque and Northern Ireland insurgencies. However, such recommendations were broadly marginalized in favour of a medico-pastoral paradigm which effectively treated the radical disposition as a 'virus'[3] with extra-territorial origins, to which young Europeans (Muslim or otherwise) were both 'at risk' and 'risky' (see Roex and Vermeulen, Chapter 5 in this volume).

In this sense, the de/radicalization model presupposes a vulnerable, adolescent subject whose psychosocial development into productive democratic citizenship is in danger of interruption. As Fadil and De Koning (Chapter 2 in this volume) aver, such a psychologizing discourse hyper-individualizes insurgency, bracketing structural causes of collective opposition in favour of therapeutic evaluations of personal trajectories. Deradicalization experts proffer a 'staircase' metaphor of successive steps towards terrorism (see De Graaf, Chapter 4 in this volume),[4] along which social workers or community mediators might pre-emptively intervene before a proverbial point of no return. Annelies Moors (Chapter 10, in this volume) focuses particularly on the media representation of European female emigrants to the Syria (*al-muhajirat*) as simultaneously under-agentive victims of unscrupulous men and over-agentive traitors who have consciously chosen widowhood or even martyrdom over Western sex-gender norms. The moral panic accompanying such emigration has paralleled those declarations of national or civilizational existential crises in the wake of periodic public furores over schoolgirls wearing *hijab* or European men and women converting to Islam. From one perspective, conversion and participating in an Islamic revival movement are purposive acts of self-making; from another, they demonstrate just how vulnerable the liberal, secular subject may be.

Indeed, the radicalization paradigm projects Europe itself as precarious, under threat from within, in perpetual danger of imminent collapse. Belgian policymakers specifically defined 'radicalization' as 'changes in society that stand in contradiction with the democratic order', as that which cannot be contained within democracy proper (see Fadil, De Koning and Ragazzi, Introduction to this volume). To a certain extent, anxieties over such challenges have a long history in, and are arguably constitutive of, the European social and political project. As much as post-war Europe – as a secular-Christian liberal ideal – positively aspired to transcend national divides and fulfil Enlightenment hopes of perpetual peace through the freedom of mobility of people, commodities and ideas, it also negatively established itself as a defensive bulwark against communism from the

East and American cultural-political imperialism from the West, both of which were taken to be proximate existential threats. Such a formulation of 'Fortress Europe' was amplified in the wake of decolonization, with migrants and asylum seekers from the Global South increasingly constituted as barbarians at the gates, particularly during periods of economic downturn. The condition of possibility for an internal common market and unified polity was the hardening of external borders. As Greg Feldman and Marco Jacquemet have ethnographically illustrated,[5] the controversial operations of Frontex and other coordinated programs of migrant interdiction exemplify both the power and pitfalls, the balance and breakdowns, the virtues and violence of European unification.

In contrast, the radicalization paradigm now approaches the ultimate source of Europe's vulnerability as located within the continent, as emanating from Europe's own failures and contradictions. It questions the power of European secular-liberal states to successfully integrate (read assimilate) diverse polities and to domesticate cultural, religious and ideological differences into a depoliticized private sphere. It frets over the fiscal inability of providential states to fulfil earlier promises of social welfare and mobility, to provide the occupational bases for a fulfilling sense of national identity. If the 'clash of civilizations' hypothesis posited symmetrical worldviews competing for hearts, minds and geopolitical dominance, the radicalization paradigm recalls early twentieth-century apocalyptic concerns over 'the decline of the west'[6] in which Europe's material decadence and moral senility were understood to render it susceptible to youthful passions emanating from abroad. While the radicalization *dispositif* certainly does not presuppose a philosophy of world history (whether as civilizational succession, in the case of Spengler, or dynastic cyclicity as in the earlier model of Ibn Khaldun), it does similarly imply that the liberal, secular ethic underlying post-war Europe has become complacent and incapable of motivating new generations of Europeans. It calls for a prompt and heavy-handed intervention lest radical, illiberal ideologies fill the void, young Europeans succumb to the utopian promises of the Islamic State, and Europe as a whole wakes up to discover itself in a state of 'submission' to an expansive Islam.[7]

Such an anxious discourse of European vulnerability is generative of new subjectivities. It justifies heavy-handed policing, surveillance, judicial detentions and the general erosion of civil liberties, sometimes in the guise of state-of-emergency exceptions but increasingly as the new European normal, all in the name of protecting citizens from themselves and others. Such disciplinary regimes are underwritten by and productive of new fields of expertise and knowledge production – terrorism studies or de/radicalization research – as well as a new class of experts who take advantage of new EU funding streams. Such researchers constitute what Foucault called 'specific intellectuals',[8] akin to J. Robert Oppenheimer, and are called into existence to address or manage what is taken to be a particular social problem rather than operating as either a 'universal' class in itself or as a group which organically emerges to articulate the interests of a dominant or subaltern class fraction. Funding agencies like the German Institute of Radicalization and De-radicalization Studies (GIRDS) blur the lines between the academy, private think tanks and state administrations.

But the radicalization paradigm does not only produce expanded forms of state discipline. As Mieke Groeninck (Chapter 3), among several other authors in this volume, details, it also calls forth new kinds of community actors and spokespeople from within marginalized and suspect communities, particularly among Muslim-born or converted Europeans. The latter in particular serve as interlocutors with the state and its administrations, and are called on to translate across cultural-religious divides, intervene with local youth deemed to be on the radicalism staircase, and publicly perform communal penance when attacks have occurred. In some cases, like the French Council of the Muslim Faith, Muslim interlocutors work with state officials to outline a set of religious practices deemed compatible with liberal-secular norms, as an Islam *of* France or Belgium or the UK – to differentiate a 'good' Islam from its 'bad' variants.[9] At its extreme, the radicalization *dispositif* empowers 'ex-Muslims' and other converts from radical traditions with disproportionate discursive presence and impact. Creating like-minded organizations in the UK, France, Germany, the Netherlands, and elsewhere, these public intellectuals have become secular zealots, equating Islam with radicalism *tout court* and joining forces with former-Trotskyists-turned-neoconservatives like the French *nouveaux philosophes* Alain Finkielkraut, Bernard-Henry Lévy and Pascal Bruckner.

In other words, the de/radicalization assemblage actually produces radicalism, not as a reaction to the state, but at the heart of the state itself. It transforms the inclusive potentialities of liberalism into exclusionary measures of legitimate belonging. In the process, as Wendy Brown details,[10] toleration itself shifts from a charitable form of Christian patronage to a compulsory demand on Muslims and other suspect groups to renounce putatively cultural tendencies to patriarchy, anti-Semitism and homophobia as the condition of possibility of their acceptance within Europe. In the face of feared radicalization from within, European states double down on the twinned traditions of Christianity and secularism as the defining features of continental identity and liberal civilization more broadly. Once a fringe group, the radical right now all but dominates electoral politics, setting the tone for immigration and border policies, turning national identity into a public obsession, and making Islamophobia simply good European common sense. As the volume's authors imply, the radicalization hypothesis may very well prove to be a self-fulfilling prophecy. Increasingly the pressing question is not how to fight radicalism within Europe, but rather how might we, in the name of true democracy and social justice, work to de-radicalize the European state.

Notes

1 Kundnani, 'Radicalisation: The Journey of a Concept'; Neumann 'The Trouble with Radicalization'.
2 Paul A. Silverstein, 'The New Barbarians: Piracy and Terrorism on the North African Frontier', *CR: The New Centennial Review* 5, no. 1 (2005): 179–212.
3 Kundnani, 'Radicalisation: The Journey of a Concept', p. 21.

4 Moghaddam, 'The Staircase to Terrorism'.
5 Greg Feldman, *The Migration Apparatus: Security, Labor, and Policymaking in the European Union* (Stanford, CA: Stanford University Press, 2011); Marco Jacquemet 'Crosstalk 2.0: Asylum and Communication Breakdown', *Text and Talk* 31, no. 4 (2011): 475–98.
6 Oswald Spengler, *The Decline of the West* (Oxford: Oxford University Press, 1991 [1918]).
7 See Bruce Bawer, *While Europe Slept: How Radical Islam Is Destroying the West from Within* (New York: Broadway Books, 2006); Michel Houellebecq, *Submission* (New York: Picador, 2015); and Bat Ye'or, *Islam and Dhimmitude: Where Civilizations Collide* (Madison, NJ: Fairleigh Dickinson University Press, 2001).
8 Michel Foucault, 'Truth and Power', in *Power/Knowledge: Selected Interviews and Other Writings, 1972-1977*, ed. Colin Gordon (New York: Pantheon Books, 1980).
9 Mahmood Mamdani, *Good Muslim, Bad Muslim: America, the Cold War, and the Roots of Terror* (New York: Pantheon Books, 2004).
10 Wendy Brown, *Regulating Aversion: Tolerance in the Age of Identity and Empire* (Princeton, NJ: Princeton University Press, 2006).

BIBLIOGRAPHY

Aarns, Pim, and Ineke Roex. *'Als ik iemand beledigd heb, dan was dat mijn bedoeling':*
Sharia4Belgiums ideologie en humorgebruik. Amsterdam: University of Amsterdam
Press, 2017.

Abels, Paul. 'Inlichtingen- en veiligheidsdiensten en terrorismebestrijding'. In *Inlichtingen-*
en Veiligheidsdiensten, edited by Beatrice de Graaf, E. R. Muller and J. A. van Reijn.
Brussels: Wolters Kluwer, 2010.

Abram, Simone. 'The Time It Takes: Temporalities of Planning'. *Journal of the Royal*
Anthropological Institute 20, no. 1 (2014): 129–47.

Adang, Camilla, Hassan Ansari, Maribel Fierro and Sabine Schmidtke, eds., *Accusations of*
Unbelief in Islam: A Diachronic Perspective on Takfir. Leiden and Boston, MA: Brill,
2015.

Aerts, Stijn, and John Nawas. 'Hoe Islamitisch is Islamitisch radicalisme'. In *De Lokroep van*
IS: Syriëstrijders en (De)radicalisering, edited by Patrick Loobuyck. Kalmthout:
Pelckmans, 2015.

Aggarwal, Neil Krishan. *Mental Health in the War on Terror: Culture, Science, and*
Statecraft. New York: Columbia University Press, 2015.

Akkerman, Tjitske, Maarten Hajer and John Grin. 'The Interactive State: Democratisation
from above?' *Political Studies* 52, no. 1 (2004): 82–95.

Al-Alwani, Taha Jabir. *Islam: Conflit d'opinions – Pour une éthique du désaccord*. Paris:
Éditions Al-Qalam, 2010 [1986].

Alexanderson, Kris. '"A Dark State of Affairs": Hajj Networks, Pan-Islamism, and Dutch
Colonial Surveillance during the Interwar Period'. *Journal of Social History* 47, no. 4
(2014): 1021–41.

Ali, Arshad Imitaz. 'Citizens under Suspicion: Responsive Research with Community
under Surveillance'. *Anthropology & Education Quarterly* 47, no. 1 (2016): 78–95.

Alimi, Eitan Y., Lorenzo Bosi and Chares Demetriou. *The Dynamics of Radicalization*.
Oxford and New York: Oxford University Press, 2015.

Allen, Lori. 'Getting by the Occupation: How Violence Became Normal during the Second
Palestinian Intifada'. *Cultural Anthropology* 23, no. 3 (2008): 453–87.

Allievi, Stefano. 'Shifting Significance of the Halal/Haral Frontier: Narratives on the Hijab
and Other Issues'. In *Women Embracing Islam: Gender and Conversions in the West*,
edited by Karin van Nieuwkerk. Texas: University of Texas Press, 2006.

Amar, Paul. 'Turning the Gendered Politics of the Security State Inside Out?' *International*
Feminist Journal of Politics 13, no. 3 (2011): 299–332.

Amghar, Samir. 'Salafism and Radicalization of Young European Muslims'. In *European*
Islam: Challenges for Public Policy and Society, edited by S. Amghar, A. Boubekeur and
M. Emerson. Brussels: Centre for European Policy Studies, 2007.

Amiraux, Valérie. 'Academic Discourses on Islam(s) in France and Germany: Producing
Knowledge or Reproducing Norms?' In *Islam and the West: Judgement, Prejudices,*
Political Perspectives, edited by Werner Ruf. Münster: Agenda Verlag, 2002.

Amir-Moazami, Shirin, and Armando Salvatore. 'Gender, Generation, and the Reform of
Tradition: From Muslim Majority Societies to Western Europe'. In *Muslim Networks*

and Transnational Communities in and across Europe, edited by S. Allievi and J. Nielsen. Leiden and Boston, MA: Brill, 2003.

Amoore, Louise. 'Data Derivatives: On the Emergence of a Security Risk Calculus for Our Times'. *Theory, Culture & Society* 28, no. 6 (2011): 24–43.

Amoore, Louise. *The Politics of Possibility: Risk and Security beyond Probability*. Durham, NC, and London: Duke University Press, 2013.

Amoore, Louise. 'Risk before Justice: When the Law Contests Its Own Suspension'. *Leiden Journal of International Law* 21, no. 4 (2008): 847–61.

Aouragh, Miriyam. 'Digital Anthropology'. In *The International Encyclopedia of Anthropology*, edited by H. Callan. Chichester: Wiley-Blackwell, 2018.

Archetti, Cristina. 'Terrorism, Communication and New Media: Explaining Radicalization in the Digital Age'. *Perspectives on Terrorism* 9, no. 1 (2015): 49–59.

Ariès, Philippe. *Centuries of Childhood*. Harmondsworth: Penguin Books, 1962.

Asad, Talal. 'Comments on Conversion'. In *Conversion to Modernities: The Globalization of Christianity*, edited by Peter van der Veer. New York: Routledge, 1996.

Asad, Talal. *Formation of the Secular: Christianity, Islam, and Modernity*. Stanford, CA: Stanford University Press, 2003.

Asad, Talal. *Genealogies of Religion: Discipline and Reasons of Power in Christianity and Islam*. Baltimore, MD: Johns Hopkins University Press, 1993.

Asad, Talal. *The Idea of an Anthropology of Islam*. Occasional Papers Series. Washington, DC: Georgetown University Center for Contemporary Arab Studies, 1986.

Asdal, Kristin, Brita Brenna and Ingunn Moser. *Technoscience: The Politics of Intervention*. Oslo: Unipub, 2007 [1986].

Austin-Broos, Diane. 'The Anthropology of Conversion: An Introduction'. In *The Anthropology of Religious Conversion*, edited by Andrew Buckser and Steven Glazier. Lanham, MD: Rowman & Littlefield, 2003.

Bacchi, Carol. 'The Turn to Problematization: Political Implications of Contrasting Interpretive and Poststructural Adaptations'. *Open Journal of Political Science* 5, no. 1 (2015): 1–12.

Bachmann, Reinhard, and Andrew C. Inkpen. 'Understanding Institutional-Based Trust Building Processes in Inter-Organisational Relationships'. *Organisation Studies* 32, no. 2 (2011): 281–301.

Backes, Uwe, and Eckhard Jesse, eds., *Vergleichende Extremismusforschung*. Baden-Baden: Nomos, 2005.

Backes, Uwe. *Politischer Extremismus in demokratischen Verfassungsstaaten: Elemente einer normativen Rahmentheorie*. Opladen: Westdeutscher Verlag, 1989.

Badier, Walter. *Émile Henry: De la propagande par le fait au terrorisme anarchiste*. Chaucre: Éditions libertaires, 2007.

Baker, Tom, and Jonathan Simon. *Embracing Risk: The Changing Culture of Insurance and Responsibility*. Chicago, IL: University of Chicago Press, 2002.

Baker-Beall, Christopher. 'The European Union's Fight against Terrorism: A Critical Discourse Analysis'. PhD diss., Loughborough University, 2010.

Baker-Beall, Christopher, Charlotte Heath-Kelly and Lee Jarvis, eds., *Counter-Radicalisation: Critical Perspectives*. Oxon and New York: Routledge, 2015.

Bakker, Edwin, and Roel de Bont. 'Belgian and Dutch Jihadist Foreign Fighters (2012–15): Characteristics, Motivations, and Roles in the War in Syria and Iraq'. *Small Wars & Insurgencies* 27, no. 5 (2016): 837–57.

Bakker, Edwin, and Seran de Leede. 'European Female Jihadists in Syria: Exploring an under-Researched Topic'. *ICCT Background Note*. The Hague: ICCT, 2015.

Balibar, Etienne. 'Is There a "Neo-Racism"?' In *Race, Nation, Class: Ambiguous Identities*, edited by E. Balibar and I. Wallerstein. London and New York: Verso, 1991.

Balibar, Etienne, and Immanuel Wallerstein. *Race, Nation, Class: Ambiguous Identities*. London and New York: Verso, 1991.

Barth, Fredrik, ed., *Ethnic Groups and Boundaries: The Social Organization of Culture Difference*. Long Grove, IL: Waveland Press, 1998.

Bauer, Alain. 'Le djihad "uberisé"'. *Sécurité Globale* 5, no. 1 (2016): 113–18.

Baumann, Gerd, and Andre Gingrich. *Grammars of Identity/Alterity: A Structural Approach*. New York and Oxford: Berghahn Books, 2004.

Bawer, Bruce. *While Europe Slept: How Radical Islam Is Destroying the West from Within*. New York: Broadway Books, 2006.

Bax, E. H. 'Oriëntaties van lager geschoolde werkloze en werkende mannelijke jongeren: Een vergelijkend onderzoek'. *Mens en Maatschappij* 54, no. 4 (1979): 361–84.

Beach, Stephen W. 'Social Movement Radicalization: The Case of the People's Democracy in Northern Ireland'. *The Sociological Quarterly* 18, no. 3 (1977): 305–18.

Bear, Laura. 'Doubt, Conflict, Mediation: The Anthropology of Modern Time'. *Journal of the Royal Anthropological Institute* 20, no.1 (2014): 3–30.

Beck, Ulrich. 'The Terrorist Threat: World Risk Society Revisited'. *Theory, Culture & Society* 19, no. 4 (2002): 39–55.

Becker, Carmen. *Learning to Be Authentic: Religious Practices of German and Dutch Muslims following the Salafiyya in Forums and Chat Rooms*. Nijmegen: Radboud University, 2013.

Beerli, Monique J. 'Saving the Saviors: Security Practices and Professional Struggles in the Humanitarian Space'. PhD diss., Sciences-Po, Paris & Geneva, 2017.

Benzakour, Mohammed. *Abou Jahjah, Nieuwlichter of Oplichter? De demonisering van een politieke rebel*. Amsterdam: L.J. Veen, 2004.

Benzine, Rachid. *Les nouveaux penseurs de l'islam*. Paris: Albin Michel, 2004.

Berbers, Anna, Willem Joris, Jan Boesman, Leen D'Haenens, Joyce Koeman and Baldwin van Gorp. 'The News Framing of the "Syria Fighters" in Flanders and the Netherlands'. *Ethnicities* 16, no. 6 (2016): 798–818.

Bernand, Marie, and Gerard Troupeau. 'Kiyās'. In *Encyclopaedia of Islam, Second Edition*, edited by P. Bearman, Th. Bianquis, C. E. Bosworth, E. van Donzel and W. P. Heinrichts. Brill Online, 2012.

Bertaux, Daniel. 'From the Life-History Approach to the Transformation of Sociological Practice'. In *Biography and Society: The Life-History Approach in the Social Sciences*, edited by Daniel Bertaux. London: Sage, 1981.

Bigo, Didier. 'Digital Surveillance and Everyday Democracy'. In *The Routledge International Handbook of Criminology and Human Rights*, edited by Leanne Weber, Elaine Fishwick and Marinella Marmo, 125–35. London: Routledge, 2016.

Bigo, Didier. 'Globalized (In)Security: The Field and the Ban-Opticon'. In *Terror, Insecurity and Liberty: Illiberal Practices of Liberal Regimes after 9/11*, edited by Didier Bigo and Anastassia Tsoukala. Abingdon: Routledge, 2008.

Bigo, Didier. 'The (In)Securitization Practices of the Three Universes of EU Border Control: Military/Navy – Border Guards/Police – Database Analysts'. *Security Dialogue* 45, no. 3 (2014): 209–25.

Bigo, Didier. 'International Political Sociology: Rethinking the International through Field(S) of Power'. In *International Political Sociology: Transversal Lines*, edited by Tugba Basaran, Didier Bigo, Emmanuel-Pierre Guittet and R. B. J. Walker, 24–48. London: Routledge, 2016.

Bigo, Didier. *Polices en réseaux: L'expérience européenne*. Paris: Presses de Sciences Politiques, 1996.

Bigo, Didier. 'Security and Immigration: Toward a Critique of the Governmentality of Unease'. *Millennium* 27, no. 1 (2002): 63–92.

Bigo, Didier, and Anastassia Tsoukala, eds., *Terror, Insecurity and Liberty: Illiberal Practices of Liberal Regimes after 9/11*. Abingdon: Routledge, 2008.

Bigo, Didier, and Daniel Hermant. 'La relation terroriste'. *Études Polémologiques* 47, no. 3 (1988).

Bigo, Didier, and Daniel Hermant. 'La relation terroriste: Cadre sociologique pour une approche comparatiste'. *Études Polémologiques* 47, no. 3 (1988): 13–79.

Bigo, Didier, and Laurent Bonelli. 'Critique de la raison criminologique'. *Cultures et Conflits*, 94–95–96 (2014): 7–26.

Bigo, Didier, Evelien Brouwer, Sergio Carrera, Elspeth Guild, Emmanuel-Pierre Guittet, Julien Jeandesboz, Francesco Ragazzi and Amandine Scherrer. *The EU Counter-Terrorism Policy Responses to the Attacks in Paris: Towards an EU Security and Liberty Agenda*. Brussels: Centre for European Policy Studies, 2015.

Bigo, Didier, Laurent Bonelli and Thomas Deltombe. *Au nom du 11 Septembre...Les démocraties à l'épreuve de l'antiterrorisme*. Paris: La Découverte, 2008.

Bigo, Didier, Sergio Carrera, Elspeth Guild and R. B. J. Walker. *Europe's 21st Century Challenge: Delivering Liberty*. Farnham: Ashgate, 2013.

Birt, Yahya. 'Promoting Virulent Envy? Reconsidering the UK's Terrorist Prevention Strategy'. *The RUSI Journal* 154, no. 4 (2009): 52–58.

Bisman, Cynthia. 'Personal Information and the Professional Relationship: Issues of Trust, Privacy and Welfare'. In *Private and Confidential? Handling Personal Information in Social and Health Services*, edited by Chris Clark and Janice McGhee. Bristol: Policy Press, 2008.

Bjørgo, Tore. *Racist and Right-Wing Violence in Scandinavia: Patterns, Perpetrators, and Responses*. Oslo: Tano Aschehoug, 1997.

Bjørgo, Tore, and John Horgan. *Leaving Terrorism Behind: Individual and Collective Disengagement*. London: Routledge, 2009.

Blaise, Pierre, and Vincent de Coorebyter. 'L'Islam et l'état Belge'. *Res Publica* 35, no. 1 (1993): 223–37.

Blommaert, Jan, and Albert Martens. *Van Blok tot Bouwsteen*. Berchem: EPO, 1999.

Blommaert, Jan, and Jef Verschueren. *Debating Diversity: Analysing the Discourse of Tolerance*. London: Routledge, 1998.

Blommaert, Jan, and Jef Verschueren. *Het Belgische Migrantendebat: De pragmatiek van de Abnormalisering*. Antwerp: IPrA Research Center, 1992.

Boccagni, Paolo. *Migration and the Search for Home: Mapping Domestic Space in Migrants' Everyday Lives*. New York: Palgrave Macmillan, 2017.

Boender, Welmoet. *Imam in Nederland: Rol, Gezag en Binding in Een Geseculariseerde Samenleving*. Amsterdam: Bert Bakker, 2007.

Bogaers, L. C. J. J. 'Politieke en religieuze radicalisering'. In *Geschiedenis van de Provincie Utrecht II*, edited by Cornelis Dekker. Utrecht: Utrecht Historische Reeks, 1997.

Bonditti, Philippe, and Christian Olsson. 'War, Violence and Security Knowledge: Between Theoretical Practices and Practical Theories'. In *International Political Sociology: Transversal Lines*, edited by Tugba Basaran, Didier Bigo, Emmanuel-Pierre Guittet and R. B. J. Walker, 228–53. London: Routledge, 2016.

Bonelli, Laurent. 'The Control of the Enemy Within? Police Intelligence in the French Suburbs (*banlieues*) and Its Relevance for Globalization'. In *Controlling Frontiers: Free Movement into and within Europe*, 193–208. London: Ashgate, 2005.

Bonelli, Laurent, and Fabien Carrié. *Radicalité engagée, radicalités révoltées: Un enquête sur les mineurs suivis par la protection judicaire de la jeunesse*. Paris: Ministère de la Justice, 2018.

Booth, Ken. 'Security and Emancipation'. *Review of International Studies* 17, no. 4 (1991): 313–26.

Borgers, Matthias J., and Elies van Sliedregt. 'The Meaning of the Precautionary Principle for the Assessment of Criminal Measures in the Fight against Terrorism'. *Erasmus Law Review* 2, no. 2 (2009): 171–95.

Borum, Randy. *Psychology of Terrorism*. Tampa, FL: University of South Florida, 2004.

Bossong, Raphael. 'The Action Plan on Combating Terrorism: A Flawed Instrument of EU Security Governance'. *JCMS: Journal of Common Market Studies* 46, no. 1 (2008): 27–48.

Bourdieu, Pierre. *La distinction: Critique sociale du jugement*. Paris: Les Éditions de Minuit, 1979.

Bourdieu, Pierre. *Outline of a Theory of Practice*. Cambridge Studies in Social Anthropology Series 16. Cambridge: Cambridge University Press, 1977.

Bourdieu, Pierre, and Terry Eagleton. 'Doxa and Common Life'. *New Left Review* I, no. 191 (1992): 111–21.

Boyer, Dominic. 'Thinking through the Anthropology of Experts'. *Anthropology in Action* 15, no. 2 (2008): 38–46.

Bracke, Sarah. 'Transformations of the Secular and the "Muslim Question": Revisiting the Historical Coincidence of Depillarization and the Institutionalization of Islam in the Netherlands'. *Journal of Muslims in Europe* 2, no. 2 (2013): 208–26.

Brems, Eva, Jogchum Vrielink and Saïla Ouald Chaib. 'Uncovering French and Belgian Face Covering Bans'. *Journal of Law, Religion & State* 2, no. 1 (2013): 69–99.

Brisard, Jean-Charles, and Kevin Jackson. 'The Islamic State's External Operations and the French-Belgian Nexus'. *CTC Sentinel* 9, no. 11 (2016): 8–15.

Brown, Katherine E., and Tania Saeed. 'Radicalization and Counter-Radicalization at British Universities: Muslim Encounters and Alternatives'. *Ethnic and Racial Studies* 38, no. 11 (2016): 1952–68.

Brown, Wendy. *Regulating Aversion: Tolerance in the Age of Identity and Empire*. Princeton, NJ: Princeton University Press, 2006.

Brubaker, Rogers. 'Categories of Analysis and Categories of Practice: A Note on the Study of Muslims in European Countries of Immigration'. *Ethnic and Racial Studies* 36, no. 1 (2013): 1–8.

Buckser, Andrew, and Steven Glazier, eds., *The Anthropology of Religious Conversion*. Lanham, MD: Rowman & Littlefield, 2003.

Buijs, Frank J., Froukje Demant and Atef Hamdy. *Strijders van Eigen Bodem: Radicale en Democratische Moslims in Nederland*. Amsterdam: Amsterdam University Press, 2006.

Bulley, Dan. '"Foreign" Terror? London Bombings, Resistance and the Failing State'. *The British Journal of Politics & International Relations* 10, no. 3 (2008): 379–94.

Bunyan, Tony. *Statewatching the New Europe: A Handbook on the European State*. London: Statewatch, 1993.

Bunyan, Tony. 'Trevi, Europol and the European State'. In *Statewatching the New Europe: A Handbook on the European State*, edited by Tony Bunyan. London: Statewatch, 1993.

Butler, Judith. *Precarious Life: The Powers of Mourning and Violence*. London and New York: Verso, 2004.

c.a.s.e. collective. 'Critical Approaches to Security in Europe: A Networked Manifesto'. *Security Dialogue* 37, no. 4 (2006): 443–87.

Callon, Michel. 'Some Elements of a Sociology of Translation: Domestication of the Scallops and the Fishermen of St. Brieuc Bay'. In *Technoscience: The Politics of Intervention*, edited by Kristin Asdal, Brita Brenna and Ingunn Moser. Oslo: Unipub, 2007 [1986].

Callon, Michel, and Bruno Latour. *La science telle qu'elle se fait: Anthologie de la sociologie des sciences de langue anglaise*. Paris: La Découverte, 1991.

Camus, Albert. *Resistance, Rebellion, and Death: Essays*. New York: Alfred A. Knopf, 2012.

Carvalho, Claudia. '"Okhti" Online – Spanish Muslim Women Engaging Online Jihad – A Facebook Case Study'. *Online: Heidelberg Journal of Religions on the Internet* 6, (2014): 24–42.

Casewit, Daoud. 'Hijra as History and Metaphor: A Survey of Qur'anic and Hadith Sources'. *The Muslim World* 88, no. 2 (1998): 105–28.

Cesari, Jocelyne. *Muslims in the West after 9/11: Religion, Politics, and Law*. Oxon and New York: Routledge, 2010.

Cesari, Jocelyne. 'The Securitisation of Islam in Europe: The Changing Landscape of European Liberty and Security'. *CEPS Challenge Research Paper*, no. 15 (2009).

Cherney, Adrian, and Jason Hartley. 'Community Engagement to Tackle Terrorism and Violent Extremism: Challenges, Tensions and Pitfalls'. *Policing and Society: An International Journal of Research and Policy* 27, no. 7 (2015): 1–14.

Chesney, Robert M. 'Beyond Conspiracy: Anticipatory Prosecution and the Challenge of Unaffiliated Terrorism'. *Southern California Law Review* 80, no. 3 (2007): 425–502.

Chesney, Robert M. 'The Sleeper Scenario: Terrorism-Support Laws and the Demands of Prevention'. *Harvard Journal on Legislation* 42, no. 1 (2005): 1–90.

Choudhury, Tufyal. *Impact of Counter-Terrorism on Communities: UK Background Report*. London: Institute for Strategic Dialogue, 2012.

Choudhury, Tufyal. 'The Radicalisation of Citizenship Deprivation'. *Critical Social Policy* 37, no. 2 (2017): 225–44.

Cohen, Robin. *Migration and Its Enemies: Global Capital, Migrant Labour and the Nation-State*. Burlington, VT: Ashgate, 2006.

Cohen, Stanley. *Visions of Social Control: Crime, Punishment and Classification*. Cambridge: Polity Press, 1985.

Collier, Stephen J., and Andrew Lakoff. 'On Regimes of Living'. In *Global Assemblages*, edited by Aihwa Ong and Stephen J. Collier, 22–39. Oxford: Blackwell, 2008.

Cook, David. *Understanding Jihad*. Berkeley, CA: University of California Press, 2005.

Cooke, Phoebe. 'Newham Imams Oppose "Divisive" Counter-Terrorism Strategy'. *Newham Recorder*, January 2016.

Coolsaet, Rik. '"All Radicalisation Is Local": The Genesis and Drawbacks of an Elusive Concept'. *Egmont Papers* 84, June (2016/b): 1–48.

Coolsaet, Rik. 'Anticipating the Post-Daesh Landscape'. *Egmont Papers* 97, October (2017): 1–50.

Coolsaet, Rik. 'Facing the Fourth Foreign Fighters Wave: What Drives Europeans to Syria, and to Islamic State? Insights from the Belgian Case'. *Egmont Papers* 81, March (2016/a): 1–52.

Coolsaet, Rik. 'Het islamitisch terrorisme: Percepties wieden en kweedvijvers dreggen'. *Justitiële Verkenningen* 31, no. 2 (2005): 9–27.

Coolsaet, Rik. 'Wat drijft de Syriëstrijder?' *Samenleving en Politiek* 22, no. 2-15 (2015): 4–13.

Coppock, Vicki, and Mark McGovern. '"Dangerous Minds"? Deconstructing Counter-Terrorism Discourse, Radicalisation and the "Psychological Vulnerability" of Muslim Children and Young People in Britain'. *Children & Society* 28, no. 3 (2014): 242–56.

Côté-Boucher, Karine, Federica Infantino and Mark B. Salter. 'Border Security as Practice: An Agenda for Research'. *Security Dialogue* 45, no. 3 (2014): 195–208.

Craight, Nic, and Emma Hill. 'Re-Locating the Ethnographic Field: From "Being There" to "Being There"'. *Anthropological Journal for European Cultures* 24, no. 1 (2015): 42–62.

Crawford, Adam. *Crime Prevention Policies in Comparative Perspective*. Cullompton: Willan, 2009.

Crawford, Adam. *The Local Governance of Crime: Appeals to Community and Partnerships*. Oxford: Oxford University Press, 1999.

Crawford, Adam. 'Plural Policing in the UK: Policing beyond the Police'. In *Handbook of Policing*, edited by Tim Newburn. Cullompton: Willan, 2008.

Crawley, Sara. 'Autoethnography as Feminist Self-Interview'. In *The Sage Handbook of Interview Research*, 2nd edn, edited by Jaber F. Gubrium, James A. Holstein, Amir B. Marvasti and Karyn D. McKinney, 143–60. Thousand Oaks, CA: Sage, 2012.

Crenshaw, Martha. 'The Causes of Terrorism'. *Comparative Politics* 13, no. 4 (1981): 379–99.

Crenshaw, Martha. 'The Psychology of Terrorism: An Agenda for the 21st Century'. *Political Psychology* 21, no. 2 (2000): 405–20.

Crepaz, Markus. *Trust beyond Borders: Immigration, the Welfare State, and Identity in Modern Societies*. Ann Arbor, MI: University of Michigan Press, 2008.

Croft, Stuart. 'Constructing Ontological Insecurity: The Insecuritization of Britain's Muslims'. *Contemporary Security Policy* 33, no. 2 (2012): 219–35.

Croft, Stuart. *Securitizing Islam: Identity and the Search for Security*. Cambridge: Cambridge University Press, 2012.

Cronin, Audrey Kurth. *How Terrorism Ends: Understanding the Decline and Demise of Terrorist Campaigns*. Princeton, NJ: Princeton University Press, 2009.

Cusson, Maurice. *L'art de la sécurité: Ce que l'histoire de la criminologie nous enseigne*. Lausanne: Presses Polytechniques et Universitaires Romandes, 2011.

Dabashi, Hamid. *Brown Skin, White Masks*. New York: Pluto Press, 2011.

Dassetto, Felice. *Facettes de l'islam Belge*. Louvain-la-Neuve: Academia-Bruylant, 1997.

Dassetto, Felice, and Albert Bastenier. *L'islam transplanté: Vie et organisation des minorités musulmanes de Belgique*. Antwerpen: EPO, 1984.

Dassetto, Felice, and Albert Bastenier. *Medias u Akbar*. Louvain-la-Neuve: CIACO, 1987.

Davidson, Naomi. *Only Muslim: Embodying Islam in Twentieth-Century France*. Ithaca, NY, and London: Cornell University Press, 2012.

Davila Gordillo, Diana, and Francesco Ragazzi. 'The Radicalisation Awareness Network: Producing the EU Counter-Radicalisation Discourse'. In *Constitutionalising the Security Union: Effectiveness, Rule of Law and Rights in Countering Terrorism and Crime*, edited by Sergio Carrera and Valsamis Mitsilegas. Brussels: Centre for European Policy Studies, 2017.

Dawson, Lorne, and Amarnath Amarasingam. 'Talking to Foreign Fighters: Insights into Motivations for Hijrah to Syria and Iraq'. *Studies in Conflict & Terrorism* 40, no. 30 (2017): 191–210.

de Certeau, Michel. *The Practice of Everyday Life*. Berkeley, CA: University of California Press, 2013.

De Goede, Marieke. 'The Politics of Preemption and the War on Terror in Europe'. *European Journal of International Relations* 14, no. 1 (2008): 161–85.

De Goede, Marieke. *Speculative Security: The Politics of Pursuing Terrorist Monies*. Minneapolis, MN: University of Minnesota Press, 2012.

De Goede, Marieke, and Stephanie Simon. 'Governing Future Radicals in Europe'. *Antipode* 45, no. 2 (2013): 315–35.

De Goede, Marieke, Stephanie Simon and Marijn Hoijtink. 'Performing Preemption'. *Security Dialogue* 45, no. 5 (2014): 411–22.

De Graaf, Beatrice. *Evaluating Counterterrorism Performance: A Comparative Study*. London and New York: Routledge, 2011.

De Graaf, Beatrice. 'Religion bites: Religieuze orthodoxie op de nationale veiligheidsagenda'. *Tijdschrift voor Religie, Recht en Beleid* 2, no. 2 (2011): 62–80.

De Graaf, Beatrice, and Alex P. Schmid, eds., *Terrorists on Trial: A Performative Perspective*. Leiden: Leiden University Press, 2016.

De Graaf, Beatrice, and Marieke de Goede. 'Sentencing Risk: Temporality and Precaution in Terrorism Trials'. *International Political Sociology* 7, no. 3 (2013): 313–31.

De Koning, Martijn. 'How Should I Live as a "True" Muslim? Regimes of Living among Dutch Muslims in the Salafi Movement'. *Etnofoor* 25, no. 2 (2013): 53–72.

De Koning, Martijn. 'The Other Political Islam: Understanding Salafi Politics'. In *Whatever Happened to the Islamists: Salafis, Heavy Metal Muslims and the Lure of Consumerist Islam*, edited by Olivier Roy and Amel Boubekeur, 153–78. London and New York: Hurst, 2012.

De Koning, Martijn. '"You Need to Present a Counter-Message" – The Racialisation of Dutch Muslims and Anti-Islamophobia Initiatives'. *Journal of Muslims in Europe* 5, no. 2 (2016): 170–89.

De Koning, Martijn. *Zoeken Naar Een 'Zuivere' Islam: Geloofsbeleving en Identiteitsvorming van Jonge Marokkaans-Nederlandse Moslims*. Amsterdam: Bert Bakker, 2008.

De Koning, Martijn, Carmen Becker, Ineke Roex and Pim Aarns. *Eilanden in een zee van ongeloof: Het verzet van de activistische da'wa-netwerken in België, Nederland en Duitsland*. Nijmegen and Amsterdam: IMES Report Series, Radboud University, 2014.

De Koning, Martijn, Joas Wagemakers and Carmen Becker. *Salafisme: Utopische Idealen in Een Weerbarstige Praktijk*. Almere: Parthenon, 2014.

De Ruyver, Brice, Marleen Easton, Jannie Noppe, Paul Ponsaers and Antoinette Verhage. *Preventie van radicalisering in België [Onderzoeksrapport]*. Antwerp: Maklu, 2011.

De Waele, Maarten, Hans Moors, Aart Garssen and Jannie Noppe, eds., *Aanpak van gewelddadige radicalisering*. Antwerpen/Apeldoorn: Maklu, 2017.

De Witte, Ludo. *Wie is er bang van Moslims? Aantekeningen over Abou Jahjah, etnocentrisme en islamofobie*. Leuven: Van Halewyck, 2004.

De Zwart, Frank. 'The Dilemma of Recognition: Administrative Categories and Cultural Diversity'. *Theory and Society* 34, no. 2 (2005): 137–69.

De Zwart, Frank. 'Pitfalls of Top-Down Identity Designation: Ethno-Statistics in the Netherlands'. *Comparative European Politics* 10, no. 3 (2012): 301–18.

De Zwart, Frank, and Caelesta Poppelaars. 'Redistribution and Ethnic Diversity in the Netherlands: Accommodation, Denial and Replacement'. *Acta Sociologica* 50, no. 4 (2007): 387–99.

Dean, Mitchell. *Governing Societies: Political Perspectives on Domestic and International Rule*. Berkshire: Open University Press, 2007.

Dean, Mitchell. *Governmentality: Power and Rule in Modern Society*. London: Sage, 1999.

Death, Carl. 'Counter-Conducts: A Foucauldian Analytics of Protest'. *Social Movement Studies* 9, no. 3 (2010): 235–51.

Decker, Scott H., and David C. Pyrooz. 'How 100 Years of Gang Research Can Inform the Study of Terrorism, Radicalization and Extremism'. *Perspectives on Terrorism* 9, no. 1 (2015): 104–12.

Della Porta, Donatella. *Clandestine Political Violence*. Cambridge: Cambridge University Press, 2013.

Della Porta, Donatella. *Social Movements, Political Violence and the State: A Comparative Analysis of Italy and Germany*. Cambridge: Cambridge University Press, 1995.

DeLuca, Kevin. 'Articulation Theory: A Discursive Grounding for Rhetorical Practice'. *Philosophy & Rhetoric* 32, no. 4 (1999): 334–48.

Demant, Froukje, Marieke Slootman, Frank Buijs and Jean Tillie. *Teruggang en uittrede: Processen van deradicalisering ontleed*. Amsterdam: IMES, 2008.

den Boer, Monica. 'Wake-Up Call for the Lowlands: Dutch Counterterrorism from a Comparative Perspective'. *Cambridge Review of International Affairs* 20, no. 2 (2007): 285–302.

Denhardt, Janet Vinzant, and Lane Crothers. *Street-Level Leadership: Discretion and Legitimacy in Front-Line Public Service*. Washington, DC: Georgetown University Press, 1998.

Donzelot, Jacques. *La police des familles*. Paris: Éditions des Minuit, 1977.

Donzelot, Jacques. *The Policing of Families*. New York: Pantheon Books, 1979.

Douglas, Mary. *Purity and Danger: An Analysis of Concepts of Pollution and Taboo*. New York: Routledge, 2002 [1966].

Dreyfus, Hubert L., ed., *Michel Foucault: Beyond Structuralism and Hermeneutics*. Chicago, IL: University of Chicago Press, 1982.

Durkheim, Émile. *The Division of Labor in Society*. New York: Free Press, 1997.

Durodie, Bill. 'Securitising Education to Prevent Terrorism or Losing Direction?' *British Journal of Educational Studies* 64, no. 1 (2015): 21–35.

Duyvendak, Jan Willem. *The Politics of Home: Belonging and Nostalgia in Europe and the United States*. Basingstoke: Palgrave Macmillan, 2011.

Duyvendak, Jan Willem, and Peter Scholten. 'Beyond the Dutch "Multicultural Model": The Coproduction of Integration Policy Frames in the Netherlands'. *Journal of International Migration and Integration* 12, no. 3 (2011): 331–48.

Edmunds, June. 'The "New" Barbarians: Governmentality, Securitization and Islam in Western Europe'. *Contemporary Islam* 6, no. 1 (2012): 67–84.

Emmelkamp, Paul, Jan Henk Kamphuis and A. Reinders. *Radicalisering van Jongeren: Een Literatuurstudie Naar de Ontvankelijkheid voor Radicalisering*. Amsterdam: Psychology Research Institute, Universiteit van Amsterdam, 2005.

Engelen, D. 'Mars door de tijd van een institutie: Een beknopte geschiedenis van de AIVD'. In *Inlichtingen & Veiligheidsdiensten*, edited by Beatrice de Graaf, E. R. Muller and J. A. Van Reijn. Brussels: Wolters Kluwer, 2010.

Ericson, Richard V. 'British Criminology: A New Subject or Old Politics'. *Canadian Journal of Criminology and Corrections* 16 (1974): 352–60.

Ericson, Richard V. *Crime in an Insecure World*. Cambridge: Polity Press, 2007.

Ericson, Richard V., and Aaron Doyle. 'Catastrophe Risk, Insurance and Terrorism'. *Economy and Society* 33, no. 2 (2004): 135–73.

Eroukhmanoff, Clara. 'The Remote Securitisation of Islam in the US Post–9/11: Euphemisation, Metaphors and the "Logic of Expected Consequences" in Counter-Radicalisation Discourse'. *Critical Studies on Terrorism* 8, no. 2 (2015): 246–65.

Evans, Tony, and John Harris. 'Street-Level Bureaucracy, Social Work and the (Exaggerated) Death of Discretion'. *The British Journal of Social Work* 34, no. 6 (2004): 871–95.

Fadil, Nadia. '"Are We All Secular/ized Yet?" Reflections on David Goldberg's "Are We All Post-Racial Yet?"' *Ethnic and Racial Studies* 39, no. 13 (2016): 2261–68.

Fadil, Nadia. 'Breaking the Taboo of Multiculturalism: The Belgian Left and Islam'. In *Thinking through Islamophobia: Global Perspectives*, edited by Abdoolkarim Vakil and Salman Sayyid. New York: Columbia University Press, 2010.

Fadil, Nadia. 'Brussels as a Landscape of Fear'. In *Islamist Movements of Europe*, edited by Frank Peter and Raphael Ortega. London: I.B. Tauris, 2014.

Fadil, Nadia. 'Not-/Unveiling as an Ethical Practice' (Report). *Feminist Review* 98, no. 1 (2011): 83–109.

Fadil, Nadia. 'Submitting to God, Submitting to the Self: Secular and Religious Trajectories of Second Generation Maghrebi in Belgium'. PhD diss., KU Leuven, 2008.

Fadil, Nadia, Farid El Asri and Sarah Bracke. 'Islam in Belgium: Mapping an Emerging Interdisciplinary Field of Study'. In *The Oxford Handbook of European Islam*, edited by Jocelyne Cesari. Oxford: Oxford University Press, 2015.

Fanon, Frantz. *Black Skin, White Masks*. New York: Grove Press, 1967 [1952].

Feddes, Allard R., Lars Nickolson and Bertjan Doosje. *Triggerfactoren in het Radicaliseringsproces*. Amsterdam: Expertise-unit Sociale Stabiliteit, Universiteit van Amsterdam, 2015.

Feeley, Malcolm M., and Jonathan Simon. 'The New Penology: Notes on the Emerging Strategy of Corrections and Its Implications'. *Criminology* 30, no. 4 (1992): 449–74.

Fekete, Liz. 'Anti-Muslim Racism and the European Security State'. *Race & Class* 46, no. 1 (2004): 3–29.

Feldman, Greg. *The Migration Apparatus: Security, Labor, and Policymaking in the European Union*. Stanford, CA: Stanford University Press, 2011.

Ferguson, Neil, and Eve Binks. 'Understanding Radicalization and Engagement in Terrorism through Religious Conversion Motifs'. *Journal of Strategic Security* 8, no. 1 (2015): 16–26.

Fermin, Alfons. *Nederlandse politieke partijen over minderhedenbeleid, 1977–1995*. Amsterdam: Thesis Publishers, 1997.

Fernando, Mayanthi. *The Republic Unsettled: Muslim French and the Contradictions of Secularism*. Durham, NC: Duke University Press, 2014.

Foner, Nancy. 'Is Islam in Western Europe like Race in the United States'. *Sociological Forum* 30, no. 4 (2015): 885–99.

Foucault, Michel. *The Archaeology of Knowledge*. New York: Pantheon Books, 1972.

Foucault, Michel. *Discipline & Punish: The Birth of the Prison*. New York: Vintage Books, 1975.

Foucault, Michel. 'Governmentality'. In *The Foucault Effect: Studies in Governmentality*, edited by Graham Burchell. Chicago, IL: University of Chicago Press, 1991.

Foucault, Michel. 'Lecture Two: 14 January 1976'. In *Power/Knowledge: Selected Interviews and Other Writings, 1972–1977*, edited by Colin Gordon. New York: Pantheon Books, 1980.

Foucault, Michel. *Security, Territory, Population: Lectures at the Collège de France, 1977–78*. London: Palgrave Macmillan, 2007.

Foucault, Michel. 'The Subject and Power'. *Critical Inquiry* 8, no. 4 (1982): 777–95.

Foucault, Michel. 'Truth and Power'. In *Power/Knowledge: Selected Interviews and Other Writings, 1972–1977*, edited by Colin Gordon, 126–28. New York: Pantheon Books, 1980.

Franklin, Sarah, and Susan McKinnon. 'New Directions in Kinship Study: A Core Concept Revisited'. *Current Anthropology* 41, no. 2 (2000): 275–79.

Franz, Barbara. 'Europe's Muslim Youth: An Inquiry into the Politics of Discrimination, Relative Deprivation, and Identity Formation'. *Mediterranean Quarterly* 28, no. 1 (2007): 89–112.

Fraser, Nancy. 'From Redistribution to Recognition'. *New Left Review* I, no. 212 (1995): 68–93.

Frissen, Thomas, and Leen d'Haenens. 'Legitimizing the Caliphate and Its Politics: Moral Disengagement Rhetoric in ISIL's *Dabiq*'. In *Authoritarian and Populist Influences in the New Media*, edited by Sai Felicia Krishna-Hensel. Abingdon: Routledge, 2017.

Funke, Manfred. 'Extremismus und offene Gesellschaft, Anmerkungen zur Gefährdung und Selbstgefährdung des demokratischen Rechtsstaates'. In *Extremismus im demokratischen Rechtsstaat*, edited by M. Funke, 15–46. Düsseldorf: Droste, 1978.

Furet, François. *Terrorisme et démocratie*. Paris: Fayard, 1985.

Garland, David. 'Les contradictions de la "société punitive": Le cas britannique'. *Actes de la Recherche en Sciences Sociales* 124, no. 1 (1994): 49–67.

Garland, David. *The Culture of Control: Crime and Social Order in Contemporary Society*. Oxford: Oxford University Press, 2001.

Geelhoed, Fiore. *Purification and Resistance: Glocal Meanings of Islamic Fundamentalism in the Netherlands*. Rotterdam: Erasmus Universiteit Rotterdam, 2011.

Gell, Alfred. *The Anthropology of Time: Cultural Constructions of Temporal Maps and Images*. Oxford and Providence: Berg, 1992.

Geschiere, Peter. *The Perils of Belonging: Autochthony, Citizenship, and Exclusion in Africa and Europe*. Chicago, IL: University of Chicago Press, 2009.

Geschiere, Peter. 'Witchcraft and the State: Cameroon and South Africa Ambiguities of "Reality" and "Superstition"'. *Past and Present* 199, no. 3 (2008): 313–35.

Geschiere, Peter. *Witchcraft, Intimacy, and Trust: Africa in Comparison*. Chicago, IL: University of Chicago Press, 2013.

Gielen, Amy-Jane. *Radicalisering en Identiteit: Radicale Rechtse en Moslimjongeren Vergeleken*. Amsterdam: Aksant, 2008.

Gignard, Alain. 'The Islamist Networks in Belgium'. In *Jihadi Terrorism and the Radicalisation Challenge in Europe*, edited by Rik Coolsaet. Aldershot and Burlington, VT: Ashgate, 2008.

Girard, René. *La violence et le sacré*. Paris: Hachette, 1982.

Githens-Mazer, Jonathan. 'Rethinking the Causal Concept of Islamic Radicalisation'. *Political Concepts: Committee of Concepts and Methods Working Paper Series* 42 (2010). Available at www.concepts-methods.org/Files/WorkingPaper/PC%2042%20Githens-Mazer.pdf.

Githens-Mazer, Jonathan. 'The Rhetoric and Reality: Radicalization and Political Discourse'. *International Political Science Review* 33, no. 5 (2012): 556–67.

Githens-Mazer, Jonathan, and Robert Lambert. 'Why Conventional Wisdom on Radicalization Fails: The Persistence of a Failed Discourse'. *International Affairs* 86, no. 4 (2010): 889–901.

Glück, Zoltan, and Setha Low. 'A Sociospatial Framework for the Anthropology of Security'. *Anthropological Theory* 17, no. 3 (2017): 281–96.

Goldberg, David Theo. 'Militarizing Race'. *Social Text* 34, no. 4 (2016): 19–40.

Goldson, Barry. '"Children in Need" or "Young Offenders"? Hardening Ideology, Organizational Change and New Challenges for Social Work with Children in Trouble'. *Child & Family Social Work* 5, no. 3 (2000): 255–65.

Goldson, Barry. '"Unsafe, Unjust and Harmful to Wider Society": Grounds for Raising the Minimum Age of Criminal Responsibility in England and Wales'. *Youth Justice* 13, no. 2 (2013): 111–30.

Gooren, Henri. 'Reassessing Conventional Approaches to Conversion: Toward a New Synthesis'. *Journal for the Scientific Study of Religion* 46, no. 3 (2007): 337–53.

Green, Nicola, and Nils Zurawski. 'Surveillance and Ethnography: Researching Surveillance as Everyday Life'. *Surveillance & Society* 13, no. 1 (2015): 27–43.

Griffel, Frank. 'What Do We Mean by Salafi? Connecting Muhammad Abduh with Egypt's Nur Party in Islam's Contemporary Intellectual History'. *Die Welt des Islams* 55, no. 2 (2015): 186–220.

Grillo, Ralph. 'Backlash against Diversity? Identity and Cultural Politics in European Cities'. *COMPAS Working Papers* 14. Oxford: Centre of Migration Policy and Society, 2005.

Groeninck, Mieke. 'Reforming the Self, Unveiling the World: Islamic Religious Knowledge Transmission for Women in Brussels' Mosques and Institutes from a Moroccan Background'. PhD diss., KU Leuven, 2017.

Grusin, Richard A. 'Premediation'. *Criticism* 46, no. 1 (2004): 17–39.

Grusin, Richard A. *Premediation: Affect and Mediality after 9/11*. New York: Palgrave Macmillan, 2010.

Guittet, Emmanuel-Pierre. *Antiterrorisme clandestin, antiterrorisme officiel*. Outremont: Athéna Editions, 2010.

Gurr, Ted Robert. *Handbook of Political Conflict: Theory and Research*. New York: Free Press, 1980.

Gurr, Ted Robert. *Why Men Rebel*. Princeton, NJ: Princeton University Press, 1970.

Gürses, Seda, Arun Kundnani and Joris van Hoboken. 'Crypto and Empire: The Contradictions of Counter-Surveillance Advocacy'. *Media Culture & Society* 38, no. 4 (2016): 576–90.

Gusterson, Hugh, and Catherine Besteman. *The Insecure American: How We Got Here and What We Should Do about It*. Berkeley, CA: University of California Press, 2010.

Hafez, Mohammed, and Chreighton Mullins. 'The Radicalization Puzzle: A Theoretical Synthesis of Empirical Approaches to Homegrown Extremism'. *Studies in Conflict & Terrorism* 38, no. 11 (2015): 958–75.

Hage, Ghassan. 'A Not So Multi-Sited Ethnography of a Not So Imagined Community'. *Anthropological Theory* 5, no. 4 (2005): 463–75.

Hage, Ghassan. 'Waiting Out the Crisis: On Stuckedness and Governmentality'. In *Waiting*, edited by G. Hage. Carlton: Melbourne University Press, 2009.

Hage, Ghassan. *White Nation: Fantasies of White Supremacy in a Multicultural Society*. New York: Routledge, 2000.

Hajer, Maarten A. *The Politics of Environmental Discourse: Ecological Modernization and the Policy Process*. Oxford: Oxford University Press, 1997.

Hajjat, Abdellali, and Marwan Mohammed. *Islamophobie: Comment les élites françaises fabriquent le 'problème musulman'*. Paris: La Découverte, 2013.

Hall, Stuart. 'Race, Articulation and Societies Structured in Dominance'. In *Black British Cultural Studies: A Reader*, edited by Houston A. Baker Jr, Manthia Diawara and Ruth H. Lindeborg. Chicago, IL: University of Chicago Press, 1996.

Hallaq, Wael B. *The Origins and Evolution of Islamic Law*. Cambridge: Cambridge University Press, 2005.

Hamm, Mark. *The Spectacular Few: Prisoner Radicalization and the Evolving Terrorist Threat*. New York: New University Press, 2013.

Harcourt, Bernard E. *Against Prediction: Profiling, Policing, and Punishing in an Actuarial Age*. Chicago, IL: University of Chicago Press, 2008.

Harris, Shane. *The Watchers: The Rise of America's Surveillance State*. New York: Penguin Books, 2010.

Hasso, Frances. *Consuming Desires: Family Crisis and the State in the Middle East*. Stanford, CA: Stanford University Press, 2011.

Hayes, Chris. *A Colony in a Nation*. New York: W. W. Norton & Company, 2017.

Haykel, Bernard. 'On the Nature of Salafi Thought and Action'. In *Global Salafism: Islam's New Religious Movement*, edited by R. Meijer. London: Hurst, 2009.

Heath-Kelly, Charlotte. 'Algorithmic Autoimmunity in the NHS: Radicalisation and the Clinic'. *Security Dialogue* 48, no. 1 (2016): 29–45.

Heath-Kelly, Charlotte. 'Can We Laugh Yet? Reading Post-9/11 Counterterrorism Policy as Magical Realism and Opening a Third-Space of Resistance'. *European Journal on Criminal Policy and Research* 18, no. 4 (2012a): 343–60.

Heath-Kelly, Charlotte. 'Counter-Terrorism and the Counterfactual: Producing the "Radicalisation" Discourse and the UK PREVENT Strategy'. *The British Journal of Politics & International Relations* 15, no. 3 (2012b): 394–415.

Heath-Kelly, Charlotte. 'Reinventing Prevention or Exposing the Gap? False Positives in UK Terrorism Governance and the Quest for Pre-Emption'. *Critical Studies on Terrorism* 5, no. 1 (2012c): 69–87.

Hibou, Béatrice, ed., *La privatisation des États*. Paris: Karthala, 1999.

Hickman, Mary J., Lyn Thomas, Henri C. Nickels and Sara Silvestri. 'Social Cohesion and the Notion of "Suspect Communities": A Study of the Experiences and Impacts of Being "Suspect" for Irish Communities and Muslim Communities in Britain'. *Critical Studies on Terrorism* 5, no. 1 (2012): 89–106.

Hillyard, Paddy. *Suspect Community*. London: Pluto Press, 1993.

Hondius, Dieke. 'Black Dutch Voices: Reports from a Country that Leaves Racism Unchallenged'. In *Dutch Racism*, edited by Philomena Essed and Isabel Hoving, 273–93. Amsterdam: Rodopi, 2014.

Honwana, Alcinda. *The Time of Youth: Work, Social Change, and Politics in Africa*. Sterling, VA: Kumarian Press, 2012.

Horgan, John. 'Deradicalization or Disengagement? A Process in Need of Clarity and a Counterterrorism Initiative in Need of Evaluation'. *Perspectives on Terrorism* 2, no. 4 (2008).

Horgan, John. *The Psychology of Terrorism*. London and New York: Routledge, 2014.

Houellebecq, Michel. *Submission*. New York: Picador, 2015.

Hoyle, Carolyn, Alexandra Bradford and Ross Frenett. *Becoming Mulan? Female Western Migrants to ISIS*. London: Institute for Strategic Dialogue, 2015.

Huey, Laura. *No Sandwiches Here: Representations of Women in Dabiq and Inspire Magazines, TSAS Working Paper Series*. Vancouver: Canadian Network for Research on Terrorism, Security and Society, 2015.

Husband, Charles, and Yunis Alam. *Social Cohesion and Counter-Terrorism*. Bristol: The Policy Press, 2011.

Huysmans, Jef. 'Security! What Do You Mean? From Concept to Thick Signifier'. *European Journal of International Relations* 4, no. 2 (1998): 226–55.

Ignatiev, Noel. *How the Irish Became White*. New York: Routledge, 2008.

Infantino, Federica. 'La frontière au guichet'. *Champ Pénal/Penal Field* 7 (2010). Available at http://journals.openedition.org/champpenal/7864 (accessed 8 March 2018).

Jackson, Richard. 'An Analysis of EU Counterterrorism Discourse Post-September 11'. *Cambridge Review of International Affairs* 20, no. 2 (2007): 233–47.

Jackson, Richard. *Writing the War on Terrorism: Language, Politics and Counter-Terrorism*. Manchester: Manchester University Press, 2005.

Jacobs, Dirk. 'Arab European League (AEL): The Rapid Rise of a Radical Immigrant Movement'. *Journal of Muslim Minority Affairs* 25, no. 1 (2005): 97–115.

Jacquemet, Marco. 'Crosstalk 2.0: Asylum and Communication Breakdown'. *Text and Talk* 31, no. 4 (2011): 475–98.

James, William. *The Varieties of Religious Experience: A Study in Human Nature*. New York: New American Library, 1958 [1902].

Jarvis, Lee, and Michael Lister. 'Disconnected Citizenship? The Impacts of Anti-Terrorism Policy on Citizenship in the UK'. *Political Studies* 61, no. 3 (2013): 656–75.

Jeandesboz, Julien. 'Beyond the Tartar Steppe: EUROSUR and the Ethics of European Border Control Practices'. In *Europe under Threat? Security, Migration and Integration*, edited by J. Peter Burgess and Serge Gutwirth. Brussels: VUB Press, 2011.

Jouili, Jeanette S. *Pious Practices and Secular Constraints: Women in the Islamic Revival in Europe*. Stanford, CA: Stanford University Press, 2015.

Jouili, Jeanette S., and Schirin Amir-Moazami. 'Knowledge, Empowerment and Religious Authority among Pious Muslim Women in France and Germany'. *The Muslim World* 96, no. 4 (2006): 617–42.

Juntunen, Tapio, and Ari-Elmeri Hyvönen. 'Resilience, Security and the Politics of Processes'. *Resilience: International Policies, Practices and Discourses* 2, no. 3 (2014): 195–209.

Kalir, Barak. 'The Development of a Migratory Disposition: Explaining a "New Emigration"'. *International Migration* 43, no. 4 (2005): 167–96.

Kanmaz, Meryem, and Mohamed El Battiui. *Moskeeën, Imams en Islamleerkrachten in België*. Brussel: Koning Boudewijnstichting, 2004.

Kapoor, Nisha. *Deport, Deprive and Extradite: 21st Century State Extremism*. London and New York: Verso, 2018.

Kassim Allo, Awol. 'The "Show" in the "Show Trial": Contextualizing the Politicization of the Courtroom'. *Barry Law Review* 15, no. 1 (2010): 41–72.

Kassimeris, George, and Leonie Jackson. 'British Muslims and the Discourses of Dysfunction: Community Cohesion and Counterterrorism in the West Midlands'. *Critical Studies on Terrorism* 5, no. 2 (2012): 179–96.

Kennedy, James, and Markha Valenta. 'Religious Pluralism and the Dutch State: Reflections on the Future of Article 23'. In *Geloven in Het Publieke Domein: Verkenningen Van Een Dubbele Transformatie*, edited by W. B. H. J. van de Donk, A. P. Jonkers, G. J. Kronjee and R. J. J. M. Plum. Amsterdam: Amsterdam University Press, 2006.

Kessler, Oliver, ed., 'Forum: International Law and International Political Sociology'. *International Political Sociology* 3, no. 4 (2010): 303–21.

Kessler, Oliver. 'Is Risk Changing the Politics of Legal Argumentation?' *Leiden Journal of International Law* 21, no. 4 (2008): 863–84.

Kessler, Oliver, and Wouter Werner. 'Extrajudicial Killing as Risk Management'. *Security Dialogue* 39, no. 2–3 (2008): 289–308.

Khosrokhavar, Farhad. *L'islam des jeunes*. Paris: Flammarion, 1997.

Kifer, Misty, Craig Hemmens and Mary K. Stohr. 'The Goals of Corrections: Perspectives from the Line'. *Criminal Justice Review* 28, no. 1 (2003): 47–69.

Kirchheimer, Otto. *Political Justice: The Use of Legal Procedure for Political Ends*. Princeton, NJ: Princeton University Press, 1961.

Kiwan, Nadia. *Identities, Discourses and Experiences: Young People of North African Origin in France*. Manchester: Manchester University Press, 2009.

Klausen, Jytte. 'Tweeting the Jihad: Social Media Networks of Western Foreign Fighters in Syria and Iraq'. *Studies in Conflict & Terrorism* 38, no. 1 (2015): 1–22.

Klijn, Annemieke, and Jeroen Winkel. 'Münster, Amsterdam en de Wederdopers'. *Groniek* 23, no. 2 (1978): 12–16.

Kolly, Maryam. 'Introduire du possible dans les métiers impossibles?' In *Gestes spéculatifs*, edited by Isabelle Stengers and Didier Debaise, 222–23. Paris: Les Presses du Réel, 2015.

Koopmans, Ruud. 'Religious Fundamentalism and Hostility against Out-Groups: A Comparison of Muslims and Christians in Western Europe'. *Journal of Ethnic and Migration Studies* 41, no. 1 (2015): 33–57.

Krasmann, Susanne. 'Law's Knowledge: On the Susceptibility and Resistance of Legal Practices to Security Matters'. *Theoretical Criminology* 16, no. 4 (2012): 379–94.

Krause, Keith, and Michael Williams. 'Broadening the Agenda of Security Studies: Politics and Methods'. *Mershon International Studies Review* 40, no. 2 (1996): 229–54.

Kroes, Rob. *Conflict en Radicalisme*. Meppel: Boom, 1971.

Kundnani, Arun. *The Muslims Are Coming! Islamophobia, Extremism, and the Domestic War on Terror*. London and New York: Verso, 2014.

Kundnani, Arun. 'Radicalisation: The Journey of a Concept'. *Race & Class* 54, no. 2 (2012): 3–25.

Kundnani, Arun. *Spooked! How Not to Prevent Violent Extremism*. London: Institute of Race Relations, 2009.

Kundnani, Arun, and Ben Hayes. *The Globalisation of Countering Violent Extremism Policies: Undermining Human Rights, Instrumentalising Civil Society*. Amsterdam: Societal Security Network, 2018.

Laclau, Ernesto, and Chantal Mouffe. *Hegemony and Socialist Strategy: Towards a Radical Democratic Politics*. London: Verso, 1985.

LaFree, Gary, and Erin Miller. 'Desistance from Terrorism: What Can We Learn from Criminology?' *Dynamics of Asymmetric Conflict* 1, no. 3 (2008): 203–30.

Lakoff, Andrew, and Stephen J. Collier. 'Ethics and the Anthropology of Modern Reason'. *Anthropological Theory* 4, no. 4 (2004): 419–34.

Lambert, Robert. *Countering Al-Qaeda in London: Police and Muslims in Partnership*. London: Hurst, 2011.

Larkin, Brian. 'Techniques of Inattention: The Mediality of Loudspeakers in Nigeria'. *Anthropological Quarterly* 87, no. 4 (2014): 989–1015.

Lassman, Peter, and Ronald Speirs, eds., *Weber: Political Writings*. Cambridge and New York: Cambridge University Press, 1994.

Laster, Kathy, and Edna Erez. 'Sisters in Terrorism? Exploding Stereotypes'. *Women & Criminal Justice* 25, no. 1–2 (2015): 83–99.

Latour, Bruno. *Reassembling the Social: An Introduction to Actor-Network-Theory*. Oxford: Oxford University Press, 2007.

Laurence, Jonathan. 'The Corporatist Antecedent of Contemporary State–Islam Relations'. *European Political Science* 8, no. 3 (2009): 301–15.

Lauzière, Henri. 'The Construction of *Salafiyya*: Reconsidering Salafism from the Perspective of Conceptual History'. *International Journal of Middle Eastern Studies* 42, no. 3 (2010): 369–89.

Lauzière, Henri. *The Making of Salafism: Islamic Reform in the Twentieth Century*. New York: Columbia University Press, 2015.

Lawlor, Leonard. 'Contestation'. In *The Cambridge Foucault Lexicon*, edited by L. Lawlor and J. Nale. Cambridge: Cambridge University Press, 2014.

Le Cour Grandmaison, Olivier. *De l'indigénat*. Paris: La Découverte/Zones, 2010.

Lechkar, Iman. 'Striving and Stumbling in the Name of Allah: Neo-Sunnis and Neo-Shi'ites in a Belgian Context'. PhD diss., KU Leuven, 2012.

Lefebvre, Henri. *The Production of Space*. Oxford: Wiley Blackwell, 1992 [1974].

Lefebvre, Henri. *La révolution urbaine*. Paris: Gallimard, 1970.

Leman, Johan. 'Van radicalisering tot jihadisering: Een antropologische kijk'. In *De Lokroep van IS: Syriëstrijders en (De)radicalisering*, edited by Patrick Loobuyck, 41–59. Kalmthout: Pelckmans, 2015.

Leman, Johan, and Renaerts Monique. 'Dialogues at Different Institutional Levels among Authorities and Muslims in Belgium'. In *Muslims in the Margin: Political Responses to the Presence of Islam in Western Europe*, edited by W. A. R. Shadid and P. S. van Koningsveld, 164–81. Kampen: Klement, 1996.

Lentin, Alana. 'Post-Race, Post Politics: The Paradoxical Rise of Culture after Multiculturalism'. *Ethnic and Racial Studies* 37, no. 8 (2012): 1268–85.

Lentin, Alana, and Gavan Titley. *The Crisis of Multiculturalism: Racism in a Neoliberal Age*. London: Zed Books, 2011.

Leveau, Rémy. 'Réflexions sur le non-passage au terrorisme dans l'immigration maghrébine'. *Études Polémologiques: Terrorisme, Pouvoirs Publics et Sociétés* 49, no. 1 (1989): 141–56.

Lévi-Strauss, Claude. *Introduction to the Work of Marcel Mauss*. London: Routledge & Kegan Paul, 1987.

Lindekilde, Lasse. 'Value for Money? Problems of Impact Assessment of Counter-Radicalization Policies on End Target Groups: The Case of Denmark'. *European Journal on Criminal Policy and Research* 18, no. 4 (2012): 385–402.

Lipsky, Michael. *Street-Level Bureaucracy: Dilemmas of the Individual in Public Services*. New York: Russell Sage Foundation, 1980.

Lofland, John, and Rodney Stark. 'Becoming a World-Saver: A Theory of Conversion to a Deviant Perspective'. *American Sociological Review* 30, no. 6 (1965): 862–75.

Loobuyck, Patrick. 'Introduction'. In *De Lokroep van IS: Syriëstrijders en (De)radicalisering*, edited by Patrick Loobuyck. Kalmthout: Pelckmans, 2015.

Luhmann, Niklas. *Trust and Power: Two Works*. Chichester and New York: John Wiley & Sons, 1979.

Maatschappelijke Ontwikkeling, Raad voor, ed., *Polarisatie: Essays Over Oorzaken en Gevolgen van Verscherpte Tegenstellingen*. Amsterdam: BV Uitgeverji SWP, 2009.

MacIntyre, Alisdair. *After Virtue*. Notre Dame, IN: University of Notre Dame Press, 1981.

Mahmood, Saba. *Politics of Piety: The Islamic Revival and the Feminist Subject*. Princeton, NJ: Princeton University Press, 2005.

Mahmood, Saba. 'Secularism, Hermeneutics, and Empire: The Politics of Islamic Reformation'. *Public Culture* 18, no. 2 (2006): 323–47.

Malkki, Leena. *How Terrorist Campaigns End: The Campaigns of the Rode Jeugd in the Netherlands and the Symbionese Liberation Army in the United States*. Helsinki: University of Helsinki, 2010.

Mamdani, Mahmood. *Good Muslim, Bad Muslim: America, the Cold War, and the Roots of Terror*. New York: Pantheon Books, 2004.

Mandel, David R. 'Radicalization: What Does It Mean?' In *Home-Grown Terrorism: Understanding and Addressing the Root Causes of Radicalisation among Groups with an Immigrant Heritage in Europe*, edited by T. Pick, A. Speckhard and B. Jacuh. Amsterdam: IOS Press, 2010.

Mann, Michael. *The Sources of Social Power*. Cambridge: Cambridge University Press, 1986.

Marinetto, Michael. 'Who Wants to Be an Active Citizen? The Politics and Practice of Community Involvement'. *Sociology* 37, no. 1 (2003): 103–20.

Martin, Thomas. 'Governing an Unknowable Future: The Politics of Britain's Prevent Policy'. *Critical Studies on Terrorism* 7, no. 1 (2014): 62–78.

Marzouki, Nadia. 'De l'endiguement à l'engagement: Le discours des think tanks américains sur l'islam depuis 2001'. *Archives des Sciences Sociales des Religions* 155 (2011): 21–38.

Massey, Doreen. 'Politics and Space/Time'. In *Place, Space and the Politics of Identity*, edited by Michael Keith and Steve Pile. London and New York: Routledge, 1993.

Massumi, Brian. 'Potential Politics and the Primacy of Pre-Emption'. *Theory and Event* 10, no. 2 (2007).

Masud, Muhammad K. 'Ikhtilaf al-Fuqaha: Diversity in Fiqh as a Social Construction'. In *Wanted: Equality and Justice in the Muslim Family*, edited by Z. Anwar. Selangor: Musawah, 2009.

Mauger, Gérard. 'Sur la "radicalisation islamiste"'. *Savoir/Agir* 37, no. 3 (2013): 91–99.

Maussen, Marcel, Veit Bader and Annelies Moors. *Colonial and Post-Colonial Governance of Islam Continuities and Ruptures*. Amsterdam: Amsterdam University Press, 2011.

Mavelli, Luca. 'Between Normalisation and Exception: The Securitisation of Islam and the Construction of the Secular Subject'. *Millennium* 41, no. 2 (2012): 159–81.

McCulloch, Jude, and Sharon Pickering. 'Pre-Crime and Counter-Terrorism: Imagining Future Crime in the "War on Terror"'. *British Journal of Criminology* 49, no. 5 (2009): 628–45.

Medvetz, Thomas. *Think Tanks in America*. Chicago, IL: University of Chicago Press, 2008.

Meeus, Wim. 'Why Do Young People become Jihadists? A Theoretical Account on Radical Identity Development'. *European Journal of Developmental Psychology* 12, no. 3 (2015): 275–81.

Meijer, Roel. *Global Salafism: Islam's New Religious Movement*. London: Hurst, 2009.

Meinhof, Ulrike. *Textes des prisonniers de la 'Fraction armée rouge' et dernières lettres d'Ulrike Meinhof*, Cahiers libres no. 337. Paris: La Découverte, 1977.

Mepschen, Paul, Jan Willem Duyvendak and Evelien Tonkens. 'Sexual Politics, Orientalism and Multicultural Citizenship in the Netherlands'. *Sociology* 44, no. 5 (2010): 962–79.

Merton, Robert K., Vanessa Merton and Elinor Barber. 'Client Ambivalence in Professional Relationships: The Problem of Seeking Help from Strangers'. In *New Directions in Helping*, Vol. 2, edited by Bella M. DePaulo, 13–44. New York: Academic Press, 1983.

Meyers, Marcia, and Susan Vorsanger. 'Street-Level Bureaucrats and the Implementation of Public Policy'. In *Handbook of Public Administration: Concise Paperback Edition*, edited by Guy B. Peters and Jon Pierre. Thousand Oaks, CA: Sage, 2007.

Miah, Shamim. 'Preventing Education: Anti-Muslim Racism and the War on Terror in Schools'. In *The State of Race*, edited by Nisha Kapoor, Virinder S. Kalra and James Rhodes. Basingstoke: Palgrave Macmillan, 2013.

Miller, David, and Rizwaan Sabir. 'Counter-Terrorism as Counterinsurgency in the UK "War on Terror"'. In *Counter-Terrorism and State Political Violence: The 'War on Terror' as Terror*, edited by Scott Poynting and David Whyte. London: Routledge, 2013.

Mills, Wright. *The Sociological Imagination*. Oxford: Oxford University Press, 2000 [1959].

Misztal, Barbara A. *Trust in Modern Societies: The Search for the Bases of Social Order*. Cambridge: Polity Press, 1996.

Modood, Tariq. *Multiculturalism*. Cambridge: Polity Press, 2007.

Moffette, David, and Shaira Vadasaria. 'Uninhibited Violence: Race and the Securitization of Immigration'. *Critical Studies on Security* 4, no. 3 (2016): 291–305.

Moghaddam, Fathali M. 'De-Radicalization and the Staircase from Terrorism'. In *The Faces of Terrorism: Multidisciplinary Perspectives*, edited by David Canter, 277–92. Chichester: John Wiley & Sons, 2009.

Moghaddam, Fathali M. *From the Terrorists' Point of View: What They Experience and Why They Come to Destroy*. Westport, CT: Praeger Security International, 2006.

Moghaddam, Fathali M. 'The Psychological Citizen and the Two Concepts of Social Contract: A Preliminary Analysis'. *Political Psychology* 29, no. 6 (2008): 881–901.

Moghaddam, Fathali M. 'The Staircase to Terrorism: A Psychological Exploration'.
    American Psychologist 60, no. 2 (2005): 161–69.
Moghaddam, Fathali M., and A. J. Marsella, eds., *Understanding Terrorism: Psychosocial
    Roots, Consequences and Intervention*. Washington, DC: American Psychological
    Association, 2003.
Möllering, Guido. 'The Nature of Trust: From Georg Simmel to a Theory of Expectation,
    Interpretation and Suspension'. *Sociology* 35, no. 2 (2001): 403–20.
Moodie, Dunbar, and Vivienne Ndatshe. *Going for Gold: Men, Mines and Migration*.
    Berkeley, CA: University of California Press, 1994.
Moors, Annelies. 'The Dutch and the Face-Veil: The Politics of Discomfort'. *Social
    Anthropology* 17, no. 4 (2009): 393–408.
Moors, Annelies. 'Unregistered Islamic Marriages: Anxieties about Sexuality and Islam in
    the Netherlands'. In *Applying Shari'a in the West: Facts, Fears and the Future of Islamic
    Rules on Family Relations in the West*, edited by Maurits Berger, 141–64. Leiden: Leiden
    University Press, 2013.
Moors, Hans, Lenke Balogh, Jaap van Donselaar and Bob de Graaff. *Polarisatie en
    Radicalisering in Nederland: Een Verkenning van de Stand van Zaken in 2009*. Tilburg:
    IVA, 2009.
Moors, J. A., E. van den Reek Vermeulen and M. Siesling. *Voedingsbodem voor
    Radicalisering Bij Kleine Etnische Groepen: Een Verkennend Onderzoek in de Somalisch,
    Pakistaanse, Koerdische en Molukse Gemeenschappen*. Tilburg: IVA, 2009.
Moosa, Ebrahim. *Ghazali and the Poetics of Imagination*. Chapel Hill, NC, and London:
    University of North Carolina Press, 2005.
Morsi, Yasser. *Radical Skin. Moderate Masks: De-Radicalising the Muslim and Racism in
    Post-Racial Societies*. London and New York: Rowman & Littlefield International, 2017.
Moskalenko, Sophia, and Clark McCauley. 'Measuring Political Mobilization: The
    Distinction between Activism and Radicalism'. *Terrorism and Political Violence* 21, no. 2
    (2009): 239–60.
Mueller, John. 'Six Rather Unusual Propositions about Terrorism'. *Terrorism and Political
    Violence* 17, no. 4 (2005): 487–505.
Muncie, John. *Youth and Crime*. London: Sage, 2004.
Murray, John. 'Policing Terrorism: A Threat to Community Policing or Just a Shift in
    Priorities?' *Police Practice and Research* 6, no. 4 (2005): 347–61.
Mythen, Gabe, and Palash Kamruzzaman. 'Counter-Terrorism and Community Relations:
    Anticipatory Risk, Regulation and Justice'. In *Regulation and Criminal Justice:
    Innovations in Policy and Research*, edited by Hannah Quirk, Toby Seddon and Graham
    Smith. Cambridge: Cambridge University Press, 2014.
Mythen, Gabe, Sandra Walklate and Elizabeth-Jane Peatfield. 'Assembling and
    Deconstructing Radicalisation in PREVENT: A Case of Policy-Based Evidence
    Making?' *Critical Social Policy* 37, no. 2 (2017): 180–201.
Mythen, Gabe, Sandra Walklate and Fatima Khan. '"I'm a Muslim, but I'm Not a Terrorist":
    Victimization, Risky Identities and the Performance of Safety'. *British Journal of
    Criminology* 49, no. 6 (2009): 736–54.
Nacos, Brigitte L. 'The Portrayal of Female Terrorists in the Media: Similar Framing
    Patterns in the News Coverage of Women in Politics and in Terrorism'. *Studies in
    Conflict & Terrorism* 28, no. 5 (2005): 435–51.
Nacos, Brigitte L. 'Young Western Women, Fandom and ISIS'. *E-International Relations* 5
    (2015). Available at https://www.e-ir.info/2015/05/05/young-western-women-fandom-
    and-isis/ (accessed 8 December 2015).

Nacos, Brigitte L., and Oscar Torres-Reyna. *Fueling Our Fears: Stereotyping, Media Coverage, and Public Opinion of Muslim Americans*. Lanham, MD: Rowman & Littlefield, 2007.

Narotzky, Susana, and Niko Besnier. 'Crisis, Value, and Hope: Rethinking the Economy'. *Current Anthropology* 55, no. 9 (2014): S4–S16.

Navaro-Yashin, Yael. *The Make-Believe Space: Affective Geography in a Postwar Polity*. Durham, NC, and London: Duke University Press, 2012.

Navest, Aysha, Martijn de Koning and Annelies Moors. 'Chatting about Marriage with Female Migrants to Syria'. *Anthropology Today* 32, no. 2 (2016): 22–5.

Neely, Brooke, and Michelle Samura. 'Social Geographies of Race: Connecting Race and Space'. *Ethnic and Racial Studies* 34, no. 11 (2011): 1933–52.

Neumann, Peter R. 'The Trouble with Radicalization'. *International Affairs* 89, no. 4 (2013): 873–93.

Neumann, Peter R., B. Rogers, R. Alonso and L. Martinez. 'Recruitment and Mobilisation for the Islamist Militant Movement in Europe'. *ICSR* 251, no. 1 (2007): 153–68.

Nisa, Eva F. 'Marriage and Divorce for the Sake of Religion: The Marital Life of Cadari in Indonesia'. In *Asian Journal of Social Science* 39, no. 6 (2011): 797–820.

O'Rourke, Jacqueline. *Representing Jihad: The Appearing and Disappearing Radical*. London: Zed Books, 2012.

O'Toole, Therese, Daniel Nilsson DeHanas and Tariq Modood. 'Balancing Tolerance, Security and Muslim Engagement in the United Kingdom: The Impact of the "Prevent" Agenda'. *Critical Studies on Terrorism* 5, no. 3 (2012): 373–89.

O'Toole, Therese, Nassar Meer, Daniel Nilsson DeHanas, Stephen Jones and Tariq Modood. 'Governing through Prevent? Regulation and Contested Practice in State–Muslim Engagement'. *Sociology* 5, no. 1 (2015): 160–77.

Ollman, Bertell. *Alienation: Marx's Conception of Man in a Capitalist Society*. Cambridge: Cambridge University Press, 1977.

Omi, Michael, and Howard Winant. *Racial Formation in the United States: From the 1960s to the 1980s*. Abingdon: Routledge, 1986.

Ong, Aihwa. *Neoliberalism as Exception: Mutations in Citizenship and Sovereignty*. Durham, NC, and London: Duke University Press, 2006.

Opitz, Sven, and Ute Tellmann. 'Katastrophale Szenarien – Gegenwärtige Zukunft in Recht und Ökonomie'. *Leviathan Sonderhefte*, 25 (2010): Sichtbarkeitsregime. *Überwachung, Sicherheit und Privatheit im 21. Jahrhundert*, S. 27–52.

Oubrou, Tareq. *Coran: Clés de lecture*. Paris: Fondation pour l'innovation politique, 2015.

Owe, Julie Ræstad. 'Runaway Jihadi Bride: Media Framing of Western Female Foreign Fighters to ISIS'. MA diss., University of Oslo, 2017.

Özyürek, Esra. 'Convert Alert: German Muslims and Turkish Christians as Threats to Security in the New Europe'. *Comparative Studies in Society and History* 5, no. 1 (2009): 91–116.

Panafit, Laurent. *Quand le droit écrit l'islam: L'intégration juridique de l'islam en Belgique*. Bruxelles: Bruylant, 1999.

Pantazis, Christina, and Simon Pemberton. 'From the "Old" to the "New" Suspect Community: Examining the Impacts of Recent UK Counter-Terrorist Legislation'. *The British Journal of Criminology* 49, no. 5 (2009): 646–66.

Pape, Robert A. *Dying to Win: The Strategic Logic of Suicide Terrorism*. New York: Random House, 2006.

Parvez, Z. Fareen. 'Debating the Burqa in France: The Antipolitics of Islamic Revival'. *Qualitative Sociology* 34, no. 2 (2011): 287–312.

Paulle, Bowen, and Barak Kalir. 'The Integration Matrix Reloaded: From Ethnic Fixations to Established versus Outsiders Dynamics in the Netherlands'. *Journal of Ethnic and Migration Studies* 40, no. 9 (2014): 1354–74.

Paxton, Robert O., and Julie Hessler. *L'Europe au XXe siècle*, translated by Evelyn Werth. Paris: Tallandier, 2011.

Perešin, Anita. 'Fatal Attraction: Western Muslimas and ISIS'. *Perspectives on Terrorism* 9, no. 3 (2015): 21–38.

Perešin, Anita, and Alberto Cervone. 'The Western *Muhajirat* of ISIS'. *Studies in Conflict and Terrorism* 38, no. 7 (2015): 1–15.

Peteet, Julie. 'Icons and Militants: Mothering in the Danger Zone'. *Signs* 23, no. 1 (1997): 103–29.

Peter, Frank. 'Political Rationalities, Counter-Terrorism and Policies on Islam in the United Kingdom and France'. In *The Social Life of Anti-Terrorism Laws: The War on Terror and the Classifications of the 'Dangerous Other'*, edited by Julia M. Eckert, 79–108. Bielefeld: transcript Verlag, 2008.

Pine, Frances. 'Migration as Hope: Space, Time, and Imagining the Future'. *Current Anthropology* 55, S9 (2014): S95–S104.

Pisoiu, Daniela. 'Coming to Believe "Truths" about Islamist Radicalization in Europe'. *Terrorism and Political Violence* 25, no. 2 (2013): 246–63.

Ponsaers, Paul, Brice De Ruyver, Marleen Easton, Antoinette Verhage, Jannie Noppe, Jo Hellinckx and Maarten Vandevelde. *Onderzoeksrapport polarisering en radicalisering: een integrale preventieve aanpak*. Brussel: Governance of Security, 2010.

Portis, Larry. 'La sociologie consensuelle et le terrorisme: De la propagande par le fait à Unabomber'. *L'Homme et la Société* 123–4 (1997): 57–74.

Prins, Baukje. *Voorbij de onschuld: Het debat over de multiculturele samenleving*. Amsterdam: Van Gennep, 2000.

Ragazzi, Francesco. 'Countering Terrorism and Radicalisation: Securitising Social Policy?' *Critical Social Policy* 37, no. 2 (2017): 163–79.

Ragazzi, Francesco. 'La lutte contre la radicalisation ou deux formes de la pensée magique'. *Mouvements* 88, no. 4 (2016): 151–58.

Ragazzi, Francesco. 'Policed Multiculturalism? The Impact of Counter-Terrorism and Counter-Radicalization and the "End" of Multiculturalism'. In *Counter-Radicalisation: Critical Perspectives*, edited by Christopher Baker-Beall, Charlotte Heath-Kelly and Lee Jarvis. Oxon and New York: Routledge, 2015.

Ragazzi, Francesco. 'Suspect Community or Suspect Category? The Impact of Counter-Terrorism as "Policed Multiculturalism"'. *Journal of Ethnic and Migration Studies* 42, no. 5 (2016): 724–41.

Ramadan, Tariq. *Être musulman européen: Études des sources islamiques à la lumière du contexte européen*. Lyon: Tawhid, 1999.

Rambo, Lewis R. *Understanding Religious Conversion*. New Haven, CT: Yale University Press, 1993.

Ramirez, Debbie A. Sasha Cohen O'Connell and Rabia Zafar. *Developing Partnerships between Law Enforcement and American Muslim, Arab, and Sikh Communities: A Promising Practices Guide*. Boston, MA: Northeastern University, 2004.

Rana, Junaid. 'The Racial Infrastructure of the Terror-Industrial Complex'. *Social Text* 34, no. 4 (2016): 111–38.

Ranstorp, Magnus. *Understanding Violent Radicalisation*. London and New York: Routledge, 2010.

Rath, Jan. *Minorisering: de Sociale Constructie van 'Etnische Minderheden'*. Amsterdam: Sua, 1991.

Reddy, Maureen T. 'Invisibility/Hypervisibility: The Paradox of Normative Whiteness'. *Transformations: The Journal of Inclusive Scholarship and Pedagogy* 9, no. 2 (1998): 55–64.

Renaerts, Monique. 'L'histoire de l'islam en Belgique et la problématique de sa reconnaissance'. *Cahiers de l'Institut de philologie et d'histoire orientales* 3 (1999): 49–61.

Renard, Thomas, and Rik Coolsaet. 'From the Kingdom to the Caliphate and Back: Returnees in Belgium'. In 'Returnees: Who Are They, Why Are They (Not) Coming Back and How Should We Deal with Them? Assessing Policies on Returning Foreign Terrorist Fighters in Belgium, Germany and the Netherlands'. *Egmont Papers* 101 (2018): 19–40.

Requate, Jörg, and Philipp Zessin. 'Comment sortir du "terrorisme"? La violence politique et les conditions de sa disparition en France et en République Fédérale d'Allemagne 1970–1990'. *European Review of History—Revue Européenne d'Histoire* 14, no. 3 (2007): 423–45.

Reynolds, Sean, and Mohammed Hafez. 'Social Network Analysis of German Foreign Fighters in Syria'. *Terrorism and Political Violence* (2017): 1–26. Published online at https://doi.org/10.1080/09546553.2016.1272456 (accessed May 2018).

Rietjens, Paul. 'België, de EU en het jihadi-terrorisme'. *Studia Diplomatica*, VX (2007), Supplement 1.

Rights Watch UK. *Preventing Education? Human Rights and UK Counter-Terrorism Policy in Schools*. London: RWUK, 2016.

Rights Watch UK. 'Radicalisation and De-Radicalisation'. *Perspectives on Radicalisation and Political Violence: Papers from the First International Conference on Radicalisation and Political Violence.* London: RWUK, 2008.

Robert, Dominique. 'Actuarial Justice'. In *Encyclopedia of Prisons and Correctional Facilities*, edited by M. Bosworth, 11–14. Thousand Oaks, CA: Sage, 2005.

Roberts, David, and Minelle Mahtani. 'Neoliberalizing Race, Racing Neoliberalism: Placing "Race" in Neoliberal Discourses'. *Antipode* 42, no. 2 (2010): 248–57.

Robinson, Cedric. *Black Marxism: The Making of the Black Radical Tradition*. Chapel Hill, NC: University of North Carolina Press, 2000 [1983].

Roediger, David. *The Wages of Whiteness: Race and the Making of the American Working Class*. New York: Verso, 2007.

Roex, Ineke. *Leven als de profeet in Nederland: Over de Salafi-beweging en democratie.* Amsterdam: Amsterdam University Press, 2013.

Roex, Ineke, Sjef van Stiphout and Jean Tillie. *Salafisme in Nederland: Aard, Omvang en Dreiging.* Amsterdam: IMES, Universiteit van Amsterdam, 2010.

Romein, Jan. *Machten van dezen tijd*. Amsterdam: Wereldbibliotheek, 1932.

Rommelspacher, Birgit. *'Der Hass hat uns geeint': Junge Rechtsextreme und ihr Ausstieg aus der Szene.* Frankfurt am Main: Campus Verlag, 2006.

Rose, Nikolas S. 'The Death of the Social? Re-Figuring the Territory of Government'. *International Journal of Human Resource Management* 25, no. 3 (1996): 327–56.

Rose, Nikolas S. *Powers of Freedom: Reframing Political Thought*. Cambridge and New York: Cambridge University Press, 1999.

Rothstein, M. A. 'Privacy and Confidentiality'. In *Routledge Handbook of Medical Law and Ethics*, edited by Y. Joly and B. M. Knoppers. Oxon and New York: Routledge, 2014.

Roy, Olivier. 'Euro-islam: De jihad van binnenuit?' *Justitiële Verkenningen* 31, no. 2 (2005): 28–46.

Roy, Olivier. *L'islam mondialisé*. Paris: Seuil, 2002.

Roy, Olivier. *La sainte ignorance: Le temps de la religion sans culture.* Paris: Seuil, 2008.

Sageman, Marc. *Leaderless Jihad: Terror Networks in the Twenty-First Century.* Philadelphia, PA: University of Pennsylvania Press, 2008.

Sageman, Marc. *Understanding Terror Networks.* Philadelphia, PA: University of Pennsylvania Press, 2004.

Saghaye-Biria, Hakimeh. 'American Muslims as Radicals? A Critical Discourse Analysis of the US Congressional Hearing on "The Extent of Radicalization in the American Muslim Community and that Community's Response"'. *Discourse & Society* 23, no. 5 (2012): 508–24.

Said, Edward W. *Orientalism: Western Conceptions of the Orient.* London: Penguin, 1995 [1978].

Salazar, Noel. 'Imagining Mobility at the "End of the World"'. *History and Anthropology*, 24, no. 2 (2013): 233–52.

Salazar, Noel. 'Key Figures of Mobility: An Introduction'. *Social Anthropology* 25, no. 1 (2017): 5–12.

Saltman, Erin Marie, and Melanie Smith. *Till Martyrdom Do Us Part: Gender and the ISIS Phenomenon.* London: Institute for Strategic Dialogue, 2015.

Saltzburg, Stephen A. 'Privileges and Professionals: Lawyers and Psychiatrists'. *Virginia Law Review* 66, no. 3 (1980): 597–651.

Sayyid, Bobby S. *A Fundamental Fear: Eurocentrism and the Emergence of Islamism.* London: Zed Books, 1997.

Schiffauer, Werner. 'Vom Exil-zum Diaspora-Islam: Muslimische Identitäten in Europa'. *Soziale Welt* 55, no. 4 (2004): 347–68.

Schiffauer, Werner. 'Vor Dem Gesetz: Der staatliche umgang mit dem legalistischen Islamismus'. In *Subjektbildung: Interdiziplinäre Analysen Der Migrationsgesellschaft*, edited by Paul Mecheril. Bielefeld: transcript Verlag, 2014.

Schinkel, Willem. *Denken in een Tijd van Sociale Hypochondrie: Aanzet tot een Theorie Voorbij de Maatschappij.* Kampen: Klement, 2007.

Schinkel, Willem, and Marguerite van den Berg. 'Polariserend en moraliserend: Burgerschap in de inburgering'. In *Polarisatie: Essays Over Oorzaken en Gevolgen van Verscherpte Tegenstellingen*, edited by Raad voor Maatschappelijke Ontwikkeling. Amsterdam: BV Uitgeverji SWP, 2009.

Schmid, Alex P. 'Radicalisation, De-Radicalisation, Counter-Radicalisation: A Conceptual Discussion and Literature Review'. *International Centre for Counter-Terrorism.* The Hague: ICCT, 2013.

Schöck, Cornelia. 'Belief and Unbelief in Classical Sunnī Theology'. In *Encyclopaedia of Islam, THREE*, edited by K. Fleet, G. Krämer, D. Matringe, J. Nawas and E. Rowson. Brill Online, 2007.

Scholten, Peter. *Framing Immigrant Integration: Dutch Research-Policy Dialogues in Comparative Perspective.* Amsterdam: Amsterdam University Press, 2011.

Sedgwick, Mark. 'The Concept of Radicalization as a Source of Confusion'. *Terrorism and Political Violence* 22, no. 4 (2010): 479–94.

Seligman, Adam B. *The Problem of Trust.* Princeton, NJ: Princeton University Press, 1997.

Sharma, Aradhana, and Akhil Gupta, eds., *The Anthropology of the State: A Reader.* Malden, MA, and Oxford: Blackwell, 2006.

Sharma, Sanjay, and Jasbinder Nijjar. 'The Racialized Surveillant Assemblage: Islam and the Fear of Terrorism'. *Popular Communication* 16, no. 1 (2018): 72–85.

Shearing, Clifford. 'Punishment and the Changing Face of the Governance'. *Punishment & Society* 3, no. 2 (2001): 203–20.

Shepard, Todd. *The Invention of Decolonization: The Algerian War and the Remaking of France*, 2nd edn. Ithaca, NY, and London: Cornell University Press, 2008.

Siebers, Hans. 'The Impact of Migrant-Hostile Discourse in the Media and Politics on Racioethnic Closure in Career Development in the Netherlands'. *International Sociology* 25, no. 4 (2010): 475–500.

Silke, Andrew, and Katherine Brown. '"Radicalisation": The Transformation of Modern Understanding of Terrorist Origins, Psychology and Motivation'. In *State, Society, and National Security: Challenges and Opportunities in the 21st Century*, edited by Shashi Jayakumar, 129–50. Singapore: World Scientific Publishing, 2016.

Silverstein, Paul A. *Algeria in France*. Bloomington, IN: Indiana University Press, 2004.

Silverstein, Paul A. 'The New Barbarians: Piracy and Terrorism on the North African Frontier'. *CR: The New Centennial Review* 5, no. 1 (2005): 179–212.

Simmel, Georg. *The Philosophy of Money*. London: Routledge, 1990.

Simmel, Georg. 'The Stranger'. In *Georg Simmel on Individuality and Social Forms*, edited by M. Janowitz. Chicago, IL: University of Chicago Press, 1972 [1908].

Simon, Jonathan. 'Choosing Our Wars, Transforming Governance: Crime, Cancer, Terror'. In *Risk and the War on Terror*, edited by Louise Amoore and Marieke de Goede. London: Routledge, 2008.

Slootman, Marieke, and Jean Tillie. 'Processen van radicalisering: Waarom sommige Amsterdamse moslims radicaal worden'. *Instituut voor Migratie- en Etnische Studies*. Amsterdam: IMES, 2006.

Snouck Hurgronje, Christiaan. *Nederland en de Islâm: Vier voordrachten, gehouden in de Nederlandsch-Indische Bestuursacademie*. Leiden: E. J. Brill, 1911.

Soja, Edward. *Seeking Spatial Justice*. Minneapolis, MN, and London: University of Minnesota Press, 2010.

Somers, Bart, Bart De Wever, Hans Bonte and Jan Creemers. *Beheersen van Moslimradicalisering: Handreiking voor Beleid en Praktijk*. Mechelen, Antwerp, Vilvoorde and Maaseik, 2013.

Spalek, Basia. 'Community Policing, Trust, and Muslim Communities in Relation to "New Terrorism"'. *Politics & Policy* 38, no. 4 (2010): 789–815.

Spalek, Basia, and Laura Zahra McDonald. 'Terrorism and Counterterrorism: Spotlight on Strategies and Approaches'. *Arches Quarterly* 5, no. 9 (2012): 20–28.

Spalek, Basia, and Robert Lambert. 'Muslim Communities, Counter-Terrorism and Counter-Radicalisation: A Critically Reflective Approach to Engagement'. *International Journal of Law, Crime and Justice* 36, no. 4 (2008): 257–70.

Spengler, Oswald. *The Decline of the West*. Oxford: Oxford University Press, 1991 [1918].

Spivak, Gayatri. 'Can the Subaltern Speak?' In *Marxism and the Interpretation of Culture*, edited by C. Nelson and L. Grossberg, 271–313. Urbana, IL: University of Illinois Press, 1988.

Sprinzak, Ehud. 'The Process of Delegitimation: Towards a Linkage Theory of Political Terrorism'. *Terrorism and Political Violence* 3, no. 1 (1991): 50–68.

Spruyt, Mark. *Wat het Vlaams Blok verzwijgt*. Leuven: Van Halewyck, 2000.

Stampnitzky, Lisa. 'Disciplining an Unruly Field: Terrorism Experts and Theories of Scientific/Intellectual Production'. *Qualitative Sociology* 34, no. 1 (2010): 1–19.

Stampnitzky, Lisa. *Disciplining Terror: How Experts Invented 'Terrorism'*. Cambridge: Cambridge University Press, 2013.

Stampnitzky, Lisa. 'Experts, États et théories des champs: Sociologie de l'expertise en matière de terrorisme'. *Critique Internationale* 59, no. 2 (2013): 89–104.

Stephens, Sharon, ed., *Children and the Politics of Culture*. Princeton, NJ: Princeton University Press, 1995.

Stern, Jessica. *Terror in the Name of God: Why Religious Militants Kill*. New York: HarperCollins, 2004.

Sunier, Thijl. 'Domesticating Islam: Exploring Academic Knowledge Production on Islam and Muslims in European Societies'. *Ethnic and Racial Studies* 37, no. 6 (2014): 1138–55.

Sztompka, Piotr. *Trust: A Sociological Theory*. Cambridge: Cambridge University Press, 2000.

Taguieff, Pierre-André. 'The New Cultural Racism in France'. *Telos* 83 (1990): 109–22.

Tebble, Adam James. 'Exclusion for Democracy'. *Political Theory* 34, no. 4 (2006): 463–87.

Thomas, Paul. 'Divorced but Still Co-Habiting? Britain's Prevent/Community Cohesion Policy Tension'. *British Politics* 9, no. 4 (2014): 472–93.

Thomas, Paul. *Responding to the Threat of Violent Extremism: Failing to Prevent*. London: Bloomsbury Academic, 2012.

Tilly, Charles. 'Review of Why Men Rebel by Ted Robert Gurr'. *Journal of Social History* 4, no. 4 (1971): 416–20.

Traverso, Enzo. *The End of Jewish Modernity*. London: Pluto Press, 2016.

Travisano, Richard. 'Alternation and Conversion as Qualitatively Different Transformations'. In *Social Psychology through Symbolic Interaction*, edited by Gregory Stone and Harvey Faberman. Waltham, MA: Ginn-Blaisdell, 1970.

Trouillot, Michel-Rolph. 'The Anthropology of the State in the Age of Globalization: Close Encounters of the Deceptive Kind'. *Current Anthropology* 42, no. 1 (2001): 125–38.

Tsoukala, Anastassia. 'Security, Risk and Human Rights: A Vanishing Relationship?' *CEPS Special Report*. Brussels: CEPS, 2008.

Uitermark, Justus. 'Integration and Control: The Governing of Urban Marginality in Western Europe'. *International Journal of Urban and Regional Research* 38, no. 4 (2014): 1418–36.

van den Berg, Marguerite, and Willem Schinkel. '"Women from the Catacombs of the City": Gender Notions in Dutch Culturist Discourse'. *Innovation: The European Journal of Social Science Research* 22, no. 4 (2009): 393–410.

Van der Woude, Maartje. 'Brede benadering terrorismebestrijding'. *Openbaar Bestuur* 11, no. 19 (2009): 2–5.

Van der Woude, Maartje. 'De erfenis van tien jaar strafrechtelijke terrorismebestrijding in Nederland'. *Strafblad* 10, no. 1 (2012): 9–18.

Van der Woude, Maartje. 'Dutch Counterterrorism: An Exceptional Body of Legislation or Just an Inevitable Product of the Culture of Control?' In *The State of Exception and Militant Democracy in a Time of Terror*, edited by A. Ellian and G. Molier, 69–95. Dordrecht: Republic of Letters Publishing, 2012.

Van der Woude, Maartje. *Wetgeving in een veiligheidscultuur: Totstandkoming van antiterrorismewetgeving in Nederland bezien vanuit maatschappelijke en (rechts) politieke context*. Den Haag: Boom Juridische Uitgevers, 2010.

van Ewijk, Edith. 'Between Local Governments and Communities: Knowledge Exchange and Mutual Learning in Dutch-Moroccan and Dutch-Turkish Municipal Partnership'. PhD diss., University of Amsterdam, 2013.

Van Gemert, Frank. 'Radicaliseren de criminele Marokkaanse jongeren van weleer? Socialecontroletheorie toegepast op twee case studies'. *Proces* 2 (2006): 44–52.

Van Ginderachter, Maarten. 'Trou de mémoire: De droom van Groot-Nederland'. In *Het geheugen van de Lage Landen*, edited by Jo Tollebeek and Henk te Velde. Rekkem: Ons Erfdeel, 2009.

Van Ginkel, Bibi. 'Prosecuting Foreign Terrorist Fighters: What Role for the Military?' *ICCT Policy Brief*. The Hague: ICCT, 2016.

Van Ginkel, Bibi, and Simon Minks. 'Addressing the Challenge of Returnees: Threat Perceptions, Policies, and Practices in the Netherlands'. In 'Returnees: Who Are They, Why Are They (Not) Coming Back and How Should We Deal with Them? Assessing Policies on Returning Foreign Terrorist Fighters in Belgium, Germany and the Netherlands'. *Egmont Papers* 101, February (2018): 55–70.

Van Hear, Nicholas. 'Reconsidering Migration and Class'. *International Migration Review* 48, S1 (2014): S100–S121.

van Hoesel, P. H. M., F. L. Leeuw and J. Mevissen. *Beleidsonderzoek in Nederland: Kennis Voor Beleid; Ontwikkeling van Een Professie*. Assen: Van Gorcum, 2005.

van Leeuwen, Marianne. *Confronting Terrorism: European Experiences, Threat Perceptions and Policies*. The Hague: Kluwer Law International, 2003.

Van San, Marion. 'Onze kinderen zijn geen terroristen': families van Belgische en Nederlandse Syriëgangers over het vertrek van hun geliefden'. *Tijdschrift voor Criminologie* 57, no. 3 (2015): 300–14.

Van San, Marion, Stijn Sieckelinck and Micha de Winter. *Idealen op drift: Een pedagogische kijk op radicaliserende jongeren*. Den Haag: Boom, 2010.

Van San, Marion. 'Striving in the Way of God: Justifying Jihad by Young Belgian and Dutch Muslims'. *Studies in Conflict & Terrorism* 38, no. 5 (2015): 328–42.

Vasta, Ellie. 'From Ethnic Minorities to Ethnic Majority Policy: Multiculturalism and the Shift to Assimilationism in the Netherlands'. *Ethnic and Racial Studies* 30, no. 5 (2007): 713–40.

Veldhuis, Tinka M. *Prisoner Radicalization and Terrorism Detention Policy: Institutionalized Fear or Evidence-Based Policy Making?* London: Routledge, 2016.

Veldhuis, Tinka, and Edwin Bakker. 'Causale factoren van radicalisering en hun onderlinge samenhang'. *Vrede en Veiligheid* 36, no. 4 (2007): 447–70.

Veldhuis, Tinka, and Siegwart Lindenberg. 'Limits of Tolerance under Pressure: A Case Study of Dutch Terrorist Detention Policy'. *Critical Studies on Terrorism* 5, no. 3 (2012): 425–43.

Vermeulen, Floris. 'Suspect Communities—Targeting Violent Extremism at the Local Level: Policies of Engagement in Amsterdam, Berlin, and London'. *Terrorism and Political Violence* 26, no. 2 (2014): 286–306.

Vermeulen, Floris, and Frank Bovenkerk. *Engaging with Violent Islamic Extremism: Local Policies in Western European Cities*. The Hague: Eleven International Publishing, 2012.

Verskin, Alan. *Islamic Law and the Crisis of the Reconquista: The Debate on the Status of Muslim Communities in Christendom*. Leiden and Boston, MA: Brill, 2015.

Visser, Marian, and Jeroen Slot. *Extremisme en Radicalisering in het Amsterdamse Voortgezet Onderwijs*. Amsterdam: Gemeente, 2005.

Viswanathan, Gauri. *Outside the Fold: Conversion, Modernity and Belief*. Princeton, NJ: Princeton University Press, 1998.

Vliegenthart, Rens. *Framing Immigration and Integration: Facts, Parliament, Media and Anti-Immigrant Party Support in the Netherlands*. Amsterdam: Vrije Universiteit, 2007.

Vroon, Vanessa E. *Sisters in Islam: Women's Conversion and the Politics of Belonging: A Dutch Case Study*. PhD diss., University of Amsterdam, 2014.

Wæver, Ole. 'Securitization and Desecuritization'. In *On Security*, edited by Ronnie D. Lipschutz, 46–87. New York and Chichester: Columbia University Press, 1995.

Warren, Mark. *Democracy and Association*. Princeton, NJ: Princeton University Press, 2001.

Weber, Linda R., and Allison I. Carter. *The Social Construction of Trust*. New York: Kluwer/ Plenum, 2003.

Weber, Max. *Economy and Society: An Outline of Interpretive Sociology*. Berkeley, CA: University of California Press, 1978 [1922].

Weggemans, Daan, and Beatrice de Graaf. *Na de vrijlating: Een exploratieve studie naar recidive en re-integratie van jihadistische ex-gedetineerden*. Amsterdam: Reed Business, 2015.

Weggemans, Daan, Edwin Bakker and Peter Grol. 'Who Are They and Why Do They Go? The Radicalization and Preparatory Processes of Dutch Jihadist Foreign Fighters'. *Perspectives on Terrorism* 8, no. 4 (2014): 100–10.

Weggemans, Daan, Ruud Peters, Edwin Bakker and Roel de Bont. *Destination Syria: An Exploratory Study into the Daily Lives of Dutch 'Syria Travellers'*. Leiden: Leiden University, Institute of Security and Global Affairs, 2016.

Weil, Patrick. 'Le statut des musulmans en Algérie coloniale: Une nationalité française denature'. *EUI Working Papers HEC* 3 (2003): 1–15.

Weimann, Gabriel. 'The Theater of Terror: Effects of Press Coverage'. *Journal of Communication* 33, no. 1 (1983): 38–45.

Werner, Wouter. 'The Use of Law in International Political Sociology'. *International Political Sociology* 4, no. 3 (2010): 304–7.

Whitaker, Reg. 'A Faustian Bargain? America and the Dream of Total Information Awareness'. In *The New Politics of Surveillance and Visibility*, edited by Kevin D. Haggerty and Richard V. Ericson, 141–70. Toronto: University of Toronto Press, 2006.

Whyte, Zachary. 'Enter the Myopticon: Uncertain Surveillance in the Danish Asylum System'. *Anthropology Today* 27, no. 3 (2011): 18–21.

Wijsen, Frans. 'Indonesian Muslim or World Citizen? Religious Identity in the Dutch Integration Discourse'. In *Making Religion: Theory and Practice in the Discursive Study of Religion*, edited by Frans Wijsen and Kocku von Stuckrad. Leiden and Boston, MA: Brill, 2016.

Wiktorowicz, Quintan. 'Anatomy of the Salafi Movement'. *Studies in Conflict & Terrorism* 29, no. 3 (2006): 207–39.

Wimmer, Andreas, and Nina Glick-Schiller. 'Methodological Nationalism, the Social Sciences, and the Study of Migration: An Essay in Historical Epistemology'. *The International Migration Review* 37, no. 3 (2003): 576–610.

Wolf, Eric. *Pathways of Power: Building an Anthropology of the Modern World*. Berkeley, CA: University of California Press, 2001.

Wood, David Murakami, and Steve Wright. 'Before and After Snowden'. *Surveillance and Society* 13, no. 2 (2015): 132–38.

Wright, J. 'Priestly Silence: A Study of the Ministerial Experience of Confidentiality'. PhD diss., Princeton University, 2000.

Yancy, George. *Black Bodies, White Gazes: The Continuing Significance of Race*. Lanham, MD: Rowman & Littlefield, 2008.

Yanow, Dvora, and Marleen van der Haar. 'People Out of Place: Allochthony and Autochthony in the Netherlands' Identity Discourse—Metaphors and Categories in Action'. *Journal of International Relations and Development* 16, no. 2 (2013): 227–61.

Ye'or, Bat. *Islam and Dhimmitude: Where Civilizations Collide*. Madison, NJ: Fairleigh Dickinson University Press, 2001.

Young, Kate, Carol Wolkowitz and Roslyn McCullagh. *Of Marriage and the Market: Women's Subordination in International Perspective*. London: CSE Books, 1981.

Young, Robert. *White Mythologies*. New York: Routledge, 2004 [1991].

Yuval-Davis, Nira. *Gender and Nation*. London: Sage, 1997.

Zakaria, Rafia. 'Women and Islamic Militancy'. *Dissent* 62, no. 1 (2015): 118–25.

Zedner, Lucia. 'Citizenship Deprivation, Security and Human Rights'. *European Journal of Migration and Law* 18, no. 2 (2016): 222–42.

Zedner, Lucia. 'Pre-Crime and Post-Criminology?' *Theoretical Criminology* 11, no. 2 (2007): 261–81.

Zemni, Sami. 'The Shaping of Islam and Islamophobia in Belgium'. *Race & Class* 53, no. 1 (2011): 28–44.

Zieleniec, Andrzej. *Space and Social Theory*. London: Sage, 2008.

Zizek, Slavoj. 'Tolerance as an Ideological Category'. *Critical Inquiry* 34, no. 4 (2008): 660–82.

INDEX